QUESTIONING EU CITIZENSHIP

The question of supranational citizenship is one of the more controversial in EU law. It is politically contested, the object of prominent court rulings and the subject of intense academic debates.

This important new collection examines this vexed question, paying particular attention to the Court of Justice. Offering analytical readings of the key cases, it also examines those political, social and normative factors which influence the evolution of citizens' rights. This examination is not only timely but essential given the prominence of citizen rights in recent political debates, including in the Brexit referendum. All of these questions will be explored with a special emphasis on the interplay between immigration from third countries and rules on Union citizenship.

Volume 83 in the Series Modern Studies in European Law

Modern Studies in European Law

Recent titles in this series:

Marketing and Advertising Law in a Process of Harmonization
Edited by Ulf Bernitz and Caroline Heide-Jörgensen

The Fundamental Right to Data Protection:
Normative Value in the Context of Counter-Terrorism Surveillance
Maria Tzanou

Republican Europe
Anna Kocharov

Family Reunification in the EU
Chiara Berneri

EU Liability and International Economic Law
Armin Steinbach

The EU and Nanotechnologies: A Critical Analysis
Tanja Ehnert

Human Rights Between Law and Politics:
The Margin of Appreciation in Post-National Contexts
Edited by Petr Agha

The European Union and Social Security Law
Jaan Paju

The Rule of Law in the European Union: The Internal Dimension
Theodore Konstadinides

The Division of Competences between the EU and the Member States:
Reflections on the Past, the Present and the Future
Edited by Sacha Garben and Inge Govaere

Unity in Adversity: EU Citizenship, Social Justice and the Cautionary Tale of the UK
Charlotte O'Brien

The Use of Force and Article 2 of the ECHR in Light of European Conflicts
Hannah Russell

Environmental Crime in Europe
Andrew Farmer, Michael Faure and Grazia Maria Vagliasindi

For the complete list of titles in this series, see
'Modern Studies in European Law' link at
www.bloomsburyprofessional.com/uk/series/modern-studies-in-european-law

Questioning EU Citizenship

Judges and the Limits of Free Movement and Solidarity in the EU

Edited by
Daniel Thym

·HART·
PUBLISHING
OXFORD AND PORTLAND, OREGON
2017

Hart Publishing
An imprint of Bloomsbury Publishing Plc

Hart Publishing Ltd
Kemp House
Chawley Park
Cumnor Hill
Oxford OX2 9PH
UK

Bloomsbury Publishing Plc
50 Bedford Square
London
WC1B 3DP
UK

www.hartpub.co.uk
www.bloomsbury.com

Published in North America (US and Canada) by
Hart Publishing
c/o International Specialized Book Services
920 NE 58th Avenue, Suite 300
Portland, OR 97213-3786
USA

www.isbs.com

First published 2017

British Library Cataloguing-in-Publication Data
A catalogue record for this book is available from the British Library.

ISBN: HB: 978-1-50991-468-5
ePDF: 978-1-50991-465-4
ePub: 978-1-50991-466-1

Library of Congress Cataloging-in-Publication Data

Names: Thym, Daniel, editor.

Title: Questioning EU citizenship : judges and the limits of free movement and solidarity in the EU / edited by Daniel Thym.

Description: Oxford ; Portland, Oregon : Hart Publishing, an imprint of Bloomsbury Publishing Plc, 2017. | Series: Modern studies in European law | Includes bibliographical references and index.

Identifiers: LCCN 2017038515 (print) | LCCN 2017039066 (ebook) | ISBN 9781509914661 (Epub) | ISBN 9781509914685 (hardback : alk. paper)

Subjects: LCSH: Citizenship—European Union countries. | Freedom of movement—European Union countries.

Classification: LCC KJE5124 (ebook) | LCC KJE5124 .Q47 2017 (print) | DDC 342.2408/3—dc23

LC record available at https://lccn.loc.gov/2017038515

Typeset by Compuscript Ltd, Shannon

Contents

List of Contributors

KM (Karin) de Vries is Assistant Professor of Constitutional Law at the Vrije Universiteit, Amsterdam, where she specialises in the law on migration, citizenship and human rights. She previously worked as a PhD candidate at the Vrije Universiteit Amsterdam and was a Max Weber Fellow at the European University Institute.

Sara Iglesias Sánchez is Legal Secretary, Court of Justice of the European Union.

Dimitry Kochenov is Professor of EU Constitutional Law at the University of Groningen, The Netherlands.

Dora Kostakopoulou is Professor of European Union Law, European Integration and Public Policy at the University of Warwick, UK.

Sandra Mantu is a Researcher at the Centre for Migration Law, Radboud University, Nijmegen, The Netherlands. Her research focuses on EU citizenship and its links with state nationality and social rights. She is co-editor of the *European Journal of Migration and Law*. Her latest monograph is *Contingent Citizenship: The Law and Practice of Citizenship Deprivation in Interntional, European and National Perspectives* (Leiden, Brill, 2015).

Paul Minderhoud is Associate Professor at the Centre for Migration Law (CMR) of the Radboud University, Nijmegen, The Netherlands. The CMR is a Jean Monnet Centre of Excellence. His main research interests concern the legal and socio-legal aspects of immigration and social security. He is co-editor of the *European Journal of Migration and Law*.

Dr Clíodhna Murphy is Lecturer in the Department of Law at Maynooth University, Ireland.

Niamh Nic Shuibhne is Professor of European Union Law at the University of Edinburgh, UK. Her research examines questions of substantive EU law from a constitutional perspective, with a particular focus on principle-based analysis of free movement law. She is one of the joint editors of the *Common Market Law Review*.

Ettore Recchi is Professor of Sociology at Science Po (Paris) and a member of the Observatoire Sociologique du Changement (OSC). His main research interests are European integration, international mobility and social stratification. His last monopgraph is: *Mobile Europe: The Theory and Practice of Free Movement in the EU* (Basingstoke, Palgrave, 2015).

Stephanie Reynolds is Lecturer in Law, School of Law and Social Justice, University of Liverpool, UK.

Urška Šadl is Professor at the European University Institute in Florence, Italy, and a research fellow at the Courts Centre of Excellence for International Courts in Copenhagen, Denmark.

Suvi Sankari LL.D is an Academy of Finland Postdoctoral Researcher, working at the Faculty of Law, University of Helsinki; a member of the Nordic Network of Legal Empirical Scholars; and member of the Finnish Academy research project 'European Bonds: The Moral Economy of Debt'.

Susanne K Schmidt is Professor of Political Science at the University of Bremen, Germany. She served as dean of the Bremen International Graduate School of Social Sciences from 2009–12. She has published widely on questions of European integration, including the role of the Commission, competition and liberalisation policies in the EU, and mutual recognition as a new mode of governance.

Francesca Strumia is Senior Lecturer in Law at the University of Sheffield, UK.

Daniel Thym is Professor of Public, European and International Law and Director of the Research Centre Immigration and Asylum Law at the University of Konstanz, Germany.

Ferdinand Wollenschläger is Professor of Public Law, European Law and Public Economic Law at the Faculty of Law, University of Augsburg, Germany.

1

Introduction: The Judicial Deconstruction of Union Citizenship

DANIEL THYM

I. POLITICAL, LEGAL AND CONCEPTUAL CONTESTATION

SUPRANATIONAL CITIZENSHIP is politically contested, the object of prominent court rulings and has given rise to intense academic debate. The contributions to this volume scrutinise these contestations with a special emphasis on the position of the Court of Justice (ECJ) whose more restrictive recent judgments indicate that something fundamental may have changed. Analysing the contents and context of the case law, which have been the subject of numerous academic contributions, this book will broaden its outlook to political, social and normative factors that can influence the evolution of citizens' rights, including the Brexit referendum and broader debates about immigration. Doing so will embed institutional practices into an analytical framework highlighting links between European Union (EU) citizenship and the ongoing crisis of the European project and examining dynamics which may help rationalise the continuous reconfiguration of citizens' rights.

Citizens' rights are contested from different sides. First, it is questioned *politically* in several Member States mainly due to its alleged effect on the welfare state. Without doubt, free movement had been discussed on earlier occasions, including by academic commentators. It was controversial during the original Treaty negotiations and caused debate about so-called posted workers in the 1990s,[1] but the intensity of the discussion increased after the 2004 EU enlargement to eastern and central Europe. After initial debate in, among others, France and Italy,[2] storm clouds have gathered in recent years. The question of welfare benefits became one of the hottest political topics in the public debate prior to the

[1] See the historic study by S Goedings, *Labor Migration in an Integrating Europe* (The Hague, SDU Uitgevers, 2005) chs 3–5; and P Davies, 'Posted Workers' (1997) 34 *CML Rev* 571.

[2] *cf* C Barnard, 'Unravelling the Services Directive' (2008) 45 *CML Rev* 323, 325–31; and H O'Nions, 'Roma Expulsions and Discrimination' (2011) 13 *European Journal of Migration and Law* 361.

Brexit referendum.[3] But it was and is not only the British who are sceptical. The German coalition government also promised to 'reduce incentives for migration into the social protection systems'[4] and proceeded with the adoption of restrictive laws,[5] while the Visegrád countries take the opposite stance and promise strong support for a 'cornerstone of EU integration'.[6] Moreover, the debate about free movement tends to be overshadowed by wider debates about migration and asylum, not least as a result of ongoing migratory pressures in the Mediterranean region which culminated in the crisis of the Common European Asylum System during the 2015/16 period.

Second, Union citizenship is challenged *legally* in a number of judgments which put a preliminary end to years of debate about access to social benefits by citizens who are not economically active. The theme is not new: it had been at the heart of many landmark rulings which defined the Court's early citizenship case law. Cases like *Martínez Sala*, *Grzelczyk*, *Förster* or *Vatsouras* are well known among experts in EU law.[7] More recently, *Brey*, *Dano*, *Alimanovic* and *Commission v the UK* effectively reversed this trend. They will be analysed in the second part of this volume. But it's not only the social benefits judgments which are contested legally. Analysing the case law, another common thread stands out: the immigration status of family members from third states took centre stage in prominent rulings such as *Baumbast*, *Carpenter*, *Metock*, *Ruiz Zambrano*, *Dereci* and *Rendón Marín*.[8] By considering such immigration issues this volume will broaden its analysis to the linkage between Union citizenship and immigration policy which plays a prominent role in many contemporary debates about the EU. This linkage will be at centre of the contributions to the third part.

Third, the *normative* concept underlying Union citizenship is being scrutinised as a result of the alleged change of direction in the Court's case law and the sense of crisis within which the EU has been engulfed in recent years.[9] The contributions to this volume will show that the normative infrastructure of supranational citizenship is bound to remain unstable. It is defined by an inbuilt tension between the national and the European level[10] and does not reside on a clear-cut normative

[3] See the contribution by Stephanie Reynolds, chapter 4 in this volume.

[4] See CDU/CSU/SPD, Deutschlands Zukunft gestalten, Koalitionsvertrag 18. Legislaturperiode, December 2013, 108.

[5] See the chapter by Stephanie Reynolds, chapter 4 in this volume.

[6] *cf* Joint Statement of the Visegrád countries, Council doc 17395/13 of 4 December 2013.

[7] For an analytical overview, see M Dougan, 'The Bubble that Burst: Exploring the Legitimacy of the Case Law on the Free Movement of Union Citizens' in M Adams et al (eds), *Judging Europe's Judges: The Legitimacy of the Case Law of the European Court of Justice* (Oxford, Hart Publishing, 2013).

[8] See D Thym, 'Family as Link. Explaining the Judicial Change of Direction on Residence Rights of Family Members from Third States' in H Verschueren (ed), *Residence, Employment and Social Rights of Mobile Persons: On How EU Law Defines Where They Belong* (Antwerp, Intersentia, 2016).

[9] See Editorial Comments, 'The Critical Turn in EU Legal Studies' (2015) 52 *CML Rev* 881; and L Azoulai, 'Solitude, désoeuvrement et conscience critique' (2015) *Politiques européennes* 82, 82–86.

[10] See R Bauböck, 'Why European Citizenship? Normative Approaches to Supranational Union' (2007) 8 *Theoretical Inquiries in Law* 453.

justification.[11] It also reflects the wider uncertainty about how to relate European integration to the rest of the world, especially insofar as questions of immigration are concerned.[12] This book cannot resolve these controversies, but it can help elucidate the role of the law and of its patron, the ECJ, in these processes. Union citizenship arguably embodies the historic mission of 'ever closer union'[13] and it is, therefore, a perfect angle to examine wider trends defining the crisis of the European project at this juncture.

II. DECONSTRUCTING SUPRANATIONAL CITIZENSHIP

By establishing the 'citizenship' of the Union, the Treaty of Maastricht introduced a concept which had often served as a projection sphere for political visions of a good life and a just society. It is the aspirational openness of the citizenship concept that explains why it has long steered the call for wider social and political inclusion.[14] It served as a normative anchor in debates about the abolition of serfdom and slavery, the gradual extension of the right to vote and the construction of the welfare state.[15] More recently, women, ethnic minorities or gays and lesbians have fought for emancipation by invoking 'citizenship'.[16] That is not to say that there is a uniform citizenship concept: its meaning remains theoretically contested and politically disputed.[17] All I say is that rules on citizenship can serve, like human rights norms, as channels to feed normative arguments into legal debates.[18] The inherent openness of the citizenship concept supports progressive change by means of dynamic interpretation.

It is the aspirational openness of the citizenship concept that explains the relevance of norms and ideas in the formation of the citizenship concept, which,

[11] See the contributions to L Azoulai et al (eds), *Constructing the Person* (Oxford, Hart Publishing, 2016); and F de Witte, *Justice in the EU: The Emergence of Transnational Solidarity* (Oxford, Oxford University Press, 2015).

[12] See D Kostakopoulou, 'EU Citizenship: Writing the Future' (2007) 13 *European Law Journal* (*ELJ*) 623.

[13] Recital 1 of the preamble of the original EEC Treaty of 1957, the present Treaty on the Functioning of the European Union and the Charter of Fundamental Rights.

[14] *cf* R Dahrendorf, 'Citizenship and Beyond' (1974) 41 *Social Research* 673; and S Sassen, *Territory, Authority, Rights: From Medieval to Global Assemblages* (Princeton, NJ, Princeton University Press, 2006) ch 6.

[15] For Europe, see P Magnette, *Citizenship. The History of an Idea* (Oxford, ECPR Press, 2005) chs 4, 5; and for the US, J Shklar, *American Citizenship* (Harvard, MA, Harvard University Press, 1991).

[16] See S Strasser, 'Rethinking Citizenship' in B Halsaa et al (eds), *Remaking Citizenship in Multicultural Europe* (Basingstoke, Palgrave, 2012).

[17] See L Bosniak, 'Citizenship Denationalized' (2000) 7 *Indiana Journal of Global Legal Studies* 447, 450–53; and S Benhabib, 'Claiming Rights Across Borders' (2009) 103 *American Political Science Review* 691, 697–99.

[18] For academic practice, see D Thym, 'Frontiers of EU Citizenship' in D Kochenov (ed), *EU Citizenship and Federalism: The Role of Rights* (Cambridge, Cambridge University Press, 2017); and, generally, M Kumm, 'The Idea of Socratic Contestation and the Right to Justification' (2010) 4 *Law & Ethics of Human Rights* 141, 144–52.

in the specific context of the EU, are defined by the institutional setting and the practice of different actors.[19] A sound legal-doctrinal exegesis is necessary, but our analysis should strive further and embrace broader constitutional explorations precisely because citizens' rights convey normative values and express basic choices of societies, which can change over time.[20] The conceptual openness of Union citizenship was one factor facilitating progressive interpretation by the ECJ, although such outcome was and is no foregone conclusion. The broader social and political context may similarly support restrictive tendencies, thematic shifts or judicial changes of direction.[21] Dead ends, standstill and decline are conceptually as likely as further expansion.[22] The different chapters in this book will show that the case law discloses such reorientation and that political actors and social practices can have an impact on legal change.

Against this backdrop, the title to this introduction employs the term 'deconstruction' not as a normative bias that supranational citizenship is bound to fail or that the alleged judicial retrenchment should be criticised. Rather, it uses the 'deconstruction' metaphor as an investigative device to encourage an examination of the legal, political and social practices and forces which may influence the outcome of legal disputes. In that respect, our terminology accepts the basic message of postmodern deconstruction theory in the tradition of Jacques Derrida which aimed to show the synthesised character of Western values and concepts.[23] The same can be said about the overall title of this volume on 'questioning EU citizenship'. To scrutinise citizens' rights is much more than a simple exercise of legal interpretation: it relates the legal and normative reconfiguration of citizenship to the broader state of the EU at this critical juncture.

A brief overview of the evolution of Union citizenship demonstrates that this dynamic potential is nothing new. When it was introduced by the Treaty of Maastricht, the initial reaction was temperate. Early comments criticised the rules for not adding much substance. Citizenship was perceived to be essentially a label attached to free movement and direct elections to the European Parliament. Commentators highlighted the 'weakness'[24] of its legal framework and castigated

[19] See D Kostakopoulou, 'Ideas, Norms and European Citizenship' (2005) 68 *MLR* 233; and the conclusion to this volume.

[20] *cf* RM Cover, 'Foreword: *Nomos* and Narrative' (1983) 97 *Harvard Law Review* 4, 11–44; and A von Bogdandy, 'Founding Principles of EU Law: A Theoretical and Doctrinal Sketch' (2010) 16 *ELJ* 95, 98–100.

[21] See J Shaw and N Miller, 'When Legal Worlds Collide: An Exploration of What Happens when EU Free Movement Law meets UK Immigration Law' (2013) 38 *EL Rev* 137; and D Kostakopoulou, 'Co-Creating European Union Citizenship' (2012/13) 15 *Cambridge Yearbook of European Legal Studies* 255, 259–66.

[22] *cf* J Ferguson, 'Decomposing Modernity' in J Ferguson (ed), *Global Shadows: Africa in the Neoliberal World Order* (Durham, NC, Duke University Press, 2006).

[23] *cf* J Derrida, *De la grammatologie* (Paris, Éditions de Minuit, 1967); and, on law, J Derrida, 'Force of Law' in D Cornell et al (eds), *Deconstruction and the Possibility of Justice* (Abingdon, Routledge, 1992).

[24] See S O'Leary, *The Evolving Concept of Community Citizenship* (The Hague, Kluwer, 1996) 304–07.

the new status as a misnomer bound to remain an 'empty gesture', a sort of 'cynical public relations exercise' on the part of the High Contracting Parties.[25] It is well known that the situation changed in the late 1990s when the Court started interpreting citizens' rights,[26] reflecting the earlier experience with the free movement of workers and other persons which had been interpreted generously by the EU legislature and the ECJ ever since the 1970s.[27]

In one of its first prominent judgments on citizenship, the ECJ arguably hinted at the forward-looking potential when it stated that Union citizenship 'is *destined to be* the fundamental status'.[28] This prospective dynamism did not come as a surprise. In contrast to the more hesitant observers, some commentators had predicted early on that the new status would not permanently remain an empty normative shell.[29] They expected the citizenship label to have a transformative impact. Ever since, citizenship judgments have constituted one of the most ambitious and tantalising lines of the ECJ case law, which was discussed in numerous academic articles. In doing so, commentators often described the evolution in a transformative manner from the (old) 'market citizenship' towards (new) 'real, social or political citizenship' including access to social benefits, voting rights and the free movement for people other than workers.[30] On this basis, the more recent cases were received with disappointment.[31] The assumption behind such academic descriptions is that the evolution of citizens' rights should present a process of gradual but steady advance.

This volume takes seriously the normative argument behind calls for progressive expansion, but concentrates on rationalising, nonetheless, why the institutional

[25] *cf* JHH Weiler, 'European Citizenship and Human Rights' in JA Winter et al (eds), *Reforming the Treaty on European Union: The Legal Debate* (The Hague, TMC Asser, 1996) 57, 68, 73.

[26] For an overview, see Kostakopoulou, 'EU Citizenship. Writing the Future' (n 12); and D Kochenov, 'The Essence of EU Citizenship Emerging from the Last Ten Years of Academic Debate' (2013) 62 *ICLQ* 97.

[27] See S Kadelbach, 'Union Citizenship' in A von Bogdandy and J Bast (eds), *Principles of European Constitutional Law*, 2nd edn (Oxford, Hart Publishing, 2009) 445–48.

[28] ECJ, C-184/99, *Grzelczyk*, EU:C:2001:458, para 31 (emphasis added), which in French, the working language of the Court, read '*a vocation à être*'; the English language version of later judgments employ the formulation 'is intended to be'.

[29] See J Shaw, 'Citizenship of the Union: Towards Post-National Membership?' in *Collected Courses of the Academy of European Law, Vol VI-1—European Community Law* (The Hague, Kluwer Law International, 1998) 278–96; and C Tomuschat, 'Staatsbürgerschaft—Unionsbürgerschaft—Weltbürgerschaft' in J Drexl et al (eds), *Europäische Demokratie* (Baden-Baden, Nomos, 1999) 75.

[30] By way of example, see D Kochenov, 'The Citizenship Paradigm' (2012/13) 15 *Cambridge Yearbook of European Legal Studies* 197; J Shaw, 'Citizenship. Contrasting Dynamics at the Interface of Integration and Constitutionalism' in P Craig and G de Búrca (eds), *The Evolution of EU Law*, 2nd edn (Oxford, Oxford University Press, 2011); E Spaventa, 'Seeing the Wood Despite the Trees? On the Scope of Union Citizenship and its Constitutional Effects' (2008) 45 *CML Rev* 13, 14–30; and A Tryfonidou, *Reverse Discrimination in EC Law* (The Hague, Kluwer Law International, 2009) ch 4.

[31] N Nic Shuibhne, 'Limits Rising, Duties Ascending: The Changing Legal Shape of Union Citizenship' (2015) 52 *CML Rev* 889; S Giubboni, 'Free Movement of Persons and European Solidarity: A Melancholic Eulogy' in H Verschueren (ed), *Residence, Employment and Social Rights of Mobile Persons. On How EU Law Defines Where They Belong* (Antwerp, Intersentia, 2016) 78–88; and A Farahat, 'Solidarität und Inklusion' (2016) *Die Öffentliche Verwaltung* 45.

practice is moving in a different direction. It is not conceived of as a counterbalance to seemingly restrictive tendencies,[32] but tries to explain analytically how such constraints unfold and which factors might help explain this development. In doing so, it will focus both on the legal small print and wider political debates. Two contextual factors will be taken up in many contributions: the implications of the Brexit referendum or the nexus between Union citizenship and immigration law on the status of third-country nationals, which defined controversial citizenship cases even before the mass migration of refugees from the Middle East and Africa tested the resolve of the European project during 2015/16.

III. THE TRADITION OF 'INTEGRATION THROUGH LAW'

In the EU, the inherent volatility of the citizenship concept is reinforced by the traditional method of 'integration through law' which influenced the making of Union citizenship. In the EU, the law has often been employed as an instrument for change,[33] reflecting the dynamic vision of the overarching Treaty objective of 'ever closer union'. The belief in the effectiveness of the legally driven modification of social and economic realities was strengthened in the 1990s by the success of the single market programme.[34] In retrospect, the quarter century between the Single European Act and the entry into force of the Treaty of Lisbon appears as a period of almost continuous Treaty changes, which reached its climax in the effort to foster the steady advance towards some sort of political union through a legally binding Charter of Fundamental Rights and the (failed) project of a Constitutional Treaty.[35] The introduction of Union citizenship was an integral part of these endeavours.

When the Treaty of Maastricht introduced the new status it arguably built upon the tradition of 'integration through law' with a view to moving towards the political dream of building some sort of federal Europe, which had always been

[32] For a different approach see the recent contribution by D Kochenov, 'On Tiles and Pillars: EU Citizenship as a Federal Denominator' in D Kochenov (ed), *EU Citizenship and Federalism: The Role of Rights* (Cambridge, Cambridge University Press, 2017).

[33] See the classic account by M Cappelletti, M Seccombe and JHH Weiler (eds), *Integration Through Law*, Vol I-1 (Berlin, De Gruyter, 1986); *Europe and the American Federal Experience. Volume 1: Methods, Tools and Institutions* and the more recent, critical assessment by JHH Weiler, 'Deciphering the Political and Legal DNA of European Integration' in J Dickson and P Eleftheriadis (eds), *Philosophical Foundations of European Union Law* (Oxford, Oxford University Press, 2012) 149–56.

[34] See R van Gestel and H-W Micklitz, 'Revitalizing Doctrinal Legal Research in Europe' (2011) EUI Working Papers LAW No 2011/05, 11–2.

[35] *cf* N Walker, 'Legal Theory and the European Union' (2005) 25 *OJLS* 581, 585; and J Hunt and J Shaw, 'Fairy Tale of Luxembourg? Reflections on Law and Legal Scholarship in European Integration' in D Phinnemore and A Warleigh-Lack (eds), *Reflections on European Integration* (Basingstoke, Palgrave, 2009) 94.

understood to include a special status for citizens.[36] This objective had been present ever since the 1970s when heads of state and government promoted further integration through citizens' rights, including free movement for people other than workers and direct elections to the European Parliament,[37] thereby laying the groundwork for the introduction of Union citizenship in the Maastricht Treaty. Clearly, there had never been widespread agreement on the contours of an eventual political union and there was little discussion about the significance of the citizenship label at the time of its introduction,[38] but this did not unmake the normative potential of the new rules.[39] This historic pedigree implies, however, that the interpretation of Treaty rules may reflect the success or failure of the European project more broadly.[40] Contributions to this volume will take up corresponding challenges epitomised by the Brexit referendum.

An underlying reason for the more recent retrogression of Union citizenship may be the inherent limits to what an institutional practice of 'integration though law' can achieve. Treaty changes, new legislation and innovative court judgments alone are not capable of bringing about an enhanced degree of pan-European identity or solidarity: establishing a fundamental status called 'citizenship' or enacting a legally binding charter of fundamental rights are no self-fulfilling prophecies.[41] Legal rules, judgments and academic treatises participate in the constant reconstruction of their meaning, but cannot change them single-handedly; they need to be embedded in social structures and political life.[42] This is not to say that judgments and other legal practices are irrelevant (although some will minimise or deny their significance). Court judgments can be instruments for real-life changes, at least insofar as they relate back to political debates and reflect wider social struggles.[43] That is why several contributions to this volume will connect the analysis of court judgments to broader constitutional trends to political and social practices at national and European level.

[36] For a survey of political visions during the 1930s and 1940s, see D Rabenschlag, *Leitbilder der Unionsbürgerschaft* (Baden-Baden, Nomos, 2009) 28–43; for the 1960s, see A Evans, 'European Citizenship' (1982) 45 *MLR* 497, 499–504.

[37] See A Wiener, *Building Institutions* (Boulder, CO, Westview, 1998) chs 2, 3; and W Maas, *Creating European Citizens* (Lanham, MD, Rowman & Littlefield, 2007) ch 2.

[38] See P Magnette, *La citoyenneté européenne* (Bruxelles, Editions de l'Université de Bruxelles, 1999) ch 5.

[39] *cf* J Habermas, *Zur Verfassung Europas—Ein Essay* (Frankfurt, Suhrkamp, 2011) 63–64.

[40] See the contribution by Daniel Thym, chapter 6 in this volume.

[41] See the pointed critique by U Haltern, 'Pathos and Patina' (2013) 9 *ELJ* 14; and JHH Weiler, 'To Be a European Citizen: Eros and Civilization' in JHH Weiler, *The Constitution of Europe* (Cambridge, Cambridge University Press, 1999).

[42] *cf* C Möllers, 'Pouvoir Constituant—Constitution—Constitutionalisation' in A von Bogdandy and J Bast (eds), *Principles of European Constitutional Law*, 2nd edn (Oxford, Hart Publishing, 2009) 175–77; and D Chalmers, 'The Persona of EU Law' in L Azoulai et al (eds), *Constructing the Person* (Oxford, Hart Publishing, 2016).

[43] See M Everson, 'A Citizenship in Movement' (2014) 15 *German Law Journal* (*GLJ*) 965, 966–67.

IV. METHODOLOGY: THE LAW, ITS CONTEXT AND EXPLANATIONS FOR CHANGE

As aforementioned, the ECJ famously declared that Union citizenship was 'destined to be the fundamental status',[44] thereby arguably hinting at an underlying dynamism of the citizenship concept discussed above. More recently, however, it did not follow that route: it seems to have abandoned the forward-looking potential and backtracked on some of its earlier positions, most prominently in cases regarding the transnational access to social benefits. This judicial retrenchment coincides with political challenges for the European project including the success of the Brexit referendum and ongoing debates about immigration. It leaves us with the query of how to rationalise interpretative changes. This volume confronts this question in an attempt to understand the role of the law and its patron, the ECJ, in the reconfiguration of one of the most visible and symbolic areas of Union activities: the free movement of persons.

Our analysis aims to elucidate the factors that define the political, legal and conceptual contestation of Union citizenship by focusing on the evolving case law of the ECJ. This court-centred analysis is justified, since judges have been principal actors over the years, both in terms of advancing citizens' rights and in situations of restrictive closure.[45] In addressing the role of judges, our enquiry will combine specific themes with more general pieces with a view to locating the significance of the law and contextual factors in the practice of evolving supranational citizenship. The contributions to the second and third parts will scrutinise two subject areas in relation to which the case law was particularly controversial in recent years: social benefits and immigration. This double focus is innovative in itself. While the question of social benefits is well established as a theme in academic research on EU citizenship, the interaction between citizens' rights and rules on immigration is not discussed regularly, although the perspective of immigration allows us to connect the study of Union citizenship to the rich and controversial literature on immigration law and policy.

Examining the evolution of the case law on social benefits and the interaction with immigration policy requires the contributors to take problems of legal interpretation seriously. The normative surplus of the citizenship concept discussed earlier can be contrasted with the rather sober Treaty language, which had always combined aspirational rules, such as the general right to free movement for all citizens, with restrictive formulations emphasising limits and conditions.[46] Doctrinal incongruity extends to the legislative prescriptions in the Citizenship

[44] *Grzelczyk* (n 28) para 31.

[45] For a broader analysis not limited to Union citizenship and free movement, see the contributions to Adams et al (n 7).

[46] See the double reference to individual rights and 'limitations' and 'conditions' in Art 21 TFEU; for an inherent ambiguity in the ECJ's reasoning, see U Šadl, '*Ruiz Zambrano* as an Illustration of How the Court of Justice of the European Union Constructs its Legal Arguments' (2013) 9 *European Constitutional Law Review* 205, 221–24.

Directive 2004/38/EC on the basis of which the Court delivered its recent controversial rulings.[47] At the same time, textual indecision is one reason why doctrinal hermeneutics alone cannot resolve legal disputes. Contributors will have to consider, instead, contextual factors influencing the case law, in the case of social benefits as in relation to immigration. Doctrinal openness implies that citizens' rights allow, like many constitutional norms, for interpretative metamorphoses.[48] It is this openness and corresponding fluctuations of the case law which are at the centre of this book.

The objective of rationalising legal change will take centre stage in the first part and in the conclusion. Contributors will discuss factors shaping the reconfiguration of supranational citizenship at a more abstract level of analysis. In doing so, they will apply mixed methods in order to shed light on diverse factors and on the complex dynamics which can influence the interpretative evolution of legal rules. While some chapters will apply a contextually embedded legal analysis, others will adopt an extralegal standpoint. A common focal point of many contributions will be the significance of social practices and political discourses. Susanne K Schmidt and Francesca Strumia will scrutinise the impact of the political process and of wider discourses more generally, including in the run-up to the Brexit referendum. Their focus on political contestation overlaps with Daniel Thym's constitutional analysis of broader trends, while Niamh Nic Shuibhne traces the ambivalent role of constitutional arguments on, among other things, the Charter of Fundamental Rights in the evolving case law.

Ettore Recchi's sociological analysis will highlight the significance of citizenship practices and their impact on identificatory patterns on the basis of empirical data. Like Recchi, Urška Šadl and Suvi Sankari employ an innovative dataset with court judgments and Advocates General opinions to test the factors that might explain the outcome of citizenship cases. Dimitry Kochenov complements the multidisciplinary approach in the first part with a normative investigation to demonstrate that the contours and outcome of more recent cases epitomise what the author perceives as the vacant ethical foundations of EU citizenship. Kochenov's theoretical orientation is shared by Karin de Vries and Clíodhna Murphy who connect the debate on Union citizenship to debates about the legal status of immigrants more generally. These diverse perspectives will be brought together in a generic argument of how to explain the evolution of the case law in the concluding contribution to this volume by Dora Kostakopoulou and Daniel Thym.

[47] See the contribution by Ferdinand Wollenschläger, chapter 9 in this volume; and K Hailbronner, 'Union Citizenship and Access to Social Benefits' (2005) 42 *CML Rev* 1245, 1247–65.

[48] See A von Bogdandy and I Venzke, 'Beyond Dispute: International Judicial Institutions as Lawmakers' (2011) 12 *GLJ* 979, 984–93; and A Stone Sweet, 'The European Court of Justice' in P Craig and G de Búrca (eds), *The Evolution of EU Law*, 2nd edn (Oxford, Oxford University Press, 2011) 126–28.

V. OUTLINE OF THE BOOK

The argument in this book unfolds in three stages, combining a more general survey of factors which may help explain judicial change with two thematic focuses on equal treatment and the perspective of immigration law. The first shot is fired by Susanne K Schmidt, who argues that detailed prescriptions in earlier citizenship case law led to an 'over-constitutionalisation', leaving little room for political contest and choice. In her view, this curtailed the opportunities to influence the integration process and stretched the legitimacy of judicial decision-making. Mirroring the experience of court-centred constitutionalism in the US, she maintains that granting rights without political backing runs the risk of promoting a 'hollow hope'. Her thesis is of immediate appeal, as it presents itself as a factor among others which might help explain the outcome of the Brexit referendum, notwithstanding the historical contingency of the British case.

In an original argument, Dimitry Kochenov demonstrates how the Court's focus on individual circumstances can result in a conceptual and practical dead-end which contradicts the normative foundations of equal citizenship theories. Kochenov contrasts the emphasis on individual circumstances in the contemporary case law of the Luxembourg court with the wider trend towards personhood as the benchmark for citizenship practices across the world. While distinctions based on legal status give way to widespread equal treatment through a de facto extension of citizens' rights to many categories of foreigners elsewhere, individual circumstances serve, in the hands of the ECJ, as a tool of rationalising the de facto exclusion of persons officially holding the status of Union citizenship. On the basis of a well-articulated commitment to equal citizenship, Kochenov decries this development in the European case law as an expression of inescapable normative individualism imposed on those in need.

Against the backdrop of the Brexit debate, Stephanie Reynolds exposes how the Court failed, in her eyes, to develop a strategy to accommodate the single market and Union citizenship. She demonstrates this by looking at the legality of the safeguard mechanism limiting access to in-work benefits in the erstwhile interim settlement between the British Government and the European Council in the run-up to the Brexit referendum. On the basis of a thorough assessment of a long list of free movement and citizenship judgments, Reynolds shows that, in contrast to conventional wisdom, it is not the doctrinal foundations of the single market which have 'infected' the citizenship case law, but the latter that has inspired a compromise formula—including the personal circumstances benchmark analysed by Kochenov in the previous chapter—which is now being reintegrated into the free movement case law. This runs the danger of undoing earlier innovations on the principled equal treatment of workers in the single market.

The novel emphasis on individual circumstances also plays a prominent part in the chapter by Daniel Thym, who shows that the institutional practice, both by the ECJ and the Commission, fluctuates between two models of how to operationalise the supranational citizenship concept: one based on residence and the other focusing on social integration. He tests the pertinence of this approach in relation to ongoing disputes about social benefits, political participation and the significance of nationality, as well as migration and collective identities. Thym shows that the move from one model to another is intimately connected to broader constitutional trends, such as the euro crisis, the failure of the Constitutional Treaty and arguments about immigration. He reconstructs more restrictive recent trends as building blocks of an EU that accepts the limits of the federal vision and that moves, instead, towards the acceptance of diversity.

While many contributions concentrate on external factors that may explain judicial change, Urška Šadl and Suvi Sankari pierce the veil of the ECJ as a purportedly uniform institution through a quantitative study of prominent citizenship cases, analysing these in relation to the internal organisation and professional background of both judges and advocates general. Alongside a thorough assessment of the thematic reorientation of the case law, Šadl and Sankari identify a growing significance of chamber judgments and a trend towards following the advocate general more often than previously. They also highlight a fascinating connection between restrictive judgments and a professional background in politics of either the reporting judge or the advocate general. This finding offers empirical evidence for the more theoretical hypotheses put forward in other chapters of the volume that the more restrictive recent twist in the citizenship case law may be explained, in part at least, by the broader political climate.

Ettore Recchi develops the argument brought forward by other contributors that the case law does not always adequately reflect social practices on the ground. He supports his findings using an original dataset on the identification of (im)mobile Union citizens with the European project. He finds, unsurprisingly, that those moving across borders tend to identify more with the EU, although the degree of influence of the corresponding 'transaction thesis' is less pronounced than one might expect. Moreover, the broader theoretical framework of his rich analysis indicates that the nexus between mobility and identification can result in a backlash when the immobile (who also tend to be less well-off economically) associate mobility with the transnational elite and direct their opposition, as a result, at the European project, including transnational movement for economic purposes. In that respect, the desire for EU-level identification associated with supranational free movement may ultimately backfire and thus undermine the overall legitimacy of the European project.

The chapters in the first part on how to explain judicial change conclude with a discourse analysis by Francesca Strumia, who traces how the legal and conceptual ambiguity of Union citizenship can be influenced by changing narratives at national and at European level concerning cross-border movements and the overall set-up of the EU as a supranational policy. She shows to what extent the emergence of hybrid statuses, both in ECJ case law and in domestic immigration laws, can serve as a gateway for broader political debates to influence the evolution of citizens' rights and migration statuses. Mirroring findings by other contributors, Strumia highlights a combination of factors both exogenous and endogenous to the case law which may explain why institutional practice has become more restrictive in recent years in light of broader political debates.

The contributions to the second part delve into the most pertinent issue that defines the ECJ case law: equal treatment, social benefits and human rights. Ferdinand Wollenschläger explains how the more restrictive recent turn reflects an inbuilt ambiguity of the legal regime on the free movement of those who do not work. While the ECJ may have used this ambiguity to correct the legislature in earlier cases, it has more recently yielded to the prerogative of the political domain to decide controversial issues. This nuanced outlook is based on an interpretation of the case law which assumes that the criterion of economic self-sufficiency requires an assessment of the individual case and does not, therefore, exclude all those who do not work from social benefits indiscriminately. Wollenschläger's argument is a powerful reminder that court judgments do not come out of the blue, but are influenced by the black letter and the doctrinal construction of supranational rules on free movement, even if these rules are ambiguous.

While Wollenschläger concentrates on the (il)legality of residence as a precondition for equal treatment, Paul Minderhoud and Sandra Mantu revisit the seminal judgments which lie at the heart of recent political and legal debates about Union citizenship and access to social benefits. They explain why Wollenschläger's focus on (il)legal residence is an important variable, the significance of which the ECJ does not always recognise. This contributes to widespread confusion about the practical implications of important rulings. Most importantly, however, Minderhoud and Mantu emphasise the continued relevance of economic activity as the hallmark of free movement in the single market, which the overarching constitutional concept of Union citizenship could not undo. The strength of their chapter is the emphasis on broader trends, which they then link back to the specific contents of seminal judgments.

Niamh Nic Shuibhne follows a similar path, although she concentrates on an aspect which arguably presents itself as one of the hot topics in years to come: the interface between citizens' rights and the human rights in the Charter of Fundamental Rights. This angle has an intuitive appeal, since both Union citizenship and the Charter are essential and relatively new components of the supranational legal order and lie at the heart of the EU's constitutional self-image. The ECJ has approached both instruments differently in recent years: while the Charter has gained visibility and significance, citizens' rights have been developed reticently in recent practice. In a thorough analysis, Nic Shuibhne demonstrates inconsistencies in the interaction between the two instruments and discusses possible explanations, including the practical predominance of secondary legislation for activating the Charter. For proponents of advancing citizens' rights, the chapter advises that it may be expedient to 'rebrand' free movement cases as human rights cases, thereby building on the dynamism of the latter.

The third part builds on Niamh Nic Shuibhne's broader outlook, however concentrating on a different theme often neglected in debates about Union citizenship: its interaction with immigration rules of those who do not have the nationality of an EU Member State. In doing so, Sara Iglesias Sánchez analyses the relevance of the Charter of Fundamental Rights for third-country nationals, which, at closer inspection, is much more nuanced than the simple distinction between citizens' rights and other human rights in the field of free movement and political participation suggests. On the basis of a profound knowledge of the ECJ's case law, she identifies subtle distinctions with the potential to enhance the legal status of third-country nationals. Iglesias Sánchez navigates skilfully through the often obscure field of application and demonstrates that, in contrast to what one might expect intuitively, the Charter applies to third-country nationals more extensively than to Union citizens due to the broad reach of immigration and asylum legislation adopted at EU level in recent years.

The interplay between Union citizenship and migration law is not limited to human rights. At the same time, the integration benchmark which defines much of the case law on Union citizenship is crucial to the legal status of third-country nationals: the concept of social integration has been a hallmark of policy debates about immigration policy for more than a decade. On this theme, Karin de Vries highlights a fascinating development in legislation and case law on immigration statuses of third-country nationals. She identifies an 'integration exception', which the legislature and courts use to demarcate the (un)equal treatment of third-country nationals. Mirroring the chapter by Kochenov, she criticises the normative direction of these rulings: instead of employing equal treatment as an instrument to foster social integration, the EU legislature and the ECJ have recourse to uneven de facto integration as a justification for limiting equal treatment, thus turning the original vocation of equal citizenship on its head.

Clíodhna Murphy follows a similar line of thought in analysing the case law of the European Court of Human Rights (ECtHR) on residence security and equal treatment for foreigners, which—in another striking parallel to the ECJ's citizenship case law—elevates integration requirements as a precondition for full membership. Normatively, the human rights court in Strasbourg thus rejects a clear-cut equality-based membership paradigm in accordance with the theoretical position of Joseph Carens, which Murphy finds theoretically attractive. The ECtHR, by contrast, embraces qualitative membership criteria put forward by David Miller. Murphy's rich analysis is a strong reminder of the fruitfulness of linking the academic scrutiny of Union citizenship to broader debates about immigration, which define many contemporary policy debates about the EU.

It is trite to say that a legal development is complex and full of unexpected turns and, yet, Union citizenship shows how the identification of such complexity can help us to rationalise legal change. In the conclusion to this volume, Dora Kostakopoulou and Daniel Thym contend that the inherent instability of citizens' rights presents itself as an expression of non-simultaneity when the coexistence of heterogeneous stages of social, political and economic development direct events in diverse directions. The apparent change in the case law can be rationalised, on the basis of the arguments put forward by the different authors in the previous chapters, as an eruption of the simultaneity of the non-simultaneous. If that is correct, the same contradictions may guide future developments in yet another direction: 'alternate takes' are real. Kostakopoulou and Thym show that they can be observed, notably in the field of fundamental rights. On the basis of the Charter, citizens' rights are being reconstructed in scenarios which often are not limited to situations of cross-border movements.

Part I

Rationalising Judicial Change

2

Extending Citizenship Rights and Losing it All: Brexit and the Perils of 'Over-Constitutionalisation'

SUSANNE K SCHMIDT

I. INTRODUCTION[1]

EU CITIZENSHIP WAS a 'symbolic' addition to the Maastricht Treaty but a 'visionary' goal for the European community from its early days. Direct rights of belonging to the EU in addition to—and eventually supplanting—national citizenship rights are a necessary and crucial cornerstone to realising 'an ever closer union'. After EU citizenship found entry into the EU Treaty, it was largely the European Court of Justice (ECJ) that shaped the concomitant rights through its case law.

The UK's referendum decision for a Brexit had many causes, among them rising inequality and lack of investment into public services under a strict austerity regime in the aftermath of the financial crisis in 2008.[2] But among the many reasons for the Brexit decision immigration reined high, in particular, the contestation of equal rights for EU citizens.

Within the history of European integration, the Brexit decision presents the most serious backlash so far. In as much as EU citizenship was an important consideration in this decision, it is interesting to take it as an instance to reflect the limits of 'integration through law'.[3] That is why this chapter discusses the consequences of over-constitutionalisation and case law of the Court on EU citizenship, focusing first on its constraints on the legislative process of the Citizenship

[1] Research for this chapter has been funded by Norface (462-14-040). I thank Torben Schmengler for research assistance, Benjamin Werner for comments and Britta Plote for language correction.

[2] www.theguardian.com/politics/2009/apr/26/david-cameron-conservative-economic-policy1. But see also: blogs.lse.ac.uk/politicsandpolicy/how-does-austerity-look-in-retrospect/.

[3] M Cappelletti, M Seccombe and JHH Weiler (eds), *Integration Through Law: Europe and the American Federal Experience. Volume 1: Methods, Tools and Institutions* (Berlin, Walter de Gruyter, 1986).

Directive of 2004 (2004/38/EC), and then on the UK's administrative practice in dealing with non-contributory social benefits for EU citizens.

Within political science, several analyses have focused on the populist mobilisation process accompanying the referendum.[4] The more structural, legally driven background of the decision has received less attention. The conditions of the EU's polity are particularly prone to a development, I argue, where rights evolve exclusively outside the support of the legislative process. This is due to the 'over-constitutionalisation' that characterises the EU's polity.[5] By declaring the direct effect and supremacy of the Treaty in the early 1960s, the Court effectively transformed the intergovernmental Treaty into a constitution that overrules all law of Member States. In contrast to national constitutions, however, the Treaty includes ample policy goals. When interpreting the Treaty, the Court necessarily transforms and develops these policy goals, which subsequently shape integration. It is here that the power of the Court as an 'engine of integration' lies.

The advent of EU citizenship proved an addition to the Maastricht Treaty with large promise to transform the integration process. Yet the Court's intervention had side-effects legal academics often ignore. As the court-driven, non-majoritarian decision-making weakens 'voice', the relevance of 'exit' is strengthened.[6] Moreover, rights developed exclusively in the inner judicial-legal sphere run the danger of remaining a 'hollow hope'.[7] Without sufficient backing by societal actors, rights cannot drive societal change. As such, the tale of EU citizenship and the Brexit may also be insightful for overarching considerations of the conditions under which an international rule of law can be built successfully. It becomes apparent that deriving details of eligibility of benefits directly from a constitution has certain pitfalls: courts are hardly legitimated for outright distributive decisions so that they grant rights on the basis of an individual assessment of merit. For administrations, these individual assessments are difficult to administer, while the legislature cannot replace them with a clear set of rules should these contradict case law principles having constitutional status. While deriving EU citizenship rights from the Treaty offered the promise of deepening integration and overcoming the importance of national welfare states, over-constitutionalisation poses clear problems for the Court, the legislature and national administrations alike.

In the following, I begin by summarising the development of EU citizenship rights through the case law of the Court, and show how 'over-constitutionalisation'

[4] SB Hobolt, 'The Brexit Vote: A Divided Nation, a Divided Continent' (2016) 23 *Journal of European Public Policy* 1259.

[5] D Grimm, 'The Democratic Costs of Constitutionalisation: The European Case' (2015) 21 *European Law Journal* (*ELJ*) 460.

[6] AO Hirschman, *Exit, Voice, and Loyalty: Responses to Decline in Firms, Organizations, and States* (Cambridge, MA, Harvard University Press, 1970).

[7] GN Rosenberg, *The Hollow Hope: Can Courts Bring about Social Change? American Politics and Political Economy* (Chicago, IL, University of Chicago Press, 1993).

constrained the legislative process of the Citizenship Directive. Also subsequent to codification in this directive, the Court continued developing rights autonomously in the judicial-legal field. Given over-constitutionalisation, the requirements of the Citizenship Directive have to be read in the light of case law development. Implementing rights derived from case law, however, poses particular challenges for administrations. In its case law, the Court decides disputes on the basis of individual assessments and balancing with a view to proportionality. For administrations engaged in the management of mass applications such individual assessments are difficult to administer, as I will show with the British example. 'Governing by case law', I conclude, poses important challenges on the ground. In short, I argue that the characteristics of the UK polity with its tradition of common law and parliamentary sovereignty were particularly conducive to emphasising the constraints of over-constitutionalisation.

II. SHAPING CITIZENSHIP RIGHTS BETWEEN THE WILL OF THE COURT AND THE LEGISLATOR

The Treaty of Rome's free movement of workers and the freedom of establishment grant far-reaching rights of non-discrimination throughout the Community for those being economically active. As early as the 1960s, an extension had been debated in order to expand rights of free movement to all EU citizens.[8] Free movement rights were seen 'as a vehicle of both economic and political integration'.[9] With decision-making stalling in the Council, progress was left to the Court, for instance with the case of *Levin*,[10] which extended the rights of workers to those not earning enough for self-subsistence as long as work was 'effective and genuine' and not only 'purely marginal and ancillary'. In *Kempf*,[11] the Court granted rights to income supplement.[12] Following the case law development, Member State governments agreed to the inclusion of EU citizenship in the Treaty of Maastricht, while emphasising the supplementary nature of EU citizenship and national control over citizenship laws. While for the Member States, citizenship was a 'symbolic' addition to the Treaty,[13] for the European Parliament, for the

[8] A Hofmann, *Strategies of the Repeat Player—The European Commission between Courtroom and Legislature* (Berlin, epubli GmbH, 2013) 217.

[9] AJ Menéndez, 'European Citizenship after Martínez Sala and Baumbast. Has European Law Become More Human but Less Social?' in M Poiares Maduro and L Azoulai (eds), *The Past and Future of EU Law: The Classics of EU Law Revisited on the 50th Anniversary of the Rome Treaty* (Oxford, Hart Publishing, 2010) 10.

[10] Case 53/81 *Levin*, EU:C:1982:105.

[11] Case 193/85 *Kempf*, EU:C:1986:223.

[12] Hofmann (n 8) 227.

[13] M Aziz, 'Implementation as the Test Case of European Union Citizenship' (2009) 15 *Columbia Journal of European Law* 281.

Court and after some time also for the Commission, it laid the basis for broadening European rights.

A. Adjudicating Symbols: The Case Law on Citizenship

Embedding citizenship rights in the Treaty lost its symbolic character before long. For the legal profession, much united in its teleological legal interpretation of the Treaty, citizenship rights promised to transfer the allegiance of individuals from the nation state to the EU:

> Notwithstanding this, the political elite of Europe has mismanaged the EU's constitutional process by failing to place the citizen at the center. This failure is especially important, since without the support of its citizens, European integration as a democratic project becomes meaningless. The same cannot be said regarding the judicial elite, who have championed the cause of citizenship to a considerable extent.[14]

In the major journals of EU law, the number of articles on citizenship increased. A comparison of publications on citizenship with those on subsidiarity in two major European law journals shows this very well. Subsidiarity had been introduced alongside citizenship into the Treaty of Maastricht, and it came with high hopes as to its capacity to reduce the centralisation tendencies of integration—albeit focusing on the legislative process and aiming to constrain the Commission in putting forward legislative proposals on issues that would be better dealt with

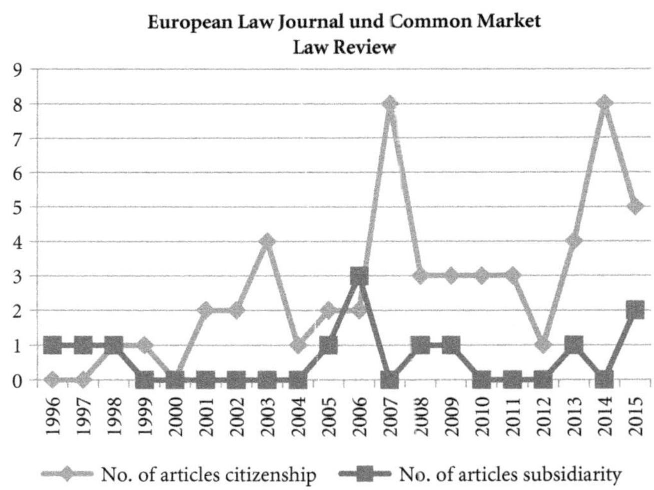

Figure 1: Publications on citizenship and subsidiarity

[14] ibid.

at the Member State level. How integration is pushed by case law has been ignored in this debate. The comparison of publications in two major law journals—the *Common Market Law Review* and the *European Law Journal*—shows that attention in the legal profession to citizenship with 53 articles in the 20 years from 1996 to 2015 by far outnumbered attention to subsidiarity with only 12 articles.[15]

The number of publications reflects the Court's increasing development of case law on citizenship. Interestingly, the Commission was largely passive at the start, not pursuing infringement procedures and only joining preliminary references.[16] In these, it argued in favour of extending residence rights, but sided with Member States' interests in restricting access to social benefits. The first important case was *Martinez Sala*,[17] where the Court held that an economically inactive Union citizen lawfully residing in Germany had to have equal access to child-raising allowance.[18] And in *Baumbast*[19] the Court found that EU citizens enjoy the right of residence and movement by direct application of Article 18(1) of the Treaty establishing the European Community.[20] Menéndez argues: The 'main concrete implications of *Martinez Sala* and *Baumbast* for the supranational citizen has been access to non-contributory social benefits'.[21]

In 2001, and before *Baumbast*, the important case of *Grzelczyk*[22] was decided during the negotiations of the Citizenship Directive. In it, the Court confirmed a right of residence for economically inactive Union citizens requiring assistance, in this case, a French student in Belgium, under the condition of not being an 'unreasonable burden'.[23] In doing so, the Court diverted from the Student Directive 93/96/EEC that denied social assistance to students.[24] Similar, in *Bidar*[25] the Court argued that assistance needed to be given to students under certain conditions.[26] The following graph shows the quantitative case law development of citizenship rights in the last 20 years, resulting in 115 judgments up until 2016.[27]

[15] Search terms: subsidiarity and citizenship. Due to differences in the online presentation of the journals, these terms were searched in the titles of the *CMLR* and in the titles and abstracts of the *ELJ*.

[16] Hofmann (n 8) 233, 242f, 245.

[17] Case C-85/96 *Martinez Sala*, EU:C:1998:217.

[18] A Tryfonidou, 'Further Steps on the Road to Convergence among the Market Freedoms' (2010) 35 *EL Rev* 36, 39.

[19] Case C-413/99 *Baumbast*, EU:C:2002:493.

[20] M Wind, 'Post-National Citizenship in Europe: The EU as a "Welfare Rights Generator"?' (2009) 15 *Columbia Journal of European Law* 239, 256, 259; Menéndez (n 9) 13ff; F Wollenschläger, 'A New Fundamental Freedom beyond Market Integration: Union Citizenship and its Dynamics for Shifting the Economic Paradigm of European Integration' (2011) 17 *ELJ* 1.

[21] Menéndez (n 9) 18.

[22] Case C-184/99 *Grzelczyk*, EU:C:2001:458.

[23] Tryfonidou (n 18) 39.

[24] K Hailbronner, 'Die Unionsbürgerschaft und das Ende rationaler Jurisprudenz durch den EuGH?' (2004) 31 *Neue Juristische Wochenschrift* 2185, 2186.

[25] Case C-209/03 *Bidar*, EU:C:2005:169.

[26] Wind (n 20) 243, 262.

[27] Curia website: curia.europa.eu/juris/recherche.jsf?language=en. Number of judgments ECJ 'citizenship of the Union'. The website does not provide for 'subsidiarity' as a subject matter.

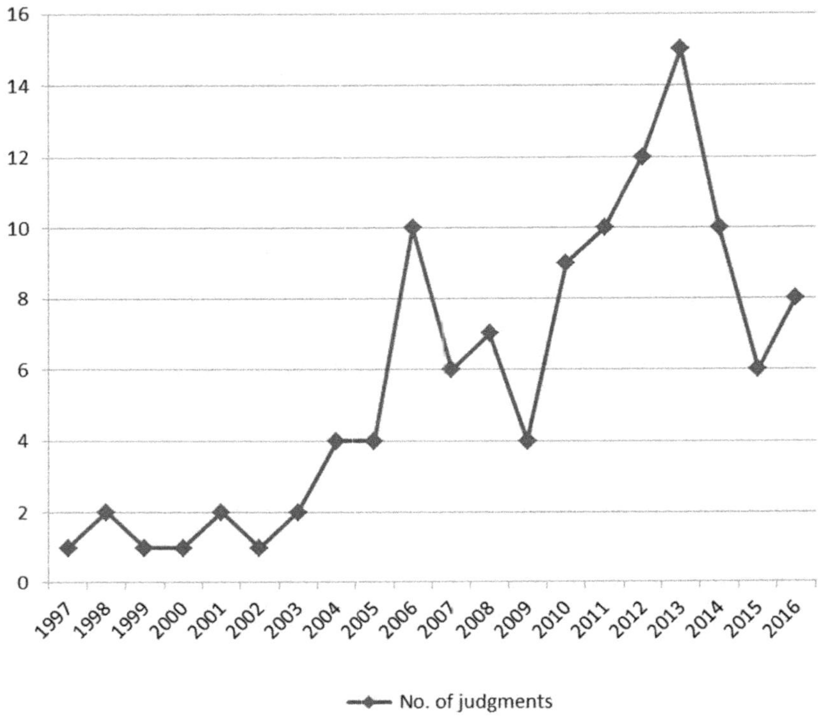

Figure 2: ECJ judgments on citizenship

B. Legislating in the Shadow of Over-Constitutionalisation

The Citizenship Directive (2004/38/EC) is the major legislative piece spelling out the rights of EU citizens. It draws a distinction according to length of residence. During the first three months, every EU citizen may reside in any EU Member State, without any claim to be supported by the host state. After five years' permanent residence, EU citizens enjoy equal status to nationals. In the interim period, EU citizens and their families can stay for more than three months conditional on having health insurance and sufficient resources. However, the Directive does not exclude access to social benefits before five years of residence. Its imprecision on this crucial issue reflects the nuanced understanding of eligibility of the ECJ in *Grzelczyk*. In this spirit, the Directive mentions eight times that EU citizens shall not become 'an unreasonable burden on the social assistance system of the host member state' (eg, Article 7 (1)), drawing on the Court's argument in the *Grzelczyk* case[28] and later in *Trojani*.[29]

[28] Hailbronner (n 24) 2187.

[29] Case C-456/02 *Trojani*, EU:C:2004:488; Wind (n 20) 243, 262. As Hofmann points out, the Court refers here, in fact, to a recital of Directive 90/364: 'Whereas beneficiaries of the right of residence must not become an unreasonable burden on the public finances of the host Member State'; Hofmann (n 8) 171.

The interaction of the legislative process and the Court's case law shows the specific conditions of policymaking in the EU very well. Courts are called upon to interpret rules and to give guidelines for this interpretation. But it is not upon the Court to set up a rule in a case like *Grzelczyk* that anyone after, say, three years, is entitled to full equal rights. In order to keep its rulings acceptable, the Court has to be oriented on the individual case, employing a proportionality analysis. In its cases, typically, the Court refers to guidelines such as: 'unreasonable burden';[30] 'a real link' to the territory;[31] 'a certain degree of integration'[32] and for those needing support when seeking employment, it argues assessing the 'genuine chance of being engaged',[33] linking the privileged status of a worker under the free movement to 'effective and genuine activities, to the exclusion of activities on such a small scale as to be regarded as purely marginal and ancillary'.[34] It is here that over-constitutionalisation makes an important difference. The various considerations which the Court draws upon in balancing the individual court case, are not only guidelines for the courts and administrations of Member States when applying EU law, but they subsequently also constrain the EU legislature. This becomes particularly apparent when regarding the way the European Commission refers to the case law in its reports and proposals for new legislation.[35] Once there is case law where the Court has regarded the criterion of a 'real link' already after 'X' months or years of residence, the EU legislature cannot require residence of 'X+1'. Similarly, once the Court has regarded employment of 'X' hours as not 'marginal and ancillary', the EU legislature can hardly determine that the status of worker under the Treaty is reserved to all those meeting their economic subsistence level. Once the Court has interpreted the Treaty, this is the law of the land. As Member States can hardly change the Treaty, they can only hope that the Court changes its interpretation.

The imprecise wording of the Directive mirrors the predicament of Member States after *Grzelczyk*. Member States were neither keen to open up their welfare systems in general to persons in need such as *Grzelczyk*, nor could they overrule the Court's interpretation of the Treaty with secondary law.[36] *Grzelczyk* already allowed access to benefits after three years. In the Citizenship Directive, Member States agreed on full rights after five years of legal residence. In the important Article 21(2) on equal treatment, economically inactive persons with no permanent residence status were no longer explicitly excluded from access to welfare assistance—only maintenance grants for students remained restricted. Agreement on the Directive was achieved shortly before the accession of 10 new Member States in May 2004.

[30] *Grzelczyk* (n 22) para 6.
[31] Case C-224/98 *D`Hoop*, EU:C:2002:432, para 38.
[32] *Bidar* (n 25) para 57.
[33] Case C-292/89 *Antonissen*, EU:C:1991:80, para 22.
[34] *Levin* (n 10) para 17.
[35] See, eg, The report of the Commission 'On progress towards effective EU Citizenship 2011–2013', COM(2013) 270 final: ec.europa.eu/justice/citizen/files/com_2013_270_en.pdf.
[36] F Wasserfallen, 'The Judiciary as Legislator? How the European Court of Justice Shapes Policy-Making in the European Union' (2010) 17 *Journal of European Public Policy* 1128, 1140.

In its imprecision concerning eligibility to benefits, the Citizenship Directive illustrates the problems of over-constitutionalisation very well. The Court had held that an individual assessment was necessary to determine eligibility, in the light of a certain degree of 'financial solidarity'[37] As Article 14(3) determines, '[a]n expulsion measure shall not be the automatic consequence of a Union citizen's or his or her family member's recourse to the social assistance system of the host Member State'. This very much mirrors the *Grzelczyk ruling.* Wasserfallen[38] emphasises that several Member States were reluctant to confirm the contentious case law of the Court in the Directive. Instead, they opted for legal uncertainty as to the eligibility of benefits in the Directive. Member States welcomed, however, the occasion to signal to the Court that they did not approve of rights of EU nationals to social assistance. As any other court, the ECJ is dependent on support for the implementation of its rulings and its general legitimacy so that it can be assumed to be somewhat responsive to the preferences of Member State governments. Signalling preferences to the Court in the context of the Citizenship Directive was important in view of the attention of EU law academia to the citizenship extension and in the expectation of further cases at the ECJ.

The extent of equal rights is spelled out in Article 24: 'Article 24 was widely understood as an attempted override' against the case law, Davies argues.[39] Paragraph 2 sets out that Member States are not obliged to grant social assistance during the first three months, 'or where appropriate, the longer period provided for in Article 14(4)b', ie, up to five years. It is plausible that Member States felt under pressure to agree in view of the upcoming Eastern accession.

At the same time, the Commission changed sides to a position favouring access to benefits, making it more likely that it would engage in infringement procedures in the future, pushing for EU citizenship rights. In the case *Collins*[40] concerning access to the UK's Jobseeker's Allowance (JSA), the Commission had argued that EU citizens had to have access to JSA even if there was no connection to the Member State (AG Colomer, No 57).[41] In late 2003, it handed an infringement procedure against Belgium to the Court,[42] opposing the requirement of sufficient personal means as a precondition for residence of EU citizens.[43] Next to the *Collins* case, Britain was directly involved with the *Bidar* court case concerning benefits for students. Case law on access of EU citizens to welfare services increasingly

[37] *Grzelczyk* (n 22) para 44; S Giubboni, 'Free Movement of Persons and European Solidarity' (2007) 13 *ELJ* 360.

[38] Wasserfallen (n 36) 1141.

[39] G Davies, 'Legislative Control of the European Court of Justice' (2014) 51 *CML Rev* 1579, 1600.

[40] Case C-138/02 *Collins*, EU:C:2004:172.

[41] B Schreinermacher, *Die Aushandlung Europäischer Gesetzgebung vor dem Hintergrund der Rechtsprechung des Europäischen Gerichtshofs* (Bremen, Universität (Diss), 2013) 101.

[42] Case C-408/03 *Commission v Belgium*, EU:C:2006:192.

[43] In his Opinion in *Collins* AG Colomer, however, took the problem of abuse of citizenship rights seriously, arguing that Member States could restrict access to welfare services with transparent, non-discriminatory means (No 75).

defined these rights on the European instead of the national level. Thus, in *Collins* the Court argued that rights of residence given by the Member States are merely declaratory, not legally constitutive,[44] since residence rights are being 'conferred directly by the Treaty' (No 40). The pressure on Member States thus grew, making the signalling of preferences more important to them.

For Member States anxious to control welfare state expenditures, a directive that stayed opaque as to the extent of entitlements was far better than one granting equal rights on the terms of the *Grzelczyk* judgment. Given that Member States disagreed with many aspects of the Directive, the text was bound to be ambiguously worded, reflecting the underlying political compromises.[45] Schreinermacher argues that case law can be more autonomy-regarding than secondary law.[46] Courts cannot legitimately set general rules as to social entitlements, but give guidelines on how the Treaty's rules need be interpreted.[47] Actors favouring far-reaching rights and liberalisation should therefore opt for codification, while actors favouring restrictions should prefer case law.

C. Adjudicating between Precedent and Legislation: Development after the Citizenship Directive

The case law development following the Citizenship Directive showed that the Court was more responsive to developing citizenship rights in cooperation with lower courts and the legal profession than to the signalling of Member States' preferences.[48] Wiesbrock argues that legal scholars and practitioners, notably the Attorneys General, established through self-citation a core of citizenship rights that are far removed from what Member States intended:

> The interpretation and analysis of the Court's judgments by legal scholars has to a large extent served to justify the expansive case law of the Court. EU legal scholars have generally defended the 'quasi-legislative' role of the Court … EU legal scholars, who have an active interest in the extension and increasing importance of EU law, have thought to present the progression towards more extensive free movement rights as an inevitable step towards further integration.[49]

[44] H Groß, 'Das Gesetz über die allgemeine Freizügigkeit von Unionsbürgern' (2005) 25 *Zeitschrift für Ausländerrecht und Ausländerpolitik* 81, 83.

[45] Interviews: Permanent Representative Austria, 26 June 2009; German Federal Ministry of Labour and Social Affairs, 17 November 2009; European Civil Action Service, 27 October 2010.

[46] Schreinermacher (n 41) 234–35.

[47] Sieberer argues that constitutional courts are most assertive in relation to liberal individual rights (against the state), and push for entitlements only when argued in a non-discrimination framework. U Sieberer, 'Strategische Zurückhaltung von Verfassungsgerichten. Gewaltenteilungsvorstellungen und die Grenzen der Justizialisierung' (2006) 16 *Zeitschrift für Politikwissenschaft* 1299.

[48] Davies (n 39) 1599.

[49] A Wiesbrock, 'The Self-perpetuation of EU Constitutionalism in the Arena of Free Movement of Persons: Virtuous or Vicious cycle?' (2013) 2 *Global Constitutionalism* 125, 148.

In *Vatsouras*,[50] the Court had already overruled the recent Citizenship Directive by arguing that financial benefits intended to facilitate access to the labour market are not 'social assistance' in the meaning of Article 24(2) of the Directive but required equal treatment under the free movement of workers, as long as a 'real link' to the labour market could be established (Nos 38–40).[51] As a consequence, Member States' welfare state reforms focusing on labour market activation carried the unintended implication of opening up financial support to EU citizens.[52]

Brey[53] is the most recent case in which the Court actively pushed for EU citizens' access to non-contributory benefits. It involved a German pensioner, recently residing in Austria who had applied for the Austrian supplementary pension. Thus, at issue was the question whether the sufficient financial means that the Citizenship Directive requires for lawful residence may include non-contributory social benefits of the host state. The Court held in *Brey* that national authorities had to provide 'an overall assessment of the specific burden which granting that benefit would place on the social assistance system as a whole by reference to the … individual situation of the person concerned' (No 77). Thus, Member State authorities could not simply argue that the fact that someone applied for social benefits implied that the person failed the requirement of sufficient resources, therefore, losing their rightful residence.

It was only in 2014, after mounting political discussion of possible welfare migration following full free movement rights for Bulgaria and Romania[54] that the Court became more restrictive in opening non-contributory social benefits to economically inactive EU citizens. Several preliminary references questioned German legislation that excluded EU citizens from basic social benefits. *Dano*[55] concerned a Romanian who had moved to Germany, never intending to work. The ECJ drew the line here and affirmed Germany's right to deny social benefits. In the following case of *Alimanovic*[56] decided in September 2015, the Court backed that unemployment benefits can be restricted to six months for those having worked less than a year, and *García-Nieto*[57] confirmed Germany's restrictions of its non-contributory Hartz IV social benefit to nationals during the first three months of residence. Moreover, shortly before the Brexit referendum in June 2016, the Court decided that the Commission's infringement procedure[58] against the UK's right to reside test (see below) was not violating the Treaty.

[50] Case C-22/08 and 23/08 *Vatsouras*, EU:C:2009:344.

[51] C Barnard, *The Substantive Law of the EU. The Four Freedoms*, 3rd edn (Oxford, Oxford University Press, 2010) 285.

[52] Davies (n 39) 1600.

[53] Case C-140/12 *Brey*, EU:C:2013:565.

[54] M Blauberger and SK Schmidt, 'Welfare Migration? Free Movement of EU Citizens and Access to Social Benefits' (2014) 1 *Research & Politics* 1.

[55] Case C-333/13 *Dano*, EU:C:2014:2358.

[56] Case C-67/14 *Alimanovic*, EU:C:2015:597.

[57] Case C-299/14 *Garćia-Nieto*, EU:C:2016:114.

[58] Case C-308/14 *Commission v UK*, EU:C:2016:436.

In these cases, the ECJ refrained from judicial activism, allowing limits to 'financial solidarity'. The rulings settled several questions concerning the right of access to benefits. In fact, empirical research shows that support for Europe is low, if citizens perceive their national welfare systems are under threat from the EU.[59] Widening eligibility to EU citizens ultimately carries the risk that Member States react by cutting down on social benefits in general,[60] transforming the question of European citizenship into one of domestic re-distributional conflict.

Where does this leave us? Equal rights of EU citizens under the free movement of workers are very broad, not requiring economic self-sufficiency. These citizens have to be treated on a par with nationals regarding access to social benefits. Those not intending to work, in contrast, do not have the right to access benefits, as the Court put clearly in its more recent case law. Given over-constitutionalisation, Member States could not overrule the case law of the Court in the legislative process of the Citizenship Directive. Secondary law cannot alter the Court's interpretation of the Treaty. But Member States aimed to signal their preferences to the Court; and after some time, the Court showed itself more responsive to the wish of Member States to restrict access to benefits for those who have recently settled and are economically inactive.

III. WHEN OVER-CONSTITUTIONALISATION TOUCHES THE GROUND: THE PROBLEMS OF THE UK

Over-constitutionalisation, it has been argued, shifts decision-making to the Court as a non-majoritarian actor. The discussion of the Citizenship Directive shows the constraints the EU legislator faces from over-constitutionalisation and the case law of the Court. 'Covert integration' results, taking place under the radar of public scrutiny. In fact, Héritier argues that covert integration is prone to being contentious, possibly leading to a backlash.[61] European law, however, not only constrains the European level of the EU's polity. Given supremacy and direct effect, it immediately impacts also at the Member State level. National courts, administrations and legislatures are bound to respect EU law, including all case law. How this plays out depends on the institutional conditions of the Member States. In the following section, I discuss these conditions present in the UK. As we will see, there is good reason to believe that the constraints of over-constitutionalisation were

[59] L Beaudonnet, 'A Threatening Horizon: The Impact of the Welfare State on Support for Europe' (2014) 53 *Journal of Common Market Studies* 457.

[60] FW Scharpf, 'Legitimacy in the Multilevel European Polity' (2009) 1 *European Political Science Review* 173; A Wiesbrock, 'Granting Citizenship-related Rights to Third-Country Nationals: An Alternative to the Full Extension of European Union Citizenship?' (2012) 14 *European Journal of Migration and Law* 63, 93.

[61] Scharpf (n 60); Wiesbrock, 'Granting Citizenship-related Rights to Third-Country Nationals' (n 60) 93.

particularly forceful in the UK. This is due to characteristics of the British polity, its parliamentary sovereignty and its common law tradition, as well as its specific kind of welfare state. The UK is predisposed to being sensitive to the effects of over-constitutionalisation, I argue. With the UK drawing in many EU citizens after Eastern accession, these effects became politically salient.

A. The British Polity

The UK's tradition of parliamentary sovereignty dates back to the seventeenth century. It implies Parliament to be free to legislate in any policy field, with courts not being able to challenge its decisions, and future parliaments to be free to reverse laws. Given the underlying contradiction with Union membership—where supreme EU law has to be accepted by Parliament—the European Communities Act of 1972 recognised supremacy of EU law under the assumption that future parliaments, in principle, could repeal this decision. Parliamentary sovereignty, thus, entails an underlying incompatibility of the British polity with the set-up of the EU,[62] while, for instance, the German tradition of constitutional sovereignty, with the Constitutional Court as the recognised arbiter of last resort, faces fewer frictions.[63] At the same time, parliamentary sovereignty implies that domestic courts are unlikely to challenge parliamentary decisions. As judicial review is regarded as rather illegitimate,[64] we can expect that domestic courts in the UK are less likely than, say, German courts, to challenge national policy as to its legality under EU law.

Another important institutional characteristic of the UK is its common law tradition. 'Case law … has been the key tenet of the common law tradition, to the point that cases and precedents can be considered de facto if not de jure the main repositories of Anglo-American law.'[65] It is typical for common law countries that legal principles set up by judges are treated as law, without a backing of the legislature being necessary.[66] In view of the EU's over-constitutionalisation, where many important policy decisions result from case law, we can therefore expect that the British common law system is particularly well adapted to translating these rules into policy. As I will argue, we can detect this familiarity with case law when we

[62] M Elliot, 'United Kingdom: Parliamentary Sovereignty Under Pressure' (2004) 2 *International Journal of Constitutional Law* 545.

[63] H Abromeit, 'Volkssouveränität, Parlamentssouveränität, Verfassungssouveränität: Drei Realmodelle der Legitimation staatlichen Handelns' (1995) 36 *Politische Vierteljahresschrift* 49.

[64] M Wind, DS Martinsen and GP Rotger, 'The Uneven Legal Push for Europe. Questioning Variation when National Courts go to Europe' (2009) 10 *European Union Politics* 63.

[65] U Mattei and LG Pes, 'Civil Law and Common Law: Toward Convergence?' in KE Whittington, RD Kelemen and GA Caldeira (eds), *The Oxford Handbook of Law and Politics* (Oxford, Oxford University Press, 2008) 273.

[66] J Dainow, 'The Civil Law and the Common Law: Some Points of Comparison' (1966/67) 15 *American Journal of Comparative Law* 419.

regard the way that the British administration converted ECJ case law principles into practice when administering EU citizens' access to non-contributory social benefits.

B. The British Welfare Sate

The EU requires of its Member States to abstain from discriminating on the basis of nationality. This challenges the continuing national organisation of welfare. In order to fulfil their redistributive functions, national welfare states depend on closure. There is therefore an underlying tension between free movement and migration.[67] In fact, the EU is unique among the regional organisations in granting unrestricted free movement rights.[68] EU legislation has set up coordination rules to reconcile national welfare states with the free movement of workers. The different worlds of welfare found in Europe[69] face different challenges in accommodating free movement rights. If we draw a distinction in the financing among contribution- and tax-based, it becomes apparent that Member States with welfare systems relying on contributions face fewer problems than those giving out tax-financed benefits. While the former can determine eligibility non-discriminately on the basis of paid contributions, the latter has to achieve the necessary closure with a view to its territory, making it much more difficult not to draw on criteria violating the prohibition to discriminate on the basis of nationality.

The UK's welfare state relies in part on tax-financed, non-contributory welfare. In order to give incentives for taking up work, even if it is low paid, it focuses on in-work benefits. According to Ruhs,[70] when compared with Sweden, which neither imposed transitory restrictions on labour migration after 2004, the British, and also the Irish, systems are particularly vulnerable for attracting lower-skilled migration, which also lowers the benefits from labour migration. This is caused by the combination of a welfare state with tax-financed in-work benefits and a very flexible labour market. Not only is the labour market relatively unregulated; in addition, there is hardly any state enforcement of labour market regulations.[71] Another peculiarity of the UK welfare state is that there is no precise data as to its claimants:[72] 'There is no single, authoritative source of information

[67] H Entzinger, 'Open Borders and the Welfare State' in A De Guchteneire and P Pécoud (eds), *Migration without Borders: Essays on the Free Movement of People* (Oxford, Berghahn Books, 2007).

[68] C Sieber-Gasser, 'Variationen der regionalen Personenfreizügigkeit: die schrittweise Öffnung des Arbeitsmarktes' (2013) 18 März *Jusletter* 1.

[69] G Esping-Andersen, *The Three Worlds of Welfare Capitalism* (Princeton, NJ, Princeton University Press, 1990).

[70] M Ruhs, 'Is Unrestricted Immigration Compatible with Inclusive Welfare States? The (Un)Sustainability of EU Exceptionalism' (2015) Centre on Migration, Policy and Society, Working Paper 2015/125, 24.

[71] ibid.

[72] M Sumption and S Altorjai, *EU Migration, Welfare Benefits and EU Membership* (Oxford, The Migration Observatory, University of Oxford, 2016) 3.

that is currently publicly available providing a comprehensive picture of the number of claims, benefits received, and groups affected by specific policy proposals on migrants' access to benefits'. On the basis of the inexistent national registration of inhabitants, the UK relies on estimations of its population and welfare recipients. The available estimates found that EU citizens' share of in-work benefits are higher than their proportion in the overall population, while their claims to out-of-work benefits are lower.[73] This mirrors equal rights under the EU free movement of workers, while EU citizens do not immediately enjoy equal treatment with nationals.

Given the characteristics of its system, the UK took measures to shelter its welfare state relatively early on. The UK had already, under the Conservative Government in 1994, introduced a habitual residence test in order to counter fears of possible 'benefit tourism'. Originally, income support had been granted irrespective of length of stay in the UK. The habitual residence has a base in the European regulation of social benefits (now 883/2004), where it is used to establish the responsible Member State. The way in which the UK defined habitual residence draws heavily on criteria the ECJ established in its case law. Consequently, the underlying legislation does not clearly define habitual residence, but the test takes into account as criteria the length of residence, prospects of employment, existing links to the UK, and the intention to settle there.

The test did not only apply to those having worker status coming from EEA countries, so that British citizens returning to the UK also had to pass the test in order not to violate EU non-discrimination rules. In fact, a review of the test under the Labour Government in the late 1990s criticised that returning UK citizens were most affected by the test. At the time, Labour cut residence requirements from five to two years in response. Nevertheless, in 2008 almost 3,000 British citizens failed the test.[74]

IV. THE UK AFTER EASTERN ENLARGEMENT

After the 2004 enlargement, the UK was one of the few Member States (together with Ireland and Sweden) not using the transitional option of suspending the free movement of labour for 2+3+2 years. This happened on the basis of a forecast that 'net flows of migrants from new member states into the UK would be between 5,000 and 13,000 per year between 2004 and 2010.'[75] However, the Workers Registration Scheme (WRS), being installed for the EU-8 workers in the transition period, showed that 'between May 2004 and September 2006, around 487,000

[73] Ruhs (n 70) 22.

[74] S Kennedy, 'The Habitual Residence Test' (House of Commons Library, 2011).

[75] C Drew and D Sriskandarajah, *EU Enlargement in 2007: No Warm Welcome for Labor Migrants* (Migration Policy Institute, 2007).

A-8 nationals registered to work in the UK'.[76] Not all of those registering took long-term residence in the UK, of course. Official estimates see a rise in residents of EU-8 nationality in the UK from 125,000 in 2004, to 690,000 in 2008, and 1,336,000 in 2014.[77] 2013 and 2014 were also the first years, where residents from the EU 27 countries outnumbered residents of non-EU nationality (2,938,000 compared with 2,406,000), since the Annual Population Survey began in 2004. Altogether, the non-British resident population grew from 5 per cent in 2004 to 8.4 per cent in 2014.

Alongside the unprecedented and unexpected migration to the UK, ongoing reforms of the welfare state, notably on eligibility criteria, sought to make the system more robust against migration.[78] Directly linked to Eastern enlargement, in 2004 the habitual residence test was complemented by a new right-to-reside test. In contrast to habitual residence, UK nationals are exempted from this test. The right-to-reside test applies first; the habitual residence is checked only afterwards. The right-to-reside test is relevant to different benefits like JSA, child and housing benefits, and seeks to ensure that those EU citizens settling in the UK are either self-sufficient or economically active.[79] After the Citizenship Directive came into force in 2006, the habitual residence test was altered in order to allow for the initial three months of residence.[80]

The way the UK administration handles the habitual residence and the right-to-reside tests were subject to several court proceedings. Exempting UK nationals makes the right-to-reside test directly discriminatory. However, the restrictive position was confirmed by the UK Supreme Court in mid-2011 in the *Patmalniece* case,[81] as granting equal benefits would for the UK result in an undue financial burden. Such a restrictive interpretation of national discriminatory principles by domestic courts clearly shields national policies from the pressure of EU law. Thus, British courts, in the tradition of parliamentary sovereignty, granted leeway to government for administering social policy. The Commission, in contrast, was highly critical of the British right-to-reside test as it exempts UK citizens. It started an infringement procedure in 2010.[82] The government claimed that without the right-to-reside test, it could have to spend up to £ 2.5 billion a year in additional benefits—an estimate by the Secretary of State for Work and Pensions, Iain Duncan Smith, that was very critically discussed and disputed.[83] It was in

[76] ibid.

[77] www.ons.gov.uk/peoplepopulationandcommunity/populationandmigration/internationalmigration/articles/populationbycountryofbirthandnationalityreport/2015-09-27. Figure 2.

[78] C O'Brien, 'The Pillory, the Precipice and the Slippery Slope: The Profound Effects of the UK's Legal Reform Programme Targeting EU Migrants' (2015) 37 *Journal of Social Welfare and Family Law* 111.

[79] S Kennedy, *EEA Nationals: The 'Right to Reside' Requirement for Benefits* (House of Commons Library, 2011): researchbriefings.parliament.uk/ResearchBriefing/Summary/SN05972, 4.

[80] Kennedy, 'The Habitual Residence Test' (n 74) 4–5.

[81] *Patmalniece v SSWP* [2011] UKSC 11.

[82] Kennedy, *EEA Nationals: The 'Right to Reside' Requirement for Benefits* (n 79) 15–16.

[83] ibid 8–9.

January 2013 that Prime Minister David Cameron promised a referendum on the question of membership in the EU until 2017, should he remain in office. In this debate on a reform of the EU, questions of access of EU citizens to the welfare state were a central cause for concern.

The Commission did not budge in view of increasing British Euroscepticism and took its case against the right-to-reside test to the Court in 2013.[84] While the Commission originally had argued for a discrimination of EU nationals relating to different benefits (State Pension Credit, income-based JSA, Child Benefit and Child Tax Credit), after the ruling in *Brey* it restricted the infringement procedure to Child Benefit and Child Tax Credits. Against the Commission's claim, Advocate General Cruz Villalón in his Opinion in the case in October 2015, argued the test to be a proportionate measure that could be justified by the need to protect public finances (No 75; 99). The Court followed this view in June 2016, shortly before the Brexit referendum, emphasising its more recent case law that backs Member States' restrictions of access to their tax-financed social systems. It was during the pending of this court case and in line with the increasingly Eurosceptic political climate that the UK government aimed to reduce the access of EU citizens to different social benefits through various legislative reforms.

It is remarkable of these reforms, in how far the British administration took up and operationalised the requirements that the ECJ had set up in its case law. In late 2013, the government announced a revised habitual residence test with more individualised questions, guided by an intelligent IT system, including queries regarding efforts to get into work.[85] This can be regarded as a response to the individual assessments that the Court normally requires in its case law, for instance in *Brey*. From 2014 onwards, JSA was cut for the first three months of stay in the UK. This showed the original generosity of the UK welfare system. The allowance is paid only for the following three months, which is still more permissive than the German law. After six months, the jobseeker has to show 'genuine chances of being engaged'.[86] The UK requires EU foreigners to provide 'compelling evidence' that they are likely to find employment—otherwise, they lose their JSA, and their right of residence. For this purpose, the UK introduced a Genuine Prospect of Work test to start in mid-2014 for new applicants to JSA.[87] In 2015, the test was extended to those who were already claiming JSA.

Moreover, since 2014, the jobseeker status no longer entitles one to housing benefits. The UK government argued that in view of 3,000 EEA citizens claiming housing benefits, this could imply savings of about £10 million a year.[88] Access to child benefits and tax credits was also cut in 2014 for the first three months

[84] *Commission v UK* (n 58).

[85] S Kennedy, 'People from Abroad: What Benefits Can They Claim?' (House of Commons Library, 2015) 8–9.

[86] *Antonissen* (n 33).

[87] Kennedy 'People from Abroad' (n 85) 17 ff.

[88] ibid 24.

of residence.[89] In order to follow the case law requirement to assess whether work is not 'only marginal and ancillary', the government has set minimum earning thresholds. EU citizens automatically qualify as workers when proving earnings of £150 per week, which corresponds to 24hours a week at the National Minimum Wage. Only those earning less are assessed individually, for which detailed guidelines of the responsible Department for Work and Pensions (DWP) exist.[90]

With the gradual introduction of Universal Credit since 2013, further measures have followed. The Universal Credit replaces the six major means-tested benefits (Income-based JSA, Income-related Employment and Support Allowance, Income Support, Working Tax Credit, Child Tax Credit and Housing Benefit). Classifying it as social assistance made it easier for the government to exclude EU citizens, compared with unemployment-related benefits where the free movement of workers requires more far-reaching rights for EU citizens. Legislation in June 2015 details that EU citizen jobseekers do not qualify for Universal Credit.[91]

In summary, for assessing whether someone is a habitual resident, possessing 'genuine chances of being engaged' or having work that is not 'only marginal and ancillary', the UK implemented different tests which show how the British common law tradition provides a very fertile ground for the direct implementation of European case law.[92] The UK administration clearly adapted its administrative procedures to the case law requirements. Moreover, it became apparent that the UK in part had been quite generous, for instance, in granting unemployment benefits in the first three months until 2014. This is interesting in view of the argument of Commissioner Reding in the aftermath of the criticism on possible benefit tourism by the governments of Germany, France, the Netherlands and the UK in late 2013. The Commissioner had argued that it was up to the Member States to design their welfare systems in a way that make them robust against exploitation.[93]

Alongside domestic reforms and in view of large-scale inner-EU migration, the UK government pushed for a reform of EU law, which led to a compromise at the European Council meeting in February 2016 on several changes to be enacted should the UK opt to remain in the EU in the referendum.[94] Among these was the agreement to change Regulation 883/2004 to allow for an indexation of child benefits paid to children living in other Member States as well as an amendment to Regulation 492/2011 to include a safeguard mechanism in times of extraordinary migration. In such a case, a Member State would have the option to restrict in-work-benefits for EU citizens for the first four years of residence. These concessions, however, failed to convince the British population as to the promised new balance of powers between the EU and its Member States.

[89] ibid 31.

[90] ibid 21.

[91] ibid 33.

[92] See the detailed staff guidance under: www.gov.uk/government/uploads/system/uploads/attachment_data/file/572413/dmgch0703.pdf.

[93] Politico, 6 December 2013: www.politico.eu/article/reding-offers-help-with-free-movement.

[94] Council of the European Union, European Council meeting, 18–19 February 2016— *Conclusions*.

V. CONCLUSION

In this chapter I have argued that the specific historical and political conditions of the Brexit decision in the UK should not blind us as to its general lessons for the EU. Disregarding the specifics of the UK party system with the state of the Conservative Party and the UK Independence Party (UKIP), as well as the politics of austerity under Chancellor George Osborne, general problems of the EU came to a head in the UK. Exceptionally high migration, particularly from Poland—described as possibly the largest movement between two countries in peacetime[95]—met conditions of a flexible labour market and a welfare state with several non-contributory benefits.[96] Moreover, and this has been my focus in this chapter, the conditions of the UK polity are particularly conducive to showing the constraints of the EU polity, namely the problem of over-constitutionalisation. On the background of its common law tradition, the UK has been particularly responsive to the requirements of ECJ case law regarding EU citizenship. Elaborated administrative procedures were installed in order to do justice to ECJ case law; abiding by the letter of case law, however, made these constraints transparent and opened them to questioning as to their political backing.

In the EU, there has not been a political consensus on allowing residence irrespective of economic self-sufficiency. With moves of 'covert' integration,[97] the Court and the Commission pushed for amplified rights of EU citizens; in granting these, the EU relies, however, on the willingness of Member States. With no EU financed welfare benefits, the non-majoritarian decisions at EU level rely on Member States carrying the burden.

The potential of courts to realise societal change, however, has clear limits. In his influential study, Rosenberg showed that the success of the US civil rights movement relied much less on the Supreme Court than public narratives assumed.[98] While courts are well legitimated in the balance of powers framework to push individual liberal rights and non-discrimination, courts are hardly legitimated to determine redistributive decisions. To determine how the taxpayers' money is being spent is not for courts to decide.[99]

The situation in the UK was exceptional in several respects: the size of the inflow of people after Eastern enlargement; the lack of knowledge on the extent to which EU citizens claim benefits; and the scale of politicising EU migration. The UK's common law tradition and the comparative exactness with which ECJ

[95] M Okólski and J Salt, 'Polish Emigration to the UK after 2004; Why Did So Many Come?' (2014) 3 *Central and Eastern European Migration Review* 11.

[96] Ruhs (n 70).

[97] A Héritier, 'Covert Integration in the European Union' in J Richardson and S Mazey (eds), *European Union: Power and Policy-Making*, 4th edn (London, Routledge, 2015).

[98] Rosenberg (n 7).

[99] Sieberer (n 47).

case law requirements were translated into administrative practice brought the non-majoritarian sources of claims to the fore. 'The Habitual Residence Test has been described as "notoriously opaque"'.[100]

Despite the historical contingencies of the British case, other Member States with a highly developed welfare state similarly grapple with how to restrict the payment of social benefits to recently arrived EU citizens for fear of giving incentives to EU migrants that contribute less economically than they claim in benefits. With right-wing populism gaining strength in several Member States, the question of access to benefits may also be politicised in other countries. It is thus at the national level that policy decisions are questioned that were withdrawn from majoritarian decision-making by over-constitutionalisation at the EU level.

Being bound by case law, the EU legislature has to incorporate case law principles into its secondary law as the Citizenship Directive showed. Member States were reluctant to follow the Court in its expansive interpretation of rights and left some aspects of the Citizenship Directive deliberately open. Clearly, Member States did not want full access for all EU citizens to non-contributory social benefits, but aimed to guard privileged treatment of their nationals. Nevertheless, the subsequent actions of the ECJ and the Commission disregarded some specifications of the Citizenship Directive, pushing initially towards an increasingly equalised status of EU citizens with nationals.

The Citizenship Directive, thus, could not provide the opportunity to define citizenship rights in line with political consensus, as it could not overcome the constraints of over-constitutionalisation. It is the great weakness of the EU that it also proved unwilling and unable to respond to British demands for a greater flexibility of rules when British membership was at stake in the referendum. The EU did not want to be taken hostage in the domestic discussion of a Member State. Were integration less shaped by 'covert' integration, this would be more defendable. But the discussion on 'exit' evolved around a topic, the access of recently settled EU-citizens to non-contributory benefits, where the EU had not listened much to 'voice'. The legislature was bound by case law. And the Court was slow to realise the limits of acceptance of its citizenship jurisprudence. With the UK leaving, incredible damage is done to the Union, to the UK and to EU citizens living in the UK as well as UK citizens living in the rest of the EU.

Thus, another opportunity was missed to reconcile liberal and republican rights concerning the rights of EU citizens.[101] It is highly likely that in the medium term the EU will have to take up this challenge and find more transparent rules on how to reconcile free movement and national welfare states. The economic heterogeneity of the EU-27/28 appears too large for rules enacted and interpreted in the context of the more homogeneous EU-6/9/12/15. As 'a certain degree of

[100] Kennedy, 'The Habitual Residence Test' (n 74) 16.
[101] Scharpf (n 60).

financial solidarity between nationals of a host Member State and nationals of other member states' (*Grzelczyk*, No 44) can become an 'unreasonable burden' (*Bidar*, No 57), it must be up to majoritarian decision-making outside the constraints of over-constitutionalisation to draft clear guidelines showing when EU citizens can expect to be treated as equals in other Member States. It cannot be left to the Court to determine the extent of solidarity, as it is upon political actors to take the responsibility and to solicit the support of the electorate.

3

The Citizenship of Personal Circumstances in Europe

DIMITRY KOCHENOV*

APPROACHED FROM THE citizenship point of view, the EU's is a curiously atypical legal system which construes the ongoing shift from citizenship to personhood in global constitutional law[1] in such a way that the advent of the person, while boasting, globally, a powerful ability to remedy the harsh edges of the arbitrary exclusionary legal fiction of citizenship by embracing those who do not qualify to benefit from it, plays quite the opposite role: it disables the protections of EU citizenship. In other words: while, globally, what can be loosely termed 'personhood' comes to the rescue when citizenship cannot help, thus creating de facto citizens where the de jure legal status is not extended, in the hands of the Court of Justice of the European Union (ECJ), quite spectacularly, personhood serves as a tool of rationalising the de facto exclusion from the rights and protections of EU citizenship. This curious turn, which this chapter aims to document and discuss, has two consequences. First, it annihilates citizenship as a meaningful legal status in the European Union,[2] since its declared benefits and protections can always be overridden by personal circumstances of the holder: precisely what citizenship, at its inception, was supposed

* I am grateful to Robert Schütze, Christoph Schönberger, Kristin Surak and Daniel Thym, and also to Gráinne de Búrca, Daniela Caruso, Vlad Perju and other participants of the EU Law Professors Seminar at Boston College Law School in November 2016 where this work was first presented. The assistance of Ryan Chavez, Harry Panagopoulos, and Jacquelyn Veraldi is kindly acknowledged. This paper was finished during my tenure as Franz Weyr Fellow at the Centre for Law and Public Affairs (CeLAPA), Institute of State and Law of the Academy of Sciences of the Czech Republic in the Fall of 2016. I am grateful to Petr Agha for the kind invitation and hospitality.

[1] L Bosniak, 'Persons and Citizens in Constitutional Thought' (2010) 8 *International Journal of Constitutional Law* 9. *cf* D Kostakopoulou, *The Future Governance of Citizenship* (Cambridge, Cambridge University Press, 2008). For analyses of the European perspective see L Azoulai, 'L'autonomie de l'individu européen et la question du statut' (2013) EUI Working Paper LAW 2013/14: hdl.handle.net/1814/29098; L Azoulai, E Pataut and S Barbou des Places (eds), *Ideas of the Person and Personhood in European Union Law* (Oxford, Hart Publishing, 2016).

[2] Let alone the 'fundamental status' the ECJ has proclaimed it to be: Case C-184/99 *Grzelczyk v centre public d'Aide sociale d'Ottignies-Louvain-la-Neuve*, EU:C:2001:458, para 31. See also, eg Case C-413/99 *Baumbast and R v Secretary of State for the Home Department*, EU:C:2002:493; Case C-34/09 *Gerardo Ruiz Zambrano v Office national de l'emploi (ONEm)*, EU:C:2011:124, para 41.

to make impossible.[3] Second, it deprives of protections of citizenship precisely those who need it most, since they become invisible in the eyes of the powers that be.[4] As a result citizenship in Europe is becoming a 'citizenship of personal circumstances'—a figure of inescapable individualism imposed on those in need,[5] who are thereby detached from other citizenry and branded out as not good enough in the eyes of the Union—leaving little space to the grand ideals of the past.

I. THE GLOBAL THINNING OF CITIZENSHIP EXPLAINED

'Citizenship' for the purposes of this chapter is defined in traditional legal-political terms, following the classical expression of Rogers Brubaker as 'an Instrument and object of closure'.[6] Citizenship is thus the chalk of the line between the 'outs' and the 'ins'; an indispensable element of the legal 'world-making':[7] having asked for one's citizenship, we are usually clear about whether that person counts in full in the eyes of our law. Not being in possession of the local citizenship, whether admitted willingly or not, has always been tinted with a slight touch of presumed barbarity.[8] By definition, the world outside the Union borders is worse than our world: in the EU, the prospect of being expulsed into that wild wider reality outside our borders came to be protected by law better than living at home undisturbed:[9] the apotheosis of parochial thinking lying nevertheless at the essence of citizenship as a legal status. It is thus unavoidable and fundamental, that citizenship, above all, is a legal status: Pierre Bourdieu is right that the law is very effective in pre-empting the recognition of what lies outwith the realm of the reality it has mandated and created,[10] branding as non-existent any fact of social reality not overlapping with the legal truth,[11] however harsh is the world shaped by the latter.[12] The necessarily arbitrary nature of how the line between the

[3] P Caro de Sousa, 'Quest for the Holy Grail' (2014) 20 *European Law Journal* (*ELJ*) 499; D Kochenov, 'Neo-Mediaeval Permutations of Personhood in Europe' in L Azoulai, E Pataut and S Barbou des Places (eds), *Ideas of the Person and Personhood in European Union Law* (Oxford, Hart Publishing, 2016).

[4] C O'Brien, 'Civis Capitalist Sum: Class as the New Guiding Principle of EU Free Movement Rights' (2016) 53 *CML Rev* 937; D Kochenov, 'On Tiles and Pillars: EU Citizenship as a Federal Denominator' in D Kochenov (ed), *EU Citizenship and Federalism: The Role of Rights* (Cambridge, Cambridge University Press, 2017) 3.

[5] See also A Somek, 'Europe: Political, Not Cosmopolitan' (2014) 20 *ELJ* 142.

[6] WR Brubaker, *Citizenship and Nationhood in France and Germany* (Cambridge, MA,, HUP, 1992) 34.

[7] P Bourdieu, 'The Force of Law: Toward a Sociology of the Juridical Field' (1987) 38 *Hastings Law Journal* 814, 838.

[8] J Tully, *On Global Citizenship: James Tully in Dialogue* (London, Bloomsbury Academic, 2014).

[9] Case C-434/09 *Shirley McCarthy v Secretary of State for the Home Department*, EU:C:2011:277; S Iglesias Sánchez, 'A Citizenship Right to Stay? The Right Not to Move in a Union Based on Free Movement' in D Kochenov (ed), *EU Citizenship and Federalism: The Role of Rights* (Cambridge, Cambridge University Press, 2017).

[10] Bourdieu (n 7).

[11] JM Balkin, 'The Proliferation of Legal Truth' (2003) 26 *Harvard Journal of Law & Public Policy* 9.

[12] JM Balkin, 'Agreements with Hell and Other Objects of Our Faith' (1997) 65 *Fordham Law Review* 1703.

citizens and the non-citizens is drawn in any society has not escaped the attention of commentators.[13] Indeed, next to the production and reproduction of exclusion, the in-built arbitrariness arose as the second key feature of the status of citizenship.

Citizenship, as a legal status of attachment to public authority,[14] is always distributed uniquely by the authority itself. It does not depend on any sentiments and feeling of the citizenry, of course: as a Dutchman having spent a lot of time in the US I can perceive of myself as an ideal American (and even be accepted by my American-born friends as such), but this fact—just as not caring about my Dutch subjecthood or the monarch that much[15]—has no bearing on the legal status I hold. This status entails the enjoyment of a set of citizenship rights including, but not limited in the majority of jurisdictions, to the right to stay and work in the territory under the jurisdiction of the authority in question, including the right not to be deported;[16] political rights; and the entitlement to non-discrimination among citizens, ie, the holders of a formal legal status of citizenship under a particular authority. Non-discrimination is of special importance in this context: while it is frequently positioned as a right, it is also, unquestionably, implied in the status as such. Remove the formal requirement of equality before the law and characterising the resulting legal arrangement as a citizenship one would be most difficult to say the least: citizenship being premised on, precisely, the creation of a legal abstraction out of the actual people with all the differences that being a person implies, will fail to emerge if any other differences between the citizens, beyond the formal legal status they hold, became an indispensable precondition informing their duties and entitlements.[17]

That the legal fiction so necessary for any modern constitutional system to survive is essentially arbitrary in nature is exceedingly difficult to ignore in a world where the whole ethos of the law is about asking for good reasons behind this or that element of the legal reality proclaimed by the powers that be. Indeed, constant questioning of authority's mantras is what reinforces modern democracy[18] and, at the level of the law, makes the Rule of Law possible.[19] After the advent of the 'culture of justification' coming to replace 'the culture of authority'[20] arbitrariness

[13] A Shachar, *Birthright Lottery* (Cambridge, MA, HUP, 2009).

[14] The formal level of the authority does not matter, usually: R Bauböck, 'Global Justice, Freedom of Movement and Democratic Citizenship' (2009) 51 *Archives européennes de sociologie* 1.

[15] D Kochenov, 'Mevrouw de Jong Gaat Eten' (2011) EUI Working Paper RSCAS 2011/06: hdl.handle.net/1814/15774.

[16] B Anderson, MJ Gibney and E Paoletti, 'Citizenship, Deportation and the Boundaries of Belonging' (2011) 15 *Citizenship Studies* 547.

[17] C Joppke, *Citizenship and Immigration* (Cambridge, Polity Press, 2010) 96–110 (and the literature cited therein).

[18] M Kumm, 'The Idea of Socratic Contestation and the Right to Justification' (2010) 4 *Law & Ethics of Human Rights* 141.

[19] G Palombella, *È possibile la legalità globale?* (Bologna, Il Mulino, 2012); G Palombella, 'The Rule of Law and its Core' in G Palombella and N Walker (eds), *Relocating the Rule of Law* (Oxford, Hart Publishing, 2009).

[20] M Cohen-Eliya and I Porat, *Proportionality and Constitutional Culture* (Cambridge, Cambridge University Press, 2013).

is not quite the answer even in the world of the likes of Trump and May. Defending arbitrariness by allusions to the necessary nature of the outcomes it produces in a democracy—ie, a body politic—cannot convince since it simply substitutes one arbitrariness (the body of those with a citizenship status) with another (the body of those who are politically involved and should have a citizenships status to participate).

Consequently, and most logically, too, as we look back, the key trend in the citizenship evolution over the last decades has been to underplay citizenship's former glory by reaching beyond the arbitrariness of the legal fiction lying at its base. This process had two key facets, which were profoundly interrelated. It consisted, first, of the extension of the rights formerly reserved for citizens only also to those who would not have the formal legal status as well as ensuring that all those in possession of the formal legal status could in fact enjoy citizenship rights, even women, minorities and naturalised citizens. As a consequence, the borderline between citizenship rights and human rights came to be rethought under pressure, inter alia, from the rise of human rights ideology[21] and the evolution of the basic relationship between the authority and the population under its control, citizens and non-citizens included.[22]

Second, we can witness a gradual extension of the status—either de jure or de facto—to the groups of those who were previously randomly excluded. Such extension happened both in the courts of law[23] and via legislative developments.

[21] G Frankenberg, 'Human Rights and the Belief in a Just World' (2014) 12 *International Journal of Constitutional Law* 35.

[22] Y Soysal, *Limits of Citizenship* (Chicago, IL, University of Chicago Press, 1994). It comes as no surprise that residence—especially long-term residence in the territory of a particular state—came to acquire a special significance in this context: G Davies, '"Any Place I Hang My Hat?" or: Residence is the New Nationality' (2005) 11 *ELJ* 43, 55; D Thym, 'Residence as *de facto* Citizenship? Protection of Long-term Residence under Article 8 ECHR' in R Rubio-Marin (ed), *Human Rights and Immigration* (Oxford, Oxford University Press, 2014).

[23] While the law used to be precisely so categorical, the rise of Art 8 ECHR jurisprudence prohibiting, in numerous cases, deportations to the country of citizenship, has created something akin to a de facto nationality, altering the legal reality to a great degree. See, for one of the first notable examples, the Concurring Opinion of Judge Martens in *Beldjoudi* (*Beldjoudi v France* (1992) Series A no 191-B; *Jeunesse v Netherlands* App no 12738/10 (ECHR, 3 October 2014). This trend, although markedly counter-orthodox in citizenship matters, and deeply empowering at the individual level, has been criticised in the literature (eg, D Thym, 'Respect for Private and Family Life under Article 8 ECHR in Immigration Cases: A Human Right to Regularize Illegal Stay?' (2008) 57 *ICLQ* 87. *cf* Thym, '*Residence as de facto Citizenship?* (n 22)) and is not yet a mainstream position of the European Court of Justice: S Adam and P Van Elsuwege, 'EU Citizenship and the European Federal Challenge through the Prism of Family Reunification' in D Kochenov (ed), *EU Citizenship and Federalism: The Role of Rights* (Cambridge, Cambridge University Press, 2017). The trend definitely adds to the picture of the ongoing contestation of the normative foundations of citizenship and is observable also in the practice of the UN Human Rights Committee (UNHRC), which is in tune with the ECtHR practice: UNHRC, 'Stewart v Canada' (1996) Communication No 538/1993 ('no one shall be arbitrarily deprived of the right to enter his own country' (quoting Art 12(4) of the International Covenant on Civil and Political Rights (ICCPR), GA Res 2200A (XXI), UN Doc A/6316 (23 March 23 1976)). See also UNHRC, 'General Comment 27, Freedom of Movement (Article 12)' 2 November 1999, UN Doc CCPR/C/21/Rev.1/Add.9. According to the Committee, the scope of 'his own country' in the sense of Art 12 ICCPR is broader than 'his country of nationality' (para 20).

Most importantly, the revision of nationality laws to make these more inclusive and tolerant of multiple nationalities facilitated a move away from the previous paradigm of exclusive allegiances.[24]

The consequence of this quest against arbitrariness leaping into the territory of citizenship, which is, in itself, an arch-example of arbitrariness in action, is the unavoidable thinning of citizenship as a legal status associated with an entitlement to rights, as well as the radical decrease in citizenship duties.[25] This is not surprising at all: striving to make less arbitrary and less exclusionary the legal fiction whose aim, precisely, is to justify arbitrary exclusion from territory, society and, not infrequently, dignity (through the denial of equality before the law), can only result in a legal fiction which is a less meaningful one. This is how we came to the advent of the 'citizenship-lite' in Christian Joppke's thoughtful analysis.[26] The high point of this development is the turn in constitutional theory to the figure of the person as opposed to a citizen, a no small feat in constitutional law.[27] Let us trace the key steps of this development.

The gradual extension of the scope of those enjoying the rights of citizenship among the actual bearers of the status is a well-known story of women, the indigenous peoples and other minorities. The gradual extension of those enjoying the status of citizenship in full is, again, the story of the 'coloureds' 'unfit for citizenship', of migrants and of the colonial subjects. Once it became unacceptable not to extend the rights of citizenship to settled minority categories, not allowing them to pass on citizenship became obviously problematised, just as the right of other minorities to enjoy access to the status as such.[28]

As the gap between the scope of nominal citizens and the scope of citizens with citizenship rights was drastically diminishing (women got the right to vote and pass on the citizenship status to their descendants, for instance),[29] coupled with the extension of the status of citizenship to the formerly excluded minority groups (think of the extension of the full Australian citizenship to the aboriginals, for instance),[30] the ideological distinction between citizens and non-citizens in a society expectedly came to be problematised and contested, bringing about the

[24] PJ Spiro, *At Home in Two Countries: The Past and Future of Dual Citizenship* (New York, New York University Press, 2015); PJ Spiro, 'Dual Citizenship as Human Right' (2010) 8 *International Journal of Constitutional Law* 111. Again, exceptions are obviously there, even in the European Union, but the global trend towards multiple nationality toleration around the world is as clear as day, as Professor Spiro has masterfully proven. For a critical analysis of exceptional cases in the EU, see D Kochenov, 'Double Nationality in the EU: An Argument for Tolerance' (2011) 17 *ELJ* 323.

[25] D Kochenov, 'EU Citizenship without Duties' (2014) 20 *ELJ* 482.

[26] C Joppke, 'The Inevitable Lightening of Citizenship' (2010) 51 *European Journal of Sociology* 37.

[27] Bosniak, 'Persons and Citizens in Constitutional Thought' (n 1).

[28] S Munshi, 'Immigration, Imperialism, and the Legacies of Indian Exclusion' (2016) 28 *Yale Journal of Law & the Humanities* 51.

[29] M Goldhaber, *A People's History of the European Court of Human Rights* (New Brunswick, Rutgers University Press, 2007) 15–26.

[30] D Mercer, '"Citizen Minus?": Indigenous Australians and the Citizenship Question' (2003) 7 *Citizenship Studies* 421.

increasing extension of rights, coupled with a grant of a (theoretical) possibility to acquire citizenship status to any settled resident of any modern liberal democratic state: the majority of jurisdictions today do not know formerly commonplace disqualifications related to race and religion, for instance.

In other words, while the proclamation of equal rights of citizenship at the inception of citizenship was precisely the ideological tool to facilitate de facto socio-economic exclusion of huge chunks of society and the legitimation of authority in charge of the preservation of the status quo as TH Marshall explained,[31] and was thus not even remotely overlapping with the actual reality on the ground, where citizenship actually endowed with rights was the privilege of a radical minority in a society—usually white males able to pass the property census[32]—the two key trends outlined above—the gradual extension of rights and the extension of the status—brought the actual reality on the ground closer to the initial rhetorical ideal, also empowering further contestations of exclusions within the ambit of citizenship—think about the sexual citizenship story, for instance,[33] or the ongoing animal citizenship debate.[34]

This, in turn, led to the relative—and necessarily welcome, given its harshly arbitrary and exclusionary beginnings—trivialisation of the status of citizenship as well as a more faithful correspondence between the actual society under the authority in question and citizenry under the same authority. Once the rigidity of the citizens–non-citizens divide in terms of the corresponding rights and entitlements is questioned, abuses of power using this divide as the chief legal tool are made difficult. History knows plentiful examples of such unfortunate deployment of the citizenship status. Think, for instance, of Nuremberg laws excluding Germany's Jewry from the status to justify their formal exclusion from the key rights of citizenship.[35] South-African *apartheid* 'homelands', designed to distribute fake citizenships of non-recognized all-black puppet states, like Bophuthatswana and Transkei[36] to grant minorities 'full rights abroad'[37] are equally good examples.

[31] TH Marshall, 'Citizenship and Social Class' in TH Marshall (T Bottomore (eds)), *Citizenship and Social Class* (London, Pluto Press, 1992).

[32] Women, although formally holding a citizenship status, were excluded not only from political rights, but also from the possibility of keeping their status after marrying a foreigner or a stateless person or passing it on to their children. *cf* for US law examples, P Weil, *The Sovereign Citizen* (Philadelphia, PA, Penn Press, 2012).

[33] Ŭ Belavusaŭ, 'EU Sexual Citizenship: Sex beyond the Internal Market' in D Kochenov (ed), *EU Citizenship and Federalism: The Role of Rights* (Cambridge, Cambridge University Press, 2017) (and the literature cited therein).

[34] S Donaldson and W Kymlicka, *Zoopolis: A Political Theory of Animal Rights* (Oxford, Oxford University Press, 2011); WA Edmundson, 'Do Animals Need Citizenship?' (2015) 13 *International Journal of Constitutional Law* 749.

[35] K Rundle, 'The Impossibility of an Exterminatory Legality: Law and the Holocaust' (2009) 59 *University of Toronto Law Journal* 65, 69–76.

[36] At some point Wikipedia had the irony of mentioning Nelson Mandela among the 'notable citizens' of this 'state', which is not, per se, legalistically incorrect.

[37] See, eg, South African, Bantu Homelands Citizenship Act, 1970, which instituted the denaturalisation of the black majority during the apartheid era. *cf* J Dugard, 'South Africa's Independent Homelands: An Exercise in Denationalization' (1980) 10 *Denver Journal of International Law & Policy* 11.

More recently, Latvian and Estonian policy of humiliation of Russian, Ukrainian and Jewish minorities, based precisely on the same strategy of the denial of citizenship to supply a justification of exclusion from key rights did not work equally well: under pressure from the international institutions the majority of formerly 'citizenship' rights came to be extended to the minorities as 'human' rights.[38] Not yet the right to vote, the right to a name[39] or the right to speak the mother tongue at work,[40] but the trend is clear: 'they are not citizens' is not an automatically enforced valid pretext any more to abuse minority populations—at least it does not come unquestioned.

Crucially and inseparably from the story of the status and rights, the same evolution affected citizenship duties, too. Traditionally the main vehicle of transposition of the purely legal truths into the reality of day-to-day lives through coercion, mass schooling and conscription, duties of citizenship are undergoing an astonishingly speedy recess in the majority of the liberal democratic jurisdictions around the globe, as 'forging a good citizen', ie, punishing those deviating from the legal truth enforced by teachers, the army and the police (and, crucially, the complacency of the well-meaning law-abiding masses),[41] is not any more a defensible task of the state. In the majority of the liberal democratic jurisdictions there is no conscription,[42] no more citizenship-based taxation,[43] and no more harassment of dual nationals,[44] to give just a few examples. As long as the duties and the civic virtues promoted by any state are necessarily designed to quash the recognition of minority (and sometimes even majority, like was the case with women all around the world and the black majority in South Africa) groups in society,[45]

[38] P Järve, 'Sovetskoje nasledije i sovremennaja ètnopolitika stran Baltii' in V Poleshchuk and V Stepanov (eds), *Ètnopolitika stran Baltii* (Moscow, Nauka, 2013); D Kochenov and A Dimitrovs, 'EU Citizenship for Latvian Non-Citizens: A Concrete Proposal' (2016) 38 *Houston Journal of International Law* 1.

[39] UNHRC, 'Raihman v Latvia' 2010 Communication No 1621/2007; on the problematic stance of the European international courts vis-a-vis this right, see A Łazowski, E Dagilytė and P Stasinopoulos, 'The Importance of Being Earnest: Spelling of Names, EU Citizenship and Fundamental Rights' (2015) 11 *Croation Yearbook of European Law & Policy* 1.

[40] D Kochenov, V Poleshchuk and A Dimitrovs, 'Do Professional Linguistic Requirements Discriminate? A Legal Analysis: Estonia and Latvia in the Spotlight' (2011) 10 *European Yearbook of Minority Issues* 137.

[41] P Szobar, 'Telling Sexual Stories in the Nazi Courts of Law: Race Defilement in Germany, 1933 to 1945' (2002) 11 *Journal of the History of Sexuality* 131, pointing out that the persecution of the 'Arian-Jewish' couples relied entirely on the information provided by the good willing citizens. Countless similar examples from a variety of jurisdictions could be provided.

[42] The countries still keeping conscription stick out as highly atypical and experience very specific threats, perceived or real. Think about Estonia, Greece, Israel and the Ukraine.

[43] With a marked exception of the US, filing income taxes all around the world is residence-, not citizenship-based. *cf* JR Harvey, 'Worldwide Taxation of United States Citizens Living Abroad—Impact of FATCA and Two Proposals' (2014) 4 *George Mason Journal of International Commercial Law* 319; T Denson, 'Goodbye, Uncle Sam? How the Foreign Account Tax Compliance Act is Causing a Drastic Increase in the Number of Americans Renouncing Their Citizenship' (2015) 52 *Houston Law Review* 967.

[44] See n. 24.

[45] A similar argument has been made in the context of constitutionalism as such: J Tully, *Strange Multiplicity: Constitutionalism in an Age of Diversity* (Cambridge, Cambridge University Press, 1995).

any arguments for their goodness and necessity all but fail to tell the whole truth, stopping at the retelling of the ideological mantras of the unity of *demos* and political community, as polished as they are comfortable, and ignoring the functions of such duties in the actual societies on the ground.[46]

Turning to the conceptualisation of citizenship through the 'acts of citizenship' is most appropriate in this context: the majority of those behind the constitutional moments are precisely the ones failing to buy what the authority is preaching: those *not* accepting the power of the duties narrative, ie, the 'activist' citizens in Engin Isin's terms[47]—from Dr Martin Luther King and President Vaclav Havel to Colonel von Stauffenberg the list of such figures can be extended *ad infinitum*. It is thus a most welcome development that citizenship is not centred on duties any more, thus becoming less totalitarian, more inclusive and forward looking.[48] It is not, thus,—in theory at least—based on idealised masculinities, given that the main duty has always been to kill for the authority that happened to draft you.[49] Nineteenth-century scholars would find it most surprising and counterintuitive that full citizenship, including a package of rights associated therewith is attainable without conscription and sacrifice, let alone extended to the legally 'unfit' who cannot be conscripted at all, like women or minorities, for instance.[50] With the waning away of the need to rationalise discrimination and de facto inequalities within the de jure status of equals, which seems to be the key function, with which the duties of citizenship have traditionally been endowed, the modern state certainly lost some of the stakes in the grand citizenship narrative of *egalité*, *liberté* and *fraternité* for the very select few on the preset terms of goodness which have to be shared by all at the gunpoint.

II. THE ADVENT OF PERSONHOOD AS A DE FACTO ALTERNATIVE TO CITIZENSHIP THINKING

The residue of pre-human rights thinking predating the tectonic shifts in the understanding and practice of citizenship is still around, however, and could explain, inter alia, the backlash the world seems to be experiencing in the field of the regulation of access to the status of citizenship: naturalisations are more

[46] For an example of such idealising see, eg, R Bellamy, 'A Duty-Free Europe? What's Wrong with Kochenov's Account of EU Citizenship Rights' (2015) 21 *ELJ* 558 (and the literature cited therein).

[47] E Isin, 'Citizenship in Flux: The Figure of the Activist Citizen' (2009) 29 *Subjectivity* 367.

[48] For a more systematic treatment, see Kochenov, 'EU Citizenship without Duties' (n 25).

[49] JR Abrams, 'Examining Entrenched Masculinities in the Republican Government Tradition' (2011) 114 *West Virginia Law Review* 165; C Snyder, *Citizen-Soldiers and Manly Warriors: Military Service and Gender in the Civic Republican Tradition* (Lanham, MD, Rowman & Littlefield, 1999). In the European context, see, Bełavusaŭ (n 33).

[50] Taney CJ has famously used the legal inability of the African Americans in the US to assume the duties of citizenship (based on a statute reserving the membership in the militias to white males) as a justification for not extending rights to them: *Scott v Sandford* [1857] 60 US (19 HOW) 393, 420–21.

and more dependent on the elaborate *rites de passage* in the form of 'culture' and 'values' tests, which settled foreigners are required to pass to acquire the formal status of citizenship.[51] The assumption behind such tests is as problematic as it is commonplace: the culture from across the border is a barbarian non-equivalent of our own.[52] Putting this assumption to practice is even more difficult, however, than embracing it rationally, as the core value of any liberal democracy today is tolerance. Tolerance is what all the 'specificity testing' is necessarily bound to come down to.[53] In this sense testing the specificity of the highly unique Danish culture and of an even more unique Swiss one amounts, in fact, to testing one and the same thing. What such tests supposedly are testing, then, is whether someone is ready to concede that she is a second-rate human being since she is used to having her croissant plain, as opposed to with cream in the morning and be punished by sitting a test about the croissant with cream losing her time to remedy her inherent barbarian lack of dignity before naturalisation becomes a fact attested by proper documentation. Whether she eats it with cream or not after naturalisation is no one's concern in a tolerant society. Most problematically however, the 'integration tests' which keep on proliferating, fully reflect the core thinking behind citizenship anywhere in the world: the presumption of virtually irremediable difference between societies serving as a pretext to disqualify those with a different formal legal attachment from key legal entitlements and recognition.

Exclusion being the core normative foundation of citizenship, it is not a surprise that the status of citizenship enjoyed a more and more wobbly pedestal of glory, as of late, in constitutional theory, rivalled by its more physical and biological double: the person.[54] Once the legal figure of a citizen gives way to a legal recognition of a physical reality of an ordinary human, constitutionalism cannot any more be the same. And this is exactly the move we are increasingly witnessing, which is very strongly attuned, logically, to the several lines of developments outlined above.

The core issue of importance here is very basic and has to do with the traditional approaches to the core aspects of legitimacy in a political community: the justification of violence and of the obligation to submit to violence of the

[51] R van Oers, E Ersbøll and D Kostakopoulou (eds), *A Re-definition of Belonging? Language and Integration Tests in Europe* (Leiden, Martinus Nijhoff, 2010).

[52] However nasty, this assumption seems to be 'natural': MJ Lerner, 'The Justice Motive: Some Hypotheses as to its Origins and Forms' (1977) 45 *Journal of Personality* 1, esp 29. For the whole picture, see, MJ Lerner and S Clayton, *Justice and Self-Interest* (Cambridge, Cambridge University Press, 2011).

[53] This presents traditional accounts of citizenship in a radically new light: L Bosniak, 'Citizenship Denationalized' (2000) 7 *Indiana Journal of Global Legal Studies* 447. See also M Kuisma, 'Rights or Privileges? The Challenge of Globalization to the Values of Citizenship' (2008) 12 *Citizenship Studies* 613; M Wolf, 'Will the Nation-State Survive Globalization?' (2001) 81 *Foreign Affairs* 178; K Rubinstein and D Adler, 'International Citizenship: The Future of Nationality in a Globalised World' (2000) 7 *Indiana Journal of Global Legal Studies* 519; RD Lipschutz, 'Members Only? Citizenship and Civic Virtue in a Time of Globalization' (1999) 36 *International Politics* 203.

[54] Bosniak, 'Persons and Citizens in Constitutional Thought' (n 1).

public authority as a necessary element of being 'free' going back to Jean Bodin[55] and rooted in the Christian soteriology of the day.[56] If only citizens and no one else are counted as the constituents of the collective whence legitimacy emanates—call it *demos*, the nation, political community—then the picture of what the state and, necessarily, the law is about will be quite different, necessarily, compared with a situation when humans are counted, non-citizens included. Indeed, why not put humans, persons, at the basis of *demos*, the nation, political community? While legal and social truths are bound to overlap for the law to be effective[57]—and knowing the bio-power of the contemporary state in shaping the life itself to the whims of fashion of the day[58]—making citizens is still much easier and less problematic than acknowledging humans.

Making a citizen is an ideology-inspired legal exercise, implying a choice among the available bodies who could be useful or not for the achievement of the goals of the authority at any given time, whatever these are. Those bodies which are less useful are simply excluded and do not exist in the eyes of the law. Exclusions can run along any lines: geography of origin, race, religion, education, language, time; you name it, and a legal-historical example will be found. The citizenship's capacity to exclude is its core function, which means that, in the 'golden days' of citizenship—the mythical days of the concept's unquestioned authority—the exclusion at the level of the *legal status* could only rarely be questioned: equality is *among* citizens, remember? As a consequence, working with citizens the authority enjoys an almost universal carte blanche: you create ethnic electorates,[59] you assign the status of those who are not white enough to your liking to the 'ancestral homelands' referred to above,[60] you declare those you send away as ideologically[61] or racially deficient as non-citizens.[62] The long history of flagrant discriminations is rich and diverse. Under the citizenship paradigm the core question before looking at rights, entitlements, duties and equality claims is: *who* is a citizen in this society? Those who are not citizens are entitled to nothing and this is legally and politically right, even if frequently also morally unjust.

Not the same at all with the persons: recognising the person as a figure of importance for the purposes of constitutional law, as a component part of the *demos*,

[55] *cf* JH Franklin, *Jean Bodin and the Sixteenth-Century Revolution in the Methodology of Law and History* (Cambridge, Cambridge University Press, 1963), discussed in detail in K Kim, *Aliens in Mediaeval Law* (Cambridge, Cambridge University Press, 2000) 193.

[56] Kim (n 55) 193.

[57] Bourdieu (n 7).

[58] ML Flear, 'Developing Euro Biocitizens through Migration for Healthcare Services' (2007) 14 *Maastricht Journal of European and Comparative Law* 239.

[59] RC Visek, 'Creating Ethnic Electorate through Legal Restorationism: Citizenship Rights in Estonia' (1997) 38 *Harvard International Law Journal* 315.

[60] Dugard (n 37).

[61] L Chamberlain, *The Philosophy Steamer: Lenin and the Exile of the Intelligentsia* (London, Atlantic Books, 2006).

[62] Rundle (n 35).

however humble this relative innovation can seem, in fact revolutionises the legal understanding of our society since it opens the status assignment decisions which cannot in the majority of cases be contested under the citizenship paradigm, up for criticism and legal contestation. Moreover, it also flips the sequence of the status-rights interactions. The core question here is *why* this person is not entitled to a particular right. A simple 'she is not a citizen' answer will no longer suffice under the personhood paradigm: a substantive analysis will clearly be required. It goes without saying that the distinction between the 'status' and 'rights' taken by lawyers for granted is profoundly artificial and is not on all occasions justifiable.

Once humanity and personhood, not the formal legal status of citizenship, emerges as the key factor in the rights assignment play, the relevance of the formal status of citizenship as such is profoundly reinvented, if not outright diminished, as we have seen in the Article 8 jurisprudence of the European Court of Human Rights for instance (ECtHR).[63] Those who are French *in fact* by the way their lives are lived and how their social world is constructed, even if not recognized as de jure French, even bearing foreign citizenships, will stay in France protected by the ECtHR.[64] The recognition of rights attached to personhood can thus lead even to the protection of what used to be the sacred core of the citizenship rights, like the residence in the territory of a state, among the non-citizens. Under this logic a place in the nation is not 'deserved' by passing humiliating tests of the knowledge of the non-existent cultural uniqueness or a random act of birth in particular circumstances, but by *being part of a society*. The threat of the loss of rights, then, assessed in the context of a concrete life project, will be the key factor of importance for the courts to consider, not the legal status of citizenship. Moreover, the harsh consequences of the loss of rights can even prevent the state from denaturalising a person,[65] or depriving a non-citizen of the core citizenship rights acquired de facto through the engagement with the society in which she lives.[66] Such a blending of legal and social reality would be unheard of before the twenty-first century.[67] The two logics—citizenship and personhood—find themselves in a stark opposition to each other. The cleavage runs between either taking legal or,

[63] Adam and Van Elsuwege (n 23). But see Thym, 'Respect for Private and Family Life (n 23).

[64] *Beldjoudi* (n 23); *Jeunesse* (n 23); see also the discussion in n 23 above. *cf*, for a meticulous overview of the contemporary ECtHR practice, see Thym, 'Residence as *de facto* Citizenship? (n 22).

[65] The European Court of Justice case of *Rottmann* is the best example, probably: Case C-135/08 *Janko Rottman v Freistaat Bayern*, EU:C:2010:104. The absolute majority of commentators have ignored the fundamental point granting this case overwhelming importance: it is a decision about the status which is based on the rights this status is associated with, an impossibility in the classical citizenship world, as the borderline between the legal and social reality, which is the fundamental starting point of pretty much all citizenship theorising, simply disappeared in the Court's reasoning, illustrating the shift we are discussing very well.

[66] eg Adam and Van Elsuwege (n 23). See, also n 23 above.

[67] B de Hart, 'Regulating Mixed Marriages through Acquisition and Loss of Citizenship' (2015) 662 *Annals of the American Academy of Political and Social Science* 170; B de Hart, 'The Morality of Maria Toet: Gender, Citizenship and the Construction of the Nation-State' (2006) 32 *Journal of Ethnic and Migration Studies* 49.

which is quite a different matter, social facts as a starting point, thus providing a choice between parallel realities and their respective truths. This is the legal recognition of social facts in the growing array of contexts that pushes personhood as such, not necessarily connected to the formal status of citizenship, to prominence, with the far-reaching implications for the relevance of the classical normative picture of citizenship which we know from political theory textbooks.

III. THE RISE OF THE CITIZENSHIP OF PERSONAL CIRCUMSTANCES IN THE EU

The European Union, while officially—and even theoretically[68]—heralding a break with at least some of the classical functions of citizenship, has indeed achieved a most radical break with this tradition, but the question of whether it is to the better or to the worse remains open. The recognition of personhood as opposed to citizenship only, while it can no doubt be empowering, can also provide a vehicle for the dismantlement of important protections normally associated with the citizenship status, especially the equality before the law. In fact, EU law as designed and as practised, ie, far from the realm of exceptions, plays the role which runs counter the normative foundations traditionally regarded as underpinning the citizenship concept, but also, crucially for this chapter, departs from the personhood approach in a remarkable way, by turning such a departure *against* the extension of rights.

Such (no doubt well-meaning)[69] intrusion into the illusory, if not deceptive, as demonstrated above, garden of normative coherence is to the better, but also to the worse: besides opening up to Europeans new categories of rights outside the realm of their own states,[70] it has also questioned the essential elements of national citizenship, including the preferential relationship between the citizen and the state and, crucially, both aspects of Rogers Brubaker's now classical definition of citizenship. This chapter began with citizenship as 'an instrument and an object of closure'.[71] The EU dismantled it by demanding inclusion of other EU citizens into the national community guided by the principle of non-discrimination on the basis of nationality, thus 'abolishing'[72] the legal relevance of Member State nationalities in a huge array of crucial areas of human activity where EU law applies. The EU has also removed, to a great degree, the Member States' ability to regulate migration of EU citizens, with a very clear outcome for the relevance

[68] Kostakopoulou, *The Future Governance of Citizenship* (n 1).

[69] On the positive potential see, eg, D Kostakopoulou, 'European Union Citizenship: Writing the Future' (2007) 13 *ELJ* 623; FG Jacobs, 'Citizenship of the European Union—A Legal Analysis' (2007) 13 *ELJ* 591; F Wollenschläger, 'A New Fundamental Freedom beyond Market Integration: Union Citizenship and its Dynamics for Shifting the Economic Paradigm of European Integration' (2011) 17 *ELJ* 34.

[70] D Kochenov, '*Ius Tractum* of Many Faces: European Citizenship and the Difficult Relationship between Status and Rights' (2009) 15 *Columbia Journal of European Law* 169.

[71] Brubaker (n 6) 34.

[72] Davies, '"Any Place I Hang My Hat?"' (n 22).

and function of the nationalities of the Member States to go beyond providing a bridge to the *ius tractum* status of EU citizenship,[73] ie, serving as the means to *acquire* the supranational status. Third, and crucially, EU law, through the European Arrest Warrant, deactivated what is usually perceived of as one of the last remaining purely *citizenship*—as opposed to human—rights: the right not to be deported.[74] With no right to stay at home guaranteed under EU law, which pushes you to move states to save your rights or your family,[75] combined with the European Arrest Warrant taking precedence, if need be,[76] over national constitutional protections, EU citizenship, quite astonishingly, it may seem, does not carry with it a notion of a home[77] and possibly even forecloses—extreme circumstances aside—the national-level legal attempts to come to safeguard such a notion.[78] As a consequence, on the one hand, the standard normative correlation between national citizens and the societies in the Member States came under strong pressure: the ability of the French State to distribute the token of Frenchness, the French passport, in this context cannot possibly hide the fact that France does not control who is de facto French for pretty much all the purposes,[79] with the implications for the essence of the *demos* and the legitimation/justification of political power at both national and European level (especially given the exclusion of the European not-quite-foreigners from the national-level franchise).[80] On the other hand, the ability of anyone to stay within the realm of his or her national legal system protected by it from expulsion to a foreign land is equally shattered. EU law, attentive as ever to personal CVs, perceived 'links to the host state society'[81] and travel itineraries thus does not only reward the movers regarded as useful in the context of the internal market, but also 'un-protects' the static citizens even at the national level. Ironically, this happens precisely at the time when the importance of de facto citizenship's recognition is growing exponentially, acquiring a radically new *positive* significance in the world of personhood constitutionalism, as seen above.

I am not saying that deciding to crack states open in this way is a bad thing. For once, it has exposed plenty of untenable assumptions usually taken for granted which underlie and solidify the essence of the notion of citizenship and, by

[73] Kochenov, '*Ius Tractum* of Many Faces (n 70).

[74] Anderson, Gibney and Paoletti (n 16).

[75] N Nic Shuibhne, '(Some of) the Kids Are All Right' (2012) 49 *CML Rev.* 349; Iglesias Sánchez, 'A Citizenship Right to Stay?' (n 9) 371.

[76] At least as the official story goes, eg Case C-399/11 *Stefano Melloni v Ministerio Fiscal*, EU:C:2013:107.

[77] eg *McCarthy*, *Dereci*, *Alokpa*.

[78] Unless, ironically, the home is presumed by law to be abroad: *Alokpa*; *Petruhhin*.

[79] The exceptions include political rights at the national level and holding high offices. cf. D Kochenov and J Lindeboom, 'Pluralism through its Denial', in M Avbelj and G Davies (eds), Research Handbook on Legal Pluralism in EU Law (Cheltenham: Edward Elgar, 2018) (forthcoming).

[80] F Fabbrini, 'The Political Side of EU Citizenship in the Context of EU Federalism' in D Kochenov (ed), *EU Citizenship and Federalism: The Role of Rights* (Cambridge, Cambridge University Press, 2017); J Shaw, *The Transformation of Citizenship in the European Union* (Cambridge, Cambridge University Press, 2007).

[81] C O'Brien, 'Real Links, Abstract Rights and False Alarms' (2008) 33 *EL Rev* 643.

extension, the national community from the exclusivity and fragility of the national culture to the meaningfulness of the allegations that social security systems are conditioned on *demos* uniformity[82] and, most importantly, the correlation between the functioning of democracy and citizenship as opposed to personhood *sensu stricto*. Are such assumptions worth fighting for? Certainly, EU law's cracking open of states is overwhelmingly empowering for those people who are willing and ready to benefit from what is on offer—from a Lithuanian serving coffee in Wales to an Irish farmer acquiring land in Romania, or a Scottish physicist working on the CERN's accelerator complex. Enforcing old assumptions would unquestionably imply trimming the life chances of such people.[83]

What I am saying is that both aspects of the most accepted definition of citizenship in the literature today fail to find reflection in what the nationalities of the Member States have become after the advent of EU citizenship, which could probably provide one of the explanations for the gradual undermining of the latter which we are facing coming both from the level of the national law, especially in the UK, and this is long before Brexit,[84] and also at the supranational level, where the ECJ seems to be minded to water down the core of the supranational legal status,[85] turning it, step by step, into a structural irrelevance in the context of the European law edifice. In Niamh Nic Shuibhne's analysis[86] which does not leave the realm of EU law, such backlash was only to be expected and is in fact nothing but a faithful adherence to the federalist principles.[87] While this conclusion can be convincingly criticised, as Eleanor Spaventa has shown,[88] it is beyond any doubt that the backlash can be explained in a sound way by looking at the overwhelming impact of EU law on what citizenship of the Member States is now about.

The main problem with citizenship in the EU at the moment, it seems, is not confined to pushing the Member States to rethink which communities of people

[82] M Keating, 'Social Citizenship, Solidarity and Welfare in Regionalised and Plurinational States' (2009) 13 *Citizenship Studies* 501.

[83] The UK seems to be en route to doing precisely that: D Kochenov, 'EU Citizenship and Withdrawals from the Union: How Inevitable is the Radical Downgrading of Rights?' in C Closa (ed), *Troubled Membership: Dealing with Secession from a Member State and Withdrawal from the Union* (Cambridge, Cambridge University Press, 2017) (forthcoming).

[84] J Shaw, N Miller and M Fletcher, *Getting to Grips with EU Citizenship: Understanding the Friction between UK Immigration Law and EU Free Movement Law* (Edinburgh, Edinburgh Law School Citizenship Studies, 2013).

[85] O'Brien, '*Civis Capitalist Sum*' (n 4); E Spaventa, 'Earned Citizenship—Understanding Union Citizenship through its Scope' in D Kochenov (ed), *EU Citizenship and Federalism: The Role of Rights* (Cambridge, Cambridge University Press, 2017); Ŭ Belavusaŭ and D Kochenov, 'Kirchberg Dispensing the Punishment: Inflicting "Civil Death" on Prisoners in *Onuekwere* and *MG*' (2016) 41 *EL Rev* 557. See also chapter 11, Nic Shuibhne's contribution to this volume.

[86] N Nic Shuibhne, 'Recasting EU Citizenship as Federal Citizenship: What are the Implications for the Citizen when the Polity Bargain is Privileged?' in D Kochenov (ed), *EU Citizenship and Federalism: The Role of Rights* (Cambridge, Cambridge University Press, 2017).

[87] C Schönberger, 'European Citizenship as Federal Citizenship—Some Citizenship Lessons of Comparative Federalism' (2007) 19 *European Review of Public Law* 63; G Neuman 'Fédéralisme et citoyenneté aux Etats Unis et dans l'Union européenne' (2003) 21 *Critique Internationale* 151.

[88] Spaventa (n 85).

they are in charge of and should perceive of themselves as serving. It goes even deeper, since the 'replacement' citizenship at the EU level—never mind the 'shall not replace'[89] language of the Treaty, which can only make legalistic, 'who issues the passport' kind of sense, failing to capture the essence of the deeper ongoing processes discussed in the preceding parts. While EU citizenship has the potential to 'take over', de facto, from the nationalities of the Member States, it seems to be based on entirely different principles, compared with any other citizenship in contemporary world. It is a citizenship conditioned on a market endorsement and the performance of ethically questionable acts, like venturing out across the invisible inter-state borders within the internal market.[90] Is this the idea of a good life worth living shared by the absolute majority of Europeans?

Rather than a celebration of the abstract humanity of the bearer through the extension of rights based on a formal legal status aimed at ignoring the actual differences between the holders, EU citizenship, on the contrary, virtually never protects the weak and the needy based on their humanity and legal status,[91] but uniquely connects such protection with the perceived cross-border or economic aspects of the lives in question. In this sense, this is a citizenship where a turn to personhood *results in the limitation rather that the extension of the amount of rights* associated with the status. Importantly, one cannot wholeheartedly claim that this only happens at one level of governance, leaving the level of the Member States *sensu stricto* unaffected. This 'citizenship of personal circumstances' has in fact legally dislodged in many respects ideologically sound national-level statuses, which are, precisely, *not* dependent on the performance of ideologised ethically and morally contingent acts, like contributing to the internal market in any way whatsoever.

The supranational-level citizenship undermining the national ones cannot, thus, withstand even the most basic criticism based on human dignity and human worth; these cannot depend on a used bus ticket: either you move in space or not is necessarily irrelevant from a moral or ethical perspective. Most reasonable suggestions voiced in the literature to disconnect the logics of citizenship from the

[89] Art 20(1) TFEU makes the following clarification: 'Citizenship of the Union shall be additional to and not replace national citizenship'.

[90] Not all borders count, of course, as the ECJ explained: Case C-212/06 *Government of Communauté française and Gouvernement wallon v Gouvernement flamand*, EU:C:2008:178. See also Opinion of AG Sharpston, EU:C:2007:398 paras 143–44. *cf* P Van Elsuwege and S Adam, 'Situtations purement internes, discriminations à rebours et collectivités autonomes après l'arrêt sur *l'Assurances soins flamande*' (2008) 44 *Cahiers de droit européen* 655.

[91] O'Brien, '*Civis Capitalist Sum*' (n 4); Caro de Sousa (n 3). Holding the formal status of EU citizenship remains essential, however, for acquiring virtually any supranational rights in Europe, as the third-country nationals are essentially confined to the pre-EEC Treaty reality, where the EU as a 'single working and living space', to borrow from Golynker, does not exist at all: O Golynker, 'European Union as a Single Working-Living Space' in A Halpin and V Roeben (eds), *Theorising the Global Legal Migration* (Oxford, Hart Publishing, 2009) 151. *cf*, D Kochenov and M van den Brink, 'Pretending there is No Union: Non-Derivative Quasi-Citizenship Rights of Third-Country Nationals in the EU' in D Thym and M Zoeteweij-Turhan (eds), *Rights of Third-Country Nationals under EU Association Agreements: Degrees of Free Movement and Citizenship* (Leiden, Brill/Nijhoff, 2015) 66.

market-inspired reading of the jurisdictional boundaries between the legal orders in Europe by either making the internal market logic irrelevant for the enjoyment of citizenship rights,[92] or, by giving the right *not* to move full recognition among the entitlements of EU citizenship deserving legal protection,[93] remained unanswered calls in a highly ideological context of European integration where the foundational ideal of the good, however ethically vacant and non-obvious—ie, the binding requirement to move about, is predetermined and seemingly immune from contestation.[94] It is a citizenship without respect designed to bring down those whom the internal market does not need and thus perceives of as disposable and unworthy of protection, recognition and respect.[95] EU citizenship, in failing to endow with protections all those who possess the formal legal status, looking instead at the particular acts they engage in, instead, is the antithesis of what citizenship is about.[96] The worth of the legal truth of status assignment here frequently remains almost entirely inconsequential.

This being said, this is all about giving recognition to the person, of course, as opposed to the classical reality the departure from which was discussed in the preceding parts. The interesting thing with EU citizenship, however, is that the departure from the classical legalistic understanding of citizenship is actually used to the effect of *depriving* persons of rights under this pretext, rather than empowering them, which is the general constitutional trend outside the EU's constitutional context, as described above. Instead of using the logic of the shift from the purely legal to social reality to extend additional protections to those whom the legalistic framework renders invisible, EU citizenship deploys the same to the opposing end: to pre-empt the extension of rights. In this sense EU citizenship is a negative departure from the abstract citizenship ideal, looking beyond the strictly legal truth of the supranational-level status only to undermine the latter's effects should the dogmatic ideal of a 'good market citizen',[97] which is by

[92] E Sharpston, 'Citizenship and Fundamental Rights—Pandora's Box or a Natural Step Towards Maturity?' in P Cardonnel, A Rosas and N Wahl (eds), *Constitutionalising the EU Judicial System* (Oxford, Hart Publishing, 2012). *cf* S Iglesias Sánchez, 'Fundamental Rights and Citizenship of the Union at a Crossroads: A Promising Alliance or a Dangerous Liaison?' (2014) 20 *ELJ* 464; D Kochenov and R Plender, 'EU Citizenship: From an Incipient Form to an Incipient Substance? The Discovery of the Treaty Text' (2012) 37 *EL Rev* 369.

[93] Iglesias Sánchez, 'A Citizenship Right to Stay?' (n 9).

[94] G Davies, 'Social Legitimacy and Purposive Power: The End, the Means and the Consent of the People' in D Kochenov, G de Búrca and A Williams (eds), *Europe's Justice Deficit?* (Oxford, Hart Publishing, 2015); Somek (n 5).

[95] Caro de Sousa (n 3); O'Brien, '*Civis Capitalist Sum*' (n 4); D Kochenov, 'Citizenship Without Respect: The EU's Troubled Equality Ideal' (2010) Jean Monnet Working Paper 08/10: ssrn.com/abstract=1793274; G Peebles, '"A Very Eden of the Innate Rights of Man"? A Marxist Look at the European Union Treaties and Case Law' (1997) 22 *Law & Social Inquiry* 581.

[96] Kochenov, 'Neo-Mediaeval Permutations of Personhood in Europe' (n 3).

[97] For an overview of the relevant case law of the ECJ, see L Azoulai, 'Transfiguring European Citizenship: From Member State Territory to Union Territory' in D Kochenov (ed), *EU Citizenship and Federalism: The Role of Rights* (Cambridge, Cambridge University Press, 2017).

definition deprived of any moral or ethical *contenu* whatsoever, not be satisfied.[98] This unexpected development demonstrates the attractiveness of the formal legalistic world of clearly formulated and meticulously enforced legal truths which citizenship has precisely been drifting away from over the last decennia, turning modern constitutionalism towards the person. How did the EU land with such an atypically modern and at the same time astonishingly medieval citizenship on its hands,[99] which is both in line with and, simultaneously, in contradiction with the global trends?

IV. UNDERMINING RIGHTS THROUGH ATTENTION TO CVs

As the integration project matured, Europe's main strength became its chief weakness. Conceived as a market to serve the ideals grander than simple economic prosperity, thus intended to benefit each and every European through becoming part of our 'legal heritage', as the Court has amply noted in *van Gend*,[100] European law failed to move on with the times. Conceived once upon a time as a stepping stone to peace, and a bunch of other valuable ideals, now reflected in Article 2 of the Treaty on the European Union (but also colonialism[101] and building a unified European nuclear force)[102] the Union gradually lowered its ambition: the means for greater progress, which was the market, fell on itself to take the chief place among the Union's ends.[103] This subtle taming of ambition, while sellable to an inattentive observer as a sign of respect vis-a-vis the Member States' sovereignty is in fact something else, it seems.

When the market is the means to achieve something greater, the limitations it imposes on the national authority are justifiable: as the official story goes, the Member States lost the political and economic upper hand in the name of liberty—an insurance policy against totalitarian twists—and prosperity—a social Europe where tomorrow is better than today—which is to come through unity. Much has changed, however, since the first version of the story had been written.

98 Caro de Sousa (n 3).

99 Kochenov, 'Neo-Mediaeval Permutations of Personhood in Europe' (n 3).

100 Case 26/62 *NV Algemene Transport- en Expeditie Onderneming van Gend & Loos v Netherlands Inland Revenue Administration*, EU:C:1963:1; see, also, FG Jacobs (ed), EU Law and the Individual (Amsterdam, North Holland 1976); O Due, 'The Law-Making of the European Court of Justice Considered in Particular from the Perspective of Individuals and Undertakings' (1994) 63 *Nordic Journal of International Law* 123.

101 P Hansen and S Jonsson, *Eurafrica: The Untold History of European Integration and Colonialism* (London, Bloomsbury Academic, 2015).

102 G Mallard, *Fallout: Nuclear Diplomacy in an Age of Global Fracture* (Chicago, IL, University of Chicago Press, 2014).

103 D Kochenov, 'The Citizenship Paradigm' (2012/13) 15 *Cambridge Yearbook of European Legal Studies* 197; Peebles (n 95).

Prosperity is not on the horizon any more, at least not for everyone,[104] liberty is none of the Union's business: the Union is not effective at all as against Polish–Hungarian-style 'illiberal democracies' as we are discovering,[105] some commotion in high places notwithstanding.[106]

Instead of the optimism of a new beginning championed by the elites of the past, Union law is now a binding and directly effective tool to tame us, European citizens, in the name of a highly specific version of the market it cherishes. In the name of the internal coherence of the market we are shielded from European human rights standards;[107] in the name of its smooth operation the market is 'apolitical.'[108] This is good for us, we are told, because the Treaties say so[109] and because politics, as much as the Treaties allow for it, is by definition the politics of means, not the politics of ends: the direction of European Unity is set in stone and not negotiable politically within the framework of the institutions the Treaties have created.[110]

Speaking of utopias, Sir Isaiah Berlin diagnosed that

> in a society in which the same goals are universally accepted, problems can be only of means, all soluble by technological methods. That is a society in which the inner life of man, the moral and spiritual and aesthetic imagination, no longer speaks at all.[111]

Our supranational legal heritage lays claim to our imagination and fails, to which the rise of all kinds of extremist movements testifies. For the first time in its history

[104] AJ Menéndez, 'The Existential Crisis of the European Union' (2013) 14 *German Law Journal* 453.

[105] A von Bogdandy and M Ioannidis, 'Systemic Deficiency in the Rule of Law: What It Is, What Has Been Done, What Can Be Done' (2014) 51 *CML Rev* 59; C Closa and D Kochenov (eds), *Reinforcing Rule of Law Oversight in the European Union* (Cambridge, Cambridge University Press, 2016).

[106] P Oliver and J Stefanelli, 'Strengthening the Rule of Law in the EU: The Council's Inaction' (2016) 54 *Journal of Common Market Studies* 1075; D Kochenov and L Pech, 'Better Late than Never? On the Commission's Rule of Law Framework and Its First Activation' (2016) 54 *Journal of Common Market Studies* 1062.

[107] Opinion 2/13 *Accession to ECHR (No 2)* EU:C:2014:2454; D Halberstam, '"It's the Autonomy, Stupid!" A Modest Defence of Opinion 2/13 on EU Accession to the ECHR, and the Way Forward' (2015) 16 *German Law Journal* 105; and P Eeckhout, 'Opinion 2/13 on EU Accession to the ECHR and Judicial Dialogue—Autonomy or Autarky?' (2015) 38 *Fordham International Law Journal* 955. See also Opinion 2/94 *Accession to ECHR (No 1)* EU:C:1996:140. The Charter of Fundamental Rights of the Union makes this situation even worse, since as long as EU citizenship is not endowed with a formal legal capacity to shape the scope of EU law by the ECJ, the Charter, by precisely *not* extending the rights to the most vulnerable who would be invisible in the context of the internal market, reinforced the sense of deprivation and injustice in the context where the Court's case law on the issue is 'convoluted and unconvincing': G Davies, 'A Right to Stay at Home: A Basis for European Family Rights' in D Kochenov (ed), *EU Citizensihp and Federalism: The Role of Rights* (Cambridge, Cambridge University Press, 2017) 468, 483. But see Nic Shuibhne, chapter 11 in this volume.

[108] MA Wilkinson, 'Politicising Europe's Justice Deficit: Some Preliminaries' in D Kochenov, G de Búrca and A Williams (eds), *Europe's Justice Deficit?* (Oxford, Hart Publishing, 2015) 111.

[109] For an analysis, see A Williams, 'Taking Values Seriously: Towards a Philosophy of EU Law' (2009) 29 *Oxford Journal of Legal Studies* 549.

[110] Davies, 'Social Legitimacy and Purposive Power (n 94).

[111] I Berlin, *The Crooked Timber of Humanity* (New York, Knopf, 1991) 15.

the Union is routinely perceived as a potentially powerful agent of injustice not only by nationalists and outcast lunatics, but also by its own servants and facilitators, professors of EU law; Gráinne de Búrca is absolutely right pointing out that the EU can be perceived as 'patent injustice'.[112] Perceptions have changed, probably, because the market without a 'mantle of ideals' is not a pretty sight:[113] the citizenship it is responsible for, having de facto overpowered the core elements of the nationalities of the Member States in a number of respects frequently punishes, instead of protecting. This is done with a most meticulous attention to detail: the 'good citizenship', which the Union cherishes,[114] rests on the intimate personal connection with the idea of the internal market and cross-border movement: virtually the only measure of someone's worthiness in the eyes of the supranational law.

The Union could try redeeming itself through making its law at least sensitive to human suffering: Sir Isaiah's 'first public obligation'. This can be done, at the very least, through allowing the *van Gend* 'legal heritage' of the citizens to play a more significant role in the system than the market logic, the latter emerging as particularly problematic in the citizenship context as long as it shapes the formal status of citizenship which can be deactivated by the failure to engage with the market sufficiently, as explained above, forming the worst and the least humane blend of the legal truth and social reality paradigms of personhood in law. In a constitutional system—even where democracy as such is out of reach[115]—rights cannot be acquired by engaging in ethically and morally irrelevant acts; mothers are not punished when disability of their children prevents them from work;[116] and tax breaks do not depend on the nationality of your former wife.[117] The core problem with EU citizenship today is precisely that the principle behind the application of the law directly penetrating countless lives is rather farcical and thus inexplicable at all from a rational humane perspective. Moreover, violence is done in the name of the perceived Member States' sensitivities, where in fact, this is the (often absurd) dull market-inspired sophistry that is at play: 'when he grows up, he might want to move across the non-existent border'.[118] Approached from this perspective the Union merely boasts a questionable legal status, which is hardly

[112] G de Búrca, 'Conclusion' in D Kochenov, G de Búrca and A Williams (eds), *Europe's Justice Deficit?* (Oxford, Hart Publishing, 2015).

[113] JHH Weiler, 'Bread and Circus: The State of European Union' (1998) 4 *Columbia Journal of European Law* 223, 231.

[114] Kochenov, 'On Tiles and Pillars' (n 4); Azoulai, 'Transfiguring European Citizenship (n 97).

[115] But see, K Lenaerts and JA Gutiérrez-Fons arguing the opposite: 'Epilogue on EU Citizenship: Hopes and Fears' in D Kochenov (ed), *EU Citizenship and Federalism: The Role of Rights* (Cambridge, Cambridge University Press, 2017).

[116] Case C-434/09 *Shirley McCarthy v Secretary of State for the Home Department*, EU:C:2011:277; Nic Shuibhne, '(Some of) the Kids Are All Right' (n 75).

[117] Case C-403/03 *Egon Schempp v Finanzamt München V*, EU:C:2005:446.

[118] *cf* Case C-148/02 *Carlos Garcia Avello v Belgian State*, EU:C:2003:539.

worthy of the glorious 'citizenship' denomination: the *Ruiz Zambrano* detour[119] was all too brief and we seem to be back to square one, to Joseph Weiler's poignant criticism of the classical status quo: the Union 'precisamente omette di compiere la transizione concettuale da una libera circolazione basata sul mercato ad una libertà basata sulla cittadinanza',[120] piling upon the ethically questionable idea of the good underlying EU law the dubious and discriminating 'citizenship of personal circumstances'.

[119] S Platon, 'Le champ d'application des droits du citoyen européen après les arrêts [*Ruiz*] *Zambrano*, *McCarthy* et *Dereçi*: De la boîte de Pandore au labyrinth du Minotaure' (2012) 48 *Revue trimestrielle de droit europeen* 21; D Kochenov, 'A Real European Citizenship; A New Jurisdiction Test; A Novel Chapter in the Development of the Union in Europe' (2011) 18 *Columbia Journal of European Law* 56.

[120] JHH Weiler, 'Europa: "Nous coalisons des Etats noun n'unissons pas des hommes"' in M Cartabia and A Simoncini (eds), *La sostenibilità della democrazia nel XXI secolo* (Bologna, Il Mulino, 2009) 82 ('precisely fails to fulfil the conceptual transition from a freedom of movement based on the market to a freedom based on citizenship').

4

(De)constructing the Road to Brexit: Paving the Way to Further Limitations on Free Movement and Equal Treatment?

STEPHANIE REYNOLDS[1]

I. INTRODUCTION

THE UNITED KINGDOM electorate sent shockwaves through Europe when it voted, in June 2016, to leave the European Union (EU). Nevertheless, that decision was represented, to some extent, as falling within the range of possibilities of a historically Eurosceptic Member State that had long positioned itself at the outer fringes of European integration. According to the Bratislava Declaration, 'while one country has decided to leave, the EU remains indispensable for the rest'.[2] In addition, the other Member States reaffirmed the need to realise citizens' 'wishes to live, study, work, move and prosper across [the] continent'.[3] When set against even more recent developments in regional and global politics, however, the referendum result seems less of an anomalous, if 'painful',[4] decision by a misfit Member State, and more part of a series of political events that, at best, suggests a fundamental disconnection between what the EU envisages for its citizens and the citizenry itself and, at worst, risks undermining the Union project as a whole. Yet at this very political juncture, at which the UK's future relationship with the Union remains far from clear, and at which anti-immigration, anti-EU and populist politics appear to be steadily but not yet decisively on the rise across

[1] I am grateful to Michael Dougan, Mike Gordon and Daniel Thym for their invaluable comments on earlier drafts of this chapter. Any errors remain my own.

[2] The Bratislava Declaration, 16 September 2016, Statement 517/16 (Institutional Affairs) 1.

[3] ibid.

[4] Statement of EU Leaders and the Netherlands Presidency on the Outcome of the UK Referendum, 24 June 2016, Press Release 381/16 (Institutional Affairs).

Europe,[5] there are frustratingly few tools to survey the Union's evolving *legal* constitutional landscape.[6]

This chapter advances that, while no longer of formal legal relevance, the UK's pre-referendum renegotiation of its relationship with the EU, agreed by the European Council in February 2016,[7] and in particular the so-called 'emergency brake' on in-work benefits contained therein (safeguard/safeguard mechanism), provides fertile ground for assessing the contemporary political and legal environments of Union citizenship and, more broadly, European integration. Further, exploration of the legality of the safeguard also provides a means of reflecting on the institutional dynamics behind the current constitutional state of play.

Having provided an overview of the mechanism in section II, the chapter will postulate, in section III, that despite doubt as to its legality upon its unveiling, the safeguard is likely to have been permitted by the Court of Justice (CJEU). However, two more significant, and still pertinent, observations arise from this finding, relating, in particular, to the Court's contribution to the present political and legal climate. First, it is the both the judicial construction and, more recent, deconstruction of Union citizenship that provides the safeguard with its clear legal foundations. Second, the seemingly paradoxical combination of initial doubt as to the Court's acceptance of the safeguard with the judicially driven constitutional evolution that ultimately grounds its legality, brings into sharp focus the increasingly constitutionalised nature of Union law and the growing dominance of the Court in the EU's institutional dynamics. Consequently, what emerges from the analysis is that the Court-driven rights of Union citizens contribute, somewhat ironically, to perceptions, rightly or wrongly, of democratic deficit within the EU, of a loss of sovereignty by the Member States, and to the growing political tension surrounding Union citizenship. Ultimately, the result of these historical, constitutional and institutional roots is that, rather than being consigned to the parallel realm of a British 'Remain' result, the safeguard mechanism continues to represent a potential Pandora's Box in terms of how Member States, either unilaterally or collectively, might seek to redefine the outer boundaries of both Union citizenship and the internal market.

[5] At the time of writing, the UK Prime Minister Theresa May triggered Article 50 TEU proceedings in March 2017, having previously indicated the UK's intention to leave the single market while seeking a bespoke deal on the customs union. The Government has yet to indicate how this might be achieved in practice. The Italian Prime Minister Matteo Renzi resigned in December 2016, following defeat in a constitutional referendum, which, for some, represented a wider opportunity for Eurosceptic parties to present their political alternative; Austria elected left-leaning President Alexander Van der Bellen over far-right, anti-immigration and anti-EU candidate Norbert Hofer; Marine le Penn, of Le Front National succeeded in reaching the second round of the French presidential elections but ultimately lost to Emmanuel Macron.

[6] Though others emerge from the other legal mechanisms borne in response to other EU 'crises', such as the European Stability Mechanism. See M Ruffert, 'The European Debt Crisis and European Union Law' (2011) 48 *CML Rev* 1777.

[7] European Council Meeting (18/19 February 2016) Brussels, 19 February 2016, EUCO 1/16, 1.

Section IV recognises that the potential re-emergence of the safeguard mechanism would nevertheless have considerable implications. Regardless of the fact that the safeguard is both legally salvageable and politically explainable, its reappearance would represent a significant change in direction for the Union, leaving the Court in an unenviable position. On the one hand, as a brake on in-work benefits would introduce blatant discrimination against Union workers, a finding of incompatibility or invalidity would seem to fall comfortably within the CJEU's institutional role. On the other hand, since its tendency to push the EU's constitutional and institutional boundaries can be viewed as a contributing factor in the Union's emerging existential crisis, the CJEU may have little choice, at this crucial juncture—at which the fundamental tenets of the Union constitution are at risk, and at which the Court would, ironically, properly act as a check on the EU's political branches—to accept some restriction on the equal treatment rights of Union workers. Interestingly, the overall analysis demonstrates that the very evolution of the internal market and Union citizenship would allow the Court to present this acceptance as fitting comfortably within its own jurisprudence.

II. AN OVERVIEW OF THE SAFEGUARD MECHANISM

The safeguard mechanism, as contained within the now formally redundant European Council Decision on a new settlement for the United Kingdom[8] (the Decision), would have introduced the possibility for Member States to restrict access to in-work benefits for newly arriving Union citizens. Employment of the safeguard would have been subject to certain processes and conditions. First, the Member State concerned would have needed to notify the Commission and Council of a 'situation affect[ing] essential aspects of its social security system, [presenting] serious … and persisting difficulties in its employment market, or [exerting] excessive pressure on the proper functioning of its public services'.[9] Second, the Commission would have needed to propose that the Council authorise utilisation of the safeguard by the applicant State. Following Council authorisation, the Member State would have been permitted to use the mechanism for a maximum period of seven years. At the individual level, in-work benefit restrictions would have been limited to the newly arrived EU citizen's first four years of employment, with access nevertheless increasing gradually as links with the host State developed over that time.[10] The rationale behind the safeguard mechanism was the apparent need to 'address the pull factor arising from a Member State's in-work benefits regime' arising from the 'diverse structure of different Member

[8] Decision of the Heads of State of Government meeting within the European Council, concerning a New Settlement for the United Kingdom within the European Union, Annex I to the Conclusions of the European Council Meeting (18/19 February 2016), Brussels, 19 February 2016, EUCO 1/16, 8.

[9] European Council (n 7) 23.

[10] ibid.

States' social security systems'.[11] The safeguard mechanism was to be employed as 'a response to situations of inflow of workers from other Member States of exceptional magnitude over an extended period of time'. It was claimed, this could be done 'without creating unjustified direct or indirect discrimination'.[12]

Despite a general presumption, before the UK Deal was published, that any restriction on the equal treatment of Union workers would require Treaty change, the Decision stated that the proposed safeguard mechanism would be realised via amendment to secondary legislation and that this would be 'fully compatible with the Treaties'.[13] Yet, by restricting the equal treatment rights of the Union *worker*, the safeguard mechanism appeared to cross a line that many would have considered to be untraverseable. Specifically, it placed limitations on the right to non-discrimination on grounds of nationality and the general free movement rights of Union citizens contained in primary Union law.[14] Moreover, by erecting clear barriers to economic integration, the safeguard appeared to strike directly at the heart of the foundational goals of the Union, developed even before Maastricht.

The safeguard mechanism would have been implemented through amendment of Article 7, Regulation No 492/2011 which requires that Union workers enjoy the same social and tax advantages as national workers.[15] In *Even*, the Court held that this provision[16] was adopted 'in implementation' of Article 45 of the Treaty on the Functioning of the European Union (TFEU) on the free movement of workers:

> For this purpose [the Regulation] provides for the abolition of all differences in treatment between national workers and workers who are nationals of other Member States as regards conditions of employment, work and remuneration and gives workers who are nationals of the other Member States … access to the same social and tax advantages from which national workers benefit.[17]

Accordingly, in *Even*, the right to equal access to social and tax advantages was presented as a concrete expression of the principle of non-discrimination contained in Article 45(2) TFEU. Consequently, the compatibility of the proposed amendment to Regulation No 492/2011 with the Treaties, in particular Article 45(2) and the more general right to non-discrimination on grounds of nationality in Article 18 TFEU, was open to more serious debate than the Decision seemed prepared to admit.

[11] ibid.

[12] ibid 19.

[13] ibid 1–2.

[14] Arts 18 and 21 TFEU respectively.

[15] Regulation (EU) No 492/2011 of the European Parliament and Council of 5 April 2011 on freedom of movement for workers within the Union [2011] OJ L141/1.

[16] In the form of Regulation (EEC) No 1612/68 of the Council of 15 October 1968 on freedom of movement for workers in the Community [1968] OJ L257/2, Art 7.

[17] Case 207/78 *Even*, EU:C:1979:144, para 21.

III. THE JUDICIAL (DE)CONSTRUCTION OF UNION CITIZENSHIP: THE COURT-FURNISHED FOUNDATIONS OF THE SAFEGUARD MECHANISM

Despite the clear tension between the purpose and proposed method of implementation of the safeguard mechanism, on the one hand, and the seemingly well-established scope and operation of primary free movement law, on the other, the drafters of the Decision nevertheless spoke directly to CJEU case law, asserting that the public interests the safeguard sought to protect fell within the Court's own jurisprudence.[18] By examining judicial responses to previous legislative modifications within the internal market, alongside the CJEU's more recent approach to EU citizenship rights, this section argues that the Court might well have accepted the mechanism, despite its legal controversies. More importantly, by conducting an in-depth investigation of the Court's case law, beyond the seminal cases that most commonly provide the focal point of assessment, this analysis is able to demonstrate that, rather than representing a cynical attempt to speak the language of the Court, the safeguard mechanism is firmly rooted in the Court-led construction of EU citizenship. In short, ironically, CJEU judgments generally viewed as progressive—in terms of pushing the constitutional boundaries of citizenship rights—simultaneously provided firm foundations for the current more retrogressive approach to those same entitlements. Meanwhile, the CJEU's institutional boundary pushing has played its own part in the political climate surrounding the safeguard's introduction.

A. Amending Free Movement Rules Via Secondary Legislation: A Brief History of the Court's Responses

Reviews of the case law by Sorensen, Davies and Horsley outline a number of approaches utilised by the CJEU when confronted with the question of the compatibility of Union secondary legislation with the Treaties.[19] First, the Court might simply find that the EU norm is valid[20] or, second, that it is invalid.[21] Third, the Court might seek to interpret the secondary legislation consistently with primary law. Fourth, the Court might find EU secondary law capable of operating within the parameters of primary law, concluding instead that the Member State's

[18] European Council (n 7) 21.

[19] K Sorensen, 'Reconciling Secondary Legislation with the Treaty Rights of Free Movement' (2011) 36 *EL Rev* 339; G Davies, 'Legislative Control of the European Court of Justice' (2014) 51 *CML Rev* 1579; T Horsley, 'Institutional Dynamics Reloaded: The Court of Justice and the Development of the Internal Market' in P Koutrakos and J Snell (eds), *Research Handbook on EU Internal Market Law* (Cheltenham, Edward Elgar, 2017).

[20] Case 15/83 *Denkavit*, EU:C:1984:183.

[21] Joined Cases 80/77 and 81/77 *Ramel*, EU:C:1978:87; Case C-363/93 *Lancry*, EU:C:1994:315.

method of implementation breaches Treaty rules.[22] Finally, a parallel system of rights, operating directly under the Treaties, while not affecting the validity of secondary Union law, might render the rules underlying the secondary legal framework nugatory.[23] Ultimately, pockets of case law could be used to support any of these approaches. However, the evolution of the jurisprudence indicates that the Court would have been most likely simply to find the safeguard mechanism valid and, more importantly, that it might be open to accepting a future safeguard in an alternative form, including one adopted unilaterally by a Member State.

i. Validity

Nevertheless, one potentially determinative feature of the safeguard contained in the Decision was its origins in *Union* secondary law. Often, *Tobacco Advertising II*[24] is presented as evidence that the Court offers more latitude to the EU legislature than to individual Member States in validity or compatibility assessments. Yet while the Court might adopt a 'decidedly deferential approach' to Union secondary norms in respect of competence control,[25] the picture in relation to compliance with the free movement provisions is rather less clear. The Court has held on several occasions that Union legislation is as subject to Treaty free movement rules as domestic norms.[26] EU secondary law is also processed in the same way, via establishment of a prima facie breach of free movement, followed by consideration of whether this can be justified in principle and practice.[27] Indeed, the Decision implicitly accepted that the safeguard mechanism would constitute a prima facie restriction of free movement, simply asserting that it would not create *unjustified* direct or indirect discrimination.[28]

Nonetheless, Sorensen has suggested that the Union legislator may enjoy more elbow room when it comes to the application of the proportionality test.[29] Crucially, a number of central features of the case law in which the Court has taken a permissive approach correspond directly to the key characteristics of the safeguard. First, the Court has held that nationality-based limitations on free movement, while sometimes permissible, 'cannot be established unilaterally by the Member States in their national rules'.[30] Accordingly, the requirement of a Commission recommendation and Council authorisation before a Member State

[22] Case 128/89 *Commission v Italy*, EU:C:1990:311.

[23] Case C-200/02 *Chen*, EU:C:2004:639; Case C-34/09 *Ruiz Zambrano*, EU:C:2011:124; Case C-120/95 *Decker*, EU:C:1998:167.

[24] Case C-380/03 *Germany v Parliament and Council*, EU:C:2006:772.

[25] Horsley (n 19).

[26] *Denkavit* (n 20); Case C-51/93 *Meyhui*, EU:C:1994:312.

[27] ibid.

[28] European Council (n 7) 19.

[29] Sorensen (n 19) 355.

[30] Case C-299/02 *Commission v Netherlands*, EU:C:2004:620, para 24.

could have triggered the emergency benefits brake appears to comply with existing institutional safeguards relating to free movement restrictions.

Second, the Court has held that market partitions may be imposed where they seek to 'maintain *a normal flow of trade*' and are taken 'in *exceptional circumstances*'.[31] The text of the Decision replicates this language verbatim in order to highlight these same situations.[32]

Third, the CJEU has previously shown a willingness to accept barriers to trade, and even restrictions on fundamental rights, so long as they are temporary.[33] Thus, an applicant State would only have been permitted to use the safeguard mechanism for seven years, while application at the individual level was limited to four. Moreover, the gradual access to in-work benefits for Union citizens over this four-year period, to reflect their growing connection with the host State labour market, is a clear effort to demonstrate adherence to suitability, necessity and general proportionality. Crucially, the Court has previously held that the Union legislature 'must be allowed a broad discretion in an area … which entails political, economic and social choices on its part, and in which it is called upon to undertake complex assessments'.[34] As a result, *Union* secondary legislative measures have often only faced the question of whether they are 'manifestly inappropriate' having regard to the objective pursued.[35] Not only would graduated access appear to meet this low threshold, but the Decision was at pains to highlight the assessment of evidence by the Union's political and administrative institutions of the UK's purportedly individual situation.[36]

ii. Invalidity

However, the Court has not always been consistent and has also shown increasing confidence in declaring Union legislation invalid for breach of Treaty free movement rules. In *Ramel*, an EU instrument that permitted France to limit imports, following the 'exceptional inflow' of wines from Italy, was invalidated.[37] In *Lancry*, the Court stated that dock dues, authorised by Union secondary legislation, could not be permitted regardless of the fact their application was temporally limited.[38] Crucially, the CJEU has been particularly unreceptive to Union legislation that permits difference in treatment between Union workers. *Pinna* concerned

[31] Case 10/73 *Rewe Zentral AG v Hauptzollamt Kehl*, EU:C:1973:111; Case 136/77 *Racke*, EU:C:1978:114.

[32] European Council (n 7) 23.

[33] C-193/94 *Skanavi*, EU:C:1996:70; in Case C-236/09 *Test Achats*, EU:C:2011:100 the Court found a provision of a Directive to be invalid because the permission it granted to discriminate on grounds of sex for a set period, contrary to Arts 21 and 23 CFR, could be renewed *indefinitely*.

[34] Joined Cases C-154/04 and C-155/04 *Alliance for Natural Health*, EU:C:2005:449 para 52.

[35] ibid; *cf* Case C-413/99 *Baumbast*, EU:C:2002:493.

[36] European Council (n 7) 34.

[37] *Ramel* (n 21).

[38] *Lancry* (n 21).

Article 73(2) Regulation No 1408/71,[39] which provided France with a time-limited exemption from the exportability of child benefit. The Court stated that:

> [T]he achievement of the objective of securing free movement for workers within the Community ... is facilitated if conditions of employment, including social security rules, are as similar as possible in the various Member States. That objective will, however, be imperilled ... if unnecessary differences in the social security rules are introduced by Community law.[40]

This stance would seem directly transferable to the circumstances of the safeguard mechanism: regardless of the time limitations in place, barriers to free movement already arise as a result of an absence of harmonisation in the field of social welfare. Further distinctions between national and EU workers, which would exacerbate the problem, cannot be permitted.[41] More broadly, there is evidence that the Court is gaining confidence in intervening where EU secondary legislation operates in breach of fundamental rights protected by the Union Charter (CFR).[42]

Thus, the picture so far is mixed. On the one hand, the Decision clearly speaks directly to the language used by the Court in those cases in which it has permitted Union-level restrictions on free movement. More broadly, the processes and justifications within the Decision largely emulated those already used for temporary restrictions on workers from recently acceded Member States, albeit via primary law.[43] On the other hand, the CJEU has rejected other EU legislation that mirrors instruments it has accepted in the past: those of a temporary nature, focused on exceptional in-flows and disturbances to the domestic market, and not explicitly turning on the question of nationality. Indeed, a permissive approach is often more likely where restrictions form part of a longer-term plan for graduated harmonisation.[44] A clearer picture—ultimately suggesting acceptance—nevertheless emerges when recent judicial developments within Union citizenship are considered.

iii. Consistent Interpretation or a Parallel Primary Law Framework?

Depending on whether it was the safeguard mechanism itself or the Member State's implementation of it that was challenged, it would be open to the Court either to interpret the safeguard as far as is possible in line with the principle of

[39] Regulation (EEC) No 1408/71 of the Council of 14 June 1971 on the application of social security schemes to employed persons and their family members moving within the Community [1971] OJ L149/02 (repealed).

[40] Case 41/84 *Pinna*, EU:C:1986:1, para 21.

[41] See also Case 20/85 *Roviello*, EU:C:1988:283.

[42] *Test Achats* (n 33); Case C-34/10 *Brüstle*, EU:C:2011:669; Joined Cases C-293/12 and C-594/12 *Digital Rights Ireland*, EU:C:2014:238. For analysis contrasting the Court's approach to competence control and fundamental rights review, see Horsley (n 19).

[43] eg Annex VI, Treaty of Accession of Bulgaria and Romania [2005] OJ L157/11.

[44] *Skanavi* (n 33); *Commission v Netherlands* (n 30).

non-discrimination, or find that, while the safeguard itself was compliant, domestic implementation was not. This would be consistent with the Court's general presumption that Union legislation does not authorise Member State acts that are in breach of the Treaty free movement rules and their derogating provisions.[45] Given the blatant discrimination the safeguard mechanism permits against non-national Union workers—authorised by the EU legislature—however, this approach seems improbable.

In assessing the originating Union legislation directly, the CJEU might have 'emasculated'[46] the safeguard mechanism as it did in relation to the derogation from equal treatment for jobseekers contained in Article 24(2) of Directive 2004/38.[47] In *Vatsouras*[48] the Court placed Jobseeker's Allowance outwith the concept of 'social assistance', contained in the Article 24(2) derogation, to ensure access to this form of support for Union citizen work-seekers, in line with its *Collins*[49] judgment. Regarding the safeguard mechanism, the Court might, for instance, have claimed exhaustive definitional authority over the concept of 'in-work benefits' or taken a generous approach when determining a 'real link' to the labour market or the manner of 'gradual' access to social support.

Alternatively, litigants might have sought to bypass the amendment to Regulation No 492/2011 by seeking equal treatment directly under primary law. Previously, this has been most visible in *Chen*[50] and *Ruiz Zambrano*,[51] in which third-country national carers were able to derive residence entitlements from the Union citizenship rights of their children, despite falling outwith the scope of Directive 2004/38.[52] In the area of the cross-border provision of healthcare, the Court has effectively created a parallel system of rights directly under Article 56 TFEU, with more easily met conditions than those operating under the more restrictive framework created by secondary Union legislation.[53] Such an approach to the safeguard seems unlikely, however, given the CJEU's recent decisions in cases such as *Dano* or *Commission v UK*, in which it has taken a literal, rather than Treaty-infused teleological, approach to Union secondary legislation and sidestepped the opportunity to bypass its requirements by means of the primary free movement and non-discrimination rules.[54]

Indeed, when the Court's most recent citizenship case law is considered, judicial receptivity to the safeguard seems increasingly probable. In *Alimanovic*

45 *Commission v Italy* (n 22).

46 Davies (n 19) 1591.

47 Directive 2004/38/EC on the right of citizens of the Union and their family members to move and reside freely within the territory of the Member States [2004] OJ L158/77.

48 Case C-22/08 *Vatsouras*, EU:C:2009:344.

49 Case C-138/02 *Collins*, EU:C:2004:172.

50 *Chen* (n 23).

51 Ruiz Zambrano (n 23).

52 In *Chen* because the mother was not dependent on the child; in *Ruiz Zambrano* because the Union citizen had not crossed an intra-EU border.

53 *Decker* (n 23).

54 Case C-333/13 *Dano*, EU:C:2014:2358; Case C-308/14 *Commission v UK*, EU:C:2016:436.

and *García-Nieto*,[55] in which it was unclear whether the social support in question was 'minimum subsistence'—for which Member States may derogate from equal treatment in respect of jobseekers—or 'financial assistance facilitating access to employment'—for which they may not, the Court was deferential to domestic definitions. This casts doubt on the suggestion above that, in line with *Vatsouras*, the Court might have claimed definitional authority over the concept of 'in-work benefits' and defined them narrowly.

Moreover, in both *Alimanovic* and *García-Nieto*, the Court took a literal approach to Directive 2004/38, using it to confirm temporally defined categories of residence, with a consequent impact on equal treatment rights.[56] Accordingly, the CJEU might well have accepted both the seven-year period for the safeguard's overall application and any potential time frame for demonstrating the growing links to the host State labour market required to unlock gradual access to welfare over a citizen's four years' employment there.

Recent CJEU decisions on Union citizenship also indicate a sea change in respect of key definitional methodologies affecting the operation of primary free movement law: specifically, the manner in which direct discrimination and other forms of market barrier are differentiated. The Decision itself openly acknowledged that the safeguard mechanism was discriminatory, but denied that this discrimination was direct in nature. Rather, it stated that the safeguard would be based on 'objective consideration independent of the nationality of the persons concerned'.[57] The importance of this distinction is obvious: it opens up the range of justificatory options for overcoming a prima facie breach of free movement. Thus, the Decision makes reference to a range of overriding requirements, in addition to the public policy derogations provided by Article 45(3) TFEU.[58]

Yet, a legal mechanism that requires non-national workers to demonstrate some supplementary link to the job market, beyond employment, which national workers need not establish before they may access social support, seems directly discriminatory. Indeed, in its early case law, the Court expressly forbade secondary EU legislation authorising particular Member States discriminating against non-national Union workers, even where there was no overt reference to nationality in its text.[59]

On the other hand, the Court has proved itself capable of legal acrobatics in other internal market contexts where it was strategically expedient to widen the range of justificatory options by categorising direct discrimination as indirect.[60] *Commission v UK* is particularly instructive here.[61] The case concerned the UK's

[55] Case C-67/14 *Alimanovic*, EU:C:2015:597; Case C-299/14 *García-Nieto*, EU:C:2016:114.
[56] ibid.
[57] European Council (n 7) 21.
[58] ibid 20.
[59] *Pinna* (n 40); *Roviello* (n 41).
[60] Case C-2/90 *Commission v Belgium (Walloon Waste)*, EU:C:1992:310.
[61] *Commission v UK* (n 54).

use of a 'right to reside' test for access to certain forms of social security. The test formed part of a wider assessment of whether an individual was 'habitually resident' in the UK, applicable to both nationals and EU citizens. However, while British nationals have overcome this threshold through nationality and residence, non-national EU citizens have had to demonstrate a 'right to reside' via residence in accordance with Directive 2004/38. Generally speaking, this meant that non-national EU citizens had to be workers, or self-employed, to be eligible, since an application for social support would suggest that non-economically active Union citizens did not meet the Directive's self-sufficiency requirements. Ultimately, the Commission simply conceded that, since the habitual residence test was applied to all, this was not direct discrimination but it remains of interest that the Court did not consider whether the 'right to reside' component constituted an additional, directly discriminatory, burden. Instead, the Court simply focused on the fact that 'habitual residence' was more easily satisfied by host State nationals and, thus, that indirect discrimination was established.[62]

The cursory manner with which the Court deals with this issue can be illustrated through an examination of the dissenting judgment of Lord Walker in the previous domestic case of *Patmalniece*,[63] also concerning the right to reside test. His Lordship accepted the test constituted indirect discrimination following the CJEU's previous approach to cumulative conditions in *Bressol*.[64] However, he questioned this classification since the right to reside assessment was 'a necessary condition … automatically satisfied by every British national'.[65] Drawing on a similar rationale for the test as used for the safeguard, the Secretary of State argued in *Patmalniece* that the 'right to reside' threshold was a justifiable means of assessing economic or social integration in the UK and of protecting the public purse against exploitation, irrespective of nationality.[66] For Lord Walker, this argument was disingenuous. The test was rooted in nationality, since *every* British national had a right to reside automatically, while non-nationals had to meet the set criteria of specific categories.[67] He noted, by way of example, that a non-economically active British citizen, recently arrived in the UK from Latvia, with no family or social connections, or financial resources in the UK would be automatically entitled to the social security in question; a recently arrived Latvian in the same situation would not. As a result, Lord Walker argued that the 'right to reside' test could not be justified.[68]

Ultimately, the majority in *Patmalniece* disagreed, finding the 'right to reside' component to be justified by the need to protect the public purse. As we have seen,

[62] ibid paras 78–79.
[63] *Patmalniece (FC) v Secretary of State for Work and Pensions* [2011] UKSC 11.
[64] Case C-73/08 *Bressol*, EU:C:2010:181.
[65] *Patmalniece* (n 63) paras 63–65.
[66] Quoted at para 76.
[67] Para 77.
[68] Para 79.

the CJEU, in *Commission v UK*, did not torture itself with these definitional anxieties in any case. Crucially, while the Advocate General engaged more deeply with the issue, his examination suggested growing acceptance of unavoidable difference in treatment based on the fact that 'as EU law currently stands, being a national of a particular Member State is not irrelevant when it comes to exercising freedom of movement and residence',[69] echoing a similar conclusion by the Court, in relation to Directive 2004/38, in *Dano*.[70]

There are important parallels between the conclusions drawn in *Commission v UK* and the strongest arguments against the legality of the safeguard. One might instinctively categorise the safeguard mechanism as directly discriminatory. Presumably, if the requirement to demonstrate a 'real link' to the Member State's labour market were applied exclusively to non-national EU workers, this would indeed be the case. However, following *Commission v UK*, should the safeguard mechanism, or its domestic implementing instrument, instead require that *all* applicants for in-work benefits demonstrate a 'real link' to the labour market, the discrimination would become indirect. This would be so even if national workers were able to establish a sufficient connection simply by reference to their nationality and residence, while non-national Union workers were required to proffer something more. Indeed, in light of *Commission v UK*, presumably, it would not be problematic if even national workers returning to the labour market after a period abroad would also automatically pass the test. As Lord Walker noted in *Patmalniece*:

> [I]it seems a discriminatory purpose does not, on the present state of the law, prevent unequal treatment being regarded as no more than indirect discrimination, which is capable of justification. There is an obvious temptation for governments, in face of understandable popular feeling (in this case, against 'benefit tourism') to try to draft their way out of direct into indirect discrimination, with a view to avoiding having to distribute large sums out of public funds … to beneficiaries whom their electors would not regard as deserving.[71]

iv. The Relevance of Union Citizenship Case Law to EU Workers' Rights

Of course, in one potentially crucial way, the safeguard mechanism went further than the recent citizenship case law. Focused on the rights of non-economically active EU citizens, that line of jurisprudence implicitly relies on the fact that, since Article 21 TFEU allows conditions to be placed on free movement by secondary law, non-compliance with Directive 2004/38 may take EU citizens outwith the scope of that provision, and therefore outside the ambit of the prohibition of nationality-based discrimination in Article 18 TFEU. By contrast, EU workers

[69] *Commission v UK* (Opinion) EU:C:2015:666 para 76.
[70] *Dano* (n 54) para 77.
[71] *Patmalniece* (n 63) para 72.

reside in their host State in accordance with the Directive and therefore clearly fall within the scope of Article 18 TFEU. Article 45(2) TFEU also prohibits nationality-based discrimination against Union workers, specifically, in relation to employment, remuneration and other conditions of work and employment. In short, there are question marks over the extent to which the citizenship case law—centred on the rights of non-economically active citizens—can be used as evidence that restrictions on the equal treatment rights of Union *workers* would be legally acceptable to the Court.

And yet, nationality-based discrimination is a surprisingly frequent feature of the Union legal framework. Four pertinent examples offer useful illustrations. First, there is little denying that the post-*Dano* case law differs fundamentally from the Court's early citizenship jurisprudence. *Martinez Sala* and *Grzelczyk*[72] made clear that individuals resident in the host State exercise their free movement rights under Article 21 TFEU, and therefore benefit from the principle of non-discrimination under Article 18 TFEU. The logical presumption arising from *Grzelczyk* and *Trojani*[73] is that, should an EU citizen not meet residence conditions, steps may (sometimes)[74] be taken to remove them. Until that point they benefit from the right to equal treatment by virtue of their citizenship. What *Dano et al* indicate is a tendency among some Member States to accept the presence of EU citizens on their territory—regardless of whether they meet the formal requirements of Directive 2004/38 and without taking steps to remove them—while discriminating against them in terms of equal access to social assistance.[75] Crucially, the Court's closer alignment of the scope of Articles 21 and 18 TFEU with the requirements of the Directive in those judgments makes such an approach permissible. Accordingly, it is not beyond the realms of possibility that a similar sea change could occur in respect of workers. Existing worker case law aside, the Court might accept a narrowing of the material scope of Article 45(2) TFEU. In-work benefits do not relate to employment or remuneration *stricto sensu* while the Court could accept the restrictive influence of any amendments to Regulation No 492/2011 on the definition of 'other conditions of work and employment'. Indeed, this would be in line with the Court's contemporary approach to Directive 2004/38.[76]

Compliance with Article 18 TFEU appears less obvious, since that provision offers a more general prohibition of discrimination. Nevertheless, Article 45 TFEU could represent a *lex specialis* of that provision, given that Article 18 is explicitly without prejudice to more focused provisions. A similar argument might be

[72] Case C-85/96 *Martinez Sala*, EU:C:1998:217; Case C-184/99 *Grzelczyk*, EU:C:2001:458.

[73] Case C-456/02 *Trojani*, EU:C:2004:488.

[74] Consider the need for support for 'temporary hardship' in *Grzelczyk*.

[75] See also Case C-140/12 *Brey*, EU:C:2013:565 or within UK domestic jurisprudence *Okafor v SSHD* [2011] EWCA Civ 499. For analysis, see D Thym, 'The Elusive Limits of Solidarity: Residence Rights of and Social Benefits for Economically Inactive Union Citizens' (2015) 52 *CML Rev* 17.

[76] eg in *Alimanovic* (n 55); and Case *García-Nieto* (n 55).

made in relation to Articles 21 and 34 of the CFR. Alternatively, as is the case for non-economically active Union citizens, emphasis could have been placed on the fact that free movement rights under Article 21 TFEU, which bring an EU citizen within the scope of Article 18 TFEU, are themselves subject to limitations in secondary law. In those States relying on the safeguard, related secondary Union legislation would then form part of the definitional framework of Article 21. Those seeking to reside in their host State outwith the confines of the safeguard would not be exercising free movement rights. This might have seemed legally tenuous in the days of *Even* or *Grzelczyk*. Yet, when viewed against the contemporary picture painted by *Dano et al*, it seems rather more plausible.

Our second example of discrimination relates to the political rights of EU citizens. Despite the prohibition of *any* nationality-based discrimination by Article 18 TFEU, Union citizens, including EU workers, may be excluded from voting in national elections in their host State. On the one hand, such voting rights might be comfortably excluded from the scope of the Treaties, which is required to trigger Article 18. On the other hand, writers have cogently argued that political disenfranchisement constitutes a clear barrier to movement, particularly since non-national EU citizens will have no say over the political institutions that, inter alia, control taxation and social security systems.[77] Indeed, given the, at times, ephemeral connections found by the Court between domestic rules and free movement, in order to bring, for example, national immigration law[78] or even legislative instruments relating to names,[79] within the scope of Union law, the position in relation to political rights appears somewhat arbitrary, at least from legal perspectives.

A third example arises in the context of EU enlargement. Direct discrimination, in relation to employment or equal treatment, against workers from newly acceding Member States, is now a permanent feature of accession agreements purportedly in order to take account of the scale of accession and the differences between Member State economies.[80] Indeed, the Decision drew links between the purported exceptional inflow of workers into the UK, and the fact that it has not always made full use of the transitional periods provided by recent accession frameworks.[81] Of course, such arrangements function at the level of primary Union law. Nevertheless, they highlight that the principle of non-discrimination against EU workers is more nuanced than the simple prohibitions contained in Articles 18 and 45(2) TFEU.

However, our final, most significant, example appears at the point at which Union citizenship and the internal market converge; specifically in the Court's treatment of jobseekers. Following the formalisation of Union citizenship at

[77] J Shaw, 'EU Citizenship and Political Rights in an Evolving European Union' (2007) 75 *Fordham Law Review* 2549.

[78] Case C-60/00 *Carpenter*, EU:C:2002:434.

[79] Case C-148/02 *García-Avello v Belgian State*, EU:C:2003:539.

[80] Treaty of Accession of Romania and Bulgaria (n 43).

[81] European Council (n 7) 34.

Maastricht, the CJEU explicitly held in *Collins*[82] that jobseekers resided in their host State legally under Article 45 TFEU and that this brought them within the scope of Article 18 TFEU.[83] Consequently, the UK's use of a habitual residence test to restrict access to Jobseeker's Allowance was permissible only because it applied 'independently of nationality'.[84] Though indirectly discriminatory, it could be justified by the legitimate need to establish a 'real link' between the host State job market and the EU citizen.

This very precise route to justification appears, however, to have been forgotten in *Vatsouras*.[85] It will be recalled that the Court was required to assess the validity of Article 24(2) Directive 2004/38—which, for jobseekers, derogated from the requirement of equal access to social assistance—against its interpretation of Articles 20 and 45 TFEU in *Collins*. Rather than find the measure invalid, the CJEU held that Jobseeker's Allowance did not constitute social assistance but was 'financial support intended to facilitate access to the job market'. This focus on maintaining access to Jobseeker's Allowance in fact permits nationality-based discrimination against jobseekers in relation to all other forms of social assistance to slip through unnoticed and, critically, via secondary Union legislation. This despite the fact that, post-*Collins*, jobseekers fall within the scope of Article 45 TFEU, and therefore within the Article 18 general prohibition of nationality-based discrimination.

Collins and *Vatsouras* accordingly provide critical insights into the legality of key aspects of the safeguard mechanism. Had the safeguard been applied exclusively to non-national Union workers, *Vatsouras* already offers limited precedent for permitted direct discrimination against Union citizens covered by Articles 45 and 18 TFEU, via secondary legislation, and without, as yet, much in the way of justificatory requirements. *Collins* and *Vatsouras* also provide stronger authority for host States to discriminate indirectly against individuals included within Articles 45 and 18 TFEU, in order to ensure a 'real link' between the applicant and the host State employment market and protect the public purse. Indeed, the application of a 'real link' test to workers—rather than workseekers—has already been permitted by the CJEU in *Geven* and *Hartmann*.[86] Thus, a safeguard mechanism requiring all applicants for in-work benefits—whether nationals or (other) EU citizens—to demonstrate a real link to the employment market could have relied on existing case law for its justification.

The only notable difference between those judgments and the safeguard would be whether the manner of assessing a 'real link' was truly indirectly discriminatory.

[82] *Collins* (n 49).

[83] Para 62. Interestingly, by contrast, the Court held at paras 26–33 that jobseekers were not workers for the purposes of equal access to social and tax advantages under Art 7, Reg No 1612/68.

[84] Para 73.

[85] *Vatsouras* (n 48).

[86] Case C-213/05 *Geven*, EU:C:2007:438; Case C-212/05 *Hartmann*, EU:C:2007:437.

The residence requirements in *Collins*, *Geven* and *Hartmann* were applied to both national and non-national EU citizens, with it simply being inherently easier for the former to meet that condition. By contrast, presumably, under the safeguard mechanism, national workers would be able to demonstrate a 'real link' to the host State job market by virtue of employment and residence, while non-national EU workers would be required to demonstrate something more: a growing connection over time. However, through the links between the internal market and citizenship case law forged in cases like *Collins* and *Vatsouras*, *Commission v UK* could be used as authority to find that sub-requirements, additional to the 'real link' test, imposed solely on EU nationals, are nonetheless indirectly discriminatory.

Ultimately, then, despite the mixed picture painted by the Court's jurisprudence, its most recent case law on Union citizenship indicates that it would have accepted the safeguard mechanism as legal. While the safeguard mechanism would clearly have gone further than the restrictions on free movement operating in the context of Union citizenship—since it imposes barriers to the movement of EU *workers*—the detailed examination of the case law conducted here demonstrates that this does not cast doubt, on the influence and authority of that body of judgments on legal assessments of the safeguard. In fact, what emerges from the above *technical* assessment of safeguard's legality is a more profound *constitutional* finding: that, while traditionally seeking to find means of securing greater rights for Union citizens, ironically, the historical development of Union citizenship rights—principally by the CJEU—furnishes the safeguard mechanism with its legal foundations.

B. The Historical and Constitutional Roots of the Safeguard

While the internal market origins of Union citizenship are well known,[87] these foundations are traditionally, and pertinently, used within the literature to question the ability of EU citizenship to recognise the personhood of non-economically active Union citizens when it still vests, largely, in movement and economic activity.[88] By contrast, analysis of the safeguard mechanism demonstrates the potentially restrictive influence of rules developed by the Court during its development of Union citizenship on the more generous principles operating in the context of the internal market. In particular, while the Court sought to extend the free movement provisions to a wider range of actors in its early (market) citizenship jurisprudence, it also offered a number of placatory limitations on

[87] For discussion, see M Everson, 'The Legacy of the Market Citizen' in J Shaw and G More (eds), *New Legal Dynamics of European Union* (Oxford, Oxford University Press 1995).

[88] C O'Brien, 'I Trade, Therefore I Am: Legal Personhood in the European Union' (2013) 50 *CML Rev* 1643; N Nic Shuibhne, 'Free Movement of Persons and the Wholly Internal Rule: Time to Move On?' (2002) 39 *CML Rev* 731.

these rights to allay potential Member State concerns about over-extension. However, the internal market foundations of Union citizenship allow for the cross-pollination of certain of these restrictions—developed in the particular context of economic inactivity—across legal structures shared by the internal market and citizenship alike. This is particularly visible within two categories of EU citizen—the service recipient and the jobseeker—since they most clearly straddle the divide between internal market and Union citizenship. However, since Union workers are *also* EU citizens, they too exercise their free movement rights simultaneously under Articles 45 and 21 TFEU. As a result, the reciprocal influence of the two spheres is inevitable.

The Court, alongside the Union legislature, recognised in the internal market's infancy that free movement would be inhibited if the human needs of the EU's economic actors were not met.[89] Therefore, as is well known, in addition to their right to carry out their economic activity, actors became able, for instance, to access social and tax advantages on an equal basis with host State nationals and to bring certain of their family members with them. Through this form of 'market citizenship', free movement emerged as a means by which a wider form of integration, beyond the economic, might be achieved.[90] Nevertheless, since these benefits could only be enjoyed by those falling within the scope of the internal market's free movement provisions, the Court sought to bring a wider range of individuals within their scope. For example, its inclusion of the service *recipient* within the ambit of Article 56 TFEU on service provision ensured access to the principle of non-discrimination to Member State nationals who would otherwise not benefit from it.[91]

Developments such as this paved a crucial road to the formal Union citizenship recognised at Maastricht. And yet, this same historical evolution forms the basis for legitimate criticism that Union citizenship is intrinsically limited in what it can offer non-economically active Union citizens. Conversely, it is also at the heart of emerging restrictions on the rights of EU workers. Specifically, in recognition of its own boundary pushing, the Court's introduction of the concept of service recipient was accompanied by the arrival and extension of a new justification—the risk of seriously undermining the financial balance of the social security system—where previously purely economic justifications had not generally been permissible.[92] More broadly, since the formalisation of Union citizenship, the

[89] eg Regulation (EU) 492/2011 and Directive 2004/38 and their previous incarnations; Case 32/75 *Cristini*, EU:C:1975:120; Case 207/87 *Even*, EU:C:1988:409; Opinion of AG Trabucchi Case 7/75 *Mr and Mrs F*, EU:C:1975:75; Case C-237/94 *O'Flynn*, EU:C:1996:206.

[90] In 1961, the Commission already recognised free movement as '*le premier aspect d'une citoyenneté européenne*', PE Deb, No 48, 135, 22 November 1961.

[91] Case 186/87 *Cowan*, EU:C:1989:47.

[92] Case C-158/96 *Kohll*, EU:C:1998:171; Case C-368/98, *Vanbraekel a.o.*, EU:C:2001.400. For discussion, see N Nic Shuibhne and M Maci, 'Proving Public Interest: The Growing Impact of Evidence in Free Movement Case Law' (2013) 50 *CML Rev* 965.

need to avoid 'unreasonable burden' on host State social assistance systems has become an ever-present justification for denying access to social support for non-economically active Union citizens.[93] As the service recipient—who continues to have one foot in the internal market and the other in Union citizenship—demonstrates, the construction of Union citizenship upon internal market foundations provides a historical synapse across which justifications can move back and forth. Accordingly, while many might reasonably have considered protection of public funds to be a legally unavailable rationale for the application of the safeguard mechanism to EU workers, it is firmly rooted in the historical development of, and interrelationship between, the internal market and Union citizenship.

Similarly, the immediate effect of the Court's decision, in *Collins*, to bring work-seekers within the scope of Article 45 TFEU as a direct result of Union citizenship is greater access to social support for individual Union citizens and, therefore, the apparent adding of flesh to the bones of Union citizenship. The novelty of the judgment nevertheless led, also, to the CJEU's acceptance of the host State's professed need to protect its social assistance schemes and to the introduction of the 'real link' criterion. Consequently, *Collins* in fact leaves jobseekers straddling Article 45 TFEU, under which Union workers are entitled to access social assistance on the same basis as national workers by virtue of their free movement rights, and Article 21 TFEU, pursuant to which the free movement and, therefore equal treatment rights, of non-economically active Union citizens may traditionally be limited. By reinforcing the links between the rights enjoyed as a Union citizen and those conferred by internal market rules, *Collins* offers a means by which rules designed in relation to economically inactive or not yet active EU citizens could transfer into the operation of the equal treatment rights of economic actors.

As noted above, this in fact happened in *Geven* and *Hartmann*.[94] There, national rules that required evidence of 'substantial work' before frontier workers could access child benefit, were permissible based on the need to demonstrate a 'real link' to the host State labour market. This approach contradicted the otherwise well-established rule that individuals are to be defined as workers, and have full access to ensuing rights, where their work is 'genuine and effective' and not 'marginal and ancillary'.[95] The transfer of Union citizenship mechanisms has therefore already, at times, reversed more inclusive approaches established in the free movement of worker context.[96]

Since *Geven* and *Hartmann*, the Court has sought to minimise the application of the 'real link' criteria to Union workers. Thus, in *Commission v Netherlands*,[97]

[93] *Trojani* (n 73); *Dano* (n 54).

[94] *Geven* (n 86); *Hartmann* (n 86).

[95] Case 53/81 *Levin*, EU:C:1982:105; Case 139/85 *Kempf*, EU:C:1986:223.

[96] N Nic Shuibhne, 'The Outer Limits of EU Citizenship Displacing Economic Free Movement Rights?' in C Barnard and O Odudu (eds), *The Outer Limits of European Union Law* (Oxford, Hart Publishing, 2009) 182.

[97] Case C-542/09 *Commission v Netherlands*, EU:C:2012:346.

participation in the labour market was found 'in principle' to offer a sufficient link to the host State to grant equal treatment rights.[98] Yet the consequence of the Court's decision not to overrule *Geven* and *Hartmann*, but to hold, instead, that work 'in principle' meets the requirements of the real link test is that the door is left open for that test to restrict the rights of Union workers in the future. Interestingly, the Court also stated in *Commission v Netherlands* that the sufficient link arose from 'the fact that, through the taxes which he pays the host Member State by virtue of his employment, the migrant worker also contributes to the financing of the social policies of that State'.[99] Arguably, the connection forged in this judgment, between the establishment of a 'real link' and one's financial contributions to the host State's social security system, is mirrored in the safeguard's 'gradual' access to welfare to reflect a 'growing connection' to the host State.

Ironically, then, the Court's constitutional boundary pushing during the evolution of Union citizenship—which historically endeavoured to extend free movement rights—now appears, through the introduction of placatory limitations on those expansions, to provide a framework for their restriction. Similarly, the CJEU's institutional boundary pushing, while initially of clear benefit to Union citizens' enjoyment of free movement rights might, nevertheless, and paradoxically, has contributed to the growing political pressure to limit them. Specifically, the achievement of a functioning internal market and an increasingly meaningful Union citizenship through the constitutionalisation of EU primary and secondary law frequently transfers essentially political decision-making to non-political institutions, while limiting the capacity of legislative organs to respond.[100] In the longer term, this approach might actually serve to damage, rather than strengthen, connections between the EU and its citizenry, particularly since the Court tends not to relinquish its institutional dominance even as it seeks to pacify the Member States.

C. The Institutional Roots of the Safeguard

Almost since its inception, the EU has faced accusations of democratic deficit. Questions over the Union's democratic legitimacy are, however, most commonly levelled at its political institutions, in particular the historically weak, through growing, power of the European Parliament.[101] However, the constitutional and institutional roots of the safeguard offer a significant example of what Grimm argues is an often overlooked factor in the Union's legitimacy deficit: the

[98] Para 65.

[99] Para 66.

[100] And, as Schmidt argues in this volume, renews pressure on *national* political institutions to act: see ch 2, p 25.

[101] eg A Follesdal and S Hix, 'Why there is a Democratic Deficit in the EU: A Response to Majone and Moravcsik' (2006) 44 *Journal of Common Market Studies* 533.

over-constitutionalisation of both primary and secondary Union law by the CJEU.[102] For Grimm, constitutions serve to furnish the basic structure and lasting principles for politics, while politics fills the spaces constitutions leave behind according to changing political preferences and circumstances.[103] Yet, the often open-textured nature of constitutional norms, he notes, creates the potential for courts to interpret them in a manner which reduces this political space, with consequential cementing effects on the law and marginalisation of the legislature.[104] Schmidt identifies the CJEU as one such court and its over-constitutionalisation of Union norms as one of the causes of disconnection between the EU and its citizenry. For her, this is particularly pertinent in the contemporary context of Brexit: 'as the court-driven non-majoritarian decision-making weakens "voice"', the relevance of "exit' is strengthened'.[105] Crucially, the evolution of the safeguard represents a clear means of charting this phenomenon.

The pivotal role played by the Court of Justice in the constitutionalisation of the EU Treaties—via assertions as to the status of EU law as a 'new legal order' that is supreme and may have direct effects in national legal systems,[106] as well as to the far-reaching obligations arising directly under the free movement provisions[107]—is well known. The benefits of this route to economic integration over the slower path, grounded in legislative harmonisation, arguably envisaged by the Treaties themselves,[108] are evident in the contemporary functioning of the internal market. The resultant changing dynamic between the Union's legislative organs, on the one hand, and its administrative and judicial branches on the other, however, is also clear. Moreover, as Grimm notes, an immediate consequence of the Court's famous *Van Gend* and *Costa* judgments is that the direct participation of the Member States in the development of the internal market through the EU's political institutions is no longer as central.[109]

The tensions that arise from this judicially driven evolution of the Union constitution are starkly visible in the Court's (in)famous *Laval* line of case law, which, when viewed through this lens, also establishes the safeguard mechanism, similarly, as the product of such tensions.[110] In these judgments, the Court held that the Posted Workers Directive[111] (PWD) offers a ceiling, rather than a floor, of

[102] D Grimm, 'The Democratic Costs of Constitutionalisation: The European Case' (2015) 21 *European Law Journal* 460.

[103] ibid 464.

[104] ibid.

[105] Schmidt (n 100); see ch 2, this volume p 18.

[106] Case 6/64 *Costa*, EU:C:1964:66; Case 26/62 *Van Gend en Loos*, EU:C:1963:1.

[107] eg Case 8/74 *Dassonville*, EU:C:1974:82; Case 120/78 *Rewe v Bundesmonopolverwaltung für Branntwein* (Cassis de Dijon), EU:C:1979:42; Case C-55/94 *Gebhard*, EU:C:1995:411.

[108] Consider, particularly, the more programmatic nature of the free provision of services and establishment under Arts 59 and 52 EEC.

[109] Grimm (n 102) 467; see also Schmidt (n 100).

[110] Case C-341/05 *Laval*, EU:C:2007:809; Case C-346/06 *Rüffert*, EU:C:2008:189 and Case C-319/06 *Commission v Luxembourg*, EU:C:2008:350.

[111] Directive 96/71/EC of the European Parliament and of the Council of 16 December 1996 concerning the posting of workers in the framework of the provision of services [1997] OJ L18/1.

protection for posted workers, despite the widely held view that the Union legislature had adopted that instrument principally as an antisocial dumping measure.[112] For the Court, the PWD gave concrete expression to the freedom to provide services, which represented a 'fundamental principle of the Union'.[113] Consequently, collective action seeking terms and conditions of employment going above and beyond the core nucleus of protection contained in the PWD was a prima facie breach of Union law. In other words, as a result of Article 56's status as a directly effective fundamental principle of EU primary law, the social objectives clearly inherent to the PWD could not contribute to the definitional framework of that broad-brush provision. Of course, the Court examined the legitimate interest in worker protection as a justification to the prima facie breach of Article 56 but, critically, this transfers the definitional scope of cross-border service provision from the legislature to the judiciary.

Importantly, 'since an interpretation of the Treaty effectively *becomes* the Treaty', as Davies reflects,[114] it can become difficult for the Union legislature to respond to the political consequences of CJEU judgments. Union efforts to address the aftermath of the *Laval* case law have been unsuccessful, somewhat ironically, after national parliaments made their first use of the Lisbon Treaty's 'yellow card' procedure to question, inter alia, whether the proposed Regulation on the exercise of the right to take collective action adequately respected the division of competences between the Union and its Member States.[115]

Regardless of whether one would agree with the factual outcome of individual cases, similar institutional dynamics are equally visible in the evolution of Union citizenship—that forms the backdrop to the safeguard—by means of the Court's (clearly pivotal) teleological approach to the Treaty's citizenship provisions. For instance, despite the fact that Article 21 TFEU makes plain that free movement rights may be limited by secondary legislation, the Court considered in *Grzelczyk* and *Baumbast* that, as a result of Union citizenship, any secondary law restrictions, as limitations on directly effective Treaty provisions, were subject to proportionality. Accordingly, a non-economically active EU citizen might still be legally resident, and entitled to equal treatment, even if she or he does not have sufficient resources,[116] or entirely comprehensive medical cover[117] as required by secondary Union law.

[112] eg EP Decision of the Committee Responsible, 2nd reading, COD/1991/0346, 24 July 1996, 'The aim is to eliminate unfair competition by ensuring that "posted" workers do not receive lower wages and are not subject to less favourable working conditions in the member state concerned'; C Barnard, 'Social Dumping or Dumping Socialism' (2008) 67 *CLJ* 262.

[113] *Laval* (n 110) para 101.

[114] Davies (n 19) 1583.

[115] Proposal for a Council Regulation on the right to take collective action within the context of the freedom of establishment and the freedom to provide services, COM(2012) 130 final; Commission Decision to withdraw the proposal: ec.europa.eu/dgs/secretariat_general/relations/relations_other/npo/letter_to_nal_parl_en.htm.

[116] *Grzelczyk* (n 72).

[117] *Baumbast* (n 35).

Those cases could, of course, be explained by the game-changing introduction of formally recognised EU citizenship into the Treaties after the secondary law instruments in question entered into force. These restrictions were nevertheless retained by subsequent Directive 2004/38. As Davies reports, the process of replacing the pre-citizenship free movement directives took place amid quite some debate about how far Union citizens' free movement rights should go and in knowledge of the existing case law.[118] Since Article 21 TFEU itself allows limits on free movement via secondary legislation, suggesting judicial deference, Directive 2004/38 might have been understood as a comprehensive statement of movement rights: 'the legislature had spoken on a subject where their authority is not in doubt, [and] where the policy context is complex and politicised'.[119] Nevertheless, while some cases appeared to show judicial responsiveness to legislative policy choices,[120] others appear to deprive the Directive of its intended consequence, subordinating it to the open-textured, judicially refined primary citizenship framework.

Our consideration, above, of how the Court might have bypassed some of the restrictive aspects of the safeguard via its approach in *Vatsouras*, offers a striking example of this. In *Vatsouras*, it seemed clear from the explicit exclusion of jobseekers from equal access to social assistance in Article 24(2) of the Citizens' Rights Directive (CRD) that the Union legislature sought to override the Court's earlier *Collins* judgment. In preserving its own case law, the CJEU clearly frustrated the intent of the Union legislature by placing Jobseeker's Allowance outwith the concept of social assistance. As Davies argues:

> [W]hile it may seem reasonable that secondary legislation is subject to primary law, it should be remembered that the Treaty says nothing about work-seekers. When the Court speaks of interpreting in the light of Article 45 TFEU, it really means interpreting in light of the castle of principles and ideas that it has built.[121]

Chen and *Ruiz Zambrano* were also explored above as offering a potential route around the requirements of the safeguard and thus also provide further examples of the dominance of principles developed by the CJEU.[122] While clearly contributing a route to residence rights crucial at the individual level, those judgments also suggest a rejection by the CJEU of arguably very clear policy choices by the EU legislature: that non-dependent ascendants are not beneficiaries of derived residence entitlements; or that, regardless of long-standing, fervent criticism, cross-border movement remains decisive in triggering Union citizenship rights.[123]

[118] Davies (n 19) 1598.

[119] ibid 1599.

[120] Compare pre-Directive 2004/38 Case C-209/03 *Bidar*, EU:C:2005:169 with post-Directive 2004/38 Case C-158/07 *Förster*, EU:C:2008:630.

[121] Davies (n 19) 1601.

[122] *Chen* (n 23); *Ruiz Zambrano* (n 23).

[123] Compare and contrast also the requirements arising re: cross-border health case in *Decker* (n 23) with Regulation (EEC) No 1408/71.

The non-political mode of decision-making visible in this case law does not alter the political character of the decisions made and yet importantly, as Grimm notes, 'the political means to secure democratic legitimacy and accountability are rendered inoperative'.[124]

Further, where the EU legislature has added flesh to the bones of the Treaties via secondary legislation, it also risks the 'legislative ossification' of these policy choices, and may subsequently find it hard to change direction should the political environment alter.[125] Indeed, the largest question mark over the legality of the safeguard mechanism arguably arose from the constitutionalisation of Article 7, Regulation No 492/2011, as a concrete expression of Article 45(2) TFEU in *Even*. Thus, although it was always open to the Member States to amend the Treaties to allow for discrimination against Union workers—admittedly with significant legal and political obstacles along the way—and irrespective of the fact that the safeguard struck at the heart of foundational Union goals, doubt as to its legality can itself provide ammunition to those who argue that the 'Masters of the Treaties' in fact operate within a judicial straitjacket.

In sum, the CJEU's teleological approach has done much to ensure that EU citizenship offers meaningful rights to Union citizens. From principled and moral perspectives, we might both welcome these developments and question whether they go far enough. Yet, when viewed through an *institutional* lens, the judicial evolution of Union citizenship, and more broadly the internal market, has left itself open to criticism in terms of democratic legitimacy: 'when [the] legislature constructs a limited regime, and it is widely accepted that there is no political will to extend [it], this does not disturb the path … of the case-law … the Court, in practice, trumps the law-maker'.[126] Accordingly, while the judicial evolution of Union citizenship might have been critical in coming to the aid of EU citizens in the short and medium term, the manner of its development might ironically undermine the Union's connection with its citizens in the longer term.[127] Indeed, research conducted by Blauberger and Schmidt indicates that Union citizenship rules:

> [P]romising to build the Union from below on the basis of equal legal entitlements, may, in fact, risk rousing further nationalism and decrease solidarity across the Union. The welfare state relies on reciprocity and court-driven rights cannot legitimate entitlements, which require legislative decisions.[128]

Of course, arguably the citizenship rights under the Treaties, much like fundamental rights, exist to offer crucial basic protections against changing political winds.

[124] Grimm (n 102) 470; see also Schmidt (n 100).
[125] Davies (n 19) 1597; see also Grimm (n 102) 464.
[126] Davies (n 19) 1605.
[127] See Schmidt (n 100); ch 2 this volume, p 34.
[128] M Blauberger and SK Schmidt, 'Welfare Migration? Free Movement of EU Citizens and Access to Social Benefits' (2014) *Research & Politics* 1, 6.

One could rightly argue that greater responsibility lies with other actors, particularly politicians and the media, to withstand and/or cease the perpetual othering of non-nationals within domestic debates. Despite the fact that academic research continues to indicate that non-national EU citizens are net contributors to the UK, while their take-up of benefits is disproportionately lower than the national population,[129] there is, generally speaking, political consensus in the UK on the need to address EU immigration. This was visible in David Cameron's renegotiation and by both the Remain and Leave campaigns in the run-up to the referendum.[130]

Yet, the Court has played its own part here too. The CJEU's constitutional and institutional boundary pushing has often been accompanied by placatory limitations on those expansions, thus, at least in part, confirming popular concerns about so-called benefit tourism. Yet, crucially, rather than offering flexibility to the Member States in their implementation of CJEU-derived rules—which might serve to lessen the impact of over-constitutionalisation—the terms of the Court-proffered leeway are uncertain and ultimately remain within the control of the Union judiciary. Ultimately, this serves only to increase the administrative burden placed on Member States and mobile EU citizens, while not being particularly visible to voters.[131]

The previous subsection (III.B) provided the 'real link' test as a pertinent example of this development. To this we can add the introduction of the concept of 'social tourism' by Advocate General Geelhoed.[132] Indeed, the causal link the Advocate General drew between the lack of harmonisation in the area of social security and the risk of social tourism[133] is replicated in the safeguard mechanism, which asserts that the diverse structures of Member States' social security systems 'may [themselves] attract workers to certain Member States'.[134]

Most recently, of course, we have seen the CJEU demonstrate further receptivity to changing political sentiment in Europe. The *Dano* line of case law sees a more literal approach to Directive 2004/38 and a growing permissiveness to restrictions on the equal treatment rights of non-economically active Union citizens, which often appears diametrically opposed to the CJEU's expansive approach

[129] See S Currie, *Migration, Work and Citizenship in the Enlarged European Union* (Cornwall, Ashgate, 2008) 45; Eurofound Report, 'Social Dimension of Intra-EU Mobility: Impact on Public Services', December 2015.

[130] Remain campaign materials on immigration tended to focus on the renegotiation or on the fact the exit would not lower immigration levels, rather than on the advantages of free movement, eg: d3n8a8pro7vhmx.cloudfront.net/in/pages/688/attachments/original/1467881907/BSIE_A5_LEAFLETS_(MYTH)_v15_PRINT.pdf?1467881907. The Leave campaign was more explicit, asking voters to imagine what the UK would be like when poorer countries join the EU, given the purported strain the UK was already under. That campaign also focused on the perceived powered of the CJEU to dictate who could enter the country: www.voteleavetakecontrol.org/why_vote_leave.html.

[131] See also Schmidt (n 100) who also argues that the constraints of over-constitutionalisation were particularly prominent within the UK legal system: ch 2 this volume, pp 28–30.

[132] (Opinion) *Trojani* (n 73) paras 13 and 18.

[133] ibid para 18.

[134] European Council (n 7) 19.

post-*Grzelczyk*.[135] These newer cases, however, offer the worst of both worlds, since they neither maintain the claim that the 'fundamental status' of Union citizenship is a route to equal treatment, nor enhance its democratic legitimacy. Specifically, the more literal approach to Directive 2004/38 visible in recent judgments does not alter wider reliance on broad, and rather vague, principles.

Member States are still required to permit the entry and residence of employees whose work is 'genuine and effective'; of jobseekers who are 'seeking work and have a genuine chance of being engaged'; of non-economically active Union citizens with 'sufficient resources'; and of family members whose removal would deny a Union citizen 'the genuine enjoyment' of the rights arising from that status. Inaction from individual Member States in respect of such ambiguous Court-derived concepts continues to be legally unacceptable yet riddled with political potholes, themselves endorsed by the Court's increased recognition of apparent social tourism.[136] As placatory limitations, the CJEU offers the Member States equally ambiguous concepts, such as the 'real link' requirement or the notion of 'unreasonable burden'. The Member States' response is frequently administrative in nature,[137] with the burden often transferred to the individual Union citizen, who as part of case-by-case assessments must provide evidence that their work is 'genuine and effective';[138] that they have a 'genuine chance of becoming employed'; or that they are 'legally resident' and not an 'unreasonable burden' when applying for social assistance.[139]

Since these administrative burdens are generally only visible to those who must endure them, Union citizenship is doubly undermined: it continues to suffer from a legitimacy deficit at the constitutional and institutional level, while exacerbating the othering of Union citizens and making access to equal treatment harder on the ground. As Grimm argues, 'the stronger the challenges are, the sooner politics will re-appear to circumvent the constitution'.[140] The safeguard concretely demonstrates this: an attempt by the Member States to reassert to the citizenry their status as 'Masters of the Treaties' and reassure them of their ability to respond politically.

Given the historical development of the internal market and of Union citizenship, however, the EU's political institutions were still able to construct the safeguard in a manner which would have been legally palatable to the Court. Crucially, what emerges from the analyses conducted thus far is that the safeguard mechanism did not spring from adversity, tailored to the specific need to convince a

[135] For Schmidt (n 100) this is case of 'too little too late', in terms of judicial response to the will of political actors: see ch 2 this volume, p 27.

[136] eg *Dano* (n 54) para 76.

[137] Blauberger and Schmidt (n 128).

[138] Individuals not meeting the UK's minimum earnings threshold must provide additional evidence that their work is 'genuine and effective'. For discussion of other administrative hurdles facing EU citizens in the UK, see Schmidt (n 100); see ch 2 this volume.

[139] See the UK's 'right to reside' test, found to be lawful in *Commission v UK* (n 54).

[140] Grimm (n 102) 464.

Member State teetering on the edge of exit to remain. Rather, both the emergence and form of the safeguard have clear, and broader, historical foundations. Consequently, regardless of its formal abandonment following the UK referendum result, the UK renegotiation has demonstrated that something like the safeguard is possible and it now retains the potential energy to reappear in the future.

IV. GONE BUT NOT FORGOTTEN? SPECULATING ON THE RE-EMERGENCE OF THE SAFEGUARD

This section considers, first, what a re-emerged safeguard mechanism might look like. Released from the formalities of the Decision, the safeguard could now take a number of shapes. Notably, the content, rather than the form, of the Decision, indicates that *unilateral* decisions to discriminate against workers are now possible. The section acknowledges, second, that, regardless of the fact that it is constitutionally rooted and politically explainable, the safeguard would still represent a significant change in direction for the EU, with far-reaching repercussions should it be employed.

A. Up for Grabs: The Potential Future Shape of the Safeguard Mechanism

First, given the demonstrated legality of the safeguard as contained in the Decision, an identical mechanism could emerge at the Union level in the future. On the one hand, this seems unlikely. In the Bratislava Declaration, published shortly after the UK vote, the other 27 Member States highlighted the need 'to serve better the … wishes [of EU citizens] to live study, work, move and prosper freely across our continent and benefit from the rich European heritage'.[141] In responding to the referendum result, the emphasis was on improving communication between the EU institutions, the Member States and Union citizens, and on challenging the 'simplistic solutions of extreme or populist political forces'.[142] On the other hand, in late 2016, the Commission announced less ambitious proposals for reform to the Social Security Regulation that would place some restrictions on EU workers' ability to aggregate contributions for unemployment benefit across Member States.[143]

Crucially, some Member States continue to face pressure domestically to tackle perceived problems with intra-EU migration and, in particular, benefit tourism.[144]

[141] Bratislava Declaration (n 2) 1.

[142] ibid 2.

[143] Proposal for a Regulation of the European Parliament and Council amending Regulation No 883/2004 on the coordination of social security systems, COM(2016) 815 final, 12.

[144] eg an association of German cities stated in 2013 that low-qualified migrants without sufficient financial means and health insurance were becoming an increasing burden for several municipalities: Blauberger and Schmidt (n 128) 5.

The post-*Dano* case law demonstrates that some Member States are already testing the water in terms of increased restrictions on the free movement rights of non-economically active Union citizens. Indeed, emboldened by the *Alimanovic* ruling, in December 2016, Germany adopted new legislation restricting access to a number of social benefits for the unemployed (outwith those directly related to facilitating access to the labour market) during the first five years of an EU citizen's residence there.[145] The UK renegotiation now presents a new possibility that might previously have been viewed as untouchable: restrictions on the equal treatment rights of Union *workers*. Indeed, Austria has already voiced plans to restrict access to employment for (other) EU citizens even if it quickly backtracked.[146] The German Government is also putting pressure on the Commission to reintroduce the option for host States to limit exported child benefit to the amount that would be paid in an EU citizen's home State;[147] a mechanism that first appeared in the UK's pre-referendum renegotiations.[148] Critically, while the Decision spoke also to older CJEU case law on Union-level internal market restrictions, our analysis demonstrates that the safeguard's legal palatability is largely grounded in the Union citizenship case law: judgments concerning *unilateral* Member State restrictions on free movement. Most significantly, the safeguard's requirement that Union workers demonstrate a 'real link' to the host State labour market before gaining graduated access to its social security system, is drawn from domestic limitations on free movement rights in *Collins*, *Vatsouras* and, importantly, *Geven* and *Hartmann*. This finding is reinforced by the conceptualisation of domestic nationality-based discrimination as indirect in nature in *Commission v UK*. So long as, technically speaking, domestic rules require all applicants for in-work benefits in a given Member State to demonstrate a 'real link' to its employment market, this will be legally acceptable, regardless of whether nationals demonstrate this by virtue of their nationality and residence, while other EU citizens have to proffer something more.

Unilateral adoption of the safeguard would necessarily neglect the amendment of secondary legislation envisaged by the Decision. Prima facie, domestic restrictions on access to social assistance would seem in conflict with Article 7 Regulation 492/2011, on equal access to social and tax advantages, as well as Article 24(1) Directive 2004/38, offering a general right to equal treatment. Yet, in *Commission v UK*, the Court demonstrated a willingness to interpret legal residence as a *substantive*, internal condition for access to social security, rather than as a rule potentially in conflict with Union secondary law determining the Member State responsible for providing specific social security entitlements. A 'real link' test could be similarly viewed as a substantive condition of access to in-work benefits,

[145] Law of 22 December 2016, [German] *Federal Law Gazette* 2016 I, No 65, 3155.

[146] N Neilsen, 'Austria wants to discriminate against EU workers' *EUObserver* (12 January 2017).

[147] See: www.bgbl.de/xaver/bgbl/start.xav?startbk=Bundesanzeiger_BGBl&jumpTo=bgbl116s3155.pdf.

[148] European Council (n 7) 22.

applicable to all applicants. This would then constitute justifiable indirect discrimination, whether as a matter of primary or secondary law.

That is not to say, of course, that the reappearance of the safeguard would not have considerable repercussions for the direction of EU law.

B. The Technical, Constitutional and Institutional Implications of the Safeguard

While clearly the precise consequences of the re-emergence of the safeguard would depend on its form, a number of technical, constitutional and institutional repercussions can be identified. Moreover, the interlinked nature of these effects serves to reinforce conclusions as to the ripple effect of constitutional boundary pushing.

The re-emergence of the safeguard at Union level would raise technical questions about the relationship between secondary EU legislation, outwith the larger question of compliance with primary law discussed in previous sections. In particular, how would amendments made to Regulation No 492/2011 interact with the principle of equal treatment contained in Article 24(1) Directive 2004/38? On the one hand, the Directive increasingly dominates over other secondary Union legislation in this area of EU law.[149] On the other, this dominance tends to operate to restrict access to welfare.[150] Accordingly, it would not be out of line with the Court's current methodology, for instance, to consider amendments to Regulation No 492/2011 to supersede Article 24(1) Directive 2004/38. Interestingly, however, following the Court's decision in *Commission v UK* to treat legal residence as a substantive condition for access to welfare within domestic social security systems, conflict is more simply avoided if the safeguard reappears at the Member State, as opposed to Union, level.

The reappearance of the safeguard, at either level, raises further technical questions: how would a 'real link' to the host State labour market be assessed and how would *graduated* access to in-work benefits progress? Clearly the guidance on the 'real link' test in *Collins*, focused on habitual residence and evidence of genuine work-seeking would not be appropriate here. It seems more likely that the focus would be on duration of employment or financial contributions to the host State social security system, particularly given the Court's focus on this in *Commission v Netherlands*.[151] This raises further questions: *how much* of a contribution would Union workers be expected to make and for *how long*?

Crucially, emphasis on duration and/or financial contributions would be particularly problematic for low-paid, temporary workers, for whom access to in-work benefits is likely to be most necessary, and who might be unlikely to demonstrate the requisite links for some time. Specifically, O'Brien has argued

[149] Specifically, Reg 883/2004 in *Brey* (n 75); *Dano* (n 54).
[150] ibid.
[151] *Commission v Netherlands* (n 97).

that the analogous focus on *continuous, legal* residence for EU citizens to qualify for permanent residence[152] would indicate that some Union citizens might be required to wait much longer, in practice, than the four years featured in the Decision for full access to welfare. Only residence in accordance with Directive 2004/38—through work, self-employment, or self-sufficiency—is considered legal for the purposes of acquiring permanent resident status. Consequently, periods between employment, or time taken for caregiving would, at best, not count towards the four-year total, or worse, break continuity of residence, should a similar approach be adopted.[153] Indeed, comparable issues already arose in the context of the UK's Worker Registration Scheme, once applicable to EU8 and EU2 workers, since it required *continuous* work for 12 months before the relevant Union citizens could work and access benefits without registration.[154]

In any case, demonstrating a growing connection to the host State employment market will be more administratively burdensome for low-paid, temporary, or zero-hours contract workers, who will accumulate much more paperwork than those in permanent work. Benefits might be most easily accessed by Union workers enjoying longer-term, better-paid employment, who would meet the substantive and administrative requirements of a 'real link' test more easily. The result would be a step backwards in terms on Union integration, since similar criticism could then be levelled at free movement of workers that already faces Union citizenship: that it operates principally as a safety net 'for distressed gentlefolk during periods of temporary financial hardship' and creates tiers of citizen.[155] Yet cases such as *Collins* and *Brey*[156] indicate that Union-level examination of these consequences of the safeguard is unlikely. What is more probable is the continued finding that prima face restrictions on Union law are proportionate as a result of case-by-case assessments at the domestic level,[157] and therefore the continued transfer of the administrative burden to the Union citizen.

From this emerges a third repercussion, both constitutional and technical in nature: the fact that restrictions on in-work benefits cause a very real barrier to trade. For example, the emphasis of the Decision on the apparent 'pull factor' of the UK's 'generous' benefits system overlooks that the UK's employment market is also increasingly defined by low-paid, zero-hours contract work that is often only possible as a result of in-work benefits.[158] Consequently, restrictions on equal

[152] Case C-378/12 *Onuekwere*, EU:C:2014:13.

[153] C O'Brien, 'Why the emergency brake on migrant benefits is sexist' *The Conversation* (4 February 2016).

[154] Currie (n 129) ch 3.

[155] M Dougan, 'The Constitutional Dimension to the Case Law on Union Citizenship' (2006) 31 *EL Rev* 613, 622.

[156] *Brey* (n 75).

[157] Though, in the context of non-economically active Union citizens, even this requirement is increasingly sidelined: *Dano* (n 54); *Alimanovic* (n 55).

[158] K Puttick, 'EEA Workers' Free Movement and Social Rights after *Dano* and *St Prix*: Is a Pandora's Box of New Economic Integration and 'Contribution' Requirements Opening?' (2015) 37 *Journal of Social Welfare and Family Law* 253.

access to social assistance constitutes a genuine barrier to movement that undermines not only the ambition of Union citizenship but the foundational goals of the internal market formed at Rome. Though this chapter demonstrates that the historical evolution of the internal market provides constitutional foundations for the safeguard, those developments were still, at their core, about acknowledging that economic integration required recognition of the human needs of workers. That the safeguard would potentially represent a reconfiguration of the Union's central objectives is all the more explicit in the reference in the Decision to 'difficulties that are serious and liable to persist in the [host State's] employment market' as a potential reason for triggering the safeguard. This would introduce pure protectionism into the justificatory gamut.[159]

Such constitutional issues trigger institutional questions about interactions between the Union's legislative and judicial branches. On the one hand, we have seen that the constitutionalisation of Union primary and secondary Union law has, to some extent, contributed to the current state of affairs. As Horsley argues, since, through its transformation of the EU legal order, the Court has created for itself the role of leading policymaker in European integration, it should also accept the limits the Treaty places upon it as an institutional actor. Horsley identifies the requirement in Article 13(2) TEU, that the Union institutions practise mutual sincere cooperation, as imposing a primary law requirement on the Court to respect the policy choices of the Union legislature where appropriate.[160] Similarly, Davies argues that the concept of inter-institutional balance suggests that Treaty interpretation should be viewed as a shared activity, with both the Union's political and judicial organs contributing to what concepts within the Treaty, such as free movement, might mean.[161]

On the other hand, a brake on in-work benefits would clearly introduce obvious barriers to trade, undermining the foundational goals of the Union and well-established approaches to their achievement, long accepted by the Member States. In rejecting the employment of a safeguard mechanism, the Court would arguably be acting appropriately within its institutional role of 'ensuring that in the application of the Treaties, the law is observed', pursuant to Article 19 TEU. And yet, ironically, at the very point at which the Court might properly act as a check on the EU's political branches—since central values of the Union's constitution appear to be at risk—its own institutional boundary pushing may leave it with little choice but to accept this change in direction for the Union. This is already visible in the Court's more literal approach to Directive 2004/38 post-*Dano*. Indeed, ultimately, despite being backed into a corner, the Court's pre-emptive approach to the current political climate in that line of case law—alongside the fact that the safeguard mechanism is built on the judicially driven evolution of Union citizenship—will

[159] And creates a window for restrictions on access to employment, as reported by Neilsen (n 146).
[160] Horsley (n 19) 941, 960.
[161] Davies (n 19) 1586.

allow it to present its acceptance of any future safeguard as securely in line with its own jurisprudence.

V. CONCLUSION

Regardless of its formal irrelevance following the decision of the UK electorate to leave the EU, the emergency brake on in-work benefits, introduced as part of the UK's now abandoned renegotiation of its EU membership, provides a useful lens through which to assess the current limits of Union citizenship, the internal market and, more broadly, European integration, as well as the institutional dynamics at play there. By introducing discrimination against the Union *worker*, the safeguard mechanism appeared to do the constitutionally unthinkable. Yet the analysis demonstrates not only that the safeguard was legally salvageable, but also that it was firmly rooted in the constitutional evolution of Union citizenship from the internal market. Consequently, while the UK will now willingly relinquish the Union citizenship rights of its own nationals, it might also leave a restrictive legacy—by virtue of the backdrop to its departure—for those who remain EU citizens. It has opened a Pandora's Box in respect of how other Member States might now seek to redefine the outer boundaries of Union citizenship and the internal market in response to political pressure.

Crucially, since the legality of the safeguard is largely grounded in CJEU case law arising from domestic restrictions on free movement, there appears no reason why a Member State must wait for the re-emergence of the safeguard at the Union level. Of course, such blatant discrimination against EU workers would go further than Member State limitations have successfully gone before. Accordingly, a finding of invalidity or incompatibility in relation to any future reintroduction of the safeguard would appear an uncontroversial performance of the Court's institutional role. And yet, the Court's previous institutional boundary pushing might leave it constrained at the very moment when it might appropriately act to protect foundational principles of Union law. However, given that any future safeguard is likely to arise unilaterally from individual Member States, by means of justifiable indirect discrimination, the CJEU will be able to present the safeguard as in line with its own jurisprudence. Startlingly then, the re-emergence of the safeguard might fail on both fronts, since it would present genuine obstacles to the free movement and equal treatment rights of Union citizens, while doing little to address Union citizenship's ongoing existential crisis.

5

Why Did the Citizenship Jurisprudence Change?

URŠKA ŠADL AND SUVI SANKARI

I. SETTING THE SCENE

THE OVERALL AIM of this volume is twofold. First, it tries to deconstruct legal, political and social forces that affect the European citizenship jurisprudence generally. Second, and more particularly, it seeks to explain and contextualise the Court's shift towards a restrictive approach to free movement rights of European citizens. So far, literature has singled out two structural elements and three contextual factors, which could make the latter shift intelligible: the role of the legislator in the European Union (EU) and the role of law writ large, as well as the financial, the constitutional (Brexit) and the migration crisis.[1] The latter especially increased the pressure on the European Court of Justice (the Court) to prioritise the general interests of the Member States over the colliding interests of individual European citizens. In this chapter, we do not question this explanation or the legal claim that the citizenship jurisprudence has become more restrictive.[2] Instead, we raise the question whether two institutional factors, namely internal reorganisation and the professional composition of the Court contributed to this process of transformation alongside the external factors already identified.[3]

To answer this question, we further unpack the shift toward the restrictive approach in greater detail and situate it more precisely in time. While existing scholarship provides a detailed map of the valid citizenship law and convincing

[1] For discussion on the factors see SK Schmidt, and F Strumia in this volume, and especially the chapter by S Reynolds.

[2] For discussion of restrictive shift in this volume see P Minderhoud and S Mantu, *cf* the chapter by F Wollenschläger, essentially suggesting the Court is only posturing a turn, or that, even if there is a turn, one does not yet know whether it concerns economically non-actives.

[3] By internal organisation we mean allocation of cases and decision-making in chambers rather than in the Grand Chamber. Professional composition refers to professional, career and legal background of sitting judges and their personal characteristics, such as nationality and gender. Professional composition and career trajectories have been identified as factors that importantly contributed to the Court's legitimacy and stability of its jurisprudence.

explanations (or justifications) for the Court's change of heart, there remains a general lack of understanding of how internal and external factors interact over time and what is their combined effect on the content of the jurisprudence. To gauge this effect, we engage with the mechanisms of jurisprudential change, aka tools, which the Court (or any court) has at its disposal to develop, modify, clarify and legitimate its law-making action. These, rather than cases (judgments), become the units of systematic qualitative and quantitative analysis. We separately scrutinise the Court's approach to interpretation, the use of public policy arguments and reliance on past decisions, which are widely considered as rights-opening/pro individual. Our study focuses on:

1. The *use* of the teleological method of interpretation of relevant Treaty Articles and Directive 2004/38.
2. The *use* of the argument of the protection of public finances.
3. The change of a reference frame, meaning that references to more recent rights-limiting precedents[4] are replacing the references to the foundational jurisprudence.[5]

With regard to the internal factors that we select, the decision-making in chambers and the membership in the Grand Chamber are often mentioned as major culprits for the inconsistencies in the Court's jurisprudence, its uninformative reasoning style and its neglectful handling of precedents.[6] The professional composition of the Court matters: it greatly influences the characteristics of the case law,[7] even if one rejects legal realism and the so-called breakfast jurisprudence.[8] The focus on only two internal factors might seem excessively narrow hence the findings inconclusive. However, we do not wish to make strong claims about causality but rather point at the mutually reinforcing factors that might drive European citizenship case law.

We analyse 38 opinions of the Advocates General and 38 corresponding judgments of the Court,[9] which deal with the rights of individual European citizens,

[4] ECJ, Case C-140/12 *Brey*, EU:C:2013:565; Case C-308/14 *European Commission v United Kingdom of Great Britain and Northern Ireland*, EU:C:2016:436; Case C-299/14 *García-Nieto*, EU:C:2016:114.

[5] ECJ, Case C-85/96 *Martínez Sala*, EU:C:1998:217; Case C-184/99 *Grzelczyk*, EU:C:2001:458; Case C-224/98 *D'Hoop*, EU:C:2002:432; Case C-413/99 *Baumbast and R*, EU:C:2002:493; and Case C-209/03 *Bidar*, EU:C:2005:169. *Martínez Sala* and *Baumbast* were given classic status also by being included in M Poiares Maduro and L Azoulai (eds), *The Past and Future of EU Law: The Classics of EU Law Revisited on the 50th Anniversary of the Rome Treaty* (Oxford, Hart Publishing, 2010).

[6] JL Dunoff and MA Pollack, 'Comparative International Judicial Practices: A Manifesto' (European Society of International Law 11th Annual Conference); M de S-O-l'E Lasser, *Judicial Deliberations: A Comparative Analysis of Judicial Transparency and Legitimacy* (Oxford, Oxford University Press, 2009).

[7] D Chalmers, 'Judicial Performance, Membership, and Design at the Court of Justice' in M Bobek (ed), *Selecting Europe's Judges: A Critical Review of the Appointment Procedures to the European Courts* (Oxford, Oxford University Press, 2015).

[8] S Danzigera, J Levavb and L Avnaim-Pessoa, 'Extraneous Factors in Judicial Decisions' (2011) 108 *Proceedings of the National Academy of Science* 6889.

[9] Most cases under scrutiny address the question whether and under what circumstances those European citizens can be granted or refused rights. The usual formulation in the judgments and the

and more particularly with their claims for social advantages, including social benefits and social assistance.[10] This selection is based on the consideration that a jurisprudential shift can be identified more accurately by including the so-called headline cases, as well as cases which do not attract immediate scholarly or public attention. Our qualitative and quantitative analysis indicates that a considerable shift from the rights-opening to the rights-closing approach occurred in 2011 with *Ziolkowski and Szeja* and *Brey*, prior to *Dano*,[11] *García-Nieto*,[12] *Alimanovic*,[13] and *Commission v United Kingdom*.[14] On this basis we divide 38 cases in two groups: the group of 18 cases decided before the Court's judgment in *Ziolkowski and Szeja* and the group of 20 cases decided after that, and examine their common features against the external context in which they are situated and against the internal shifts in the organisation (the chamber system) and the professional composition of the Court. Additionally, we examine the group of most recent cases, decided since *Dano* in 2014, in our sample, which contains 11 cases, separately.

Our examination relies on literature suggesting that courts are not isolated from their environment and respond to it by adapting their jurisprudence to the changing global political and societal structures.[15] Likewise, internal struggles leave the Court with 'unfinished' judgments,[16] unclear legal compromises, and diverging interpretations of existing legal sources, including previous case law.[17]

Our findings suggest that since 2011, citizenship cases concerning claims of individual citizens in matters of residence and social advantages have increasingly been decided by the chambers of five sitting judges. By contrast, the professional membership of the Court has not changed considerably. The same could not be said about the professional background of Advocates General that delivered the opinions in the examined cases. Since 2011, the percentage of opinions delivered by Advocates General coming from academia and legal practice has decreased

opinions is whether someone would become a burden on the social assistance in any of the manifold variations (unreasonable burden, burden on the public finances). The term stems from pre-Maastricht legislation of the 1990s on free movement of economically non-active Member State nationals. It appears in all preambles of this legislation, whereas the Articles of the same legislation speak of a burden on the social assistance system. The dualism of unreasonable burden and burden was reiterated in Directive 2004/38/EC (presumably on purpose), however, the reference point of what the burden is placed on was synchronised, and is now narrower, referring only to the social assistance system in the preamble and Articles of Directive 2004/38/EC [2004] OJ L158/77.

[10] On file with the authors.

[11] ECJ, Joined cases C-424/10 and C-425/10 *Ziolkowski and Szeja*, EU:C:2011:866, *Brey* (n 4), Case C-333/13 *Elisabeta Dano and Florin Dano*, EU:C:2014:2358.

[12] *García-Nieto* (n 4).

[13] ECJ, Case C-67/14 *Alimanovic*, EU:C:2015:210.

[14] *Commission v United Kingdom* (n 4).

[15] KJ Alter, LR Helfer and MR Madsen, 'How Context Shapes the Authority of International Courts' (2016) 79 *Law & Contemporary Problems* 1.

[16] M Jacob, Precedents and Case-based Reasoning in the European Court of Justice: Unfinished Business (Cambridge, Cambridge University Press, 2014).

[17] D Sarmiento, 'Half a Case at a Time: Dealing with Judicial Minimalism at the European Court of Justice' in M Claes et al (eds), *Constitutional Conversations in Europe: Actors, Topics and Procedures* (Cambridge, Intersentia, 2012) 13.

while the percentage of opinions delivered by Advocates General with previous dominant career in politics or civil service has increased. Our findings also show a greater reliance (in the form of explicit references) on the opinions of the Advocates General, especially in chamber judgments. By contrast, the Court has not adopted an increasingly minimalist reasoning, nor has it shown a significantly greater deference to national courts. It has, however, delivered a much higher proportion of highly abstract answers to preliminary references after 2011.

These findings are illustrative of an institution with a fragmented vision of European citizenship, which is nonetheless unwilling to cede its broad jurisdiction and participation in the evolving 'new policy' in the distribution of resources between nationals and non-nationals, economically active and not economically active migrant European citizens. On the one hand, this would be difficult to attribute to the changing professional composition of the Court. On the other, the allocation of cases to the Reporting Judges and the Advocates General with background in national civil service and politics could explain a greater sensitivity of the Court to the national interests related to the questions of migration and welfare hence the restrictive turn. Given that the influence of the individual Reporting Judge on her colleagues in the chamber cannot be inferred from our observations, this conclusion is somewhat speculative. What we can observe directly is that the increase of negative outcomes coincides with the relocation of European citizenship cases from the Grand Chamber to the chambers of five judges around 2011. Although *Ziolkowski and Szeja* was the first case decided by the Grand Chamber with a negative outcome for the individuals in 2011, after 2014 the chambers of five judges have rendered twice as many judgments with negative outcomes for the individual citizen as the Grand Chamber. On this basis, we argue that the internal factors discussed above clearly underwrote the jurisprudential shift together with the external economic, constitutional and existential crises.

The contribution is structured as follows. In the second section, we briefly outline our methodology and theoretical framework. In the third section, we trace the modification of the Court's reasoning and approach to interpretation and precedent, in particular to the so-called citizenship classics. In the fourth section, we juxtapose the findings of the qualitative analysis with the changes in the professional composition of the Court and its internal organisation and professional composition (two internal factors). We also outline the timeline of external factors and try to contrast them to the critical junctures in the jurisprudence against the internal factors. We conclude in section five.

II. THEORETICAL FRAMEWORK AND METHODOLOGY

A. Framework

Our examination is anchored in the established theory of international and supranational adjudication, according to which the success of international and supranational courts in terms of compliance with their rulings, interpretive authority and institutional legitimacy depends on a mixture of internal and external factors: (1) factors within the control of states such as the composition of the tribunal, or the caseload; (2) factors within the control of the supranational tribunal itself such as its awareness of the audience, neutrality and demonstrated autonomy from political interests; and (3) factors often beyond the control of both states and jurists like the type of cases or violations and the cultural and political homogeneity of the states. While on the one hand international courts can adopt strategies that significantly increase the odds of their success, on the other hand they can also decrease their chances of success. They can lose their audience awareness by not favouring individual rights over States and by not empowering national courts.[18] Moreover, external factors such the increase in cultural and political heterogeneity within the Court's community of law—against which courts cannot be immune internally either—can further impede their legitimacy of and compliance with their rulings.[19] More recent literature on the subject furthermore suggests that international courts are forced to *constantly* relate and respond to the changing context, political and societal,[20] and that they indeed do so by legal means available (aka legal diplomacy):[21] interpretation, argumentation and judicial remedies (outcomes).

This setting might provoke an internal struggle among the members of the Court regarding its role and its judicial tasks, which will most likely only exacerbate with the changing and rapidly expanding membership and professional reconfiguration, internal reorganisation and working methods. These will prompt judges to avoid giving concrete answers to national courts and defer them to policymakers, national and European. It will leave the Court with 'unfinished' judgments.[22]

B. Methodology

In this chapter we zoom into opinions and judgments of the Court, where the term 'unreasonable burden' (in any of the language formulations) occurs in the English text or the title of the document that has been stored in the EUR-Lex database until the end of 2016.[23] To capture a broader legal context, we also consider a

[18] L Helfer and A Slaughter, 'Toward A Theory of Effective Supranational Adjudication' (1997) 70 *Yale Law Journal* 273, 308–12.

[19] ibid 362–65.

[20] Alter, Helfer and Madsen (n 15).

[21] MR Madsen, 'The Protracted Institutionalisation of the Strasbourg Court: From Legal Diplomacy to Integrationist Jurisprudence' in MR Madsen and J Christoffersen (eds), *The European Court of Human Rights between Law and Politics* (Oxford, Oxford University Press, 2011); MR Madsen, 'The Challenging Authority of the European Court of Human Rights: From Cold War Legal Diplomacy to the Brighton Declaration and Backlash' (2016) 79 *Law & Contemporary Problems* 141.

[22] Jacob (n 16).

[23] Full list on file with the authors (email: Urska.sadl@eui.eu).

range of cases that are connected to those cases directly through case citations and cases that concern related matters of free movement of persons that resonate with external audiences and are accompanied by a press release.

First, we examine the case law qualitatively to tease out the legal shifts in the case law, and especially the doctrinal effect of the rights-curbing interpretations, reasoning and precedents of the Court. However, we do not focus on individual cases but on the specific aspect of all cases included in our selection. In particular, we examine the judicial method of interpreting Treaty Articles and Directive 2004/38, the selection of cited cases, and the Court's reading of its case law—known and treated in literature as both generally applicable and expansive (the so-called citizenship classics)—as well as the changes in the use of policy reasoning as a type of substantive reasoning of the Court. We also record the outcomes of cases, either as pro-individual or against the individual. The outcome is coded as pro-individual if the Court grants a right to the individual or deems measures which limit individual rights (to move, to reside, social advantages, non-discrimination) incompatible with European law. Then, we examine whether the Advocates General and the Court both adopt a more restrictive approach to interpretation, the references to the classics (eg, to describe the state of the law in the section preceding the argumentation part, or in the argumentative part itself), and the role of public interest of the Member State in the reasoning chain. We pay particular attention to the 'timing' of particular arguments, twists in interpreting or selecting cases, as well as to case outcomes and broader issues discussed.

The methodical examination of Advocates General opinions alongside the Court's judgments is largely missing from the detailed and thought-provoking analysis of the changing trends in the case law. Moreover, in case commentaries, the Opinion is most often juxtaposed with the judgment, or the case law more generally, rather than to the Opinions of the same Advocate General or opinions on the same or similar legal issues. On the one hand, this is justified by the fact that the opinions are not binding on the Court, and would tell us little about the case law as such. On the other hand, however, the Advocates General have considerable influence on the Court, especially in the area of European citizenship, where the Advocates General carved out the basic approach of the Court in the early case law.[24] Moreover, their legal analysis often goes beyond what is absolutely necessary in terms of deciding the concrete case. Given the proverbial explanatory silence[25] of the Court, the opinions are crucial for understanding the Court's reasoning process, the context of individual cases, as well as underlying concerns.

Second, to quantify our qualitative observations we code several characteristics related to the case. More specifically, we assign codes (different labels) for the

[24] See U Šadl and S Sankari, 'The (Elusive) Influence of the Advocate General on the Court of Justice: The Case of European Citizenship' (forthcoming 2017) *Yearbook of European Law* (first view available at https://doi.org/10.1093/yel/yex001).

[25] On the silence of the CJEU see Sarmiento (n 17); S Sankari, *European Court of Justice Legal Reasoning in Context* (Groningen, Europa Law Publishing, 2013).

composition, deference of final decisions to national courts, characteristics of the outcome (pro or against individual, abstract or concrete answer, avoidance of an answer, ie, minimalism) as well as characteristics of judges and Advocates General who participate in the decision-making in the case, especially their legal background, career paths, nationality, gender and stage at the time of the decision.

We assign the code explicit deference to those cases where the Court, in the operative part, refers to the national court ([it is for the] national court [to ascertain]). We assign the code implicit deference to the cases where the Court makes references to the national court ([it is for the] national court [to ascertain]) in the grounds of the judgment but not in its operative part, relating to the choice of major premise or facts or proportionality.

Similarly, we code for minimalism. We divide minimalist rulings into two further categories. The first comprises cases where minimalism is partial, meaning that the Court defers some elements or at least the application (concrete answer) to the national court. In this sense, partial minimalism can overlap with deference. However, it is a wider category than just deference in that the Court seemingly answers questions posed but does not fully address all aspects of them. Thereby it leads the national court only half way. By contrast, the second category of minimalism is complete silence, which means that the Court implicitly or explicitly refrains from answering all or one of often many questions posed by the national court, or reformulates them restrictively (including questions of admissibility or restrictive useful answers to the national court).[26]

We also code the Court's answers as concrete or abstract. When the Court explicitly uses the following phrases: 'in the specific circumstances of the present case', or 'in those precise circumstances', or 'taking into account all the relevant factors in the individual case', or 'a person in the circumstances of the appellant in the main proceedings in the operative part of the judgment', the answer is coded as concrete. Otherwise, we code the answer as abstract.

On this basis, we gain a (quantitative) overview of the shift with regard to the legal characteristics of case law as well as of the characteristics of the case law related to the institutional factors, which we interpret and contextualise further.

III. LEGAL ANALYSIS

In this section, we focus on the legal analysis of jurisprudential shift through the lens of three mechanisms: interpretation, reasoning and treatment of citizenship

[26] When legitimately not answering a question the national court has explicitly posed only in the alternative (or 'if so', 'if the first question is answered in the negative'), and the alternative question does not warrant an answer, this does not count as complete silence. However, when the Court or the Advocate General decide—without the national court posing questions in the alternative—that an answer to a further question is not necessary in light of the answer already given, counts as complete silence.

classics (precedent). As already mentioned above, we selected these mechanisms as the most important judicial tools which allow the Court to change the direction of the jurisprudence.

A. Proliferation of Objectives

With regard to interpretation, the main change of direction is in the use of the teleological method of interpretation, in particular on the reinterpretation of the objectives of Directive 2004/38. The classic interpretive position of the Court, embodied in cases like *Baumbast*[27] and extending to *Metock*[28] and even to *Lassal*,[29] can be defined as the reading of the Treaty provisions, Directive 2004/38 and Regulation 883/2004[30] in light of their *main* purpose to facilitate the exercise of the primary and individual right to move and reside freely and to strengthen that right. By contrast, the current position of the Court is based primarily on the reading of Directive 2004/38 as intended to strengthen only the rights of those who fulfil the conditions set therein.

This modification materialised through four interpretive twists. It began with the crowding of legislative objectives. In *Ziolkowski and Szeja*,[31] the Court explicitly invoked three objectives of Directive 2004/38 in parallel: to move and reside freely, referring to recital 1 of the Directive; to facilitate the exercise of this right by providing a single legislative framework, referring to recitals 3 and 4 of the Directive; and to introduce a gradual system of residence rights, referring to the 'overall context' of the Directive.[32]

Second, in the same case, the Court constructed a tension between the aim and the context of the Directive: it juxtaposed the aim of the Directive to strengthen rights by consolidating previously fragmented regulation of free movement of persons with the context of the Directive, which was to grant these rights gradually. Thereby the Court implicitly suggested that the sub-purpose of preventing

[27] In *Baumbast* (n 5) the Court held that the aim of Regulation (EEC) No 1612/68 [1968] OJ L257/2, amended by Directive 2004/38/EC [2004] OJ L158/77, was to achieve the freedom of movement for workers, which had to comply with the principles of liberty and dignity. *Baumbast* (n 5) para 50.

[28] In *Metock* the Court insisted that according to recital 2 in the preamble, Directive 2004/38/EC [2004] OJ L158/77 aimed in particular(!) to 'strengthen the right of free movement and residence of all Union citizens' hence guaranteeing the same or better rights to Union citizens than the amended or repealed secondary legislation'. See ECJ, Case C-127/08 *Metock and Others*, EU:C:2008:449.

[29] ECJ, Case C-162/09 *Lassal*, EU:C:2010:592.

[30] The Court clarified that all provisions laid down in the Regulations on social security should be interpreted in the light of the objective pursued by their legal basis, which aimed to facilitate freedom of movement. See R Cornelissen, 'EU Regulations on the Coordination of Social Security Systems and Special Non-Contributory Benefits: A Source of Never-Ending Controversy' in E Guild, C Sergio and K Eisele (eds), *Social Benefits and Migration A Contested Relationship and Policy Challenge in the EU* (Brussels, CEPS, 2013) 84.

[31] *Ziolkowski and Szeja* (n 11) para 40.

[32] ibid paras 35–38.

unreasonable burdening of public finances (recital 10 of the Directive) could override the main purpose when the rights of those who reside from three months to five years were concerned.

Subsequently, in *Brey*, the Court reinforced the understanding of the Directive as simultaneously pursuing two apparently opposing aims: to facilitate free movement on the one hand and to set out the conditions for free movement on the other.[33] The crowding of objectives in *Brey* was possible because with the third interpretive twist the Court reduced the objective to strengthen rights from the main objective to one among many objectives of Directive 2004/38, stating that the Directive was intended 'inter alia' to facilitate the primary right to move and reside freely and its practical effectiveness.[34] With the first three interpretive twists, the Court opened the Directive *as a whole* to reinterpretation. Fourth, and finally, in *Commission v United Kingdom*, the Court interpreted the objective—newly levelled with others—to set the conditions for the exercise of citizenship rights as a legitimate interest of the Member State to protect its public finances.[35] For the relatively small group of right-holders concerned, the Court settled the question, open since the introduction of Directive 2004/38, namely whether the host Member States could protect their public finances against *abstract and cumulative* or *actual and individual* risks. The fourth and final interpretive twist—the generalisation of *Brey* and *Dano*—which favours the financial interest of the Member States over free movement, accomplishes the process of reinterpretation.

The Court complemented this interpretive position with public policy arguments. It presupposes substantial negative consequences without discussing any alternative outcomes and without the necessary support of empirical evidence. This raises the question whether the omission of the Court to reason openly hides an unstated justification for its position, which might not be economic.

B. Public Policy Arguments

European citizenship is a highly politicised area of law, prone to arguments of unpersuasive reasoning. EU law has never been blind to the financial interests of individual Member States, and their economic rationality. In particular,

[33] '[A]lthough the aim of Directive 2004/38 is to facilitate and strengthen the exercise of the primary and individual right to move and reside freely … it is also intended, as is apparent from Article 1(a) thereof, to set out the conditions governing the exercise of that right … which include, where residence is desired for a period of longer than three months, the condition laid down in Article 7(1)(b)'. *Brey* (n 4) para 53.

[34] *Brey* (n 4) para 71.

[35] *Commission v United Kingdom* (n 14) para 68: 'It is clear from the Court's case-law that there is nothing to prevent, in principle, the grant of social benefits to Union citizens who are not economically active being made subject to the requirement that those citizens fulfil the conditions for possessing a right to reside lawfully in the host Member State (see to this effect, in particular, *Brey* (n 4) para 44; and *Dano* (n 11) para 83)'.

Article 7(1) of Directive 2004/38 imposes the requirements of comprehensive sickness insurance and sufficient resources, which should prevent migrant citizens from becoming an unreasonable burden on the public finances of the host Member State.[36] In general, the Court has operationalised these requirements in the case law by introducing the concept of a sufficient degree of integration and the real or genuine link to the labour market of the host Member State,[37] as well as a certain degree of financial solidarity between the nationals of the Member States.[38] In particular, the protection of public finances was considered a legitimate concern of the Member States in *Grzelczyk*[39] and *Baumbast*,[40] as well as in *Zhu and Chen*,[41] and could in principle (but not in those cases) justify limitations of the exercise of residence rights—yet it was not considered as *telos* in the classic case law.

It is simply common sense to expect that arguments based on economic consequences of increased migration and welfare policies, and the ability of the Member States to protect their public finances, will continuously resurface in the case law, especially in cases that concern economically non-active European migrants.[42] They are the so-called public policy arguments.[43]

What public policy arguments reflect are the 'real' social considerations underlying formal legal sources. However, when a public policy argument is based on specific consequences, it becomes a so-called slippery slope argument.[44] It can still be valid (and persuasive) but it must be based on temporally and spatially relevant

[36] Prior to it, for example Directive 90/364/EEC [1990] OJ L180/26 granted the right of residence to persons who have ceased to be in gainful employment, provided that they did not place an excessive burden on the public finances of the host State.

[37] *D'Hoop* (n 5) para 38; Case C-138/02 *Collins*, EU:C:2004:172, para 69; Case C-258/04 *Ioannidis*, EU:C:2005:559, para 30; *Bidar* (n 5) paras 55–56.

[38] The Court's vocabulary is largely determined by Arts 18–21 TFEU [2016] OJ C 202/01; Arts 7, 14, 24 and recitals 1, 4, 10 and 11 of Directive 2004/38/EC [2004] OJ L158/77, which refer to an unreasonable burden, a genuine link to the labour market of the host Member State, or a certain degree of financial solidarity. However, the legislation borrows from the Court's practice in this field and the origin of the concepts is not always easy to determine.

[39] *Grzelczyk* (n 5) paras 42–43.

[40] *Baumbast* (n 5) para 90.

[41] ECJ, Case C-200/02 *Zhu and Chen*, EU:C:2004:639, para 32.

[42] Nic Shuibhne and Maci discuss these arguments as public interest arguments, which Member States put forward in disputes to preserve their protectionist measures in different domains, such as competition law, free movement of goods and persons. N Nic Shuibhne and M Maci, 'Proving Public Interest: The Growing Impact of Evidence in Free Movement Case Law' (2013) 50 *CML Rev* 965.

[43] MacCormick in 1978 argued that a policy argument 'shows that to decide the case this way will tend to secure a desirable state of affairs', that is, a policy argument is rather the course of action leading to a goal than the goal itself (N MacCormick, *Legal Reasoning and Legal Theory* (Oxford, Oxford University Press, 1978) 262. Bengoetxea—siding more with Dworkin—perceives policies as closer to principles, goals in themselves, and places policy arguments in the category of dynamic criteria of interpretation, reminiscent of consequentialist arguments. For him, policy arguments are not extra-legal, like, eg, substantive arguments (eg, common knowledge, general economic, social or political topoi): J Bengoetxea, *The Legal Reasoning of the European Court of Justice: Towards a European Jurisprudence* (Oxford, Oxford University Press, 1993) 262.

[44] F Schauer, 'Slippery Slopes' (1985) 99 *Harvard Law Review* 361, 381.

empirical facts, in addition to logical inference.[45] It loses validity when it relies on simple logical inference alone, presupposing substantial negative consequences without discussing any alternative outcomes. In such cases the reasoning jumps to extreme hypotheticals and fails to engage with the issue at hand. It becomes irrational.

Most illustrative examples concern the well-known benefit/welfare/social tourism argument. The Opinion in *Dano* contains the following slippery slope:

> Although the referring court provides no precise information about the existence of such a risk,[46] it none the less refers to the limits of basic provision systems financed from taxation in the light of the amounts involved, amounts which might encourage immigration of Union citizens whose average income is considerably lower.[47]

The same approach is apparent from the Opinion in *Alimanovic*, namely that the 'granting entitlement to social assistance to Union citizens who are not required to have sufficient means of subsistence could result in relocation *en masse* liable to create an unreasonable burden on national social security systems'.[48] While the Court did not explicitly repeat these arguments it might appear from other references to the Opinion[49] that it based its judgment in *Alimanovic* on a similar logic.[50] To summarise, the Court could have validly and persuasively justified its reinterpretation of the Directive with a public policy argument. However, the argument that the Court offered was, first, based on an extreme hypothetical (fear of *en masse* migration), second, unsubstantiated with facts and, third, it did not engage in the weighing of alternatives, value and policy choices (even if they could not be empirically supported)[51] based on which a balance between

[45] RS Summers, *Form and Function in a Legal System: A General Study* (Cambridge, Cambridge University Press, 2005) 274.

[46] The risk of seriously undermining the social assistance system and insurance in the Member State.

[47] Opinion of Advocate General Wathelet in *Dano* (n 11) para 133.

[48] Opinion of Advocate General Wathelet in Alimanovic (n 13) para 91. The Advocate General equates the situation of a national of a Member State who moves to the territory of another Member State and stays there for less than three months, with a national who moves for more than three months but without pursuing the aim of seeking employment there.

[49] Explicit references in Alimanovic (n 13) to points 93–96 and 106 of the Opinion in the same case.

[50] Compare, *Dano* (n 11) para 78: 'A Member State must therefore have the possibility, pursuant to Article 7 of Directive 2004/38, OJ L158/77, of refusing to grant social benefits to economically inactive Union citizens who exercise their right to freedom of movement solely in order to obtain another Member State's social assistance although they do not have sufficient resources to claim a right of residence.' and *Dano* (n 11) para 79: 'To deny the Member State concerned that possibility would, as the Advocate General has stated in point 106 of his Opinion, thus have the consequence that persons who, upon arriving in the territory of another Member State, do not have sufficient resources to provide for themselves would have them automatically, through the grant of a special non-contributory cash benefit which is intended to cover the beneficiary's subsistence costs.'

[51] In fact, broader constitutional considerations could even speak against a strict systemic evaluation, or empiricism in the area of social policy. Social policy is arguably not an empiricist undertaking but a reflection of a compromise among the members of society reached on largely non-economic grounds. See for instance in PM Huber, 'Unionsbürgerschaft' (2013) *Europarecht* 637,

individual rights and public interests could be realised in the individual case within the legal framework of the Directive.

C. Change of a Reference Frame

Finally, the analysis suggests that the Court is replacing its reference frame, and increasingly relying on the rights-closing precedents. The tracing of references might be problematic, generally speaking. There are two caveats to the approach. First, changes in the practice of precedent citations will be reliable indicators of legal change only if precedent citations reflect the Court's actual reasoning process[52] and where citation practice will be relatively well established and consistent over time.[53] Second, if the process of change is continuous, desirable and inherent in judicial decision-making, 'genuine' indicators of change are impossible to isolate and distinguish from the 'regular' fluctuations in case citations. Law is updated because old precedents are replaced with newer ones, which have more bearing on the current legal problems just for that sake alone. Finally, the Court has a particular citation style, referencing older and most recent cases in citation strings of three cases, which more often hides rather than elucidates the evolution of the case law.

These objections notwithstanding, we can observe three trends that suggest the Court has introduced new reference points in the citizenship case law by ways of omission, reinterpretation and treating citizenship classics (*Martinez Sala*, *Baumbast*, *D'Hoop*, *Bidar* and *Grzelczyk*)[54] as opening-line references. This means that the Court increasingly cites the classics as preliminary points that do not

650–54; and J Croon, 'Comparative Institutional Analysis, the ECJ and the General Principle of Non-Discrimination' (2013) 19 *European Law Journal* 153, 163–72. That said, these arguments do not dispense with the need to substantiate the statements about serious economic consequences and financial implications, even with value judgements and non-economic considerations, especially when they are available.

[52] There is a lasting disagreement in jurisprudence on this point, which we do not discuss here. We simply assume that precedents are not selected at random by the Court and that they *grosso modo* reflect the reasoning process (that is, they are not simply a legal façade for underlying non-legal considerations and arguments).

[53] With regard to the latter point, it is widely thought that the Court has not developed sophisticated 'common law' techniques of distinguishing and overruling and only exceptionally discusses the substance of earlier decisions in greater detail. However, the Court's citation practice is remarkably stable and consistent. Hence, permutations in the strings of references are good indicators of shifts in the jurisprudence. The Court most often refers to lines of cases, or the so-called settled/well-established/consistent case law, and cites several, most often three, cases in a citation string. In other words, the Court's practice might be particular to the institution and reminiscent of a typical civil law court but follows a consistent pattern.

[54] They established a conventional framework for the review of conditions and limits to primary and directly effective citizenship rights. N Nic Shuibhne, 'Limits Rising, Duties Ascending: The Changing Legal Shape of Union Citizenship' (2015) 52 *CML Rev* 889, 894.

contribute to the ensuing actual legal discussion (opening-line references), cites them together with newer cases that do not lead to the same outcomes or rest on the same rationale (reinterpretation), or omits them altogether, even in situations where the classics would be of legal relevance (omission).[55]

An example of an opening-line reference can be found in *Dano*, where the Court repeats its famous passage that 'the status of citizen of the Union is destined to be the fundamental status of nationals of the Member States, enabling those among such nationals who find themselves in the same situation to enjoy within the scope *ratione materiae* of the EU Treaty the same treatment in law irrespective of their nationality, subject to such exceptions as are expressly provided for in that regard', referring to two classics, *Grzelczyk*, paragraph 31, and *D'Hoop*, paragraph 28. These references, however, have no tangible bearing on the Court's main line of argumentation. The Court answers the preliminary reference mainly by relying explicitly on its judgments in *Brey* and *Ziolkowski and Szeja*.[56] Neither of them departs from the premise of fundamental status or even mentions it.

An example of reinterpretation of the classics can be found in *Commission v United Kingdom* on the entitlement of European citizens to social benefits in the host Member State. The Court, when assessing the proportionality of a presumably discriminatory residence test invokes the classic rights-opening cases (*Grzelczyk*, *Bidar*) in a string/together with more recent and more restrictive cases (*Brey*, *Dano*) to argue that the test does not contradict previous case law.[57]

The judgments that are cited together in a citation string do not rest on the same rationale, and suggest opposite outcomes and opposite weighing of citizens' rights and Member State interests. In fact, *Grzelczyk*, *Bidar*, and *Brey* all build on the idea of a 'certain degree of solidarity'[58] and, moreover, all three clearly adopt a so-called individual approach to establishing whether the citizen would exceed the expectation of solidarity and become a burden on the finances of the Member State.[59] They do not—and this holds true even for *Dano*—permit *systematic* residence tests.

Finally, in *García-Nieto* the Court replaced entirely a reference frame, in which claims to equal treatment of economically non-active citizens could be made. The legal question concerns the interpretation of the scope of Directive 2004/38.

[55] For instance to *Sala* (n 5) (economically non-active EU citizens that are lawfully present in the territory of the host Member State); either *Grzelczyk* (n 5) or *Bidar* (n 5), or both (student maintenance, certain degree of solidarity and the prohibition to revoke residence automatically where the applicant applies for social assistance); and *D'Hoop* (n 5) (equal treatment, and prohibition to penalise the exercise of rights).

[56] References to *Brey* in *Dano* (n 11) paras 60 and 63, and references to *Ziolkowski and Szeja* in *Dano* (n 11) paras 70, 71 and 73.

[57] *Commission v United Kingdom* (n 14) para 80.

[58] *Bidar* (n 5) para 56; *Grzelczyk* (n 5) para 44; and *Brey* (n 4) para 72.

[59] See also the discussion on abstract and cumulative risks above (III.A).

The Court made a far-reaching decision in *García-Nieto*:[60] instead of resolving the issue within the reference framework of its older case law,[61] which narrowed the scope of Article 24(2) of Directive 2004/38,[62] it decided to resolve the question within the reference framework of its later case law, in particular *Alimanovic*[63] and *Dano*, paragraph 69, which extended the reach of the conditions of Article 24(2) of Directive 2004/38. The result of this choice of new reference points is that a Union citizen can claim equal treatment with nationals of the host Member State under Article 24(1) of Directive 2004/38 only if his residence in the territory of the host Member State complies with the conditions of Directive 2004/38 (judgments in *Dano*, paragraph 69, and *Alimanovic*).[64]

IV. JURISPRUDENTIAL SHIFT IN THE CONTEXT OF INTERNAL AND EXTERNAL CRISIS

The jurisprudential shift, which we examined qualitatively in the previous section, can be observed also quantitatively. Our examination of the judgments shows that the percentage of pro-individual outcomes dropped from 83 per cent to 55 per cent after 2011, that is, by 28 per cent, and to 27 per cent of pro-individual outcomes after 2014, that is, by 56 per cent. Similarly, the proportion of opinions with pro-individual outcomes delivered by the Advocates General has dropped from 89 per cent to 50 per cent since 2011, and to 36 per cent since 2014. Our systematic analysis of the reasoning of the Court furthermore demonstrates that the Court has not become more deferential to the national courts. Nor has the Court delivered more minimalist judgments. Another noteworthy change in the reasoning of the Court is a significant rise of abstract answers to concrete questions posed by national courts. The proportion of these has increased from 41 per cent before 2011 to 89 per cent since 2011. By way of comparison, deference to national courts and the proportion of abstract answers in the opinions of the Advocates General have remained largely unchanged. Furthermore, the Court has explicitly referred to

[60] *García-Nieto* (n 4). The benefit in question was a jobseeker benefit under A 7(1) Book II of the German Social Code. The Act is under amendment at the federal level.

[61] ECJ, Case C-22/08 *Vatsouras*, EU:C:2009:334, the judgment in *Vatsouras* relies on Collins (n 37), see N Nic Shuibhne, The Coherence of EU Free Movement Law: Constitutional Responsibility and the Court of Justice (Oxford, Oxford University Press, 2013) 75. *Vatsouras* para 45: '[B]enefits of a financial nature which, independently of their status under national law, are intended to facilitate access to the labour market cannot be regarded as constituting "social assistance" within the meaning of Article 24(2) of Directive 2004/38'.

[62] eg D Chalmers, G Davies and G Monti, *European Union Law: Text and Materials*, 2nd edn (Cambridge, Cambridge University Press, 2010) 458. Similarly, K Lenaerts, 'European Union Citizenship, National Welfare Systems and Social Solidarity' (2011) 18 *Jurisprudence* 397.

[63] *García-Nieto* (n 4) para 37: 'it should be recalled that, in the judgment in Alimanovic (ECJ, Case C-67/14 *Alimanovic* [2015] EU:C:2015:597 paras 44–46), the Court held that benefits such as the benefits at issue cannot be considered to be benefits of a financial nature which are intended to facilitate access to the labour market of a Member State, but must be regarded as "social assistance" within the meaning of Article 24(2) of Directive 2004/38, OJ L158/77'.

[64] *García-Nieto* (n 4) para 38.

the opinions of the Advocates General more often since 2011. Several judgments contain more than one reference. This is particularly evident in recent judgments with negative outcomes for the individuals, delivered after 2014. All above findings are presented in Table 1 below.

In this section, we attempt to explain and contextualise the change by first examining the professional backgrounds of the sitting judges and the decision-making in chambers. Second, we place the institutional factors alongside the political and the economic context.

A. Institutional Transformation

Institutional transformations can have non-negligible—even if indirect—effects on the development of the jurisprudence. It is easy to imagine that a sharp increase in judges with diverse educational and professional credentials and conflicting understanding of the judicial role will affect both the organisation of daily judicial work and the established working methods and find expression in the case law. In the context of the Court of Justice, the institutional transformation comprises the change in presidency of the Court after 12 years, in 2015, its internal restructuring, including a physical relocation to new premises, the reorganisation of the chamber system, a prolonged and controversial reform of the General Court, and the rather sudden increase of the number of judges without extensive training and experience in European Union law pursuant to the 2004 and 2007

Table 1: Comparing early, recent and most recent case law

	Group 1 (early)	**Group 2 (recent)**	**Group 3 (most recent)**
Chamber judgments	28%	67%	45%
Grand Chamber judgments	72%	44%	55%
Number of sitting judges	10	8	10
Seniority of AG at the time of delivery of opinion	5.5 years	5.45 years	5.45 years
Seniority of JR at the time of delivery of judgment	5.5 years	8.75 years	8.9 years
Number of references to the AG	0.5	1.15	1.45
Reference to AG opinion in the judgment	50% of judgments	60% of judgments	63% of judgments
Pro-individual outcomes CJ	83%	55%	27%
Pro-individual outcomes AG	89%	50%	36%
Number of observations	20% of MS	16% of MS	14% of MS

enlargements. In addition, the mere establishment of a panel in 2009 in Article 255 TFEU could have an impact on the nomination and the selection of post-Lisbon judges. These factors importantly play into the case law along with the types of questions referred by the national courts or the maturity of a specific area of law. The key question is whether they accelerated the restrictive turn in the European citizenship case law.

Our findings, presented in Table 1 above, show two notable institutional developments. First, the proportion of judgments decided by the Grand Chamber has decreased since 2011 (Group 2, in the second column) from 72 per cent of cases to 44 per cent of cases. Second, fewer judges participated in the decision-making in Group 2: eight as opposed to 10 in Group 1. Since 2014 (Group 3), however, the number of judges has again increased to 10 sitting judges per case on average and the percentage of cases, decided by the Grand Chamber, has increased to 55 per cent.

Table 2 below presents the findings with regard to the professional background of judges. We can observe that among the judges who participated in the decision-making in the selected cases, the percentage of participating academics has doubled since 2011 (from 16 per cent to 33 per cent), while the percentage of sitting judges coming from the ranks of judiciary has declined. The proportion

Table 2: Percentage of different judicial backgrounds of judges participating in the decision-making in early, recent and most recent cases (percentage of 'votes'), the backgrounds of the Advocates General and Reporting Judges (JR)

Sitting Judges	**Group 1**	**Group 2**	**Group 3**
AC	16%	33%	32%
JUD	38%	28%	29%
LP	3%	4%	2%
POL	43%	35%	37%
Reporting Judges			
AC	17%	10%	0%
JUD	0%	5%	0%
LP	28%	15%	9%
POL	56%	65%	91%
Advocates General			
AC	33%	25%	9%
JUD	0%	0%	0%
LP	44%	40%	27%
POL	22%	35%	64%

of judges participating in the decision-making in the selection with the main career background in legal practice and politics or the civil service has remained relatively stable. By contrast, the percentage of opinions delivered by the Advocates General with an academic background has dropped significantly, to only 9 per cent since 2014. The percentage of opinions delivered by the Advocates General with a background in national politics and the civil service has increased significantly, from 22 per cent before 2011, to 35 per cent after 2011 and 64 per cent after 2014. The most significant finding, however, relates to the Reporting Judges. Since 2014, 91 per cent of cases have been reported by judges with a background in national politics and the civil service. The judges with an academic background have been Reporting Judges in 10 per cent of opinions since 2011 and in none since 2014. With regard to individual Members of the Court, more opinions have been delivered by Advocate General Wathelet, and assigned to two Reporting Judges, Berger and Lapuerta. Judges Makarczyk and Klucka were replaced in 2009 before their terms expired and Küris, who served a full term, was not reappointed in 2010. The general findings with regard to the professional composition of the sitting judges are presented more systematically in Table 2. Group 1 comprises cases decided before 2011; Group 2 cases decided since 2011; and Group 3 the most recent cases, decided since 2014. All cases in Group 3 are also part of Group 2. We treat them separately to evaluate the persistence of the restrictive turn. We discuss the findings in more detail in section C below, after we place them into the broader political and economic context (section B below).

B. The Chronology of Mounting Crisis

The transformations of the European citizenship jurisprudence occurred in a highly specific political and economic context. The classic case law in this field was established well before the 2007–08 global financial crisis and the ensuing unprecedented policy action programmes and measures on the European level. The intergovernmental action ratified by the Court to contain the crisis provoked political and ideological disagreement over their appropriateness and democratic legitimacy, and in turn the Court's authority faced increasing political and scholarly challenges for these and other unpopular judgments handed out in 2007–15.[65] And while the devastating societal consequences of the economic crisis for many Europeans and the controversy over austerity measures still reverberated across Europe in 2015, unprecedented numbers of migrants started arriving from the Middle East. The latter highlighted the failure of the EU's mechanisms intended to

[65] Having laid out the groundwork on the internal market by *Viking* and *Laval* (ECJ, Case C-438/05, EU:C:2007:772; Case C-341/05 EU:C:2007:809), followed by *Ruiz Zambrano* (ECJ, Case C-34/09, EU:C:2011:124) and two EMU-related cases, complex with regard to competence and technicality (ECJ, Case C-370/12 *Pringle*, EU:C:2012:756; Case C-62/14 *Gauweiler*, EU:C:2015:7), the Court's popularity was not at an all-time high.

deal with such issues, as well as notable differences in Member States' attitudes to them. This did no favours to the overall legitimacy of the Union and its law, and in turn also allowed local politics to project the problem on Brussels.

The coinciding crises increased the pressure from different political corners of the individual Member States to control migration more effectively, wrapping the movement within the Union with that from the outside. The rhetoric of taking back control or repatriating competences featured prominently in the UK Government's reviews of balance of competences produced from 2012 onwards.[66] Member States were keen to preserve the 'Western' standard of living and their autonomy and ability to maintain the habitual high level of welfare—or rather workfare—and reserve it for their 'own' citizens. This added pressure to revisit the Court's interpretations over the extent of equal treatment of Member State nationals. Coincidently, the public discourse, mushrooming since the enlargements in 2004 and 2007, took a rather explicit and unfriendly if not an outright hostile turn in some Member States from 2013 onwards. Social benefits for economically non-active European citizens and study maintenance fees have sparked a great deal of public controversy in Germany, Austria and Denmark. Child benefits to mobile EU workers became a cause célèbre in the United Kingdom (and in Austria) in spite of their estimated limited economic relevance.[67] In the UK, mobility overall became a burden *per se*, formulated in terms of repatriating immigration control, in spite of the fact that it was never wholly lost and no concrete comprehensive numbers on costs and benefits of mobility were ever produced.[68] Moreover, throughout all this, the Court was also on tenterhooks (internally and externally) over the reform of the EU court system that started in 2011, increasingly so for two years since late 2013.[69] In the anticipation of Brexit in June 2016 the crisis turned constitutional-slash-existential.[70]

With the exception of the Lisbon Treaty entering into force at the end of 2009, the legal framework governing European citizenship rights has not changed since

[66] Review documents are available at: www.gov.uk/government/collections/review-of-the-balance-of-competences.

[67] See chapter by SK Schmidt in this volume. The UK's requirements for a renegotiated deal with the EU are documented in European Council Conclusions (18 and 19 February 2016, EUCO 12/16): www.consilium.europa.eu/en/press/press-releases/2016/02/19-euco-conclusions/, 22 and 33; on public discussion, see eg S Booth, C Howarth and P Swidlicki, 'How to Save EU Free Movement: Make it fair to keep it free' (2014) 11 *Open Europe Report*; J Doyle 'Tax credits "turned UK into a honeypot for EU immigrants": worker on minimum wage could receive additional £330 a week' *The Daily Mail* (25 November 2014): www.dailymail.co.uk/news/article-2848128/Tax-credits-turned-UK-honeypot-EU-immigrants-Worker-minimum-wage-receive-additional-330-week.html; and P Oltermann, 'Germany among EU countries keen to copy UK child benefit peg' *The Guardian* (23 February 2016): www.theguardian.com/world/2016/feb/23/germany-angela-merkel-eu-countries-keen-copy-uk-child-benefit-peg.

[68] On the absence of data on the UK covering both revenue and expenditure, A Iliopoulou-Penot, 'Deconstructing the Former Edifice of Union Citizenship? The Alimanovic Judgment' (2016) 53 *CML Rev* 1007, 1029.

[69] A Alemanno and L Pech, 'Thinking Justice Outside the Docket: A Critical Assessment of the Reform of the EU'S Court System' (2017) 54 *CML Rev* 129, 138–39.

[70] In his State of the Union address on 14 September 2016, European Commission President Juncker declared that: 'Our European Union is, at least in part, in an existential crisis'.

2006 (Directive 2004/38). Hence, forces external to the law should largely account for the jurisprudential shift, which became visible after 2011. However, the classic case law in this field was developed prior to the implementation deadline of new secondary legislation in 2006 and, moreover, time in itself is a factor in that it was developed mainly by different judges and Advocates General than those who served during and from 2012. The Court members' selection panel introduced by the Lisbon Treaty, Article 255 TFEU, became operational from early 2010 onwards, but during its first three years did not give a single unfavourable opinion on a Court candidate.[71]

Although a simple timeline can be drawn this way of the (overlapping) events that establish the external as well as internal context for the Court, it is a crude tool that does not alone allow deducing causality between events and twists in the Court's case law. It is nevertheless possible to argue that external pressure on the Court mounted during 2008–11, reached its peak in 2012 and prompted the Court to change the direction of the citizenship jurisprudence, and did not subside until the British referendum in June 2016. Namely, even in mundane times national governments, whose interests are hypothetically negatively affected by the Court's decisions, will put pressure on the Court by the use of national media or economic threats.[72] This tendency will most likely not disappear in times of crisis. These strategies will only intensify in times of grave financial crisis. The Member States will want more flexibility to define the fundamental interests of their own societies and restrict or expand public spending. They will expect the Court to apply laxer proportionality review to their protectionist measures, which limit free movement and individual rights, or discriminate between nationals and non-nationals, and find them compatible with European law. It is not hard to imagine that such events will further accelerate developments, more favourable to national interests, in the jurisprudence.

C. Summing Up

How can the findings be interpreted? Generally, they imply, first, that the Court has become more sensitive to broader—mainly economic—concerns of the Member States in individual cases. More concretely, the restrictive approach, which limits individual rights to social advantages in the host Member State, is clearly observable on the level of outcomes. This could indicate that the Court increasingly adopts decisions which do not aggravate the economic situation in

[71] H de Waele, 'Not Quite the Bed that Procrustes Built: Dissecting the System for Selecting Judges at the Court of Justice of the European Union' in M Bobek (ed), *Selecting Europe's Judges: A Critical Review of the Appointment Procedures to the European Courts* (Oxford, Oxford University Press, 2015) 44–47.

[72] D Terris, CPR Romano and L Swigart (eds), *The International Judge. An Introduction to the Men and Women Who Decide the World's Cases* (Oxford, Oxford University Press, 2007) 173.

the Member States, even hypothetically speaking. Second, the Court has not been more deferential to national courts: it has not let the national courts weigh the individual and national interest in concrete situations more often, or given the national courts the authority to perform comprehensive and autonomous proportionality tests within the national context. At the same time, the Court has not been more unwilling to solve broader problems of interpretation comprehensively than before 2011. The proportion of minimalist judgments has increased only slightly, by 6 per cent, and remains relatively low at 44 per cent. Third, and almost paradoxically, the Court has become more unwilling to provide clear and concrete solutions to preliminary questions. Instead, it has provided highly abstract answers, unrelated to the situations at hand. This might indicate that the Court is in favour of coherent and general (legislative) rather than partial, judicial, case-to-case solutions.

One could argue that the changing profile of judges who have participated in the decision-making process since 2011 corroborates this sensitivity to the broader economic context of the Court and a new openness to the political process with uncertain outcomes for individual citizens. Explicit reliance on the opinions of the Advocates General, who overtly invoke negative implications of granting equal rights to migrant European citizens, in particular increased immigration from less affluent parts of the European Union, sends an additional signal to the Member States and European political institutions that the Court will not resist but assist the political process.

Literature has dubbed European citizenship as an 'unhappy misnomer'[73] and a product of 'academic imagination'.[74] O'Brian recently questioned whether it ever existed outside scholarly imagination sparked by a handful of rulings from Luxembourg? (The emperor was naked.) So conceived, citizenship as protection of rights was destined to fail, and the external crisis could only speed up but not trigger this process. The internal working of the Court as well as the profile of its members and especially the assignment of cases to chambers with Reporting Judges and Advocates General less determined to block national policy choices were a necessary precondition for the restrictive turn.

V. CONCLUSION

There were times where the Court could do no wrong: if it was 'deferential', it was giving impetus to the legislative action and to a comprehensive approach to individual rights. If it was 'activist,' it was because it was protecting individual rights, bearing the burden of integration where political institutions have faltered. These

[73] The term is used by AJ Menéndez, 'Which Citizenship? Whose Europe?—The Many Paradoxes of European Citizenship' (2014) 15 *German Law Journal* 907.

[74] ibid; C O'Brien, '*Civis Capitalist Sum*: Class as the New Guiding Principle of EU Free Movement Rights' (2016) 53 *CML Rev* 937, 974.

are times where the Court is judged harshly, also by its habitual allies, most notably the national courts.

The jurisprudence ebbs and flows. Change is an intrinsic element of judicial law-making everywhere. However, it can safely be concluded that the citizenship jurisprudence of the Court took a decisive turn, which will be difficult to reverse. The implications are significant. In legal terms, the new approach means less favourable legal treatment of economically inactive migrants, jobseekers and third-country family members. In existential terms it might be the beginning of the end of the aspiration to 'the good life,' which has characterised the European project since its inception.[75]

Qualitatively, the shift encompasses three main modifications. First, the Court altered its use of teleological interpretation, which had far-reaching consequences: stressing different objectives of the interpreted texts or previously less used objectives of Treaty Articles and provisions of Directive 2004/38, and finding a new balance between the particular and the general objectives. Second, the Court complemented this interpretive position with policy arguments. It presupposed substantial negative consequences without discussing any alternative outcomes and without the necessary support of empirical evidence. Third, the Court effectively created a new reference frame by selecting new reference points of interpretation and argumentation. Most conspicuously, rights-closing reference points such as *Brey* have practically replaced the classic rights-opening reference points in the argumentative parts of the judgments, and have achieved (in a very short time) the status of 'settled case law'. New precedents support negative outcomes for whole groups of economically non-active citizens.

The practice of decision-making in chambers importantly encourages and sustains this type of decision-making. Namely, while the professional membership of the Court has not changed considerably, the same could not be said about the professional background of the Advocates General who delivered the opinions in the examined cases. Since 2011, the percentage of opinions delivered in cases under examination by the Advocates General coming from academia and legal practice has decreased, while the percentage of opinions delivered by the Advocates General with a previous dominant career in politics or the civil service has increased. Substantive references to the Advocates General have become much more common in the most recent cases.

When juxtaposed with the context in which they occurred, our findings can be understood as a politically savvy response from an institution, which is losing political power, authority and legitimacy. Content wise, they indicate that the Court, especially when sitting in chambers, has a fragmented vision of European citizenship on the one hand and a strong 'jurisdictional claim' to re-define and co-design a new system of European solidarity on the other.

[75] F de Witte, Justice in the EU: The Emergence of Transnational Solidarity (Oxford, Oxford University Press, 2015).

6

The Evolution of Citizens' Rights in Light of the European Union's Constitutional Development

DANIEL THYM

I. INTRODUCTION

THE CONSTITUTIONAL FOUNDATIONS of Union citizenship are bound to remain unstable due to the doctrinal and conceptual ambiguity of supranational citizens' rights. If that is correct, change need not present a linear progress towards 'more' citizenship, reflecting the EU's famous self-description as 'ever closer union'.[1] It could similarly result in friction, dead ends and retrogression. On this basis, this chapter sets out to explain the evolution of citizens' rights as a reflection of broader trends. Our heuristic device for rationalising the constitutional embeddedness will be a juxtaposition of two competing models of the concept of transnational mobility. Their impact on the case law and institutional practice will be exemplified through closer scrutiny of three thematic leitmotifs defining most accounts of citizenship with regard to solidarity, political participation and identity.

Having reminded readers of the underlying reasons for the legal and conceptual ambiguity of Union citizenship, it will be demonstrated that institutional practice fluctuates between two models: one based on residence and the other focusing on social integration. As ideal types, these models influence the resolution of specific questions, although positions of policy actors will most likely reflect a blend, thereby reinforcing the overall trend towards constant variation and conceptual indeterminacy (below II). The pertinence of this approach will be tested in relation to ongoing disputes about social benefits and transnational solidarity (III), political participation and the significance to nationality (IV) as well as migration

[1] Recital 1 of the preamble of the original EEC Treaty of 1957, the present Treaty on the Functioning of the European Union and the Charter of Fundamental Rights.

and collective identities (V). It will be shown that the evolution of citizens' rights in these areas is intimately connected to broader constitutional trends, such as the euro crisis, the failure of the Constitutional Treaty or arguments about immigration among the wider public. Answers to specific questions in the case law and the political process can be rationalised as building blocks of a European Union (EU) that accepts the limits of the federal vision by accommodating the continued diversity among Member States.

II. TWO COMPETING MODELS

Citizens' rights are no abstract category: they are intricately connected to a social context. Until recently in Western thought, this context concerned membership in statal communities and it remains uncertain whether the citizenship concept can be applied to a supranational polity such as the EU and whether doing so requires conceptual adaptation. This question has preoccupied the scholarly literature over past years and notable differences persist until today.[2] Against this background, this section suggests rationalising the evolution of citizens' rights through the juxtaposition of divergent visions of transnational mobility whose identification can serve as a heuristic device for reconstructing institutional practices.

This approach builds on the work of the American migration scholar Hiroshi Motomura who demonstrated that the US perspective on immigration evolved over time by distinguishing between three ways of construing the relationship between incoming migrants and US society: legal rules may be perceived, alternatively, as a quasi-automatic 'transition', as a 'contract' obliging newcomers to comply with certain conditions, or as an 'affiliation' when immigrants gradually get involved with the nation's life.[3] Such a constructivist account recognises that different ideals coexist and can change over time. It can be particularly useful in relation to Union citizenship whose significance remains contested.[4]

To identify different visions of transnational membership is not to say that the European Court of Justice (ECJ) or other EU institutions hold a uniform citizenship concept. Arguably, it is not the function of judges to actively engage in theoretical debate: they should resolve legal disputes.[5] We cannot expect a Grand Chamber of 15 judges to have a uniform understanding or to reflect on it openly in their judgments. Although the standard invocation of Union citizenship as

[2] For an overview, see D Kostakopoulou, 'European Union Citizenship: Writing the Future' (2007) 13 *European Law Journal (ELJ)* 623; and D Kochenov, 'The Essence of EU Citizenship Emerging from the Last Ten Years of Academic Debate' (2013) 62 *ICLQ* 97.

[3] See H Motomura, *Americans in Waiting* (Oxford, Oxford University Press, 2006).

[4] The argument in this section builds upon D Thym, 'The Elusive Limits of Solidarity: Residence Rights of and Social Benefits for Economically Inactive Union Citizens' (2015) 52 *CML Rev* 17, 33–39.

[5] *cf* CR Sunstein, *One Case at a Time* (Cambridge, MA, Harvard University Press, 1999).

'fundamental status' may be taken to hint at an underlying theory on the part of the ECJ, it might not exist.[6] This does not prevent academic commentators, however, from reconstructing the theoretical infrastructure. Such academic reconstructions are ideal types which are modelled upon judgments and policy initiatives as legal phenomena and which accentuate theoretical features for analytical purposes. They are not mutually exclusive and the positions of policy actors will most likely reflect a blend, combining elements of different ideal types. Arguably, the discrepancies underlying many free movement rulings can be explained by this mixture; judges drift along.

In this section, I will present the methodological background (below A) and discuss, on this basis, two visions of transnational membership which I shall call the 'residence model' (B) and the 'integration model' (C). Their explanatory potential is limited to the EU context, where transnational mobility constitutes the hallmark of supranational citizens' rights to this date. It is not the purpose of this chapter to rationalise the meaning of citizenship more generally. Implications of the two models will be illustrated later in relation to three thematic leitmotifs that feature prominently in contemporary citizenship accounts: social solidarity, political participation and questions of collective identification.[7] Doing so will link the discussion of Union citizenship to broader constitutional trends.

A. Methodological Background

There was and remains nothing inevitable in the evolution of Union citizenship. Even within a nation-state context, the notion of citizenship is a prime example of an essentially contested project which lends itself to different visions of what we mean by citizenship. In the EU, this volatility is reinforced by the transformative character of the European integration process and corresponding uncertainties about its *finalité*, which reinforce the inherent openness of the citizenship concept in the context of EU integration.[8] Methodologically, these characteristics can be integrated into legal accounts on the basis of a contextually embedded doctrinal constructivism which accepts, in contrast to US-style legal realism, that legal concepts can have a semi-autonomous significance.[9]

Corresponding legal analyses are based on a reconstruction of the case law and its doctrinal foundations, thereby ideally supporting a better understanding of

[6] *cf* A Williams, *The Ethos of Europe* (Cambridge, Cambridge University Press, 2011).

[7] On recurring themes in debates about citizenship, see L Bosniak, 'Citizenship Denationalized' (2000) 7 *Indiana Journal of Global Legal Studies* 447; and R Bellamy, *Citizenship. A Very Short Introduction* (Oxford, Oxford University Press, 2008).

[8] For further comments see the introduction to this volume, section II.

[9] See T Horsley, 'Reflections on the Role of the Court of Justice as the "Motor" of European Integration' (2013) 50 *CML Rev.* 931, 934–54; and G Beck, *The Legal Reasoning of the Court of Justice of the EU* (Oxford, Hart Publishing, 2012).

the systematic coherence of the law and its internal inconsistencies.[10] Doing so assumes that doctrinal arguments and constraints should be taken seriously in a discursive community involving academics in the constant reconstruction of the legal infrastructure.[11] Meanwhile, abstract legal concepts, such as free movement, citizenship or human rights, require a broader constitutional analysis in a process Armin von Bogdandy has aptly described as a doctrinal argument about constitutional principles.[12] This chapter follows this approach by extrapolating the constitutional infrastructure guiding the interpretation of the supranational rules on Union citizenship.

Such focus on questions of doctrinal interpretation and constitutional reconstruction does not imply that legal debates exist in splendid isolation. To the contrary, constitutional principles such as citizenship convey a set of normative values and express basic choices of societies, which can change over time.[13] Citizens' rights, like human rights, present fields of the law resonating with broader social and political developments. Their conceptual openness was one factor facilitating progressive interpretation by the ECJ that has been described by academic observers as a process of judicial transformation transcending the original rationale of market integration.[14] However, such an outcome was and is no foregone conclusion. The broader social and political context may similarly support restrictive tendencies, thematic shifts or judicial changes of direction.[15] Our analysis will show that the evolution of Union citizenship discloses such reorientation and that political actors and social practices can influence these interpretative metamorphoses.

B. 'Residence Model'

The novelty factor of Union citizenship lies in its supranational character. It grants rights to transnational movement, equal treatment and political participation across state borders, thereby overcoming the Westphalian model of territorial

[10] See R van Gestel and H-W Micklitz, 'Why Methods Matter in European Legal Scholarship' (2014) 20 *ELJ* 292.

[11] See M Kumm, 'On the Past and Future of European Constitutional Scholarship' (2009) 7 *ICON* 401, 406–11.

[12] See A von Bogdandy, 'Founding Principles of EU Law: A Theoretical and Doctrinal Sketch' (2010) 16 *ELJ* 95, 98–100.

[13] See RM Cover, 'Foreword: *Nomos* and Narrative' (1983) 97 *Harvard Law Review* 4, 11–44.

[14] See E Spaventa, 'From *Gebhard* to *Carpenter*' (2004) 41 *CML Rev* 743, 764–68; and S Kadelbach, 'Union Citizenship' in A von Bogdandy and J Bast (eds), *Principles of European Constitutional Law*, 2nd edn (Oxford, Hart Publishing, 2009) 461–66.

[15] See D Kostakopoulou, 'Co-creating European Union Citizenship' (2012/13) 15 *Cambridge Yearbook of European Legal Studies* 255, 259–66; and J Shaw and N Miller, 'When Legal Worlds Collide: An Exploration of What Happens when EU Free Movement Law meets UK Immigration Law' (2013) 38 *EL Rev* 137.

sovereignty. The individual right to free movement for broadly defined categories of economic activity and corresponding guarantees of equal treatment, which up until now pinpoint the essence of citizens' rights, do not abolish political communities at national level, but oblige them to treat Union citizens similarly to nationals. When Union citizens move, territorial presence often replaces the formal link of nationality as the demarcation line between insiders and outsiders participating in solidary communities.[16] Below I will discuss to what extent this model can help us rationalise the evolution of citizens' rights at EU level.

Academic discourse on EU law presents us with two visions behind the residence model that coincide insofar as the rights of Union citizens are concerned, but which can diverge in relation to individuals from outside the EU—reflecting an underlying ambiguity as to how to relate European integration to the rest of the world. While some propagate the emergence of a generic model of stakeholder citizenship that is conceptually not restricted to the EU context and may pave the way for the general realignment of membership,[17] others describe the EU and its citizenship in (con-)federal terms.[18] This discrepancy takes centre stage when we analyse migration law towards third-country nationals,[19] but it is less relevant for the distinction between the 'residence model' and the 'integration model', since both the federal and the universalist frame of reference converge on the treatment of intra-European mobility.

C. 'Integration Model'

The 'integration model' rejects the quasi-automatic acquisition of citizens' rights whenever someone takes up habitual residence. Instead, it highlights qualitative factors connecting individuals to a political community, which often includes an expectation that one should actively pursue incorporation into societal structures. Success or failure of this venture may regulate the degree of residence security and equal treatment under EU law.[20] From this perspective, the Union is more

[16] For an early description of this idea, see G Davies, '"Any Place I Hang My Hat" or: Residence is the New Nationality' (2005) 11 *ELJ* 43, 47–49.

[17] See esp D Kostakopoulou, *The Future Governance of Citizenship* (Cambridge, Cambridge University Press, 2008) ch 4; and Y Soysal, *Limits of Citizenship* (Chicago, IL, University of Chicago Press, 1994) ch 8.

[18] This approach is particularly common among scholars from continental Europe, such as C Schönberger, *Unionsbürger* (Tübingen, Mohr Siebeck, 2005); Kadelbach (n 14) 469–75; or AP van der Mei, *Free Movement of Persons within the European Community* (Oxford, Hart Publishing, 2003).

[19] See D Thym, 'Citizens and Foreigners in EU Law: Migration Law and its Cosmopolitan Outlook' (2016) 22 *ELJ* 296, 302–06.

[20] See L Azoulai, 'Transfiguring European Citizenship: From Member State Territory to Union Territory' in D Kochenov (ed), *EU Citizenship and Federalism: The Role of Rights* (Cambridge, Cambridge University Press, 2017).

than an emancipatory 'playground of opportunities'[21] enhancing the freedom of choice of individuals through the pursuit of one's preferences; here, not anyone residing abroad is automatically considered an insider like under the 'residence model' discussed above. Rather, the 'integration model' emphasises the value of social cohesion as a precondition for democratic allegiance and social solidarity. It makes access to social benefits and other rights associated with membership in a specific community conditional upon certain prerequisites without which equal treatment with nationals will be denied.

It is important to note that there is a variety of theoretical explanations for the significance of social cohesion which can result in different responses to specific questions.[22] In particular, social cohesion does not necessarily imply ethno-cultural closure and may support quite the reverse, namely changing self-perceptions of European societies in response to transnational mobility and cultural diversity. The argument for social cohesion is not about classic nationalism: it recognises, rather, that political communities require a sense of shared identity if our societies are to be more than the sum of their parts.[23] Despite the inherent emphasis on liberty, the doctrinal infrastructure of EU free movement law embraces important expressions of the 'integration model', which the Court has strengthened in a number of controversial judgments concerning access to social benefits and the limits of residence security in recent years. It is a central objective of this chapter to try to clarify this reorientation of the case law.

III. SOCIAL BENEFITS AND TRANSNATIONAL SOLIDARITY

Equal access to social benefits has received much attention in scholarly treatises on Union citizenship over the years. Judgments delivered by the ECJ on cases such as *Martínez Sala*, *Grzelczyk*, *Förster* or, most recently, *Dano* and *Alimanovic* feature prominently in academic accounts of Union citizenship. Moreover, the issue presents itself as a perfect thematic prism to elucidate the conceptual (re-)orientation of supranational citizenship, since welfare provision represents a core ingredient of modern statehood and corresponding citizens' rights.[24] It epitomises the component of individual rights which lies at the heart of many citizenship theories, in particular those written by legal academics. Our analysis will proceed in two steps highlighting the Court's position first (below A) and discussing contextual factors that may explain the change of direction thereafter (B).

[21] Kochenov, 'The Essence of EU Citizenship' (n 2) 130.

[22] For an overview see M Moore, 'Cosmopolitanism and Political Communities' (2006) 32 *Social Theory and Practice* 627; or S Song, 'Three Models of Civic Solidarity' in RM Smith (ed), *Citizenship, Borders, and Human Needs* (Pennsylvania, PA, Penn Press, 2011).

[23] See C Joppke, *Citizenship and Immigration* (Cambridge, Polity Press, 2010) ch 4.

[24] See TH Marshall, *Class, Citizenship, and Social Development* (Garden City, NY, Doubleday, 1964).

A. Judicial Change of Direction

Access to social benefits is a perfect test case to highlight the pertinence of the 'residence model' and the 'integration model' described above, since their distinct features coincide with changing parameters of the free movement rules. There is a noticeable difference between the classic position of EU law on the equal treatment of those who are economically active (below i) and the integration requirements for other citizens which have been fortified in a number of more recent judgments (ii).[25]

i. 'Residence Model'

The classic foundation of the residence model can be found in the recitals of implementing legislation on the free movement of workers: widespread equal treatment is perceived as a means to facilitate social integration, thus allowing migrant workers to enjoy the same rights from day one as a matter of principle.[26] On this basis, the Court reaffirmed in a number of judgments delivered over past decades that Union citizens who are working in another Member State 'shall enjoy the same social and tax advantages as national workers'.[27] This trend towards residence-based equality was reaffirmed by the social security coordination regime that links special non-contributory cash benefits to the place of residence through legislation. This also applies to individuals other than workers.[28] The ECJ endorsed this approach by the legislature in light of primary law, since non-contributory benefits are 'closely linked with the social environment'.[29] This has important ramifications for our topic: mobility is perceived to entail a changing of the guard in the realm of welfare benefits, since the state of residence is expected to take over whenever someone moves across borders.

A strict version of the residence model would focus, in line with social security coordination, on the place of 'habitual residence' to determine the state bearing responsibility for social assistance: the crucial question would be 'where the habitual centre of their interests is to be found'.[30] We would have to distinguish, for that matter, between temporary 'visitors', who are physically present but retain habitual residence elsewhere, and 'residents', who relocate their centre of

[25] The argument in this section builds upon Thym, 'The Elusive Limits of Solidarity' (n 4) 33–39.

[26] *cf* Recital 5 Regulation (EEC) No 1612/68 [1968] OJ L257/2 and today's Recital 6 Regulation (EU) No 492/2011; see also ECJ, *Cowan*, 186/87, EU:C:1989:47, paras 16–17.

[27] Art 7(2) Regulation (EU) No 492/2011 in line with Regulation (EEC) No 1612/68.

[28] See Art 70 of Regulation (EC) No 883/2004.

[29] ECJ, *Bartlett et al*, C-537/09, EU:C:2011:278, para 38; for further reading see M Dougan, 'Expanding the Frontiers of European Union Citizenship by Dismantling the Territorial Boundaries of the National Welfare States?' in C Barnard and O Odudu (eds), *The Outer Limits of European Union Law* (Oxford, Hart Publishing, 2009) 144–50.

[30] Definition of the term 'habitual residence' in ECJ, C-90/97, *Swaddling*, EU:C:1999:96, para 29; for details see van der Mei (n 18) 161–64.

interests enduringly.[31] Social security experts maintain that the ECJ should have moved down this road in *Brey* and *Dano* when it had to decide on the equal treatment of citizens residing abroad without being economically active there.[32]

Things turned out differently. Instead of relying on the residence-based rationale of Regulation (EC) No 883/2004 to resolve the dispute, the ECJ effectively diminished its relevance by arguing that the Social Security Coordination Regulation should be construed, first and foremost, as a coordination instrument that identifies the legal order applicable and does not harmonise national rules governing access to specific social benefits.[33] This meant that other rules took over. The latter gave more flexibility to the Court on the basis of the EU Treaties and the Citizenship Directive 2004/38/EC, although their contents had often been applied in a manner which effectively extended domestic welfare systems to all those who are physically present as residents. *Martínez Sala*, *Trojani* and *Grzelczyk* are the most pertinent examples of such residence-based reasoning by the ECJ on the basis of the regular rules on the free movement of persons.[34] However, this was not the only possible outcome: the same rules could be interpreted in a way that directs the case law in a different direction.

ii. 'Integration Model'

In the *Förster* ruling, the ECJ embarked upon a fully-fledged version of the 'integration model' for the first time when it made equal access to study grants for EU citizens living abroad conditional upon 'a certain degree of integration',[35] thereby denying equal access to study grants to Union citizens who had resided in the host State for less than five years.[36] Without doubt, the integration criterion had been developed by the Court in a number of earlier judgments, but these had employed it in a way that focused on territorial presence in line with the 'residence model'.[37] *Förster* departed from this line of reasoning by making equal treatment conditional upon other qualitative factors.

[31] For practical examples, see Commission, *Practical Guide: The Legislation that Applies to Workers* (2013), section 3.

[32] See H Verschueren, 'Preventing "Benefit Tourism" in the EU: A Narrow or Broad Interpretation of the Possibilities Offered by the ECJ in *Dano*?' (2015) 52 *CML Rev* 363, 377–81; and A Farahat, 'Solidarität und Inklusion: Umstrittene Dimensionen der Unionsbürgerschaft' (2016) *Die Öffentliche Verwaltung* 45, 47–49.

[33] See ECJ, *Brey*, C-140/12, EU:C:2013:565, paras 39–43; reaffirmed by ECJ, *Commission v United Kingdom*, C-308/14, EU:C:2016:436, paras 63–67; and the critique by H Verschueren, 'Free Movement or Benefit Tourism: The Unreasonable Burden of Brey' (2014) 16 *European Journal of Migration and Law* 147, 159–64.

[34] See ECJ, *Martínez Sala*, C-85/96, EU:C:1998:217; ECJ, *Trojani*, C-456/02, EU:C:2004:488; and ECJ, *Grzelczyk*, C-184/99, EU:C:2001:458.

[35] ECJ, *Förster*, C-158/07, EU:C:2008:630, para 49.

[36] *cf* Art 24(2) Directive 2004/38/EC, whose compatibility with primary law the ECJ reaffirmed in *Förster*, ibid, paras 51–55.

[37] See, in particular, ECJ, *Collins*, C-138/02, EU:C:2004:172, para 72; ECJ, *Bidar*, C-209/03, EU:C:2005:169, paras 58–62; and ECJ, *Ioannidis*, C-258/04, EU:C:2005:559, para 35.

The essence of the integration model concerns the rejection of equal treatment whenever someone fails to satisfy the 'real/genuine link'[38] or 'certain degree of integration'[39] standard established by the Court.[40] Doctrinally, it is construed as an objective consideration for justifying unequal treatment under Article 18 TFEU, Article 24 Directive 2004/38/EC, Article 4 Regulation (EC) No 883/2004 or Article 7 Regulation (EU) No 492/2011 which the Court interprets in parallel.[41] Nonetheless, inspection of the case law shows that it is difficult to identify clear patterns on the basis of the ECJ case law about how the integration criterion should be applied to specific scenarios.[42]

The inherent difficulties in the application of the real link standard to individual cases may have been one deciding factor for the Court to opt for a clear-cut answer in *Dano* and *Alimanovic* when it flatly denied equal treatment to certain categories of Union citizens irrespective of the circumstances of the individual case, since it construed the rejection of equal treatment to flow directly from Directive 2004/38/EC[43]—a conclusion it justified, among others, by the high degree of legal certainty and transparency for domestic authorities and individuals concerned.[44] It is difficult to imagine a more radical deviation from the residence model: territorial presence is deemed irrelevant under EU law; unlawful presence in another Member States brings about no legally significant link to the host society.[45]

It should be noted that the integration model has implications for both incoming and outgoing citizens when it comes to social benefits. While the former may be excluded from welfare provision (as in *Förster*), the latter can rely on the integration argument to 'export' benefits when moving abroad. Conceptually, limitations on incoming citizens and generosity for outgoing nationals are two sides of the same coin if social affiliation—not territorial presence—guides the scope of transnational rights.[46] Against this background, it was conceptually coherent that the ECJ allowed students in a number of judgments throughout the years to export study grants, which host societies can withhold from incoming foreigners.

[38] ECJ, *D'Hoop*, C-224/9, EU:C:2002:432, para 38; and ECJ, *Collins* (n 37) para 67 for jobseekers.

[39] *Bidar* (n 37) para 57 for other Union citizens.

[40] On the emergence of a coherent concept, see M Jesse, 'The Value of "Integration" in European Law' (2011) 27 *ELJ* 172, 174–82.

[41] See Thym, 'The Elusive Limits of Solidarity' (n 4) 23–24.

[42] See M Dougan, 'The Bubble that Burst' in M Adams et al (eds), *Judging Europe's Judges: The Legitimacy of the Case Law of the European Court of Justice* (Oxford, Hart Publishing, 2013) 140–45; and Thym, 'The Elusive Limits of Solidarity' (n 4) 45–49.

[43] See ECJ, *Dano*, C-333/13, EU:C:2014:2358, para 77; ECJ, *Alimanovic*, C-67/14, EU:C:2015:597, paras 59–60; and N Nic Shuibhne, 'Limits Rising, Duties Ascending: The Changing Legal Shape of Union Citizenship' (2015) 52 *CML Rev* 889, 908–11.

[44] *Alimanovic* (n 43) para 61; and ECJ, *García-Nieto et al*, C-299/14, EU:C:2016:114, para 49.

[45] See also D Thym, 'When Union Citizens Turn into Illegal Migrants: The *Dano* Case' (2015) 40 *EL Rev* 249, 256–58.

[46] See R Bauböck, 'Global Justice, Freedom of Movement and Democratic Citizenship' (2009) 50 *European Journal of Sociology* 1, 19–22; and Davies (n 16) 49–54.

It delivered a remarkable line of rulings emphasising the responsibility of the home state through benefits' exportation in various domains.[47]

B. Constitutional Context

There are at least three contextual factors which help rationalise the move towards the integration model in light of the broader constitutional outlook. First, the Court may have yielded to the EU legislature, since it should be remembered that the initial enthusiasm for equal treatment was shared by the legislature, whose generous interpretation of the Treaty regime throughout the 1960s preceded later Court judgments.[48] That is not to say that the Court wasn't innovative; it certainly was, but its attention mostly focused on national rules in domestic legal orders. Judges often corrected Member States, but there were few instances throughout the years in which it positioned itself consciously against the EU legislature in free movement cases. The most prominent examples are *Grzelczyk* and *Baumbast*, when it scrutinised free movement legislation in light of primary law.[49]

It went along these lines in *Vatsouras*, although judges shied away from declaring the restriction in Article 24(2) of the Citizenship Directive to be an outright violation of the EU Treaties.[50] Corresponding uncertainties about the implications of the judgments ultimately led to another reference by the same German court in *Alimanovic* in response to which the ECJ decided not to challenge the exemption on the basis of primary law any longer.[51] The same holds for *Förster* where judges indirectly confirmed statutory rules on not granting study grants before the acquisition of permanent residence status.[52] In *Dano*, the ECJ was confronted with deliberate ambiguity on the part of the EU legislature and opted for a conservative standpoint.[53] Doing so had the side effect of rendering it easier to satisfy the demands of the British Government in the run-up to the Brexit referendum.[54] It could be interpreted, therefore, as an act of defiance towards the potential future

[47] See N Rennuy, 'The Emergence of a Parallel System of Social Security Coordination' (2013) 50 *CML Rev* 1221, 1232–50; and Dougan (n 29) 136–62.

[48] See D Thym, 'Family as Link. Explaining the Judicial Change of Direction on Residence Rights of Family Members from Third States' in H Verschueren (ed), *Residence, Employment and Social Rights of Mobile Persons. On How EU Law Defines Where They Belong* (Antwerp, Intersentia, 2016) 16–18; and S Goedings, *Labor Migration in an Integrating Europe* (The Hague, SDU Uitgevers, 2005).

[49] See M Dougan, 'The Constitutional Dimension to the Case Law on Union Citizenship' (2006) 31 *EL Rev* 613.

[50] *cf* ECJ, *Vatsouras & Koupatantze*, C-22/08 and C-23/08, EU:C:2009:344, paras 33 et seq.

[51] See the contribution by Ferdinand Wollenschläger, chapter 9 in this volume.

[52] *Förster* (n 35) para 55 notes Art 24(2) Directive 2004/38/EC which did not apply directly to the case *ratione temporis*.

[53] See the chapter by Paul Minderhoud and Sandra Mantu, chapter 10 in this volume.

[54] See the chapter by Stephanie Reynolds, chapter 4 in this volume.

will of the EU legislature on a highly politicised topic. In short, the restrictive turn could be an expression of judicial restraint.[55]

Second, the doctrinal infrastructure of the free movement rules for workers and those who do not work may be similar, but their constitutional context differs markedly. While the former (Articles 45, 49, 56, 59 TFEU) have been an integral part of the common market ever since the original Treaty of Rome, the latter (Article 21 TFEU) are closely linked to the concept of Union citizenship brought about by Treaty of Maastricht. Its introduction reiterated the political dream of building some sort of federal Europe, which culminated in the move towards the Constitutional Treaty. Against this background, it can be argued that both the initial enthusiasm of the Court's early citizenship case law and later hesitation reflect a broader integrationist reorientation,[56] in particular for those who are not economically active. Potential feedback loops between the Court's case law and the evolution of political union will be discussed below.

Third, there is no uniform concept of solidarity underlying equal access to social benefits, since we have to distinguish between work-related benefits and broader social assistance to anyone in accordance with most domestic welfare systems. Granting equal treatment to workers was and is largely uncontroversial, since most Member States gradually embraced territoriality instead of nationality as the door-opener for various forms of social benefits after the Second World War.[57] Equal treatment for incoming workers was also meant to prevent downward pressure on legislation protecting the domestic population.[58] One may certainly question the outer limits of this equality, such as in-work benefits for part-time workers or the level of payments for children living abroad.[59] But such disputes about the fringes should not distract from the essentially economic rationale of equal treatment for workers in line with classic free movement law and corresponding equal treatment guarantees for those who are economically active.

By contrast, there may be no solid normative vision of how transnational solidarity should be construed outside the labour market (it does certainly not follow from the basic agreement on how to treat workers). Floris de Witte has shown that the equal treatment of workers, which one may reconstruct theoretically as an expression of a Durkheimian organic solidarity, does not necessarily pre-empt our

[55] See K Lenaerts, 'The Court's Outer and Inner Selves: Exploring the External and Internal Legitimacy of the European Court of Justice' in M Adams et al, *Judging Europe's Judges: The Legitimacy of the Case Law of the European Court of Justice* (Oxford, Hart Publishing, 2013) 17–28; Dougan, 'The Bubble that Burst' (n 42) 145–53; and V Hatzopoulos, 'Actively Talking to Each Other: The Court and the Political Institutions' in M Dawson et al (eds), *Judicial Activism at the European Court of Justice* (Cheltenham, Edward Elgar, 2013).

[56] See Dougan, 'The Bubble that Burst' (n 42) 150–51.

[57] See M Ferrera, *The Boundaries of Welfare* (Oxford, Oxford University Press, 2005); and T Kingreen, *Soziale Rechte und Migration* (Baden-Baden, Nomos, 2010).

[58] See Goedings (n 48) 122–26; and S O'Leary, 'Free Movement of Persons and Services' in P Craig and G de Búrca (eds), *The Evolution of EU Law* (Oxford, Oxford University Press, 2011) 508–11.

[59] Both questions featured prominently in the reform package agreed upon in the run-up to the Brexit referendum; see chapter 4 by Stephanie Reynolds in this volume.

position on transnational solidarity for those in need.[60] Similar rights for those who are economically inactive require a broader vision of social justice beyond the paradigms of the single market. Certainly, the Court could have constructed such vision, but it could not draw, when doing so, on the basic political consensus for workers. Again, it may be no surprise therefore, that the innovative judgments were delivered during a period of optimism in the late 1990s and early 2000s, while the more restrictive turn coincided with the economic crisis which engulfed the eurozone after 2010.[61] At the time, it became more visible that the EU lacked a meaningful social policy, about the emergence of which commentators had been cautiously optimistic a decade earlier.[62]

IV. MEMBERSHIP IN POLITICAL COMMUNITIES

In recent Western thought, citizenship has most commonly been associated with membership in political communities.[63] These communities have traditionally been states and the transfer of the citizenship idea to the European Union may necessitate, therefore, conceptual translation exploring how far established patterns of state membership can be applied to the EU.[64] Recent events reinforced the uncertainty whether such conceptual translation may succeed. This section explores corresponding changes (below A) and relates them to broader constitutional trends characterising the ongoing crisis of the European project (B).

A. Evolution of Citizens' Rights

The most visible expression of membership in a political community is the right to vote, but it also presupposes the status defining someone as a member of this community and giving her a basic right to remain.[65] In both respects, we can observe a reorientation of supranational citizens' rights in the evolution of the EU Treaties and case law. While residence abroad appeared as the central axis for political participation and the right to remain for many years (below i), attachment to the state of origin was reinforced more recently (ii).

[60] See F de Witte, *Justice in the EU: The Emergence of Transnational Solidarity* (Oxford, Oxford University Press, 2015) ch 3.

[61] *cf* S Giubboni, 'Free Movement of Persons and European Solidarity: A Melancholic Eulogy" in H Verschueren (ed), *Residence, Employment and Social Rights of Mobile Persons: On How EU Law Defines Where They Belong* (Antwerp, Intersentia, 2016) 80–81.

[62] *cf* C Barnard, 'EU "Social" Policy' in P Craig and G de Búrca (eds), *The Evolution of EU Law* (Oxford, Oxford University Press, 2011).

[63] See D Leydet, 'Citizenship' in *Stanford Encyclopedia of Philosophy*, Fall 2011 edition: plato.stanford.edu/entries/citizenship.

[64] *cf* N Walker, 'Postnational Constitutionalism and the Problem of Translation' in JHH Weiler and M Wind (eds), *European Constitutionalism Beyond the State* (Cambridge, Cambridge University Press, 2003).

[65] See Bosniak (n 7) 456–63, 470–79.

i. 'Residence Model'

The Treaty of Maastricht endowed the newly established category of Union citizenship with distinct rights, including the right to vote in municipal and European elections while living in another Member State.[66] This transnational right to vote presents an obvious move towards residence as the decisive factor for political participation. At the time, it could be expected that the voting rights in municipal and European elections might be followed by further moves towards a European democracy. A legal expression of this forward-looking dynamic was today's Article 25 TFEU which called on the EU institutions 'to strengthen [Union citizenship] or to add to the rights' by means of a simplified Treaty revision procedure.[67] In contrast to the original excitement,[68] the provision turned out to be a dead letter and was not activated a single time over the past 25 years.

Undoubtedly, the Lisbon Treaty intended to strengthen political participation through, among other things, the introduction of a citizens' initiative and more ambitious Treaty language[69] but, as discussed below, this did not change much in practice. Regarding the right to vote, attempts failed to move further towards the residence model.[70] Luxembourg rejected voting rights for EU citizens in national elections in a referendum[71] and the Commission adopted a recommendation requesting Member States to retain the right to vote for nationals living abroad[72]—instead of taking up the citizens' initiative to extend transnational participation in the country of residence.[73] This episode may not be of crucial relevance, but it presents anecdotal evidence for the decline of the 'residence model'.

Along similar lines, EU citizenship was not considerably reinforced as a basic status. The official designation as 'Citizenship *of the Union*' may relate the individual to the Union's territory as a whole,[74] but this does not unmake the primary relevance of state nationality. It is sometimes forgotten that corresponding concerns were one of the reasons for the initial Danish rejection of the Maastricht Treaty: Danish voters worried that the EU would interfere with nationality laws.[75]

[66] See today's Art 22 TFEU.

[67] Art 25 TFEU in line with the original Art 8e(2) as amended by the Treaty of Maastricht ([1992] OJ C224/36).

[68] *cf* S O'Leary, *The Evolving Concept of Community Citizenship* (The Hague, Kluwer, 1996) 308–14.

[69] See P Craig, *The Lisbon Treaty* (Oxford, Oxford University Press, 2010) 66–71; and J Shaw, 'Citizenship: Contrasting Dynamics at the Interface of Integration and Constitutionalism' in P Craig and G de Búrca (eds), *The Evolution of EU Law* (Oxford, Oxford University Press, 2011) 597–608.

[70] For corresponding proposals, see F Fabbrini, 'Voting Rights for Non-Citizens' (2011) 7 *European Constitutional Law Review* 392, 404–05.

[71] *cf* on the 2015 referendum, M Finck, 'Towards an Ever Closer Union Between Residents and Citizens?' (2015) 11 *European Constitutional Law Review* 78.

[72] See Commission Recommendation 2014/53/EU ([2014] OJ L32/34).

[73] *cf* the Citizens' Initiative 'Let me vote' (No ECI(2013)000003), which failed to gather enough signatures in 2013/14.

[74] See Azoulai (n 20) section I.

[75] See D Howarth, 'The Compromise on Denmark and the Treaty on European Union' (1994) 31 *CML Rev* 765, 772–73.

As a result, the European Council adopted a decision, which was integrated into primary law five years later, that EU citizenship 'shall complement and not replace national citizenship'.[76] It is true that this was reformulated by the Treaty of Lisbon in line with the erstwhile Constitutional Treaty, although it remained unclear whether the sematic shift from Union citizenship 'complement[ing]' to 'be[ing] additional' to nationality implied substantive change.[77]

Against this background, it did not come as a surprise that the Court trod carefully when scrutinising nationality laws. In *Rottmann*, it may have obliged Member States to take into account the consequences of any deprivation of nationality for citizens' rights under EU law, while being cautious not to limit state discretion extensively.[78] Notwithstanding the need for a proportionality test, it reaffirmed the domestic prerogative for acquiring or losing Union citizenship together with nationality in light of international law.[79] This seemed to change when the *Ruiz Zambrano* judgment set out to reinforce the legal significance of Union citizenship by proclaiming that citizens may invoke the status against measures of their home State depriving citizens of the genuine enjoyment of the substance of rights[80]—a criterion reformulated later as relating to situations 'where [Union citizens] would have to leave the territory of the Union'.[81] To derive from Union citizenship a quasi-automatic guarantee to remain on EU territory presented us with a rich expression of the 'residence model'.

ii. 'Integration Model'

It is well known among experts of EU law that the Court may have positioned itself for a great leap forward in *Ruiz Zambrano*, but changed direction in later rulings, thereby retreating from the initial move towards the residence model.[82] The practical relevance of the 'substance of rights test' was effectively limited to the situation of minor citizens with third-country national family members.[83] Moreover, the conceptual significance of the new approach was restricted when the Court emphasised that the guarantee to remain in the Union did not imply that a family could stay in Luxembourg where it was residing, since the children

[76] Art 17(1) EC Treaty as amended by the Treaty of Amsterdam ([1997] OJ C340/173) differed from Art 8(1) EC Treaty as amended in Maastricht (n 67).

[77] See A Schrauwen, 'European Citizenship in the Treaty of Lisbon' (2008) 15 *Maastricht Journal* 55, 59–60; and Shaw (n 69), 598–600.

[78] ECJ, *Rottmann*, C-135/08, EU:C:2010:104, para 40 noted the decision of the European Council in response to the first Danish referendum.

[79] *cf Rottmann*, ibid, para 39; and ECJ, *Micheletti*, C-369/90, EU:C:1992:295, para 10.

[80] *cf* ECJ, *Ruiz Zambrano*, C-34/09, EU:C:2011:124, para 42.

[81] ECJ, *Dereci et al*, C-256/11, EU:C:2011:734, para 65.

[82] For an overview, see D Kochenov, 'The Right to Have What Rights? EU Citizenship in Need of Clarification" (2013) 19 *ELJ* 502; and M Wendel, 'Aufenthalt als Mittel zum Zweck' (2014) *Die Öffentliche Verwaltung* 133.

[83] See chapter 11 by N Nic Shuibhne in this volume; and Thym, 'Family as Link' (n 48) 25–28.

held French passports and could be expected, therefore, to return to France.[84] Union citizenship may connect the individual to Union territory, but the residual responsibility rests with the home State, in line with the public international law.[85] Thus, judges accentuated social affiliation instead of territorial presence as the guiding principle for citizens' rights, in line with its conclusion on the EU–Turkey association agreement that 'the acquisition of the nationality of the host Member State represents, in principle, the most accomplished level of integration'.[86]

Along similar lines, the ECJ realigned the significance of social affiliation in an area that had defined much of its early case law on free movement: the public policy exception on the basis of which Member States can expel Union citizens. Judges employed the concept of social integration to interpret the legal position of mobile citizens under the newly established permanent residence status in Directive 2004/38/EC: if citizens disappoint the integration objective, they obtain fewer rights and can be expelled more easily in light of 'integration-based reasoning'.[87] In *Dias*, this implied that formal factors (presence of national residence certificates) are outweighed by qualitative considerations (absence of sufficient resources) because 'the integration objective … is based not only on territorial and time factors but also on qualitative elements'.[88] This approach has been reaffirmed in other (but not all) judgments on permanent residence.[89]

The ECJ also employed the integration criterion to bolster its novel approach to the issue of public security.[90] This was manifest in the conclusion in *G*, that the seemingly precise 10-year rule for enhanced protection against expulsion should be understood as a proxy for a complex assessment of qualitative factors as a result of which periods of imprisonment need not to be taken into account.[91] The doctrinal impact of these judgments should not be overestimated, since they primarily concerned those residing for more than five years and have no immediate bearing on the ECJ's well-established case law on other scenarios.[92] Yet, they signal a conceptual shift away from residence-based equality towards an output-oriented assessment that links citizens' rights to the degree of integration.[93]

[84] *cf* ECJ, *Alokpa & Moudoulou*, C-86/12, EU:C:2013:645, para 34.

[85] See ECJ, *McCarthy*, C-434/09, EU:C:2011:277, para 29; for a thorough analysis, see F Haag, 'Die Letztverantwortung des Herkunftsmitgliedstaates im Unionsbürgerrecht' in D Thym and T Klarmann (eds), *Unionsbürgerschaft und Migration im aktuellen Europarecht* (Baden-Baden, Nomos, 2017).

[86] ECJ, *Demirci et al*, C-171/13, EU:C:2015:8, para 54.

[87] ECJ, *Lassal*, C-162/09, EU:C:2010:592, para 37 following AG Trstenjak, ibid, para 80.

[88] ECJ, *Dias*, C-325/09, EU:C:2011:498, para 64.

[89] Contrast ECJ, *Onuekwere*, C-378/12, EU:C:2014:13, paras 34–36 and ECJ, *Tahir*, C-469/13, EU:C:2014:2094, paras 33–34 to ECJ, *Ogieriakhi*, C-244/13, EU:C:2014:2068.

[90] See Azoulai (n 20).

[91] *cf* ECJ, *G*, C-400/12, EU:C:2014:9, paras 29–36.

[92] Doctrinally, the new approach remains limited—so far, at least—to Arts 16 and 28, not to Arts 7 and 27 of Directive 2004/38/EC.

[93] Similarly, see S Robin-Olivier, 'Libre circulation des travailleurs' (2011) 3 *Revue trimestrielle de droit européen* 599, 604–07; Nic Shuibhne (n 43) 916–26; and E Spaventa, 'Once a Foreigner, Always a Foreigner' in H Verschueren (ed), *Residence, Employment and Social Rights of Mobile Persons. On How EU Law Defines Where They Belong* (Antwerp, Intersentia, 2016).

B. Constitutional Context

Two contextual factors may help rationalise the move towards the integration model in light of the broader constitutional outlook. They concern the limited bearing of the traditional method of integration through law in the realms of democracy (below i) and the general crisis of legitimacy in which the EU has been engulfed in recent years (ii).

i. The Limits of Integration through Law

The process of EU integration has always relied on the transformative potential of 'integration through law' by employing the law as an instrument for change.[94] Union citizenship was an integral part of this endeavour: a special status for citizens with direct elections to the European Parliament and free movement for others than workers had been an integral part the political dream of building some sort of federal Europe through successive Treaty amendments and corresponding institutional practices,[95] which also informed the move towards Union citizenship in the Treaty of Maastricht.[96] We can perceive, on this basis, the introduction of citizens' rights as an effort of social engineering to enhance the democratic legitimacy of the European project by way of constitutional fiat. If that is correct, the counter-argument is apparent: it highlights failures and pitfalls of the legal rules in practice.[97] To establish a fundamental status called 'citizenship' is not a self-fulfilling prophecy. Citizens' rights need to be embedded into social structures and political life in order to fill the legal rules with substance.

At the time of the Treaty of Maastricht, it could be argued more convincingly than today that transnational voting rights might be a first move towards a supranational democracy based on enhanced participation and a genuine political culture with pan-European political parties and public discourses.[98] Success was certainly no foregone conclusion, but a cautious optimism prevailed among many observers at the time.[99] The experience of comparative federalism showed that citizens' rights can have unifying effects.[100] Yet there is nothing automatic in such a process: whether and if so, to what extent Union citizenship commands

[94] See Thym, 'Introduction' in this volume, section III.

[95] cf A Wiener, Building Institutions (Boulder, CO, Westview, 1998) chs 2, 3; and F Wollenschläger, *Grundfreiheit ohne Markt: Die Herausbildung der Unionsbürgerschaft im unionsrechtlichen Freizügigkeitsregime* (Tübingen, Mohr Siebeck, 2007).

[96] See, again, Thym, 'Introduction' in this volume, section III.

[97] See U Haltern, 'Pathos and Patina' (2003) 9 *ELJ* 14, 26–32; and J Přibáň, 'The Juridification of Identity' (2009) 16 *Constellations* 44, 47–53.

[98] For the original optimism, notwithstanding principled caveats, see the German Federal Constitutional Court, Judgment of 12 October 1993, Cases 2 BvR 2134/92 and 2159/92, *Treaty of Maastricht*, BVerfGE 89, 155, 184–85.

[99] See, by way of example, J Habermas, 'Remarks on Dieter Grimm's "Does Europe Need a Constitution?"' (1995) 1 *ELJ* 303.

[100] See the comparison by Schönberger (n 18).

centripetal forces cannot be deduced from a simple comparison with nineteenth-century state-building. Contextual factors may prevent history repeating itself—and these factors seem to have pointed in the opposite direction in recent years.

It was mentioned earlier that there is a notable parallel between the aspirational Court judgments on Union citizenship and the rise of the Constitutional Treaty, whose failure might have paved the way for a more restrictive turn.[101] This trend seems to have gathered momentum as a result of the euro crisis and the rise of Euroscepticism across the continent. Arguably, events over past years have shown that even an ideal institutional setting for voting rights and other participatory elements would not necessarily give rise to a meaningful European democracy. Empirical studies show that citizens either do not use their rights in the first place or do not identify with the supranational polity when doing so.[102] Citizens' rights have resulted in a limited degree of shared feelings of mutual belonging among the citizens of Europe capable of sustaining, as an identificatory infrastructure for solidarious communities, broader redistributive policies.[103] From an empirical perspective, the *legal* construction of Union citizenship need not coincide with the *social* construction of European identity.

ii. A Vision for the Union as a Whole

A first analysis of the Brexit referendum reveals a division between mobile and immobile citizens, since it was the latter who disproportionately supported the 'leave' campaign.[104] This coincides with earlier findings that those exercising their free movement rights are inclined to be more supportive of EU integration, while those who do not tend to be more critical.[105] By contrast, much of the academic literature focused on the mobile citizen living in another Member State, while ignoring the broader societal and political effects of the decision, by many citizens, to stay at home,[106] which, coincidentally, was a crucial consideration in the Spaak report paving the way for the Treaty of Rome.[107] A holistic analysis will have to overcome this primary attention to those crossing borders. The doctrinal proposal

[101] See Dougan, 'The Bubble that Burst' (n 42) 150–51.

[102] See A Favell, 'European Citizenship in Three Eurocities' (2010) 30 *Politique européenne* 187, 191–202.

[103] *cf* R Bellamy, 'Evaluating Union Citizenship: Belonging, Rights and Participation within the EU' (2008) 12 *Citizenship Studies* 597, 601–06; and G Delanty, 'European Citizenship' (2007) 11 *Citizenship Studies* 63.

[104] See R Bauböck in EUDO Citizenship Forum 'Free Movement under Attack' (2016).

[105] See the chapter 7 by Ettore Recchi in this volume; T Kuhn, Experiencing European Integration: Transnational Lives and European Identity (Oxford, Oxford University Press, 2015) ch 7; and N Fligstein, Euro-Clash: The EU, European Identity, and the Future of Europe (Oxford, Oxford University Press, 2010).

[106] For a rich discussion see S Iglesias Sánchez, 'A Citizenship Right to Stay?' The Right Not to Move in a Union Based on Free Movement' in D Kochenov (ed), *EU Citizenship and Federalism: The Role of Rights* (Cambridge, Cambridge University Press, 2017).

[107] *cf* Editorial Comments (2014) 51 *CML Rev* 729, 730; and Goedings (n 48) 121–23.

to apply citizens' rights to purely internal situations was rejected by the Court for reasons which arguably concerned the preservation of the federal balance of power.[108] The challenge remains how to relate the analysis of citizens' rights to wider effects for societies as a whole.

Such broader outlook would connect discussions about transnational mobility to the state of the Union as a whole. Indeed, the citizenship case law is not the only area in which judges in Luxembourg shied away from fostering a supranational vision of social justice by means of Treaty interpretation: not assessing austerity measures in light of the Charter of Fundamental Rights is another example.[109] Thus, the reticence on the part of the Court to explore further the constitutional potential of Union citizenship may reflect a more general concern that guarantees in the EU Treaties cannot resolve the problems the EU is confronted with at this juncture. The Court may have decided implicitly not to develop a thick reading of constitutional rules on either citizenship or monetary union at time of profound economic and political crises. Anyone trying to change this will have to engage, therefore, in a general undertaking to develop a vision of social justice for the Union as a whole, not only for those moving across borders.[110]

This leaves us with the overall impression of both the EU institutions and its highest Court retracting from earlier attempts at constitutional engineering by means of enhanced citizens' rights and progressive constitutional adjudication. That need not be understood as resignation. It could be presented positively as a move towards a more confederal understanding of European integration which restrains the vision of some sort of federal Europe and accepts that the Member States will remain the primary political communities in years to come.[111] Doing so would not be a return to the closed nation-state, but build the European Union on domestic communities within a broader supranational structure of mutual respect and responsiveness.[112] The move away from residence-based voting rights and the strengthening of national citizenship in recent case law can be perceived as building block of such a European Union based on domestic political communities instead of promoting a quasi-federal vision of the EU.

V. MIGRATION, MOBILITY AND SOCIAL COHESION

Citizenship can have many meanings. Most accounts seem to concur, nonetheless, that it embraces questions of membership and belonging, although authors might

[108] For more detail, see D Thym, 'Frontiers of EU Citizenship' in D Kochenov (ed), *EU Citizenship and Federalism: The Role of Rights* (Cambridge, Cambridge University Press, 2017) 719–22.

[109] See AJ Menéndez, 'Which Citizenship?' Whose Europe?—The Many Paradoxes of European Citizenship' 2014 15 *German Law Journal* 907, 928–31.

[110] The conclusion to this volume will explore trends in this direction.

[111] See the contribution by Francesca Strumia, chapter 8 in this volume.

[112] See K Nicolaïdis, 'European Demoicracy and its Crisis' (2013) *Journal of Common Market Studies* 351; and R Bellamy, 'An Ever Closer Union of Peoples' (2013) 35 *Journal of European Integration* 499.

disagree about how the element of identity is to be construed normatively.[113] The European Union is no exception, since it has been an integral part of the redefinition of statehood after the Second World War. More recently, this 'post-national' conception of Union citizenship was confronted with the increasing salience of migration from third-states, which became a prominent feature of EU activities and in domestic policy debates. This section will explore the interaction between both developments by linking the institutional practice on citizens' rights (below A) to debates about migration at European and national level (B).

A. Evolution of Citizens' Rights

Considering controversial citizenship cases, the residence status of family members of Union citizens holding the passport of a third state appears as a common thread in judgments such as *Baumbast*, *Carpenter*, *Akrich*, *Metock*, *Ibrahim*, *Ruiz Zambrano*, *Dereci* or *Alokpa*. This linkage between Union citizenship and migration law helps us rationalise the shift, on the part of the ECJ, from enhanced residence rights (below i) to a renewed focus on questions of social integration (ii).

i. 'Residence Model'

The introduction of Union citizenship has been an integral part of the redefinition of statehood. It was meant to symbolise the benefits EU integration brings to the individual, thereby supporting the '*rapprochement* of peoples who wish to go forward together'.[114] Union citizenship can be said, therefore, to have a 'post-national' character. It appeared as a vehicle for overcoming the close nation-state with its traditional ethno-cultural definition of belonging.[115] Citizens' rights could be construed, on this basis, as emancipatory in character giving the individual the option to choose different life plans and to pursue her happiness beyond her home state. It presented, in essence, an instrument to overcome established meanings of belonging. To find conclusive evidence that such vision motivated judges is inherently difficult, but cannot be excluded.[116]

It is much easier, by contrast, to trace the interaction between Union citizenship and the residence rights of third-country national family members. Their status came into the ambit of ECJ case law only indirectly, since third-country nationals cannot rely on citizens' rights. They benefit from free movement in the

[113] See the chapter 13 by Karin de Vries; and chapter 14 by Clíodhna Murphy, in this volume.

[114] European Union, Report by Leo Tindemans to the European Council, Bulletin of the EC Supplement 1/76, 27 (emphasis in the original).

[115] See Kostakopoulou, *The Future Governance of Citizenship* (n 17) ch 4; and Soysal (n 17).

[116] For instructive reading, see de Witte (n 60) 22–37; and JHH Weiler, 'To Be a European Citizen: Eros and Civilization' in JHH Weiler, *The Constitution of Europe* (Cambridge, Cambridge University Press, 1999).

form of 'derived rights'[117] as family members of a sponsor holding an EU passport. As a result, corresponding judgments were not primarily about transnational movement for economic purposes, which constituted the formal doctrinal basis for the Court's intervention, but revolved around questions of family unity in substance.[118] For some years, it seemed as if judges in Luxembourg were protecting family unity as an end in itself. The formal linkage to free movement rights was given little attention.[119] Residence-based equality for Union citizens and third-country national family members appeared as the new hallmark of transnational citizens' rights.

ii. 'Integration Model'

In recent years, the Court of Justice has shown a noticeable sensitivity when dealing with family members from third countries. Judgments concerned diverse doctrinal scenarios, but they had one thing in common: they revealed an interpretative shift from a judicial style of argumentation based on the telos (purpose) and constitutional principles (human rights, free movement) to an examination of the wording and the general scheme of the supranational rules in question. This conclusion extends to judgments on social benefits and the more restrictive follow-up to *Ruiz Zambrano* discussed earlier in the same way as it concerns a third-country national family member.

The Court found, for instance, that a derived residence right after divorce does not come about if the partner left the Member State before initiating divorce proceedings[120] and that parents living across the border in another Member State cannot invoke derived rights.[121] It also concluded that family members do not benefit from a derived residence status whenever a Union citizens moved abroad, marries there and returns to his home state before a period of three months, since free movement had not been exercised effectively in such a scenario.[122] It is noticeable that such a conclusion puts less emphasis on family unity as an end in itself, reinforcing instead the classic concept of transnational mobility as the hallmark of free movement.[123] This did not undo the generosity of the earlier case law, which judges did not overturn, but it emphasised that citizens' rights do not bring about indefinite equal treatment whenever residing abroad.

[117] *Dereci et al* (n 81) para 55.

[118] For further comments, see Thym, 'Family as Link' (n 48) 20–31.

[119] See Spaventa, 'From *Gebhard* to *Carpenter*' (n 14) 764–68; and A Tryfonidou, 'Family Reunification Rights of (Migrant) Union Citizens' (2009) 15 *ELJ* 634.

[120] See ECJ, *Singh et al*, C-218/14, EU:C:2015:476.

[121] See ECJ, *Iida*, C-40/11, EU:C:2012:2405, paras 46–65.

[122] See ECJ, *O & B*, C-456/12, EU:C:2014:135, para 52.

[123] See E Spaventa, 'Family Rights for Circular Migrants and Frontier Workers' (2015) 52 *CML Rev* 753, 764–78; and E Pataut, 'Citoyenneté de l'Union européenne' (2014) *Revue trimestrielle de droit européen* 781, 791.

The perspective of migration law towards third-country nationals allows us to elucidate another element of the free movement case law: the qualitative approach to the 'integration' yardstick in recent rulings on social benefits and the public policy justification discussed above. Generally, the notion of 'integration' is used more frequently for cross-border movements of third-country nationals than for Union citizens. It became a central term in debates about immigration policy at national and European level from the mid-2000s onwards.[124] In the context of immigration law, the concept soon developed a life of its own emphasising the value of social cohesion besides residence-based quality; secondary legislation often employed the term in the context of opening clauses allowing Member States to make the residence status of foreigners conditional upon, for instance, integration requirements by promoting the knowledge of the national language.[125] The ECJ subscribed to this contextual approach in two judgments.[126]

B. Constitutional Context

There are at least three contextual factors which help rationalise the move towards the integration model in light of the broader constitutional outlook. First, EU law had addressed cross-border movements of people mainly from the perspective of Union citizenship for many years. This may have changed given the newly found prominence of immigration from third countries both in political debates and the EU Treaties, which have comprised supranational competences for law-making on immigration law *sensu stricto* since the Treaty of Amsterdam, on the basis of which the EU legislature adopted a number of legislative instruments that can have a direct bearing on citizenship cases.[127] On closer inspection, various judgments on family members discuss these instruments alongside free movement rules,[128] although the ECJ had brushed aside a related argument some years before.[129] These new rules on third-country nationals differ markedly from Union citizenship— mirroring discrepancies between citizens' rights and the EU–Turkish association acquis in relation to which the Court explicitly recognised

[124] For a reliable overview, see S Carrera, *In Search of the Perfect Citizen? The Intersection between Integration, Immigration and Nationality in the EU* (Leiden, Martinus Nijhoff, 2009); and chapter 13 by Karin de Vries in this volume.

[125] See Jesse (n 40) 182–88; and Carrera (n 124) ch 4.

[126] See ECJ, *P & S*, C-579/13, EU:C:2015:369; and ECJ, *K & A*, C-153/14, EU:C:2015:453; and the analysis by Clíodhna Murphy, chapter 14 in this volume; and D Thym, 'Towards a Contextual Conception of Social Integration in EU Immigration Law: Comments on *P&S* and *K&A*' (2016) 18 *European Journal of Migration and Law* 89.

[127] See Horsley (n 9) 956–63; and A Lansbergen and N Miller, 'European Citizenship Rights in Internal Situations' (2011) 7 *European Constitutional Law Review* 287, 300–01.

[128] See esp *Dereci et al* (n 81), paras 71–72; *O & B* (n 122) paras 78–81; ECJ, *Ymeraga et al*, C-87/12, EU:C:2013:291, para 42.

[129] Despite calls to the contrary by AG Geelhoed the ECJ, *Metock*, C-127/08, EU:C:2008:449, para 66 neglected the immigration dimension.

that it pursued different objectives from EU citizenship and that, therefore, 'the two legal schemes in question cannot be considered equivalent'.[130] In short, the change could be the result of an adaptation, on the part of judges, to a modified legal and constitutional context.

Second, the distinction between Union citizenship and immigration law towards third-country nationals has constitutional implications, since the latter leaves the EU legislature more discretion.[131] When adopting corresponding rules, the Member States rejected a transfer of the residence-based logic of the (early) citizenship regime to immigration law. Instead, they promoted a more contextualised meaning of social integration mentioned earlier. It can be argued that the qualitative realignment of the 'integration' yardstick in the more recent citizenship case law integrates this immigration-based logic into free movement rules (while many commentators had expected the influence to run in the opposite direction).[132] The language used by the British Government before the Brexit referendum did the same: it constantly branded Union citizens as 'migrants' and warned against instances of 'benefits tourism', thereby tearing down the semantic wall between the 'mobility' of EU citizens and the 'immigration' status of third-country nationals the Commission had tried to erect in its official communications.[133]

Third, the Court may have responded to calls from national governments after intense reactions to both the *Metock* judgment and the *Ruiz Zambrano* ruling had signalled fundamental concerns.[134] We should be careful, however, not to equate this call for proactive integration policies with right-wing populism even if it can be (mis)used for this purpose. To allow Member States to pursue integration policies within certain limits, need not contradict the 'post-national' orientation of Union citizenship, which helped overcome the closed nation-state. Supranational rules would continue to direct the reconfiguration of collective identities away from traditional notions of ethno-cultural essentialism to embrace diversity and non-discrimination,[135] without however preventing Member States from seeking a new sense of mutual trust and collective belonging on the basis of some sort of rights-based and discourse-oriented constitutional patriotism, be it at national level or for an emerging European democracy.[136] Such outlook would suit earlier

[130] ECJ, *Ziebell*, C-371/08, EU:C:2011:809, para 74.

[131] See D Thym, 'EU Migration Policy and its Constitutional Rationale: A Cosmopolitan Outlook' (2013) 50 *CML Rev* 709, 716–25.

[132] See Jesse (n 40) 188–89; and K Groenendijk, 'Recent Developments in EU Law on Migration' (2014) 16 *European Journal of Migration and Law* 313.

[133] *cf* Thym, 'When Union Citizens Turn into Illegal Migrants' (n 45) 256.

[134] See N Nic Shuibhne and J Shaw, 'General Report' in U Neergaard et al (eds), *Union Citizenship: Development, Impact and Challenges. The XXVI FIDE Congress in Copenhagen* (Copenhagen, DJØF Publishing, 2014) 139–50.

[135] See Joppke (n 23) ch 4; and Thym, 'Citizens and Foreigners in EU Law' (n 19) 314–15.

[136] See J Habermas, 'Staatsbürgerschaft und nationale Identität' (1990) in J Habermas, *Faktizität und Geltung* (Berlin, Suhrkamp, 1992); Delanty (n 103) 67; and JW Müller, *Constitutional Patriotism* (Princeton, NJ, Princeton University Press, 2007).

findings that the EU institutions started recognising the value of social cohesion at a time when the financial crisis and Brexit indicate that some sort of political union at supranational level is not forthcoming.

VI. CONCLUSION

While the legal rules on Union citizenship have been relatively stable, their interpretation changed markedly over the years and remains subject to intense debates about Court judgments and wider institutional practice. This chapter set out to rationalise these arguments in light of broader constitutional trends defining the state of the European integration process at this juncture. It employed two distinct visions of how to construe supranational citizenship as a heuristic device for reconstructing discussions on diverse subject matters such as welfare benefits, political participation, nationality law, residence security and interaction with immigration law towards citizens of third countries. Doing so allowed us to highlight a common trend underlying Court judgments and institutional practice: they epitomise a drift away from residence-based equality towards a novel emphasis on the value of social cohesion when the meaning of citizens' rights is intricately linked to the degree of integration in host societies.

How to explain this normative reconfiguration of supranational citizenship. This chapter argues that the volatile character of Union citizenship and the move towards the 'integration model' can be rationalised by the constitutional context. Although each scenario is defined by specific circumstances discussed above, there are three overarching themes connecting the evolution of citizens' rights to broader constitutional trends. First the ECJ's restrictive turn on social benefits and family members can be explained by greater deference to the legislature, which had always sent out mixed signals when it came to social benefits for Union citizens who do not work and to the immigration status of third-country nationals. Although judges in Luxembourg had emphasised the dynamic potential of Union citizenship in earlier cases, new judgments are defined by a conservative style or argumentation which accentuates the limits of Union law and recognises the significance of the new provisions on immigration law.

Second, there is a notable parallel between shifting institutional practices and the rise and fall of the Constitutional Treaty. The latter arguably presented the high point of the 'integration through law' concept which employed EU law as an instrument for political and social change. Union citizenship was an integral part of these endeavours, since it had always been aimed at fostering the link between the European project and its citizens. The momentum behind this idea seems to have been lost. This is most visible in discussions on political participation and the significance of nationality in relation to which the initial drive towards transnational equality based on residence gave way to a fortification of membership and democratic legitimacy in the Member States. Institutional practices emphasising the value of social integration appear as epitaphs of a Union losing self-confidence as a supranational polity, emphasising instead the continued significance of solidary political communities at national level.

Third, there is nothing automatic in the projection of a legal solution from one policy field to another. Thus, the equality-based reasoning behind economic market integration cannot justify access to social benefits across borders for those who do not work. To do so requires a distinct normative vision of social justice. In this respect, a general deficit of European constitutionalism became apparent in recent years. The Court of Justice hesitates to develop a thick normative understanding of supranational rules that may guide the resolution of intricate political questions. Union citizenship is not the only area in which the Court trod carefully, not least in the run-up to the Brexit referendum. It similarly showed constraint in the context of the euro crisis. The novel emphasis on social integration in the citizenship case law need not contradict this tendency. It can be explained as an expression of institutional practices which accept the limits of supranational constitutionalism while recognising that the Union should be built on functioning communities at national level. The evolution of citizens' rights can be construed as an integral part of this wider trend.

7

The Engine of 'Europeanness'? Free Movement, Social Transnationalism and European Identification

ETTORE RECCHI

I. THE SPATIAL BASES OF EUROPEAN IDENTIFICATION

ONE OF THE things that Brexit proved is that Europe's root problem is Europeans' self-identification. It is not by chance that the only (or the first?) country that has seceded from the European Union (EU) is the UK. For decades, Britons have scored on top of Eurobarometer as the EU citizens least willing to call themselves 'European'. Collective identification matters. A poor sense of 'Europeanness' means no solidarity with other Europeans. No solidarity translates into little public support to European institutions when they endeavour to impose redistributive policies or to pool Member States' resources. An appeal to German taxpayers to pay off the Greeks' debts cannot leverage—as happened after the reunification of the two Germanys—a strong bond between the two populations. There is no financial alchemy or constitutional engineering able to remedy this basic flaw of European integration.

What can make Europeans feel 'European'? What can bind them to a political-territorial community that was created top-down and only relatively recently? Historically, when nation states took up the challenge of nation-building, they used the instruments of compulsory conscription, mass education (in particular the teaching of history and geography), explicit propaganda (especially in times of crisis) and 'banal nationalism' expressed through widespread symbols and implicit fictions.[1] Today, compulsory military service has been discontinued by almost all the EU Member States (with a few after-thoughts), so that implementing it on a continental scale would hardly be feasible. As regards education, a history of Europe purged of nationalistic biases was proposed by scholars from different countries. But limited use has been made of these textbooks, which tend to

[1] M Billig, *Banal Nationalism* (London, Sage, 1995).

be hostage of national controversies about key historical characters and events.[2] As for propaganda, the European Commission has promoted a wide range of media campaigns, especially on the occasions of major changes such as the introduction of the euro. Less episodically, it is this propagandistic purpose that lies behind many of the EU's cultural policies such as the designation of the 'European Years' or a European capital of culture.[3] Last but not least, there is 'banal Europeanism' hinged on an array of different tools. Some of them have a deliberate identitarian connotation: the European flag, the European anthem, Europe Day (9 May, anniversary of the Schuman Declaration). Others were put in place for different purposes: for instance, the common currency or free movement rights. But have these policies had any effects on bolstering a European identity?

In this chapter, I concentrate on free movement, arguing that it has a very strong potential for fostering a sense of 'Europeanness'. The starting point of my argument rests on psycho-geographical knowledge, according to which humans are territorial beings. The localisation of life-worlds nurtures a sense of spatial confidence that tends to turn into spatial attachment.[4] Permanence in a physical context breeds adaptation, familiarity and eventually an attachment to it. This, in turn, substantiates the taken-for-granted nature of its institutions, thus contributing to the legitimacy of ongoing collective arrangements, including political ones.[5] In other words, people's inclination to be attached to the places where they spend or have spent their life—the places that constitute an individual's 'space-set'[6]—fits in with intentional activities of power-holders to demand legitimacy for the existing political order inasmuch as such order coincides geographically with the subjects' (or citizens') space-set. Concretely, loyalty to a given country is higher if people have a first-hand experience of that country's territory (and especially of symbolically core places). One of the latent functions of conscription has always been to socialise youth to different regions of 'their' nation. Internal migration yields a similar effect. Although some may fear it can erode community bonds,[7] in

[2] S Immerfall, K Boehnke and D Baier, 'Identity' in S Immerfall and G Therborn (eds), *Handbook of European Societies*, 2nd edn (New York, Springer, 2010).

[3] M Sassatelli, 'Imagined Europe: The Shaping of a European Cultural Identity through EU Cultural Policy' (2002) 5 *European Journal of Social Theory* 435.

[4] YF Tuan, *Space and Place: The Perspective of Experience* (Minneapolis, MN, University of Minnesota Press, 1977); RD Sack, *Human Territoriality: Its Theory and History* (Cambridge, Cambridge University Press, 1986); J Lévy, *L'espace légitime. Sur la dimension géographique de la fonction politique* (Paris, Presses de la FNSP, 1994); A Moles and E Rohmer, *Psychosociologie de l'espace* (Paris, L'Harmattan, 1998).

[5] H Popitz, *Phenomena of Power: Authority, Domination, and Violence* (New York, Columbia University Press, 2017 [1986]) ch 2.

[6] E Recchi, 'Space, Mobility and Legitimacy' in WR Thompson (ed), *Oxford Research Encyclopedia of Politics* (Oxford, Oxford University Press, 2016); E Recchi and T Kuhn, 'Europeans' Space-Sets and the Political Legitimacy of the EU' in N Kauppi (ed), *A Political Sociology of Transnational Europe* (Colchester, ECPR Press, 2013).

[7] RD Putman, *Bowling Alone: The Collapse and Revival of American Community* (New York, Simon & Schuster, 2000).

fact it spreads out the sense of belonging to a larger spatial unit—the nation. The US and Chinese instances—where internal migration and national identification are robust—are cases in point.

According to this logic, in contemporary Europe the free movement regime should facilitate the same outcome on a transnational scale. Albeit with different underlying (and not entirely explicit) theoretical premises, indeed such insight sits well with Karl Deutsch's 'transactionalist thesis' on European integration. The thesis is an upshot of Deutsch's earlier theory of nationalism.[8] In his view, nation-building comes about mainly through the construction of 'infrastructures' which facilitate economic and social exchanges within territorial boundaries. Infrastructures create 'societies', while communication and culture create 'communities'. But the latter cannot exist without the former. The sense of belonging to a nation grows out of the intensification of social relations within it. In a nation-centred world, co-nationals interact with each other more than they do with people external to the nation, thereby strengthening their sense of solidarity and common destiny. Once people start to communicate regularly and cluster across national borders, however, their spatially-bounded connections trigger a reconfiguration of collective attachments. Deutsch accordingly notes that 'boundaries are not just lines on a map … what really makes a *boundary* is a sharp drop in the frequency of some relevant transaction flow'.[9] As in the case of incipient nations, the expansion of economic, social and cultural exchanges across the boundaries of pre-existing polities is expected to lead to the formation of 'security communities'—one of which was the newborn European Economic Community, which Deutsch held could progressively endow itself with a collective identity through increased transnational interactions.[10]

II. ASSESSING THE 'FREE MOVEMENT' EFFECT

In the previous section, I sketched out two converging but theoretically distinct hypotheses. The first one draws on psycho-geographical tenets to claim that individuals with mobility experiences in different European countries are expected to be more prone to see themselves as 'European'. EU citizens who live in another Member State under the aegis of the free movement regime belong to such possibly more pro-Europe population. To test the hypothesis, I will use original survey data collected in 2004 and 2010 on intra-EU migrants and pool them with Eurobarometer data on the general, immobile population of nationals of each EU country. Statistical analysis, in the form of logistic regressions, will control

[8] KW Deutsch, *Nationalism and Social Communication: An Inquiry into the Foundations of Nationality* (Cambridge, MA, MIT Press, 1953).

[9] KW Deutsch, *Nationalism and its Alternatives* (New York, Knopf, 1969) 97.

[10] KW Deutsch et al, *Political Community and the North Atlantic Area: International Organization in the Light of Historical Experience* (Princeton, Princeton University Press, 1957).

whether—*ceteris paribus*—'EU movers' are more likely to feel attached to Europe than 'EU stayers'.[11] The second hypothesis draws on Karl Deutsch's argument of the effect of cross-border activities on individual outlooks: the more people engage in transnational practices, the more they are likely to adopt a supranational identification. To test the hypothesis, I will rely on data from Eurobarometer 73 of 2010 that record a list of 10 possible individual cross-border behaviours (from watching foreign TV to travelling abroad: see below). Multilevel logistic regression will control whether the more people act transnationally, the more they feel attached to Europe.

To begin with, I will present the analyses which compare the sense of belonging to Europe between movers and stayers. A key point to bear in mind is that EU movers form a small fraction of Europeans. EU citizens resident in another Member State hover around 3 per cent of the total population.[12] This makes it impracticable to study their characteristics, behaviours and attitudes using data from sample surveys conducted with random criteria on the entire population: even in large-scale surveys, the absolute number of sampled cases would be rather modest. A solution is to combine data from population surveys with data from ad hoc surveys on migrants that deal with the same phenomena using the same indicators. This is the strategy adopted here, by merging Eurobarometer data with data from the European Internal Movers' Social Survey (EIMSS) and Moveact surveys, which were designed to make this operation possible.[13] More specifically, I constructed a first joint matrix relative to 2004 with data from Eurobarometer 62 and the EIMSS survey on German, British, French, Spanish and Italian nationals living abroad. The second matrix has 2010–11 as its temporal reference, and pools data from Eurobarometer 73 of 2010 with data from the 2011 Moveact survey on mobile citizens of German, British, Polish and Romanian nationality.[14] It is thus possible to compare—among other things—the sense of identification with Europe of the stayers and movers of different countries at two distant moments of time.

[11] A methodological caveat is in order: cross-sectional survey data (that is, collected at one particular time) cannot be used to establish conclusively whether this possible difference is due directly to the experience of mobility or to other factors that preceded it. Only longitudinal information collected before and after migration would settle the question. However, there are theoretical reasons (illustrated in the previous section) that do justify the expectation that the experience of cross-border mobility fosters supranational identifications rather than the other way around.

[12] E Recchi, *Mobile Europe: The Theory and Practice of Free Movement in the EU* (Basingstoke, Palgrave Macmillan, 2015) 52ff.

[13] ibid 155–57.

[14] None of the 2011 Eurobarometers contain the dependent variable common to all the other surveys: the question on 'attachment to Europe'. I therefore had to rely on the survey closest in time able to ensure full comparability: the Eurobarometer 73.3 of March–April 2010. Moreover, to be precise, in the latter survey the response item was not phrased as 'Europe' but rather as the 'European Union'. This is an unfortunate change which must be factored in, but—also in consideration of the question structure, which is for the rest unaltered—I assume it to be an analogously trustworthy measurement of the European component of identification.

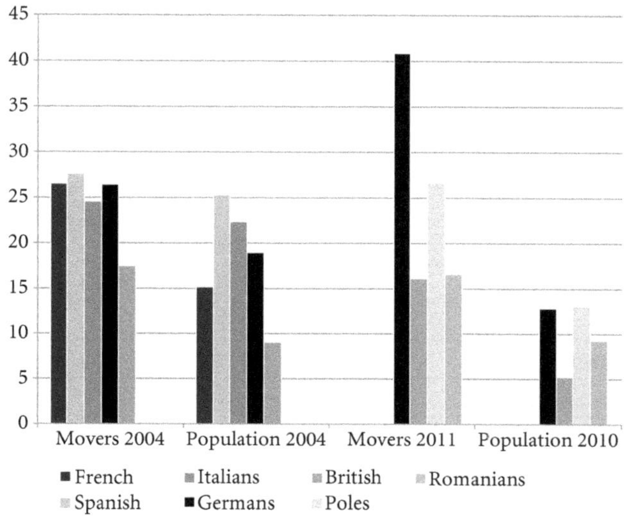

Figure 1: Feeling European: EU movers and stayers who declare themselves to be 'very attached' to Europe (2004 and 2010–11)

Sources: 2004: Eurobarometer 62 and EIMSS (N = 10,728); 2011: Eurobarometer 73 and Moveact (N=6,852).

Both surveys show that European citizens who feel 'very attached' to Europe are proportionally more numerous among those living in another Member State than in the rest of the population (Figure 1). This is the case within each nationality examined, independently of its level of identification with Europe. In absolute terms, in 2004, the Spanish respondents, both stayers and movers, accounted for the largest proportion of convinced Europeans. In 2010–11, across a different range of nationalities, the highest level of European identification was expressed by Germans among mobile citizens and Poles among non-mobile ones. Not surprisingly (especially ex post), in both 2004 and 2010–11, British respondents recorded the lowest levels of attachment to Europe. In the more recent survey, the percentage of Romanians who expressed a strong attachment to Europe was almost equally low (16.7 per cent among movers and 9.3 per cent among stayers). But there are no exceptions to the rule that attachment to Europe is more widespread among mobile citizens. Moreover, among the nationalities for which it makes sense to conduct intertemporal comparison—German and British—a decrease in the proportion of respondents strongly attached to Europe is apparent among stayers but not among movers. Indeed, in the sample of Germans resident abroad in 2011, 41 per cent of respondents were very attached to Europe.

Of course, this preliminary analysis yields only inconclusive findings, given that the difference between movers and stayers may also be due to the differing composition of the samples. To neutralise this possibility, I conducted multivariate

Table 1: Determinants of attachment to Europe in 2004 and 2010–11: logit regressions ('very attached' versus 'fairly, not very or not at all attached')

	2004	2010–11
Intra-EU mobility	1.734**	3.857**
Age (ref: > 60 yrs)		
15–30	.781*	.942
31–40	.804*	.961
41–50	.905	.803
51–60	1.112	.905
Gender (=woman)	.732**	.827*
Education (ref: Low, up to 15)		
Middle (up to 16–19)	1.304*	1.105
High (over 19)	2.032**	1.751**
Social class (ref: EGP VII)		
EGP I–II	1.383**	1.209
EGP III	1.167	.852
EGP IV	1.189	1.127
EGP V–VI	1.042	.827
Nationality (ref: German)		
French	.918	–
British	.472**	.368**
Spanish	1.214*	–**
Italian	1.060	–**
Polish	–	.698
Romanian	–	.423
Local identification	1.041	1.259*
Regional identification	3.324**	–
National identification	2.182**	2.691**

Sources: 2004: Eurobarometer 62 and EIMSS: N = 9,254; df = 19; chi-square = 3852.56; Nagelkerke R^2 = ,18. 2010–11: Eurobarometer 73 and Moveact: N = 6,344; df = 17; chi-square = 1916.80; Nagelkerke R^2 = .17. *Note:* * $p < .05$, ** $p < .01$. Coefficients are odds ratios.

analyses which control for the simultaneous effect of the main sociological factors that can influence the level of European identification. Table 1 presents the results of two logistic regression models of such factors on the dichotomous dependent variable described in Figure 1: that is, self-definition or otherwise as 'very attached to Europe'.[15] The first model refers to the 2004 sample (consisting of the Eb62 and EIMSS data), the second to the 2010–11 sample (consisting of Eb73 and Moveact data). In both cases, experiencing intra-EU mobility is one of the strongest predictors of attachment to Europe. In 2011, in fact, assuming the overall combination of the reference modalities of the control variables introduced into the model, mobility is associated with four times higher odds of feeling 'very attached' to Europe, standing out as the single most powerful independent variable of the model. As to be expected, education—in particular, up to tertiary level (that is, after the age of 19)—tends to engender a greater sense of Europeanness as well. By contrast, upper-class membership is significant in the first but not the second model. Likewise, while in the first model attachment to Europe was significantly lower among interviewees in the younger age groups, this is not the case in the 2010–11 surveys. Gender differences are in line with most of the literature: men are more inclined to describe themselves as 'European'.[16]

Unfortunately, the two datasets do not contain data relative to values and political attitudes that might be important (for instance, self-placement on the right–left scale).[17] But information regarding the other competing political-territorial identities is indeed available. Analysis reveals that strong regional and national identities—to which local ones were also added in 2011—are associated with attachment to Europe. This may be the substantive expression of a sensibility underlying the collective dimension of social life in its territorial variants. More prosaically, however, not to be excluded is the presence of a 'response set' which reduces the discriminatory capacity of these indicators. Finally, British origin is correlated negatively—and considerably so—with European identification in both surveys. It is especially negative in comparison with the reference category—German nationality—which is significantly associated with an attachment to Europe greater than that of the other nationalities in 2010–11, but not in 2004,

[15] Caution is needed when interpreting parameters of logistic regressions conducted on different samples, see: C Mood, 'Logistic Regression: Why We Cannot Do What We Think We Can Do, and What We Can Do About It' (2010) 26 *European Sociological Review* 67. As long as it cannot be assumed that unobserved heterogeneity is the same across such samples, effects cannot be compared properly. In this light, the two models examined here (and in following analyses of this chapter) must be read as two parallel takes on the issue rather than a way to gauge changes in the influence of only apparently comparable factors.

[16] B Nelson and J Guth, 'Exploring the Gender Gap: Women, Men and Public Attitudes toward European Integration' (2000) 1 *European Union Politics* 267; J Citrin and J Sides, 'More than Nationals: How Identity Choice Matters in the New Europe' in RK Herrmann, T Risse and MB Brewer (eds), *Transnational Identities: Becoming European in the EU* (Lanham, MD, Rowman & Littlefield, 2004); T Risse, *A Community of Europeans? Transnational Identities and Public Spheres* (Ithaca, NY, Cornell University Press, 2010).

[17] An emphasis on the pro-Europe impact of cross-border mobility and transnational behaviours should not blind us to socialisation effects: a recent study on EU-oriented solidarity attests that these two types of antecedents tend to interact, see: I Ciornei and E Recchi, 'At the Source of European Solidarity: Assessing the Effects of Cross-border Practices and Political Attitudes' (2017) *JCMS: Journal of Common Market Studies* DOI: 10.1111/jcms.12507.

when a more marked effect was exerted by Spanish and Italian origin (the latter with a non-significant statistical difference).

In sum, European citizens who move from one EU Member State to another feel more European than their peers who spend their lives within the boundaries of their country of birth.[18] But freedom of movement does not exhaust the opportunities for interaction across national borders created by European integration and, simultaneously, globalisation. Mobility is only one of a broad set of transnational behaviours that can spill over into a stronger European identity. Eurobarometer 73 provides an opportunity to track down a large palette of transnational practices among Europeans, as it contains a series of dichotomous items on the basis of which I constructed an additive index of 'individual transnationalism'. Indicators were divided into three categories—*strong*, *moderate* and *weak*[19] transnational behaviours—assigning them different weights in the index (15 per cent, 10 per cent and 5 per cent):

— Had worked abroad for more than three months (15 per cent).
— Had studied abroad for more than three months (15 per cent).
— Had lived abroad for more than three months (for reasons other than work or study) (15 per cent).
— Had or had had a partner who was or had been a citizen of another country (15 per cent).
— Normally spent holidays abroad (10 per cent).

[18] Moreover, studies focusing on migrants in Europe indicate that intra-EU migrants tend to identify more with Europe than third-country nationals (A Roeder, 'Does Mobility Matter for Attitudes to Europe? A Multi-level Analysis of Immigrants' Attitudes to European Unification' (2011) 59 *Political Studies* 458; D Di Mauro and I Fiket, 'Discovering Europe? Identity of Migrants in the EU' in I Tarrósy, Á Tuka, Z Vörös and A Schmidt (eds), *European Integration: Perspectives and Challenges: How 'Borderless' is Europe?* (Pécs, University of Pécs, 2014). Van Mol shows that the association between mobility experiences and European identification holds even in case of relatively short settlements, like Erasmus grants (lasting no more than 12 months), see: C Van Mol, *Intra-European Student Mobility in International Higher Education Circuits: Europe on the Move* (Basingstoke, Palgrave, 2014). Finally, even among migrants (in the German case), it is found that 'those who are spatially more mobile are those identifying the most as European', see C Teney, L Hanquinet, and K Bürkin, 'Feeling European: An Exploration of Ethnic Disparities among Immigrants' (2016) 42 *Journal of Ethnic Migration Studies* 2182, 2193.

[19] This classification of transnational behaviours according to their intensity seems to be the best one possible given the indicators available in Eb73. In theoretical terms, I have elsewhere proposed a more composite classification which rests on a fundamental distinction between transnationalism practices which depend on *physical* mobility (long/brief residence abroad) and *virtual* mobility (personal/impersonal), see: E Recchi, 'Pathways to European Identity Formation: A Tale of Two Models' (2014) 27 *Innovation: The European Journal of Social Science Research* 119. Another classification distinguishes three dimensions of transnationalism relative to background, practices and human capital, see: T Kuhn 'Individual Transnationalism, Globalisation and Euroscepticism: An Empirical Test of Deutsch's Transactionalist Theory' (2011) 50 *European Journal of Political Research*. The human capital component is not strictly speaking a transnational behaviour, and remains thus outside the present analysis. At the same time, it is evident that knowledge of foreign languages is a *sine qua non* of individual transnationalism whose identitarian consequences deserve closer scrutiny, see: J Gerhards, *From Babel to Brussels. European Integration and the Importance of Transnational Linguistic* Capital (Berlin, Berlin Studies on the Sociology of Europe ((BSSE) No 28 Freie Universität Berlin, 2012).

— Owned property abroad (10 per cent).
— Had family members living abroad (5 per cent).
— Had friends living abroad (5 per cent).
— Regularly followed news about another country (5 per cent).
— Regularly cooked typical dishes of another country (5 per cent).

The index of individual transnationalism thus constructed varies from 0 (no transnational experience) to 20 (involvement in all transnational practices). Its distribution in the sample is, in fact, markedly unbalanced. Only 6.6 per cent of the interviewees record scores over 10, while fully 48.1 per cent record 2 (the median) or less. The average score is 3.04. Multivariate analysis[20] confirms that people in the upper class, with higher educational qualifications, younger, male, and resident in large cities, were likely to have higher scores. Moreover, not surprisingly, transnationalism was found to be more widespread among people living in the richest and most globalised countries.

Table 2 sets out the results of three multilevel logistic regression models used to test the hypothesis that international mobility and transnationalism influence the sense of belonging to the EU.[21] The first model does *not* include the independent variables of interest—that is, the experience of international mobility (having lived abroad for more than three months) and the individual transnationalism index—so as to highlight their separate explanatory power.

In general, multilevel models are used if it is believed that the parameters relative to the individual factors do not vary independently but according to patterns typical of the higher-order units—in the present case, countries. The analysis is thus able to account for a more complex variability compared with the non-hierarchical models employed previously, given the larger number of countries considered (the then 27 Member States of the EU).[22] It is also possible to control for a number of potentially significant context variables: in particular, the membership or otherwise of the residence country in the EU15, postulating that European identification is stronger the longer a country has been a Member State of the EU;[23] national demographic size, presuming that smaller states have a higher

[20] Not presented here: LG Baglioni and E Recchi, 'La classe media va in Europa? Transnazionalismo e stratificazione sociale nell'Unione Europea' (2013) *SocietàMutamentoPolitica* 47.

[21] Differently from previous models, in this analysis the 'international mobility' variable is not restricted to *current* mobility but also includes past experiences, and it is not limited to movements within the EU but to any possible foreign country. Moreover, the sample is the EU-wide Eurobarometer, and not a case-control combination of two different surveys as before. All this provides an even stronger test of the mobility–supranational identity link.

[22] In the logistic regression models estimated previously, by contrast, the number of countries was too small to use hierarchical models, see MR Steenbergen and BS Jones, 'Modeling Multilevel Data Structures' (2002) 46 *American Journal of Political Science* 218, 219. Moreover, EU movers and stayers share nationality but not residence: therefore, a common dependence on the context would have been an unrealistic assumption.

[23] S Nissen, 'European Identity and the Future of Europe' in M Bach, C Lahusen and G Vobruba (eds), *Europe in Motion: Social Dynamics and Political Institutions in an Enlarging Europe* (Berlin, Sigma, 2005).

Table 2: Mobility experiences, individual transnationalism and attachment to the EU in the EU population: multilevel logit regressions ('very attached' versus 'fairly, not very or not at all attached')

	Model 1	*Model 2*	*Model 3*
	Only control variables	**Past mobility abroad (≥ 3 months)**	**Individual transnationalism index**
Individual-level variables			
International mobility (≥ 3 months)		1.654***	
Individual transnationalism index			1.103***
Gender (= woman)	.885**	.902*	.896*
Age	.986*	.983*	.978**
Age (squared)	1.000	1.000	1.000
Education (ref: Low, up to 15)			
Middle (up to 16–19)	1.078	1.082	1.059
High (over 19)	1.496***	1.461***	1.339***
Social class (ref: Inactive)			
Bourgeoisie (I)	1.408**	.757*	.820
Salariat (II)	.856	.899	.960
Routine white-collar (III)	1.038	1.073	1.112
Petty bourgeoisie (IV)	.855	.895	.932
Working class (V–VI–VII)	1.063	1.106	1.155
Internet use (7 points scale)	1.068***	1.064***	1.048***
Local identification	1.347***	1.350***	1.340***
Region/county identification	1.808***	1.844***	1.916***
National identification	4.005***	4.084***	4.380***
Country level variables			
EU15 Member State	.736	.748	.824

(continued)

Table 2: ***(Continued)***

	Model 1	*Model 2*	*Model 3*
	Only control variables	**Past mobility abroad (≥ 3 months)**	**Individual transnationalism index**
Population (thousands)	1.000	1.000	1.000
Gdp per capita (thousands, $)	1.000	1.000	1.000
Unemployment rate	1.000	.998	.996
Globalisation index (Kof)	1.004	1.004	1.005
Intercept	.017	.014	.013
Variance of random intercept	.506	.513	.507
Log-likelihood	−7708.84	−7664.49	−7561.52
Wald chi-square	1184.82	1259.70	1414.60

Source: Eurobarometer 73 (2010). n = 26,582, N = 27.

Note: * $p < .05$, ** $p < .01$, *** $p < .001$. Coefficients are odds ratios

interest in European integration;[24] per capita income and the unemployment rate, given the greater utility deriving to economically weaker countries from EU membership;[25] and the country's level of globalisation (measured with the KOF index), on the assumption that societal openness to the global dimension creates a climate conducive to supranational identities.[26]

None of the national-level variables included in the models proves significant. To single out the conditions under which a more solid European identification develops therefore requires shifting the focus to factors operating at the individual level. The model also includes an additional variable measuring the frequency of internet use among the interviewees. Although not a direct expression

[24] R Steinmetz and A Wivel, *Small States in Europe: Challenges and Opportunities* (Farnham, Ashgate, 2010).

[25] RC Eichenberg and RJ Dalton, 'Europeans and the European Union: the Dynamics of Public Support for European Integration' (1993) 47 *International Organization* 507; M Gabel and H Palmer, 'Understanding Variation in Public Support for European Integration' (1995) 27 *European Journal of Political Research* 3.

[26] JK Jung, 'Growing Supranational Identities in a Globalising World? A Multilevel Analysis of the World Values Surveys' (2008) 47 *European Journal of Political Research* 578; W Haller and V Roudometof, 'The Cosmopolitan–Local Continuum in a Cross-National Perspective' (2010) 46 *Journal of Sociology* 277.

of transnationalism (the web can be used to search for local information), the fact that this variable is significantly associated with a stronger attachment to the EU seems to bear out the central hypothesis that activities spanning over national borders foster a sense of supranational identification.

This hypothesis is decidedly corroborated when the experience of (past or current) mobility abroad (model 2) and the individual transnationalism index (model 3) are introduced. The effect of each of these variables is markedly positive and significant. But that of transnationalism, including a range of practices wider than only sojourns in another country, is even stronger—when comparing the coefficients, consider that 'mobility' is a dichotomy, while the transnationalism index varies on a 20-points scale. It is also noteworthy that the model including the social transnationalism index has a better overall fit, but the significance of upper-class membership and urban-metropolitan residence disappears. Moreover, once the social transnationalism index is introduced, the effect of education diminishes. It seems likely that in the first model the large part of class and education effects 'incorporated' transnationalism, which thus emerges as a more direct cause of supranational identification.

Overall, evidence presented in this section resonates with other analyses carried out in parallel with different datasets and modelling. Examining Eurobarometer data relative to support for the EU and data relative to the transnational practices of Europeans, Fligstein noted that the same social categories—young people, more highly educated individuals and members of the upper social strata—figure among the most pro-Europe *and* transnational citizens.[27] However, because his analysis was conducted on separate data, he was unable to prove that the two phenomena were indeed associated (ie, that the supporters of European integration and the Europeans with the most experience of mobility were the same people). A German pioneer study found that cross-border mobility and practices go hand-in-hand with cosmopolitan[28] identification. Interestingly, another German study indicates that the transnationalism–cosmopolitanism association is stronger among ordinary citizens than it is in the elite.[29] This probably reflects a ceiling effect, as the members of the elite are homogenously highly transnational.[30]

[27] N Fligstein, *Euroclash: The EU, European Identity, and the Future of Europe* (Oxford, Oxford University Press, 2008).

[28] S Mau, J Mewes and A Zimmermann, 'Cosmopolitan Attitudes Through Transnational Social Practices?' (2008) 8 *Global Networks* 1.

[29] M Helbling and C Teney, 'The Cosmopolitan Elite in Germany: Transnationalism and Postmaterialism' (2015) 15 *Global Networks* 446.

[30] It is worth noting that, both in the general public and the elites, cosmopolitanism does not come at the expense of local identities, see: V Roudometof, 'Transnationalism, Cosmopolitanism and Glocalization' (2005) 53 *Current Sociology* 113; P Gustafson, 'More Cosmopolitan, No Less Local—The Orientations of International Travellers' (2009) 11 *European Societies* 25. Local and global identifications are not incompatible and can be nested one into the other, see: J Díez Medrano and P Gutiérrez, 'Nested Identities: National and European Identity in Spain' (2001) 24 *Ethnic and Racial Studies* 753; Risse (n 16). Qualitative studies of European upper-middle classes confirm the coexistence of international travels, migration experiences, and foreign friendships with a persistent focus on the issues,

The most powerful study on the transnationalism-Europeanness association is, however, Kuhn's.[31] Her point of departure is an apparent inconsistency: at the aggregate level, transnational contacts have proliferated in Europe since the 1970s, while support for European institutions has stagnated, with some trendless fluctuations. In fact, the transnationalism-European identification association is incontrovertible at the individual level, but it does not show up in aggregate terms because it is strongly stratified. In other words, the rise in the volume of transnational activities is disproportionately due to privileged social strata, a group that also expresses strong support for the EU. Kuhn's analysis reveals that transnational practices (hinged on cross-border mobility) sustain European identification (and EU support) more than a transnational background and transnational human capital. Moreover, EU-based transnational practices affect pro-EU attitudes more than experiences of transnationalism that are geographically anchored outside the European space. Finally, the transnationalism-EU identification association is accentuated in the most globalised European countries, where highly transnational individuals are more 'Europhile' and 'non-transnationals' are more vigorously 'Eurosceptic', possibly feeling marginalised and threatened by European integration.

III. CONCLUSION

Collective politico-territorial identification is a pre-condition for the legitimacy of any political order—and all the more so of democracies. The EU has suffered from this legitimacy deficit for a long time. Is free movement an antidote to such inherent fragility? And what about cross-national practices that do not imply population resettlement but make nonetheless people move physically or virtually from one country to another? In the theoretical section of this chapter (section I), I have mobilised existing literature to argue that intra-EU migration and individual transnationalism are likely predictors of enhanced identification with Europe. In the empirical section (section II), I have shown that mass surveys—some of which were analysed in greater detail—corroborate such theoretical expectations.

However, these findings must be placed in perspective: Intra-EU mobility and individual transnationalism remain minority phenomena and this puts a brake on their culturally integrating effects, in two senses. First, demographically: individuals who have an opportunity to enlarge their 'space-sets' to a EU-wide scale are still a tiny proportion of the European population. In particular, free

debates, and identities of the place of residence (M Savage et al, *Globalisation and Belonging* (Thousand Oaks, CA, Sage, 2004); A Andreotti, P Le Galès, and FJ Moreno-Fuentes, *Globalised Minds, Roots in the City: Urban Upper-middle Classes in Europe* (Oxford, Wiley & Sons, 2014).

[31] T Kuhn, *Experiencing European Integration: Transnational Lives and European Identity* (Oxford, Oxford University Press, 2015).

movement can be an engine of 'Europeanness', but its horsepower so far has not been sufficient to act as a locomotive of further identitarian integration. Second, ideologically: because the stratified nature of intra-EU mobility and transnational practices (involving mostly the highly educated, young and more privileged strata of the population) generates an anti-mobility reaction in the most sedentary part of the citizenry. One of Kuhn's findings mentioned above—which she appropriately terms 'the Janus face' of expanding transnationalism[32]—warns that a legitimacy crisis can also be triggered by unintended backlash effects of a more mobile world. Mobility can bring about a divide between an ever more globalised upper class and a comparatively localised mass resenting the lack of transnationally generated opportunities. This 'local–cosmopolitan' polarisation, well known to classic American sociology,[33] may regain salience on a larger scale. Differences in social transnationalism lie at the roots of the politically relevant divide between 'winners and losers of globalization'.[34] In attitudinal terms, these may be mirrored in the emerging 'cosmopolitanism–sovereigntism' ideological struggle that, around the theme of the permeability of nation-state borders, is supplanting the traditionalism–libertarianism dialectic in advanced societies.[35]

Such tension is echoed in the 'boundary work' that permeates EU politics and that migration flows—especially when they reach an extraordinary intensity, as during the asylum-seekers' crisis of 2015–16 in Europe—magnify. Citizenship is inherently exclusive, and European citizenship is no exception. Inflows of aliens reinforce the salience of the 'us versus them' frame of political life in the populace, especially among those who do not share transnational practices themselves and who are the prime supporters of the 'Fortress Europe' philosophy of migration policies.[36] The less mobile are likely to accentuate mobility as an all-encompassing threat, ultimately willing to get away with all legal foundations to transnational behaviours—including the EU free movement regime. As the 'local versus cosmopolitan' divide grows larger, free movement becomes an easy target for right- and left-wing nostalgics of an idealised, more protective, state-centred world.

[32] ibid 127.

[33] AW Gouldner, 'Cosmopolitans and Locals: Toward an Analysis of Latent Social Roles. I' (1957) 2 *Administrative Science Quarterly* 281; R Merton, *Social Theory and Social Structure* (Glencoe, Free Press, 1968 [1957]) 368ff.

[34] H Kriesi et al, *West European Politics in the Age of Globalization* (Cambridge, Cambridge University Press, 2008).

[35] A Azmanova, 'After the Left–Right (Dis)continuum: Globalization and the Remaking of Europe's Ideological Geography' (2011) 5 *International Political Sociology* 384.

[36] A Geddes, *Immigration and European Integration: Beyond Fortress Europe*, 2nd edn (Manchester, Manchester University Press, 2008).

8

European Citizenship and Transnational Rights: Chronicles of a Troubled Narrative

FRANCESCA STRUMIA

I. INTRODUCTION

BORDERS, THE INTERNAL ones among the Member States, have an inconsistent texture in the European Union (EU). They are both open and closed. Guarded and forgotten. What they mark is not clear any more, except in one sense. They mark the difference between the experience of the third-country national migrants, whether the resident foreign worker, the passing tourist, or the asylum seeker, and the experience of the citizens, the European citizens. The former can be stopped and questioned at borders. They have to evidence, respectively, their right to stay, their plans to return home, their claims for international protection. The latter can be stopped. But they cannot be questioned as to their intention to stay, to go, to return.

This is the difference between immigration and free movement of persons. The former is a privilege granted by a State. The latter is a right enjoyed by a citizen. The interpretation of this right, as codified in the Treaties and in secondary EU legislation, has yielded a narrative of transnational rights that characterises European supranational citizenship as a status of belonging across national borders. This narrative is one of the most revolutionary achievements of European integration. It alters the traditional paradigms of immigration law. It consolidates and constitutionalises rights that have at best been sketched in international law. It both stretches and constrains national sovereignty, transforming the boundaries of citizenship and altering the roots of jurisdiction.

Yet this narrative of transnational rights has become contested in Europe. Populist political discourse in several corners of the EU advances ideas of closure and rebounded national citizenship that directly contrast with the former narrative.[1] The UK decision to 'Brexit' the EU can be seen as a rejection of

[1] See 'Drawbridges Up—The New Divide in Rich Countries is not between Left and Right but between Open and Closed' *The Economist* (30 July 2016).

transnational law and the rights that it implies.[2] And overall the interests of free movement and transnational solidarity underpinning the narrative of transnational rights are in a phase of retreat.[3] The narrative appears thus under threat of implosion. This calls for taking stock of its main tenets as well as its vulnerabilities, and for an assessment of its prospects. This chapter undertakes this exercise. It does so by comparing and contrasting discourses on, respectively, transnational rights and state discretion that transpire from judicial cases, legal texts and policy debates. Whilst comprehensive discourse analysis of the relevant sources is beyond the scope and objective of the chapter, its methodological aim is to narrate,[4] beyond the substance of the legal rules, the principles and preferences that they express.[5]

The first section introduces the narrative of transnational rights and considers the role of the Court of Justice of the European Union (CJEU) in weaving its main threads. The second section traces the recent evolution of this narrative. It analyses a few hybrid sub-narratives that the intersection of different political and judicial discourses has produced; and it weighs the ransom to which threats of secession subject the narrative of rights across borders. The last section focuses on the endogenous and exogenous limits of the rights narrative, laid bare by the evolutions highlighted in the previous section. And it examines the challenges and the questions that these limits pose, in the optic of preserving the narrative from eventual demise.

II. THE COURT OF JUSTICE AND THE NARRATIVE OF TRANSNATIONAL RIGHTS

The role of the CJEU in 'putting flesh on the bones' of European citizenship has been told in many ways and from several perspectives.[6] It is in judicial hands that a rather succinct list of citizenship rights has acquired a life of its own. And that a newborn concept has been glorified through the promise that it would become the 'fundamental status' for nationals of the Member States as well as the harbinger of a 'minimum degree of financial solidarity' among the Member

[2] R Michaels, 'Does Brexit Spell the Death of Transnational Law?' (2016) 17 (Brexit Supplement) *German Law Journal* 52.

[3] See, eg, C O'Brien, '*Civis Capitalist Sum*: Class as the New Guiding Principle of EU Free Movement Rights' (2016) 53 *CML Rev* 937. But see *Standard Eurobarometer 86*, Autumn 2016, 24 (suggesting that an 80% majority of the respondents has a positive view of free movement of persons).

[4] On the methodology of legal storytelling see, F Di Donato 'Constructing Legal Narratives: Client–Lawyers Stories in A Wagner and L Cheng (eds), *Exploring Courtroom Discourse—The Language of Power and Control* (London, Routledge, 2016) 111.

[5] Also see F Strumia, 'European Citizenship and EU Immigration: A Demoi-cratic Bridge between the Third Country Nationals' Right to Belong and the Member States' Power to Exclude' (2016) 22 *European Law Journal* (*ELJ*) 417.

[6] See S O'Leary, 'Putting Flesh on the Bones of European Union Citizenship' (1999) 24 *EL Rev* 68.

States and their nationals.[7] The Court's stance on European citizenship has been described, depending on the points of view, as constitutionalising or federalist,[8] market-prone,[9] or overly activist.[10] There is no question that the alchemy of supranational citizenship and free movement of persons has produced its most creative results through the jurisprudence of the Court. In particular, the Court, through its combined interpretation of Union citizenship and right to free movement, has weaved a strong narrative of rights across borders, that challenges some of the main tenets of national sovereignty, as well as immigration law.[11]

The beneficiaries of this narrative of transnational rights are, first of all, second-country nationals, that is, European citizens who exercise their right to move across the borders of the Member States. They enjoy a right to reside in any other Member State;[12] a right to be treated equally with nationals— through this guarantee of equal treatment, the narrative of rights across borders has come to embrace also non-economically active European citizens;[13]—a right to export entitlements, benefits, identities between a Member State of nationality and a Member State of residence.[14]

The narrative of rights across borders also embraces third-country nationals (TCNs) who have a family relation with a European citizen.[15] TCNs derive from European citizen family members' rights to reside in a host Member State together with their sponsor European citizen;[16] rights to return to the sponsor European citizen's Member State of origin;[17] as well as autonomous rights to remain in a

[7] See, eg ECJ, Case C-413/99 *Baumbast and R v Secretary of State for the Home Department*, EU:C:2002:493; ECJ, Case C-184/99 *Rudy Grzelczyk v Centre public d'aide sociale d'Ottignies-Louvain-la-Neuve*, EU:C:2001:458.

[8] See, eg F De Cecco, 'Fundamental Freedoms, Fundamental Rights and the Scope of Free Movement Law' (2014) 15 *German Law Journal* 383; M Dougan, 'The Constitutional Dimension to the Case Law on Union Citizenship' (2006) 31 *EL Rev* 613.

[9] See, from different perspectives, M Everson, 'A Citizenship in Movement' (2014) 15 *German Law Journal* 965, 967; D Kochenov, 'The Citizenship Paradigm' (2012/13) 15 *Cambridge Yearbook of European Legal Studies* 197; N Nic Shuibne, 'The Resilience of EU Market Citizenship' (2010) 47 *CML Rev* 1597.

[10] See, eg K Hailbronner, 'Union Citizenship and the Access to Social Benefits' (2005) 42 *CML Rev* 1245. But see M Dougan, 'The Bubble that Burst' in M Adams et al (eds), *Judging Europe's Judges: The Legitimacy of the Case Law of the European Court of Justice* (Oxford, Hart Publishing, 2013).

[11] For the development of this argument, see Strumia, 'European Citizenship and EU Immigration' (n 5).

[12] Parliament and Council Directive 2004/38/EC of 29 April 2004 on the right of the citizens of the Union and their family members to move and reside freely within the territory of the Member States [2004] OJ L158/77 (Citizenship Directive) Arts 6–7.

[13] *Grzelczyk* (n 7); ECJ, Case C-456/02 *Michel Trojani v Centre public d'aide sociale de Bruxelles (CPAS)*, EU:C:2004:488.

[14] See, eg, ECJ, Case C-499/06 *Halina Nerkowska v Zakład Ubezpieczeń Społecznych Oddział w Koszalinie*, EU:C:2008:300; ECJ, Case C-148/02 *Carlos Garcia Avello v Belgian State*, EU:C:2003:539.

[15] Strumia, 'European Citizenship and EU Immigration' (n 5) 421–23.

[16] See Citizenship Directive (n 12). Also see ECJ, Case C-200/02 *Kunqian Catherine Zhu and Man Lavette Chen v Secretary of State for the Home Department*, EU:C:2004:639.

[17] ECJ, Case C-456/12 *O v Minister voor Immigratie, Integratie en Asiel and Minister voor Immigratie, Integratie en Asiel v B*, EU:C:2014:13.

host Member State, and continue their lives there, after dissolution of a family relation in qualifying circumstances.[18]

Echoes of the narrative of rights across borders have even overcome the joint venture between citizenship and free movement and come to bear on static European citizens. The *Ruiz Zambrano* doctrine,[19] revived in a set of recent judgments,[20] talks of a substance of European citizenship that cannot be interfered with even in purely internal situations. Protection of the genuine enjoyment of this substance of supranational citizenship may dictate in certain situations rights across borders for TCN parent caretakers of minor European citizens.

In all the above-described instances, the narrative that the Court has weaved around European citizenship speaks of rights across borders. Relevant rights limit the discretion that States traditionally retain in the context of immigration and nationality law, and more broadly in respect to decisions on the management of borders and admission and exclusion of aliens within their communities. The Citizenship Directive, in defining the European citizens' 'right of entry', refers to an obligation of the Member States to grant 'leave to enter'.[21] Beyond the legislative definition, in the Court's case law the rights recognised to second-country nationals and TCNs in the penumbra of European citizenship correspond to a limitation to Member States' discretion in admitting and excluding non-nationals.[22] Relevant limitations extend also to the power of the Member States with regard to the grant and withdrawal of nationality. Whilst relevant powers remain an exclusive competence of the Member States, the Court has repeatedly found that they have to be exercised 'having due regard to EU law'.[23] This means that the discretion of the Member States in deciding who should and should not be considered a national is constrained by the need to take into account rights descending from EU law and, particularly, rights of European citizens.[24]

European citizenship's narrative thus posits, albeit only in a discrete set of situations, the existence of an individual right to cross national borders. In this sense, on the one hand it lends some support to arguments in favour of the existence of a human right to free movement.[25] On the other hand, it contrasts with a competing narrative exalting the discretion of sovereign nation-states in matters of immigration and nationality. The latter narrative is well supported in both international law and political philosophy. International law recognises unfettered discretion to

[18] Citizenship Directive (n 12) Arts 12–13; also see ECJ, Case C-218/14 *Kuldip Singh and Others v Minister for Justice and Equality* [2015] EU:C:2015:476.

[19] ECJ, Case C-34/09 *Gerardo Ruiz Zambrano v Office national de l'emploi (ONEm)*, EU:C:2011:124.

[20] See ECJ, Case C-165/14 *Alfredo Rendón Marín v Administración del Estado*, EU:C:2016:675; ECJ, Case C-115/15 *Secretary of State for the Home Department v NA*, EU:C:2016:487; ECJ, Case C-304/14 *Secretary of State for the Home Department v CS*, EU:C:2016:674.

[21] Citizenship Directive (n 12) Art 5.

[22] Strumia, 'European Citizenship and EU Immigration' (n 5) 426–28.

[23] See, eg ECJ, Case C-135/08 *Janko Rottmann v Freistaat Bayern*, EU:C:2010:104, para 32.

[24] ibid para 56. Also see Strumia, 'European Citizenship and EU Immigration' (n 5) 426–27.

[25] See, eg J Carens, *The Ethics of Immigration* (Oxford, Oxford University Press 2013) 225–54.

sovereign states to decide on the admission and exclusion of aliens, as well as to manage the borders of their territorial and political communities.[26] This sovereign power to include and exclude finds several justifications in political philosophy. Sovereign states are entitled to a measure of closure in order to protect a sustainable system of distributive justice, a communal set of scarce resources, as well as their cultural and political identity.[27] This interest in closure, and the narrative of discretion that it underpins, also have a reflection in EU law. The right to free movement of European citizens in fact admits of several limits to make room for the legitimate interests of the Member States: interests in protecting public policy, public health, public security and, crucially for purposes of current debates, the viability of the Member States' finances.[28] These interests are however construed as exceptions to the narrative of rights revolving around European citizenship.

Table 1: Competing narratives

	Second Country Nationals	**TCNs**
Rights narrative	Free movement rights	Derivative rights across borders
Discretion narrative	Discretionary exceptions to free movement rights (public policy, public security, public health, public finances etc)	Discretionary admission and exclusion through immigration and nationality regulation

This narrative of transnational rights, to which the CJEU has given the strongest prompt, resonates in part in national courts.[29] It also resonates to some extent in political discourse, where it contributes to animate both supporters and detractors from free movement of persons, at a time when the right that was once considered a European 'dream' appears to have turned, from many perspectives, into a 'nightmare'.[30] An example emerges in the media diatribe, in the aftermath of the UK EU referendum, between UK foreign secretary Boris Johnson and MEP Guy Verhofstadt. Whilst the former derided the fundamental rights nature of free movement across borders, even in the context of the European project, the latter

[26] See, eg Human Rights Committee, General Comment 15, 'The Position of Aliens under the Covenant' HRI/GEN/1/Rev.9 (Vol I).

[27] See, eg M Walzer, *Spheres of Justice: A Defense of Pluralism and Equality* (New York, Basic Books, 1983); D Miller, 'Immigration: The Case for Limits' in A Cohen and C Wellman (eds), *Contemporary Debates in Applied Ethics*, 2nd edn (Malden, Blackwell, 2014); also see Strumia, 'European Citizenship and EU Immigration (n 5) 434–35.

[28] Citizenship Directive (n 12) Arts 14 and 27.

[29] For a Belgian example, see F Strumia, 'Ruiz Zambrano's Quiet Revolution: Four Hundred and Sixty-Eight Days that Made the Immigration Case of One Deprived Worker into the Constitutional Case of Two Precarious Citizens' in B Davies and F Nicola (eds), *EU Law Stories: Contextual and Critical Histories of European Jurisprudence* (Cambridge, Cambridge University Press, 2017).

[30] See Editorial Comments, 'Free Movement of Persons in the European Union: Salvaging the Dream Whilst Explaining the Nightmare' (2015) 51 *CML Rev* 729.

declared ready to pull out the Treaty of Rome and point Mr Johnson to the very source of that right in the lines of the Treaty.[31]

Ultimately, the narrative of rights that the cases have developed around supranational citizenship places the substance of this latter citizenship in a status of belonging across national borders.[32] This status grounds a complex set of transnational rights. An architecture of obligations of mutual recognition supports these transnational rights. European citizenship grounds the obligation, on the part of the Member States, to recognise the choices of naturalisation and grant of nationality of other Member States; as well as the obligation to recognise nationals of those other Member States, who choose to reside within their borders, as part members of their communities and beneficiaries of their obligations as providers of citizenship, on equal terms with their own nationals. European citizenship also grounds obligations of recognition on the part of the citizens themselves: obligations to recognise nationals of other Member States as part members of their ingroup of citizens, and as potential addressees of their duties of communal solidarity.[33]

But recent twists and turns unveil the reluctance of the Member States, and their citizens, to take on these obligations of recognition. This reluctance points to the unsteady ground, on which the transnational rights' narrative ultimately rests.

III. A WAVERING NARRATIVE

Two evolutions in particular threaten the stability of the narrative of transnational rights. From a first perspective, recent judicial and policy choices at the supranational as well as national level have tended to blur the line between narrative of rights and narrative of discretion, yielding unexpected hybrids. From a second perspective, the withdrawal from the European Union of a Member State, following the UK EU referendum,[34] threatens to silence without appeal the transnational rights of several European citizens.

A. Hybrid Narratives

A first hybrid derives from recent turns in the Court's jurisprudence. In a string of recent cases the Court seems to have revisited some of its holdings on free

[31] For an account, see: uk.businessinsider.com/boris-johnson-making-impossible-brexit-promises-article-50-2016-11.

[32] Strumia, 'European Citizenship and EU Immigration' (n 5) 439; also see F Strumia 'Supranational Citizenship' in A Shachar, R Bauböck, M Vink and I Bloemraad (eds), *Oxford Handbook of Citizenship* (Oxford, Oxford University Press, 2017).

[33] Strumia, 'Supranational Citizenship' (n 32).

[34] On 23 June 2016, British nationals expressed a 52% preference for leaving the European Union in a referendum consultation.

movement of non-economically active citizens, increasingly yielding to the Member States' discretion to protect their public finances. Such discretion has always been a feature of EU law: free movement has never been a right for everyone and has always been conditional.[35] However, the Court in its 'classic' jurisprudence on citizenship has been the most vocal actor in stretching the right to free movement in both depth and breadth, also against Member States' signals and preferences.[36]

The Court's change of trend begins in 2010 with the *Brey* ruling.[37] In *Brey*, the Court ruled that the claim of a German pensioner for a pension supplement paid by the government of Austria—where he resided—could not be automatically denied on the basis that the claimant was not economically sufficient. Denial required a prior assessment of the claimant's individual circumstances.[38] At first sight, the Court maintained a protective approach towards the rights of the not economically active claimant. However, it clarified in a dictum that nothing prevents Member States from subjecting the eligibility of not economically active Union citizens for social benefits to a test of legal residence.[39] This dictum, whilst arguably well supported in EU Treaty and secondary law,[40] represented a first important concession to the narrative of Member States' discretion. In subsequent cases, the Court went further in recognising a margin of discretion to the Member States in excluding not economically active European citizens. In *Dano*, the Court concluded that two Romanian nationals living on benefits in Germany, without ever having worked or studied in the host country, did not meet the legal requirements to reside in a host Member State under Directive 2004/38.[41] A contrary finding—according to the Court—would have denied the legitimate interest of the Member States in protecting themselves against undue burdens on their finances.[42] The Court lent further credit to the narrative of discretion in *Alimanovic* and *García-Nieto*.[43] In these two cases, the Court qualified its *Brey* ruling, holding that, respectively, in the case of jobseekers, and in the case of migrant Union citizens in the first three months of residence in a host Member State, a claim for social assistance can be automatically denied without further individual assessments. From a different perspective, but in the same direction of giving room to Member States' discretion, the Court upheld in June 2016 the UK ordinary residence test for the grant of social benefits

[35] See, eg Council Directive 90/364/EEC of 28 June 1990 on the right of residence [1990] OJ L180; Citizenship Directive (n 12) Art 7.

[36] See, eg, *Baumbast* (n 7); *Grzelczyk* (n 7). Also see S Schmidt, chapter 2 in this book on the 'over-constitutionalisation' of free movement on the part of the Court of Justice.

[37] ECJ, Case C-140/12 *Pensionsversicherungsanstalt v Peter Brey*, EU:C:2013:565.

[38] ibid.

[39] ibid para 44.

[40] See Treaty on the Functioning of the European Union [2016] OJ C202, Art 21; also see Citizenship Directive (n 12) Art 14.

[41] ECJ, Case C-333/13 *Elisabeta Dano and Florin Dano v Jobcenter Leipzig*, EU:C:2014:2358.

[42] ibid para 74.

[43] ECJ, Case C-67/14 *Jobcenter Berlin Neukölln v Nazifa Alimanovic and Others*, EU:C:2015:597; ECJ, Case C-299/14 *Vestische Arbeit Jobcenter Kreis Recklinghausen v Jovanna García-Nieto and Others*, EU:C:2016:114.

to migrant Union citizens.[44] This line of cases has been hailed as a reversal of the Court's traditional position protective of rights of free movement and as a betrayal of some of the Court's main tenets.[45] Truth to be told, the Court is indeed partially retreating from its most daring pro-free movement stances; however it is moving within the boundaries of EU Treaty and secondary law. Relevant law, as noted above, has always subjected free movement to limits and conditions. It is undeniable, however, that the Court is watering down its narrative of transnational rights and blending it with the narrative of Member States' discretion. A strange hybrid is born as a result, that casts European citizenship under a crepuscular light.

This is not the sole hybrid that the blending of competing narratives yields. A second one results, rather than from judicial evolutions, from policy choices at Member States' level. Several Member States have enacted in the last decade 'golden residence' and 'golden passport' programmes. Relevant programmes award, respectively, residence or nationality on a fast-track basis to desirable TCNs. In particular, the beneficiaries of these programmes are investors and promising entrepreneurs, who commit to invest capital in the economy of the host country, or to use it as a hub to develop a viable business idea.[46] Beneficiaries are offered a shortcut to European citizenship, and its corollary transnational rights. The transnational rights that come with European citizenship are in fact one of the core prizes with which Member States lure potential applicants.[47]

This is particularly true for golden passport programmes, under whose terms qualifying applicants are awarded nationality directly, and with it, European citizenship. Malta and Cyprus have been pioneers in the European Union in this respect. Malta introduced its Individual Investor Programme in 2014.[48] After reforms prompted by a row with the European Commission,[49] the scheme now provides for the grant of a Maltese passport in exchange for a combined investment of €1,150,000 into the Maltese economy, 70 per cent of which is to be contributed to a National Development and Social Fund.[50] Applicants are also required to provide proof of their residence in Malta.[51] Cyprus sells its citizenship

[44] ECJ, Case C-308/14 *European Commission v United Kingdom of Great Britain and Northern Ireland*, EU:C:2016:436. In this case, the Court clarified that the Member States' margin of appreciation in assessing the legality of residence before awarding benefits covers not only social assistance, but also social security benefits.

[45] See D Thym, 'The Elusive Limits of Solidarity: Residence Rights of and Social Benefits for Economically Inactive Union Citizens' (2015) 52 *CML Rev* 17; O'Brien (n 3) 937.

[46] See F Strumia, 'New-generation Skilled Migration Policies and the Changing Fabric of Membership: Talent as Output and the Headhunting State' (2016) 4 *Investment Migration Working Paper*: investmentmigration.org/download/new-generation-skilled-migration-policies-changing-fabric-membership-talent-output-headhunting-state/.

[47] See, eg Brochure for the Malta Individual Investor Programme: iip.gov.mt/wp-content/uploads/2014/07/IIP-Brochure-v1.2_updated.pdf.

[48] Individual Investor Programme of the Republic of Malta Regulations, Legal Notice 47 of 2014: iip.gov.mt/wp-content/uploads/2014/02/LN-47-2014.pdf.

[49] See Joint Press Statement of the European Commission and the Maltese Authorities on Malta's Individual Investor Programme (IIP), 29 January 2014: europa.eu/rapid/press-release_MEMO-14-70_en.htm.

[50] Individual Investor Programme of the Republic of Malta Regulations (n 28).

[51] ibid Art 4.

at a much higher prize, as it requires an investment of at least €5,000,000 in one of a variety of qualifying instruments.[52] Qualifying investors are not required to reside in Cyprus. The Maltese and Cypriot schemes are not isolated phenomena. Similar schemes have been adopted in several Member States.[53] In some cases, relevant schemes rely on mechanisms less transparent than the Maltese and Cypriot ones. Through legal provisions allowing discretionary grants of citizenship, these schemes offer national passports, and European citizenship rights, in exchange for qualifying contributions to the national economy.[54]

It is not a novelty that States use immigration and nationality regulation to reward particularly desirable migrants.[55] And it is not a novelty that in conjunction with the effort to attract these talented migrants States give away some of their discretion in managing migration.[56] What is novel is that several Member States, in the very exercise of their discretionary power to include and exclude, have come to appropriate the narrative of transnational rights to serve their own interests. The web of transnational rights weaved through the CJEU's interpretation of EU law becomes the hook to catch wealthy, or talented migrants. Sovereign discretion is exercised precisely to fast-track relevant migrants into the status of cross-border belonging that European citizenship brings about. In signing up in this way to the narrative of transnational rights, albeit for the purpose of furthering specific sovereign interests, Member States contribute to revitalise the same narrative. And ultimately, narrative of rights and narrative of discretion become intertwined in a further, unexpected hybrid.

Table 2: Hybrid narratives

	Discretion	**Rights**
Member States	Narrative of discretion—exceptions to free movement; immigration and nationality law	Hybrid narrative of rights—discretionary award of transnational rights
CJEU	Hybrid narrative of discretion—case law yielding to discretionary exceptions	Narrative of rights—Rights to free movement for SCN; derivative rights for TCNs

[52] Scheme for Naturalisation of Investors in Cyprus by Exception: www.moi.gov.cy/moi/moi.nsf/All/1562764E412F7B6DC2257B80005235CF.

[53] For an overview, see J Dzankic, 'Investment-based citizenship and residence programmes in the EU' (2015) 8 RSCAS/EUDO Working Paper: cadmus.eui.eu/bitstream/handle/1814/34484/RSCAS_2015_08.pdf.

[54] ibid.

[55] For examples from the Kingdom of Italy in the 19th century see S Donati, *A Political History of National Citizenship and Identity in Italy, 1861–1950* (Palo Alto, CA, Stanford University Press, 2013) 87.

[56] To some extent, this was the case also with the European guest worker programmes of the 1950s and 1960s. For an overview see S Castles et al, *The Age of Migration*, 5th edn (Basingstoke, Palgrave Macmillan, 2014) 103–08.

B. Narratives Held to Ransom

Beyond the hybridisation that cross-appropriation of competing narratives has induced, European citizenship's narrative of transnational rights has come to face a further challenge. On 23 June 2016, 52 per cent of the voters in the UK EU referendum expressed a preference in favour of the UK leaving the European Union. The results of the popular consultation sparked political conflicts, social unrest and legal quandaries.[57] At the time of writing, it is expected that the UK Government will invoke Article 50 of the Treaty on European Union and begin the formal negotiations for withdrawal during the first part of 2017. Beyond the political contingencies, the Brexit saga reveals an Achilles heel of the CJEU narrative of rights. This narrative, it seems, is ultimately held to ransom by the decisions of governments at the international level, whether supported or not by popular majorities.[58] This condition raises questions as to the status of the transnational rights narrative from both a political and a legal perspective.

From a political perspective, questions arise as to the legitimacy of the silencing of transnational rights through 'the voice of others'.[59] This is in effect what happened with the UK EU referendum. The voice of a majority of the voters, but a bare minority of the UK population, sparked the decision to prospectively silence the supranational citizenship and the transnational rights of the entire UK population.[60] One can argue, and it has been extensively argued, that this is simply democracy making its course. In democratic consultations, the winner takes all. However, the result is particularly troubling in this case, as what the winner takes is not simply a bunch of seats in Parliament, the leadership of government for a number of years, or even a momentous decision in economic and political terms. What the winner takes is, rather, the right of each British national to have transnational rights through supranational citizenship.[61] The right to have rights through national citizenship could not be collectively taken away just as easily. International law entails protection of the right to a nationality, as well as safeguards against statelessness and collective expulsion.[62] Supranational

[57] For the legal quandaries see *R (on the application of Miller and another) (Respondents) v Secretary of State for Exiting the European Union (Appellant)* [2017] UKSC 5.

[58] See F Strumia, 'Brexiting European Citizenship through the Voice of Others' (2016) 17 (Brexit Supplement) *German Law Journal* 109. Article 50 of the Treaty on European Union [2016] OJ C202, prescribing the process for withdrawal of a Member State, refers to the decision to withdraw being made in accordance with the relevant Member State's constitutional requirements.

[59] Strumia, 'Brexiting European Citizenship' (n 58).

[60] Votes cast for 'leave' were 17,410,742 versus 16,141,241 votes cast for 'remain', out of a total electorate of 46,500,001: www.electoralcommission.org.uk/find-information-by-subject/elections-and-referendums/past-elections-and-referendums/ex^u-referendum/electorate-and-count-information.

[61] Strumia, 'Brexiting European Citizenship' (n 58).

[62] For the right to a nationality, see Universal Declaration of Human Rights, Art 15; for the prohibition of collective expulsion see, eg, European Convention of Human Rights Protocol no 4, Article 4. On statelessness, see Convention on the Reduction of Cases of Statelessness, 30 August 1961: www.unhcr.org/3bbb286d8.html.

citizenship enjoys no comparable protection and can thus be taken away at the diktat of political voice, without any appeal, and without any required individual consent, as a majority is sufficient to strip citizenship from all. As a paradox, its inherent narrative of rights across borders that grew to contrast governmental discretion, is left at the mercy of that very governmental discretion, and of the political process empowering governmental decisions. It is true that a unanimous governmental decision expressed in the Treaties was ultimately at the root of the narrative of transnational rights. However, that narrative has bred on the notion that the EU's subjects are not only the governments, but also the peoples of the Member States. Hence the democratic paradox.

Relatedly, from a legal perspective, the firmness of the narrative of transnational rights and of the status that it reflects is left hanging. The Court has oft repeated that Union citizenship was 'destined to be the fundamental status' for nationals of the EU Member States.[63] Renowned Advocates General have attached great expectations to that status, arguing that European citizenship was meant to be a vehicle of fundamental rights. It was to transform free movement of persons into the 'movement of free citizens'.[64] It was also to entitle each Union citizen to look to his or her supranational status as a guarantee of a modicum of fundamental rights in any part of the Union.[65] The narrative of transnational rights fulfils in part this promised destiny, as well as the expectations linked to European citizenship. However, the exposure of both the status of supranational citizenship, and of its attached narrative of rights, to sudden silencing for entire cohorts of holders, makes them legally unreliable. How can a status that can be stripped off from one day to the next based on political contingencies be legally fundamental? Who would, after a possible bitter divorce between the EU and the UK, possibly resulting in the loss of transnational rights, trust to plan one's own life across borders and believe that he or she could really belong in a supranational citizenship space?

Ultimately, if the blurring of the lines gives a gentle nudge to the coherence of the transnational rights narrative, its being held to ransom by political decisions gives a hard shake to its very premises.

IV. THE LIMITS OF THE NARRATIVE OF RIGHTS AND THE WAY FORWARD

Challenges to the coherence, as well as to the premises of the narrative of transnational rights ultimately yield a glimpse of its limits. These are both exogenous—the narrative, it seems, is not self-standing and relies on a measure of political endorsement; and endogenous—the European citizens' right to belong across

[63] See, eg *Baumbast* (n 7).

[64] ECJ, Case C-228/07 *Jörn Petersen v Landesgeschäftsstelle des Arbeitsmarktservice Niederösterreich*, Opinion of AG Jarabo Colomer, EU:C:2008:281, para 28.

[65] ECJ, Case C-168/91 *Christos Konstantinidis v Stadt Altensteig*, Opinion of AG Jacobs, EU:C:1992:504.

borders rests on unsettled legal and philosophical grounds. Exogenous and endogenous limits ultimately point to the challenges facing the narrative of transnational rights and its future prospects.

A. Exogenous Limits and the Rebuilding of Trust

Rights mirror into obligations. In the case of EU transnational rights, these are the obligations of recognition that were considered earlier: recognition, on the part of the Member States, of one another's polities, social contracts, institutions and citizens.[66] At the intersection of transnational rights and corresponding obligations of recognition, judicial rationales meet political discourses. The judicial narrative of rights, in other words, relies on a measure of political resonance. Burgeoning hybrid narratives, and the surfacing ransom to which the narrative of rights is held, reveal however denial and conditionality of recognition.

Denial of recognition is most evident with the political ransom to which the narrative of transnational rights has come to be held in the wake of the UK EU referendum. In the aftermath of the UK vote, and in preparation of the formal negotiations for withdrawal of the UK from the EU, political discourses of rejection, rather than recognition, accompany the uncertainty in which transnational rights have been left. Political rejection of the idea that European citizens could automatically hold a right to cross borders was a fundamental component of the campaign preceding the referendum. That 'regaining control of borders' and regulating immigration from EU countries would be a leit-motive of the Brexit agenda was clear ever since Prime Minister David Cameron's speech on EU immigration in November 2014.[67] Denial of recognition has escalated after the referendum, and possibly reached its apex with the British Home Secretary's—later repealed—suggestion, at the Conservative Party conference in October 2016, that companies should disclose lists of their foreign employees.[68] Whilst in the UK rejection of the immigrant other is a historical deja vu,[69] denial of recognition does not stop at the UK border. Beyond the UK, denial of recognition has found expression, for instance, in the Swiss free movement referendum saga;[70] as well as in the practices

[66] K Nicolaïdis, 'The Idea of European Demoicracy' in J Dickson and P Eleftheriadis (eds), *Philosophical Foundations of European Union Law* (Oxford, Oxford University Press, 2012) 248.

[67] David Cameron, EU speech, 28 November 2014: www.bbc.com/news/uk-politics-30250299.

[68] For an account see G Ruddick and R Mason, 'Amber Rudd Faces Backlash from Businesses over Foreign Workers' *The Guardian* (5 October 2016): www.theguardian.com/business/2016/oct/05/government-faces-backlash-from-business-leaders-over-foreign-workers. At the request of a private citizen, this has been registered by the police as a non-crime hate-speech episode.

[69] For an account of the gradual introduction of restrictions to the immigration of Commonwealth Citizens, see R Karatani, *Defining British Citizenship: Empire, Commonwealth and Modern Britain* (London, Frank Cass Publishers, 2003) 145–65.

[70] Prompted by popular initiative, a referendum on immigration was held in Switzerland in February 2014, yielding a slight majority in favour of introducing immigration quotas also for EU

of Member States adopting restrictive definitions of what counts as work, and introducing exacting legal residence tests.[71] Whilst not all directly responding to the EU citizenship narrative of rights, these surrounding political discourses re-embolden the narrative of discretion that EU citizenship had countered in the first place.

The hybridisation of the narrative of rights emphasises further its subordinate nature. Not only does the latter narrative depend on recognition, but recognition becomes conditional on the attitude and direction of the narrative of rights. In the case of the first hybrid, the Court bows to political discourses and concedes to the narrative of discretion. It impliedly admits that the narrative of rights needs to endorse a measure of denial of recognition as a condition to preserve its legitimacy. As to the second hybrid, where the Member States appropriate the narrative of rights for purposes of attracting desirable migrants, the latter narrative comes to be articulated in this case within the very frame of the narrative of discretion and discourse of recognition. It becomes a tool of the sovereign states' discretion, rather than a constraint on such discretion. A further condition looms, on which the Member States' honouring of their obligations of mutual recognition becomes impliedly dependent: that the narrative of transnational rights may be placed at the service of their sovereign interests when needed.

Conditionality and subordination of the European citizenship narrative ultimately reveal that the equilibrium of transnational rights and obligations of recognition has broken up in the EU. Whilst that equilibrium was arguably wavering already,[72] Brexit could be seen as a breaking point. Complete denial of recognition, through the choice of withdrawal from the Union, nullifies the narrative of transnational rights.

Once the debris from this wreckage comes to rest, a question will be left for researchers to address: what are the conditions to restore such equilibrium? Kalypso Nicolaïdis has long suggested that mutual recognition, intended as a rule of governance as well as a political and philosophical principle that cuts across political economy, international law and ultimately European integration, rests on a notion of managed trust.[73] She refers to a definition of trust as 'the willingness

nationals. Whilst Switzerland is outside the EU, it has a set of bilateral agreements with the EU encompassing, among others, free movement of persons. A reconciliation between the referendum result and the agreements with the EU was found in December 2016. See E Maurice, 'EU and Switzerland Agree on Free Movement' *EU Observer* (22 December 2016): euobserver.com/justice/136398.

[71] For an overview, see O'Brien (n 3) 957–61.

[72] The rejection of the Constitutional Treaty in the Dutch and French referendums, and the rejection of the Lisbon Treaty in the Irish referendum being possible signs of such denial, although the questions asked in those referendums were profoundly different in scope and direction from the question asked in the UK referendum.

[73] K Nicolaïdis, 'Trusting the Poles?: Towards a Regulatory Peace Theory in a World of Mutual Recognition' in I Lianos and I Blanc (eds), *Regulating Trade in Services in the EU and the WTO: Trust, Distrust and Economic Integration* (Cambridge, Cambridge University Press, 2012) 264–65. Also see M Maduro, 'So Close and Yet so Far: the Paradoxes of Mutual Recognition' in SK Schmidt (ed), *Mutual Recognition as New Mode of Governance* (London, Routledge, 2008) 148.

to take risks concerning the behavior of others action in spite of non-trivial probability of betrayal'.[74] Trust informs, in her vision, the cooperation of regulatory authorities and norm setters. It is a precondition, as well as an objective of cooperation. And it comes in two versions: 'blind and binding trust', illustrating the tension respectively between 'deferential and interventionist recognition'.[75] If blind trust is instinctive and can be based on mutual ignorance, binding trust is based on the combination of a minimal measure of blind trust coupled with monitoring mechanisms that ensure reciprocal knowledge among the involved institutions.[76]

Mutual trust informs several areas of EU regulatory and policy cooperation. It is critical, for instance, to cooperation in the context of criminal law, as well as to the common immigration policy.[77] In the relevant contexts, trust is at the basis of enforcement cooperation among the authorities of the Member States. In the domain of transnational rights, mutual trust takes on a different connotation. The latter domain implies, on the part of the Member States and their nationals, trust in one another's systems of values, social contracts and justice. Trust underpins in this sense the idea of mutual belonging at the basis of transnational rights, and the obligations of mutual recognition that put flesh on the bones of that idea.[78]

Nicolaïdis further hints that 'paradoxically, only the prospect of reversibility makes recognition sustainable'.[79] Yet actual reversal also induces to question the foundations of mutual trust: the crisis of recognition in the EU, of which Brexit represents both the symptom and the outburst, calls for some hard thoughts in this sense. Relevant thoughts necessarily address the nature of the compact that joins the Member States. The type of blind trust that such compact requires and the type of binding trust that it allows may shed light on the feasible scope of mutual recognition in the EU. And in turn on the prospects of supranational citizenship and its narrative of transnational rights.

The blind trust that the EU compact requires begins from a measure of understanding. The Committee on a People's Europe forcefully expressed this 30 years ago: 'Continuation of this venture rests on the assumption that future generations will also understand and appreciate one another across borders and will realize the benefits to be derived from closer cooperation and solidarity'.[80] And a notion of solidarity is needed to legitimate in turn the forms of binding trust that the EU

[74] Nicolaïdis, 'Trusting the Poles?' (n 73) 292.

[75] ibid 265.

[76] ibid 266.

[77] The tension between mutual trust and protection of human rights in the context of the common immigration policy has been taken into account in a number of judgments of the ECtHR as well as of the CJEU on 'Dublin transfers' of asylum applicants. See ECJ, Case C-411/10 *NS and Others*, EU:C: 2011:865; ECJ, Case C-578/16 *CK and Others v Republika Slovenija*, EU:C: 2017:127; Case *MSS v Belgium and Greece*, App no 30696/09 (ECtHR, 21 January 2011).

[78] Strumia, 'European Citizenship and EU Immigration' (n 5) 441–43.

[79] ibid 294.

[80] P Adonnino, 'A People's Europe. Reports from the ad hoc Committee' (1985) 7 *Bullettin of the European Communities Supplement*: aei.pitt.edu/992/.

compact envisages. Solidarity requires acknowledgement of the common pursuit of a shared collective good, and willingness to pool the risks that such common pursuit creates.[81]

To re-ground both understanding and solidarity, it seems however that a step back has to be taken at this point and that reforms to the EU compact along two sets of lines need to be pondered. On the one hand, philosophical and programmatic reforms, and on the other, institutional reforms. From the philosophical and programmatic point of view, common objectives and a shared notion of common good need to be spelled out with further honesty and precision. Andrew Williams has already denounced an integration project that proceeds through principles concerned with order and processes rather than through values driven by ethical needs.[82] In a Union without a common identity, without a common welfare, without a common language, and with a scant common ethic, a reflection is needed on what is ultimately the kernel of the common project, beyond the completion of a single market. Managing the harms of globalisation, mending the inequalities that it has highlighted and re-including the groups that it has displaced could be a possible starting point for a restatement of the integration project.[83] The re-articulation of common objectives and notions of collective good needs to go hand-in-hand, however, with continuous reassurances that identities are not at stake and that sovereignties while pooled are not obliterated.[84] Relevant objectives and reassurances need to sit at the core of an intergovernmental dialogue leading to Treaty revisions where necessary. They also need to form the spine of a clearer and more explicit narrative on the role of the European Union for its citizens, a narrative that should form part of civic education and reflection in each Member State.

From the institutional point of view, both peripheral mechanisms of intervention and central mechanisms of accountability need some rethinking. The rebuilding of trust and recognition requires that the social contracts of the Member States be to some extent interchangeable. This requires peripheral mechanisms to equalise the strength of the social protection net of the different Member States, as well as to sustain comparable opportunities for economic inclusion so as to manage incentives for mass free movement.[85] It also requires reliable, and trusted,

[81] For a possible notion of collective good, see F De Witte, *Justice in the EU: The Emergence of Transnational Solidarity* (Oxford, Oxford University Press, 2015) 169, 171–72; for an account of the EU as a recipe to enhance the Member States' problem-solving capacities, see A Sangiovanni, 'Solidarity in the European Union' (2013) 33 *OJLS* 213.

[82] A Williams, 'Taking Values Seriously: Towards a Philosophy of EU Law' (2009) 29 *OJLS* 549, 558–59.

[83] EU policies already encompass a commitment in this sense. See, eg, Regulation (EU) No 1309/2013 of the European Parliament and of the Council of 17 December 2013 on the European Globalisation Adjustment Fund (2014–2020) and repealing Regulation (EC) No 1927/2006 [2013] OJ L347, 855.

[84] 'Recognition is about respecting and reconfiguring sovereignty at the same time': Nicolaïdis, 'Trusting the Poles?' (n 73) 269.

[85] European policy on economic, social and territorial cohesion goes in this direction. See TFEU [2016] OJ C202 Arts 174–78.

central mechanisms of accountability that may monitor and sanction egregious deviations from fundamental shared principles such as the rule of law, democratic guarantees and fundamental rights.[86] It could easily be objected that several of these mechanisms—both peripheral and central—are already there, and that it is precisely their failure that foreshadowed the crises of the EU. The point is, however, that the perspective of trust and recognition offers a distinctive rationale to inform the process of their rethinking.

B. Endogenous Limits and the Nature of Transnational Rights

Even before getting to recognition at the political level, the lack of coherence that the hybridisation of the narrative of transnational rights reveals, and its subjection to the ransom of withdrawal, point to an inner vulnerability. The transnational rights that the judicial narrative has stretched and consolidated lack a clear philosophical and legal rationale that may shore them up in the face of political contingencies.

The UK litigation on the constitutional power to give notice of withdrawal from the EU under Article 50 of the Treaty on European Union sheds further light on the uncertainty of the relevant rationale.[87] The question raised in the *Miller* case is whether the executive can rely on its royal prerogative, traditionally used for managing international relations, to give the notice required under Article 50 TEU; or whether Parliament rather holds the relevant power. The answer to the constitutional question turns in relevant part on the nature of the rights that the process envisaged in Article 50 TEU is liable to affect. The executive in fact cannot use the royal prerogative to alter domestic law rights.[88] And the argument of the claimants in the *Miller* case that both the High Court and the Supreme Court have ultimately married in their judgments, is that withdrawal of the UK from the EU will inevitably affect rights that have become UK domestic law.[89]

The question of transnational rights and their nature emerged with peculiar strength in between the lines of the High Court's judgment. The High Court distinguished three classes of rights grounded in EU law that have become domestic as a result of the UK membership of the EU: rights that are capable of replication in UK domestic law; rights that UK nationals enjoy in other Member States; and rights that are not capable of replication in domestic law.[90] In all three cases,

[86] For an analysis of the shortfalls of EU mechanisms to sanction violations of the rule of law principle, see D Kochenov and L Pech, 'Monitoring and Enforcement of the Rule of Law in the EU: Rhetoric and Reality' (2015) 11 *European Constitutional Law Review* 512.

[87] *Miller* (Supreme Court) (n 57).

[88] ibid para 50.

[89] *Miller* (Supreme Court) (n 57) para 86; *(R) Miller v Secretary of State for Exiting the European Union* [2016] EWHC 2768 (Admin) (High Court judgment) para 94.

[90] *Miller* (High Court) (n 89) paras 57–66.

according to the High Court, relevant rights have become domestic law through the will of the UK Parliament and cannot be repealed by the executive through the exercise of the royal prerogative.[91] The High Court's position with regard to the rights in the second class—rights that UK nationals enjoy in other Member States—is questionable. And indeed the Supreme Court in confirming the High Court's judgment follows a slightly different line of reasoning and effectively disregards the High Court's argument about these latter rights.[92] In fact, despite the High Court's thoughtful argument, these are hardly domestic law rights: on the one hand they descend from the EU Treaties, so they are EU law rights. On the other hand, they are claimed and enforced in the courts of Member States other than the UK. At best, these are the transnational rights that UK nationals enjoy under the European citizenship's narrative of rights.[93]

The High Court's stance in this respect reaches beyond the UK constitutional question of who has the power to trigger Article 50 TEU. It rather points to the question of the necessary safeguards, under EU law, for transnational rights that withdrawal of a Member State puts in jeopardy.[94] The problem of safeguards in the context of withdrawal links back, in turn, to the nature of those transnational rights. Are these rights that were intended to be left at the disposal of the whims of international relations? Or are they part of a more solid and ingrained legal heritage of the European supranational citizens?

The CJEU has spoken of a legal heritage in this sense in some of its seminal judgments. It has suggested that the now European Union represents a 'new legal order under international law'.[95] The CJEU's doctrine, in this sense, resonates in the holding of the Supreme Court in *Miller*. The majority in *Miller* emphasises that the EU Treaties are exceptional in character, that they have peculiar legal and constitutional implications and that they are unusual.[96] In this sense, the UK Supreme Court impliedly confirms the CJEU's theory of a 'new legal order'. According to the CJEU, such legal order is intended to create rights and obligations not only for the Member States, but also for their citizens.[97] As a result, EU law is intended to confer upon individuals 'rights which become part of their legal heritage'.[98] The European citizenship narrative of rights is an expression of this very heritage.

[91] ibid para 92.

[92] *Miller* (Supreme Court) (n 57) paras 69–73.

[93] The Report of the Committee on a People's Europe referred already in 1985 to a set of 'special rights' of Community nationals; Adonnino (n 80).

[94] Also see F Strumia 'In-Between the Lines of the High Court Brexit Judgment: EU Transnational Rights and their Safeguards' *EU Law Analysis (EU Law Analysis*, 6 November 2016): eulawanalysis.blogspot.it/2016/11/in-between-lines-of-high-court-brexit.html; F Strumia 'Brexit and the Safeguard of EU Transnational Rights—Act II: the Supreme Court Position' (*EU Law Analysis*, 28 January 2017): eulawanalysis.blogspot.co.uk/2017/01/brexit-and-safeguard-of-eu.html.

[95] ECJ, Case C-26/62 *NV Algemene Transport- en Expeditie Onderneming van Gend & Loos v Netherlands Inland Revenue Administration*, EU:C:1963:1.

[96] *Miller* (Supreme Court) (n 57) para 86, 88, 90.

[97] ibid.

[98] ibid.

The ultimate foundations of that legal heritage remain, however, underspecified. And the threat that withdrawal of a Member State from the EU suddenly poses to the transnational rights that such heritage encompasses makes the quest for those foundations all the more urgent. What is at stake is not only the European citizenship narrative of rights, but the very destiny of EU law as a 'new legal order' under international law.

The research agenda that relevant challenges call for has three prongs. A first prong entails considering what obligations protection of a heritage of transnational rights poses for the Member States, both the remaining ones and the exiting one, in the context of the process of withdrawal. The Member States are bound by the Treaties to a duty of sincere cooperation with one another and with the Union.[99] One possible question is what shape this duty takes in the context of withdrawal negotiations, and with peculiar regard to the transnational rights that withdrawal arrangements affect. A second prong needs to be concerned with the philosophical and legal foundations of transnational rights, of which EU law is considered from several sides a concrete example.[100] And a final prong has to scan existing bodies of international and transnational law for possible supplementary sources of protection of the transnational legal heritage that animates the European citizenship narrative, and that contemporary trends have left exposed. In this last sense, it has been observed that supranational citizenship does not enjoy, under international law, the same level of legal protection that national citizenship and nationality attract. Whilst international law codifies the right to a nationality, nobody has a real right to a supranational citizenship.[101] The safeguards that the *Rottmann* and *Zambrano* doctrines have built under EU law for supranational citizenship are as vulnerable to be washed away as the narrative that they contribute to bolster.[102] And whilst lack of a nationality triggers international law protections against statelessness, lack of a supranational citizenship triggers at best indifference. Yet, some of the rights that supranational citizenship entails and that are at the heart of its narrative of transnational rights may warrant further protection under international law. For instance, the International Covenant on Civil and Political Rights recognises the right of every person to 'enter their own country'.[103] In the jurisprudence of the Human Rights Committee the right has traditionally been interpreted as addressed to individuals who were being wrongly excluded from their country through manipulation of their nationality condition.[104] However, a recent string of cases has taken to consider a broader

[99] See Art 4(3) TEU [2008] OJ C115/13. Also see Strumia, 'In-Between the Lines' (n 94).

[100] See K Tuori, 'Transnational Law' in M Maduro, K Tuori and S Sankari (eds), *Transnational Law: Rethinking European Law and Legal Thinking* (Cambridge, Cambridge University Press, 2014) 11; also see Michaels (n 2).

[101] See above text to n 62.

[102] See above text to nn 19 and 24.

[103] International Covenant on Civil and Political Rights, Art 12(4).

[104] See Human Rights Committee, General Comment 27 on Freedom of Movement. Also see Human Rights Committee, Communication 538/1993, *Stewart v Canada* [1993] CCPR/C/58/D/538/1993.

range of ties that qualify a country as a person's own.[105] This may perhaps lead to question whether and to what extent the holding, and the concrete exercise, of transnational rights on the part of European citizens qualifies the Member States in which they exercise those rights as 'their own country'.[106] And conversely what international law obligations are generated as a result on the part of the host Member States.

V. CONCLUSION

Echoes of populism, protectionism and resurgent nationalism, beyond threatening the European integration project, infiltrate the narrative of transnational rights that integration has yielded. They corrupt some of the narrative threads, and they cloud its prospects. This chapter has traced the hybrids that emerge as a result, and has illustrated the fragility of European citizenship's narrative of rights in the face of political contingencies.

The vicissitudes of the narrative of transnational rights call, on the one hand, for a reflection on its premises, and for the rescaling of some of the ideas, obligations and conditions that ultimately sustain the narrative. The chapter has begun an exercise in this sense through a reflection on the changing roles of trust, understanding and solidarity in the compact among the EU Member State.

On the other hand, those same vicissitudes call perhaps for a closing of the ranks. The narrative of transnational rights is a legal heritage that integration has bestowed upon the Member States and its citizens. This legal heritage is a hefty response to centuries of indulgence to the arbitrary exercise of power and to derivations of nationalism that have ultimately caused historical havoc.

True that the narrative needs a measure of political resonance, true that it cannot stand without democratic endorsement, and true that it should not threaten communal solidarity. Whilst these competing needs may require some compromise, the narrative also deserves a measure of bold firmness in its defence. At least on the part of the CJEU, which has been, after all, its first herald.

[105] See, eg Human Rights Committee, Communication 1959/2010, *Warsame v Canada* [2010] CCPR/C/102/D/1959/2010.

[106] A further source of protection for relevant rights under international law could be found in the right to private and family life under Art 8 of the European Convention on Human Rights. In this sense, see D Thym, 'Respect for Private and Family Life under Article 8 ECHR in Immigration Cases: A Human Right to Regularize Illegal Stay' (2008) 57 *ICLQ* 87.

Part II

Equal Treatment, Social Benefits and Human Rights

9

*Consolidating Union Citizenship: Residence and Solidarity Rights for Jobseekers and the Economically Inactive in the Post-*Dano *Era*

FERDINAND WOLLENSCHLÄGER

I. CONSOLIDATING UNION CITIZENSHIP

THE QUESTION OF transnational free movement rights of economically inactive persons and the latter's access to social assistance constitutes a controversial and politically sensitive issue. For it raises the question, to what extent economically inactive Union citizens are entitled to social solidarity in the host Member State. The current political climate seems rather reserved, which has also had an impact on the Court's recent jurisprudence. Turning to the legal framework, the European Union (EU) free movement regime contains a tension in this regard, making matters complicated and provoking debate: while, in order to prevent an unreasonable burden on the welfare systems of notably the wealthier Member States, self-sufficiency is demanded as a residence criterion, not possessing sufficient resources does not necessarily mean losing one's right to residence and to equal treatment. This tension goes back to the initial jurisprudence of the Court of Justice (ECJ) on Union citizenship and its subsequent codification in the Residence Directive 2004/38/EC (II). It poses a challenge for determining free movement rights of non-market actors under the current EU rules—as the Court's jurisprudence demonstrates. The main part of this chapter explores this issue further and argues that we are witnessing a consolidation phase: other than often assumed, the *Dano* judgment, at least from a legal point of view, does not constitute a paradigm shift. Moreover, the recent jurisprudence—generally speaking and this has to be stressed in view of the widespread criticism it draws[1]—takes

[1] For an overall critical view on the recent jurisprudence, see A Farahat, 'Solidarität und Inklusion: Umstrittene Dimensionen der Unionsbürgerschaft' (2016) *Die Öffentliche Verwaltung* 45; C O'Brien,

account of the current legal framework as concretised in the Residence Directive rather than questions it, notwithstanding problematic aspects of notably the *Dano* judgment (III). Methodologically, these findings are based on a legal-doctrinal analysis of the EU free movement rules and their interpretation in the ECJ's jurisprudence.[2]

II. THE INTRODUCTION OF UNION CITIZENSHIP: A TURNING POINT FOR FREE MOVEMENT OF ECONOMICALLY INACTIVE PERSONS

A. A Free Movement Right for Economically Inactive Persons: A 'Paper Declaration'?

With market freedoms already foreseeing a right of residence for market actors;[3] the ECJ awarding the same right from the mid-1980s onwards to students and recipients of services and the Free Movement Directives 90/364/EEC, 90/365/EEC and 93/96/EEC—having entered into force at the beginning of the 1990s after more than a decade of legislative procedure—closing the remaining gaps as far as economically inactive persons were concerned, the progress achieved by introducing a general right of free movement with the Treaty of Maastricht in 1993 (currently Article 21 of the Treaty on the Functioning of the European Union (TFEU)) seemed negligible. True, the existing guarantees were not absolute: the public-policy proviso allowing for expulsion of non-nationals on grounds of public order, security and health, as well as the stipulation of economic conditions to be fulfilled by economically inactive persons under the Free Movement Directives both give evidence of this. However, a general right of free movement 'subject to the limitations and conditions laid down in the Treaties and by the measures adopted to give them effect', simply seemed to carry over these restrictions. In view of this it is understandable that Article 21 TFEU was considered a 'paper

'Civis Capitalist Sum: Class as the New Guiding Principle of EU Free Movement Rights' (2016) 53 *CML Rev* 937, 943ff, 961ff, 973ff—rightly stressing possible negative consequences in terms of permitting further restrictions on the free movement regime in general, which might be seen in the current debate on the free movement of workers; A Iliopoulou-Penot, 'Deconstructing the Former Edifice of Union Citizenship? The Alimanovic Judgment' (2016) 53 *CML Rev* 1007, 1015ff; N Nic Shuibhne, 'Limits Rising, Duties Ascending: The Changing Legal Shape of Union Citizenship' (2015) 52 *CML Rev* 889. Positive: D Thym, 'When Union Citizens Turn into Illegal Migrants: The Dano Case' (2015) 40 *EL Rev* 249, 260ff. Ambivalent: A Wallrabenstein, 'Die Gleichheit der Freiheit' (2016) *Zeitschrift für europäisches Sozial- und Arbeitsrecht* 349, 357.

[2] See on 'doctrinal constructivism', A von Bogdandy, 'The Past and Promise of Doctrinal Constructivism: A Strategy for Responding to the Challenges Facing Constitutional Scholarship in Europe' (2009) 7 *International Journal of Constitutional Law* 364, 371ff; further A von Bogdandy, 'Founding Principles of EU Law: A Theoretical and Doctrinal Sketch' (2010) 16 *European Law Journal (ELJ)* 95, 98ff; A Somek, 'The Indelible Science of Law' (2009) 7 *International Journal of Constitutional Law* 424.

[3] This section follows F Wollenschläger, 'A New Fundamental Freedom beyond Market Integration: Union Citizenship and its Dynamics for Shifting the Economic Paradigm of European Integration' (2011) 17 *ELJ* 1, 15ff.

declaration'[4] and that any progress its introduction promised for European integration was considered small: 'Union Citizenship may have "constitutionalised" the Community law rights of free movement, but it has not added much that is substantially new to existing community law'.[5] These initial assessments, however, turned out to be unfounded.

First and foremost (and unlike what some commentators have proposed)[6] the reservation contained in Article 21 TFEU does not allow for any watering down of this guarantee (and hence for denying its direct effect).[7] This norm confers on every Union citizen in a clear and precise manner a right of residence and in consequence it is directly applicable.[8] After initial reluctance,[9] the ECJ confirmed this interpretation in the *Baumbast* case and subsequent decisions.[10]

However, the fact that the right of residence is subject to restrictions laid down in primary and secondary EU law illustrates that, according to the Member States' will, the former are still applicable and that Article 21 TFEU does not confer an absolute right.[11] It is equally true, however, that the right of residence's significance cannot be interpreted without considering its re-positioning in a completely new

[4] D Pollard, 'Rights of Free Movement' in NA Neuwahl and A Rosas (eds), *The European Union and Human Rights* (The Hague, Martinus Nijhoff, 1995) 116.

[5] T Kostakopoulou, *Citizenship, Identity and Immigration in the European Union: Between Past and Future* (Manchester, Manchester University Press, 2001) 66. Equally restrictive: N Bernard, *Multilevel Governance in the European Union* (The Hague, Kluwer Law International, 2002) 186f; P Magnette, *La citoyenneté europ*é*ene* (Bruxelles, Editions de l'Université de Bruxelles, 1999) 162: '"la valeur ajoutée" de la citoyenneté de l'Union apparaît nulle jusqu'à present' (the added value of Union citizenship appears to be absent at the moment); D O'Keeffe, 'Union Citizenship' in D O'Keeffe (ed), *Legal Issues of the Maastricht Treaty* (Chichester, Chancery Law Publishing, 1994) 93f; S O'Leary, 'The Relationship between Community Citizenship and the Protection of Fundamental Rights in Community Law' (1995) 32 *CML Rev* 519, 519f; S O'Leary, *European Union Citizenship: The Options for Reform* (London, Institute for Public Policy Research, 1996) 92; J Shaw, 'Citizenship of the Union: Towards Post-National Membership?' in *Collected Courses of the Academy of European Law, Vol VI-1—European Community Law* (The Hague, Kluwer Law International, 1998) 247; J Shaw, 'European Union Citizenship' (1997) 3 *European Public Law* 413, 416f; JHH Weiler, 'Les droits des citoyens européens' (1996) *Revue Du Marché Unique Européen* 35, 39.

[6] *cf* only W Kaufmann-Bühler in CO Lenz and K-D Borchardt (eds), *EGV*, 2nd edn (Köln, Bundesanzeiger Verlag, 1999) Art 18 EC, para 1—repealed, however, in the 3rd edn (2003) Art 18 EC, para 1.

[7] cf for an account of this debate F Wollenschläger, *Grundfreiheit ohne Markt. Die Herausbildung der Unionsbürgerschaft im unionsrechtlichen Freizügigkeitsregime* (Tübingen, Mohr Siebeck, 2007/2017) 126–27.

[8] *cf* only Wollenschläger, ibid 126–27.

[9] Left open in ECJ, Case C-85/96 *Martínez Sala*, EU:C:1988:217, para 60; Case C-378/97 *Wijsenbeek*, EU:C:1999:439, paras 41f; Case C-357/98 *Yiadom*, EU:C:2000:604, para 23; Case C-192/99 *Kaur*, EU:C:2001:106, paras 15, 28.

[10] ECJ, Case C-413/99 *Baumbast*, EU:C:2002:493, paras 80–81. Confirmed in Case C-456/02 *Trojani*, EU:C:2004:488, para 31; Case C-408/03 *EC v Belgium* EU:C:2006:192, para 34; Case C-50/06 *EC v Netherlands*, EU:C:2007:325, para 32; Case C-398/06 *EC v Netherlands* EU:C:2008:214, para 27.

[11] *cf Trojani* (n 10) para 32; *EC v Netherlands* [2007] (n 10) para 33; *EC v Netherlands* [2008] (n 10) para 28; Case C-33/07 *Jipa*, EU:C:2008:396, para 21; Case C-524/06 *Huber*, EU:C:2008:724, para 54; AP van der Mei, *Free Movement of Persons within the European Community* (Oxford, Hart Publishing, 2003) 46–47; O'Leary, *European Union Citizenship* (n 5) 136. The invalidity of the restrictions is advocated by V Constantinesco, 'La citoyenneté de l'Union' in J Schwarze (ed), *Vom Binnenmarkt zur Europäischen Union* (Baden-Baden, Nomos, 1993) 29–30, as well as by the Portuguese government (quoted in Opinion of AG Alber in ECJ, Case C-184/99 *Grzelczyk*, EU:C:2001:458, para 52).

normative context: The right of residence heads the TFEU's provisions on Union citizenship, a status shared by all Europeans and held independent of one's nationality and one's involvement in an economic activity. Moreover, the right of free movement has been re-evaluated: for economically active persons, it is now protected per se and not as an aspect of one's being engaged in a transnational economic activity; and for economically inactive persons, it has changed from being a guarantee enshrined in secondary law to one granted by primary law. This paradigm shift must be considered when interpreting Article 21 TFEU;[12] and indeed, it has been so considered, as the more restrictive application of the public policy proviso[13] and the economic conditions of residence demonstrate. This will be considered in the following section.

B. Reinterpretation by the Court

In order not to provide incentives for a primarily economically motivated migration and to protect the social systems of especially the wealthier Member States, the Free Movement Directives 90/364/EEC, 90/365/EEC and 93/96/EEC, in force at the time of the introduction of former Article 18 EC (= Article 21 TFEU), made the right of residence of economically inactive persons dependent on the economic conditions of sufficient means of existence and a comprehensive health insurance. Even more than was the case with the public policy proviso, these limitations were questioned in light of the new status of a Union citizenship shared by all Europeans, whether economically active or not. Consequently, these limitations were either rejected completely[14] or at least reduced to prohibiting the abuse of rights[15,16] : 'When taken seriously, Union citizenship ought to be developed in such a way that both the "rich" and the "poor" can enjoy the rights that come with it'.[17] Or: 'Non è compatibile con la ratio ultima del nuovo statuto di cittadino europeo, che è quella dell'integrazione fra i popoli degli Stati membri, la quale non può trovare "mortificazione" in logiche di bilancio'.[18]

However, the proviso contained in Article 18 EC (currently Article 21 TFEU) does not allow the economic conditions of residence set up by the (former) Free

[12] *cf* further M Dougan, 'The Constitutional Dimension to the Case Law on Union Citizenship' (2006) 31 *EL Rev* 613, 615; ECJ, Case C-378/97 *Wijsenbeek*, EU:C:1999:144, Opinion of AG Cosmas, para 80.

[13] *cf* in this regard Wollenschläger, 'A New Fundamental Freedom beyond Market Integration' (n 3) 17–18.

[14] *cf* only E Pérez Vera, 'Citoyenneté de l'Union Européenne, Nationalité et Condition des Étrangers' (1996 [1998]) 261 *Recueil des cours* 243, 350–51.

[15] J Kokott, 'Die Freizügigkeit der Unionsbürger als neue Grundfreiheit' in PM Dupuy et al (eds), *Common Values in International Law: Essays in Honour of Tomuschat* (Kehl, NP Engel Verlag, 2006) 221f; DH Scheuing, 'Freizügigkeit als Unionsbürgerrecht' (2003) *Europarecht* 744, 769–70.

[16] *cf* for an extensive account of the critique of the economic conditions of residence Wollenschläger, *Grundfreiheit ohne Markt* (n 7) 166–67.

[17] van der Mei (n 11) 220.

[18] M Condinanzi, A Lang and B Nascimbene, *Cittadinanza dell'Unione e libera circolazione delle persone* (Milan, Giuffrè, 2003) 34.

Movement Directives to be disregarded. Yet it is equally true, as a consequence of the introduction of Article 18 EC (= Article 21 TFEU), that these conditions henceforth constitute restrictions on a superordinate guarantee, ie one enshrined in primary law, meaning that the former must not restrict the latter in a disproportionate manner.[19] Hence, in accordance with the ECJ's jurisprudence, the right of free movement may be restricted with regard to the legitimate aim of protecting the financial interests of the Member States, as provided for by the economic conditions set up by the (former) Free Movement Directives. However, these conditions must be applied in accordance with the principle of proportionality: consequently, the fact that a student temporarily requires social assistance or that the health insurance does not cover all risks does not entitle the host Member State to expel a Union citizen.[20]

In the *Grzelczyk* case,[21] the ECJ had already relativised the economic conditions of residence and allowed a student temporarily not fulfilling them to invoke Article 18 EC (= Article 21 TFEU). This decision, however, was based on a different methodological approach. The ECJ interpreted the economic conditions of residence strictly in line with the criterion of financial solidarity among Member States demanded by the Directive, but did not apply the principle of proportionality.[22]

C. Consolidation by the Union Legislator

Despite all the criticism coming from the Member States of the ECJ's jurisprudence, the community legislator has written this partial relativisation of the economic conditions of residence into the new Free Movement Directive 2004/38/EC, whose Article 6 now grants an unconditional right of residence for a period of up to three months. However, if a Union citizen becomes an unreasonable burden on the host Member State's system of social assistance, she or he may be expelled (Article 14(1)).[23] The right of residence of persons who are economically inactive for more than three months continues to depend on the economic conditions of having sufficient means of existence and a comprehensive health insurance (Article 7(1)(b) and (c)).[24] However, codifying the Court's jurisprudence

[19] *cf* Wollenschläger, *Grundfreiheit ohne Markt* (n 7) 176f; further E Spaventa, 'Seeing the Wood Despite the Trees? On the Scope of Union Citizenship and its Constitutional Effects' (2008) 45 *CML Rev* 13, 26–27.

[20] *Baumbast and R* (n 10) paras 90f; *Trojani* (n 10) paras 30f; Case C-200/02 *Chen/Zhu*, EU:C:2004:639, para 33; *EC v Belgium* (n 10) paras 38f; *EC v Netherlands* [2008] (n 10) para 29.

[21] *Grzelczyk* (n 11) paras 37–38.

[22] *cf* for an extensive account of the development of the ECJ's jurisprudence Wollenschläger, *Grundfreiheit ohne Markt* (n 7) 170–71.

[23] During this three-month period, a Union citizen does not enjoy the right of national treatment in respect of social assistance (*cf* Art 24(2) of Directive 2004/38/EC).

[24] The economic 'conditions' of residence—like the public policy proviso (*cf* in this respect ECJ, Case C-48/75 *Royer*, EU:C:1976:57, paras 28f; Case C-118/75 *Watson and Belman*, EU:C:1976:106, para 20; Case C-157/79 *Regina/Pieck*, EU:C:1980:179, para 9)—should not be considered conditions in the sense that their non-fulfilment automatically terminates the right of residence; rather

in *Grzelczyk*,[25] according to Article 14(3) an 'expulsion measure shall not be the automatic consequence of a Union citizen's or his or her family member's recourse to the social assistance system of the host Member State'.[26] Hence, the latter is obliged to weigh the conflicting interests before deciding on an expulsion. Recital 16 of the Directive lists criteria to be taken into account:

> The host Member State should examine whether it is a case of temporary difficulties and take into account the duration of residence, the personal circumstances and the amount of aid granted in order to consider whether the beneficiary has become an unreasonable burden on its social assistance system and to proceed to his expulsion.[27]

Finally, a substantial innovation of the new Residence Directive has been the introduction of a permanent right of residence for a Union citizen if she or he has resided legally for a continuous period of five years in the host Member State (Articles 16 and 17).[28] Once acquired, this right does not depend on the fulfilment of economic conditions, applying to economically active and inactive persons alike. This means that it is not possible to expel a Union citizen for economic reasons, even if she or he requires social assistance for the rest of their life. Recital 17 of Directive 2004/38/EC declares in this respect:

> Enjoyment of permanent residence by Union citizens who have chosen to settle long term in the host Member State would strengthen the feeling of Union citizenship and is a key element in promoting social cohesion, which is one of the fundamental objectives of the Union.

their non-fulfilment only allows for an expulsion of the Union citizen in question. *Cf* Wollenschläger, *Grundfreiheit ohne Markt* (n 7) 180–81, 187–88. Similarly, C Schönberger, 'Die Unionsbürgerschaft als Sozialbürgerschaft' (2006) *Zeitschrift für Ausländerrecht und Ausländerpolitik* 226, 228. Disagreeing D Thym, 'Sozialleistungen für und Aufenthalt von nichterwerbstätigen Unionsbürgern' (2014) *Neue Zeitschrift für Sozialrecht* 81, 86f; Thym, 'When Union Citizens Turn into Illegal Migrants' (n 1) 259; D Thym, 'The Elusive Limits of Solidarity: Residence Rights of and Social Benefits for Economically Inactive Union Citizens' (2015) 52 *CML Rev* 17, 39ff; see further with regard to the right of permanent residence ECJ, Joined Cases C-424/10 and C-425/10 *Ziolkowski et al*, EU:C:2011:866, paras 36ff.

[25] Art 14(3) has been introduced only in the Common Position of the Council of 5 December 2003, *cf* Common Position (EC) No 6/2004 of 5 December 2003 [2004] OJ C54/12 (Arts 14 and 15). *Cf* also the Communication from the Commission to the European Parliament, SEK (2003) 1293 final, sub 3.3.2 (Arts 14 and 15).

[26] A relativisation may already be seen in the (English version of the) provision of Art 7(1)(b) Directive 2004/38/EC since it requires the Union citizen to 'have sufficient resources for themselves and their family members *not to become a burden on the social assistance system* of the host Member State during their period of residence' (emphasis by the author). The German version is worded more strictly by defining the threshold not with regard to a burden on the social assistance system, but with regard to having to rely on social assistance ('für sich und seine Familienangehörigen über ausreichende Existenzmittel verfügt, so dass sie während ihres Aufenthalts keine Sozialhilfeleistungen des Aufnahmemitgliedstaats in Anspruch nehmen müssen'). See on this divergence also Nic Shuibhne (n 1) 896–97.

[27] The indeterminacy of these criteria is criticised by K Hailbronner, 'Union Citizenship and Access to Social Benefits' (2005) 42 *CML Rev* 1245, 1260–61.

[28] *cf* in view of the five-year-criterion ECJ, Case C-162/09 *Lassal*, EU:C:2010:266, Opinion of AG Trstenjak, para 40.

III. RESIDENCE AND SOLIDARITY RIGHTS FOR JOBSEEKERS AND THE ECONOMICALLY INACTIVE UNDER THE CURRENT LEGAL FRAMEWORK

The ECJ's jurisprudence on the right to residence of economically inactive persons and its subsequent codification in the Residence Directive 2004/38/EC, which have been outlined in the previous section, imply a tension.[29] On the one hand, in order to protect the social assistance systems of the Member States (*cf* recital 10 Directive 2004/38/EC), economic conditions of residence apply. On the other hand, in view of the fundamental right of residence, these conditions are not to be understood too strictly; notably not fulfilling them does not necessarily mean losing one's right of residence.[30] Not surprisingly, this tension, touching upon the sensitive issue of access of economically inactive persons to social assistance, has led to controversial debates not only in academia, but also in the political sphere. Moreover, the ECJ had to face the challenge of how to cope with it.

Against this background, the following section will examine the acquisition and loss of residence rights by jobseekers and the economically inactive under the Residence Directive 2004/38/EC. It will focus on the situation of persons staying for longer than three months in the host Member State, but not having yet acquired the right to permanent residence. For, no economic criteria apply to the right of residence of all other Union citizens. Moreover, persons not falling within this category are also either not entitled (duration of stay < 3 months)[31] or entitled (right to permanent residence) to social assistance irrespective of the circumstances in the individual case.

After showing why residence matters (A) the relevance of the economic residence criteria, notably as interpreted in the recent jurisprudence of the ECJ, will be explored (B). Particular attention is drawn to the issue of proportionality (C).

[29] See also Thym, 'The Elusive Limits of Solidarity' (n 25) 26.

[30] See also the relativisation contained in the (English) wording of Art 7(1)(b) Directive 2004/38/EC, mentioned above (n 24).

[31] Confirmed in ECJ, Case C-299/14 *García-Nieto*, ECLI:EU:C:2016:114, paras 45ff, and rightly so as proportionate: 'Since the Member States cannot require Union citizens to have sufficient means of subsistence and personal medical cover for a period of residence of a maximum of three months in their respective territories, it is legitimate not to require those Member States to be responsible for those citizens during that period. In that context, it must also be stated that, although Directive 2004/38 requires the host Member State to take account of the individual situation of the person concerned before it adopts an expulsion measure or finds that the residence of that person is placing an unreasonable burden on its social assistance system …, no such individual assessment is necessary in circumstances such as those at issue in the main proceedings. In the judgment in *Alimanovic* …, the Court stated that Directive 2004/38, establishing a gradual system as regards the retention of the status of "worker" which seeks to safeguard the right of residence and access to social assistance, itself takes into consideration various factors characterising the individual situation of each applicant for social assistance and, in particular, the duration of the exercise of any economic activity. Therefore, if such an assessment is not necessary in the case of a citizen seeking employment who no longer has the status of "worker", the same applies a fortiori to persons who are in a situation such as that of Mr Peña Cuevas in the main proceedings.'

Moreover, the relevance of the fundamental right to social assistance guaranteed by Article 34 of the EU Charter of Fundamental Rights (CFR) is discussed (D). A final section focuses on the situation of former workers and of jobseekers finding themselves in between the spheres of market and non-market actors in view of their janus-faced status and thus posing a specific challenge (E).

A. Why Residence Matters

Residence matters. For, enjoying a right to residence does not only mean protection from expulsion. Rather, the claim to non-discrimination and the acquisition of the right to permanent residence depend upon it. First, Article 24(1) Directive 2004/38/EC grants a claim to equal treatment with the nationals of the host Member State to 'all Union citizens residing on the basis of this Directive in the territory of the host Member State'. This nexus has recently been stressed in *García-Nieto*:

> As regards access to such benefits, a Union citizen can claim equal treatment with nationals of the host Member State under Article 24(1) of Directive 2004/38 only if his residence in the territory of the host Member State complies with the conditions of Directive 2004/38.[32]

Second, according to Article 16(1), sentence 1, Directive 2004/38/EC, the right of permanent residence is granted to 'Union citizens who have resided legally for a continuous period of five years in the host Member State'. This nexus has been confirmed in *Ziolkowski et al*:

> It follows that the concept of legal residence implied by the terms 'have resided legally' in Article 16(1) of Directive 2004/38 should be construed as meaning a period of residence which complies with the conditions laid down in the directive, in particular those set out in Article 7(1). Consequently, a period of residence which complies with the law of a Member State but does not satisfy the conditions laid down in Article 7(1) of Directive 2004/38 cannot be regarded as a 'legal' period of residence within the meaning of Article 16(1).[33]

B. Relativity of the Economic Residence Criteria

The initial jurisprudence of the ECJ on Union citizenship and its subsequent codification in the Residence Directive 2004/38/EC have introduced a certain flexibility regarding the application of the economic residence criteria. The *Brey* case constitutes a recent example of this approach (i). The *Dano* case, although sometimes

[32] *García-Nieto* (n 31) para 38. Similarly, Case C-67/14 *Alimanovic*, ECLI:EU:C:2015:597, paras 51–52; Case C-333/13 *Dano*, ECLI:EU:C:2014:2358, paras 68–69.

[33] *Ziolkowski et al* (n 24) para 46. *Cf* on the issue of permanent residence which is not discussed any further here, Nic Shuibhne (n 1) 916ff.

read in the opposite sense (ii), has not altered this, even if it has emphasised the rule-exception-ratio underlying the Residence Directive (iii).

i. Brey: *The Orthodox Approach*

The Court's proportionality approach was most recently reflected in the *Brey* case handed down on 19 September 2013. It concerned German pensioners living in Austria who applied for a compensatory supplement intended to augment their retirement pension. The allowance was refused by the Austrian authorities since the claimants did not possess sufficient resources and thus did not have a right to residence as economically inactive persons under Directive 2004/38/EC.

The Court conceded, on the one hand, that

> the fact that a national of another Member State who is not economically active may be eligible, in light of his low pension, to receive that benefit could be an indication that that national does not have sufficient resources to avoid becoming an unreasonable burden on the social assistance system of the host Member State for the purposes of Article 7(1)(b) of Directive 2004/38.[34]

On the other hand, however, the Court continued by stressing that

> the competent national authorities cannot draw such conclusions without first carrying out an overall assessment of the specific burden which granting that benefit would place on the national social assistance system as a whole, by reference to the personal circumstances characterising the individual situation of the person concerned.[35]

ii. Dano: *A Paradigm Shift?*

A deviation from the orthodox approach, even a full restoration of the economic residence criteria is seen by some in the *Dano* case handed down only a little more than one year later on 11 November 2014. True, the ECJ's ruling reflects a strict reading of the economic residence criteria, since it does not discuss any relativisation in view of proportionality requirements, and moreover emphasises the Directive's goal to protect the social system of the host Member State as well as its manifestation in the limitations on the right of residence of eceonomically inactive persons:

> In order to determine whether economically inactive Union citizens … whose period of residence in the host Member State has been longer than three months but shorter than five years, can claim equal treatment with nationals of that Member State so far as concerns entitlement to social benefits, it must therefore be examined whether the residence of those citizens complies with the conditions in Article 7(1)(b) of Directive 2004/38. Those conditions include the requirement that the economically inactive Union citizen must have sufficient resources for himself and his family members.

[34] ECJ, Case C-140/12 *Brey*, ECLI:EU:C:2013:565, para 63.

[35] *Brey* (n 34) para 64.

> To accept that persons who do not have a right of residence under Directive 2004/38 may claim entitlement to social benefits under the same conditions as those applicable to nationals of the host Member State would run counter to an objective of the directive, set out in recital 10 in its preamble, namely preventing Union citizens who are nationals of other Member States from becoming an unreasonable burden on the social assistance system of the host Member State.
>
> It should be added that, as regards the condition requiring possession of sufficient resources, Directive 2004/38 distinguishes between (i) persons who are working and (ii) those who are not. Under Article 7(1)(a) of Directive 2004/38, the first group of Union citizens in the host Member State have the right of residence without having to fulfil any other condition. On the other hand, persons who are economically inactive are required by Article 7(1)(b) of the directive to meet the condition that they have sufficient resources of their own.
>
> Therefore, Article 7(1)(b) of Directive 2004/38 seeks to prevent economically inactive Union citizens from using the host Member State's welfare system to fund their means of subsistence …
>
> As the Advocate General has observed in points 93 and 96 of his Opinion, any unequal treatment between Union citizens who have made use of their freedom of movement and residence and nationals of the host Member State with regard to the grant of social benefits is an inevitable consequence of Directive 2004/38. Such potential unequal treatment is founded on the link established by the Union legislature in Article 7 of the directive between the requirement to have sufficient resources as a condition for residence and the concern not to create a burden on the social assistance systems of the Member States.
>
> A Member State must therefore have the possibility, pursuant to Article 7 of Directive 2004/38, of refusing to grant social benefits to economically inactive Union citizens who exercise their right to freedom of movement solely in order to obtain another Member State's social assistance although they do not have sufficient resources to claim a right of residence.[36]

The question remains, however, which general conclusions may be drawn from the judgment. This leads over to the next section.

*iii. Residence and Solidarity Rights for Jobseekers and the Economically Inactive in the Post-*Dano *Era*

With regard to *Dano*,[37] it has to be stressed that the outcome of the case (denial of a claim to social assistance) seems totally justifiable in view of the reported

[36] *Dano* (n 32) paras 73ff.

[37] *cf* for this (restrictive) evaluation (in terms of consequences of the *Dano* judgment) F Wollenschläger, 'Keine Sozialleistungen für nichterwerbstätige Unionsbürger? Zur begrenzten Tragweite des Urteils des EuGH in der Rechtssache Dano vom 11.11.2014' (2014) *Neue Zeitschrift für Verwaltungsrecht* 1628, 1629f; further E Eichenhofer, 'Ausschluss von ausländischen Unionsbürgern aus deutscher Grundsicherung?' (2015) *Europarecht* 73, 77–78; D Kramer, 'Earning Social Citizenship in the European Union: Free Movement and Access to Social Assistance Benefits Reconstructed' (2016) *18 Cambridge Yearbook of European Legal Studies* 270, 293ff; Thym, 'The Elusive Limits of Solidarity' (n 25) 25–26. A wider interpretation (in terms of inapplicability of the proportionality test) is assumed

facts (migration solely to gain access to social benefits).[38] Moreover, in view of the controversial debate on free movement of economically inactive persons, it might have been wise of the Court not to add fuel to the flames by relativising the clear result by proportionality considerations not relevant for the outcome.[39] Finally, the Court has stressed that the fulfilment of the economic criteria is the rule (for enjoying a right of residence as economically inactive person) and a deviation from this is only permissible in exceptional cases.[40]

However, the Court's ruling has to be criticised from a methodological perspective.[41] There is no reference to its former case law and the corresponding provisions in the Residence Directive mitigating the dividing line between market and non-market actors. Apart from this, it has to be stressed that not applying the proportionality test is not only contrary to the Court's understanding of Article 21 TFEU, but also contrary to the Residence Directive and thus not in line with EU law. While it is true that Article 7(1)(b) Directive 2004/38/EC stipulates economic residence criteria (sufficient resources and comprehensive sickness insurance), it is equally true that not fulfilling them does not necessarily terminate the right to residence. In contrast, Article 14(3) Directive 2004/38/EC explicitly states that '[a]n expulsion measure shall not be the automatic consequence of a Union citizen's or his or her family member's recourse to the social assistance system of the host Member State'. Moreover, the economic criterion itself is worded in an open way since Article 7(1)(b) Directive 2004/38/EC does not require possessing 'sufficient resources', but 'sufficient resources *not to become a burden on the social assistance system of the host Member State during their period of residence*' (emphasis added, see above, footnote 26).

In line with this, the Court has in the subsequent *Alimanovic* judgment, handed down on 15 September 2015, equated enjoying a right of residence with the prohibition of an automatic expulsion:

> Only two provisions of Directive 2004/38 may confer on job-seekers in the situation of Ms Alimanovic and her daughter Sonita a right of residence in the host Member State under that directive, namely Article 7(3)(c) and Article 14(4)(b) thereof.[42]

by Nic Shuibhne (n 1) 913–14; S Peers, 'Benefits for EU Citizens: A U-turn by the Court of Justice?' (2015) 74 *CLJ* 195, 196–97. *Cf* for a contrast of a restrictive and broad interpretation H Verschueren, 'Preventing "Benefit Tourism" in the EU: A Narrow or Broad Interpretation of the Possibilities Offered by the ECJ in Dano?' (2015) 52 *CML Rev* 363, 370ff, and in favour of the former ibid, 388–89.

[38] *cf* also Verschueren (n 37) 373. Considering the motivation for migration immaterial Thym, 'When Union Citizens Turn into Illegal Migrants' (n 1) 258–59.

[39] See also Thym, 'When Union Citizens Turn into Illegal Migrants' (n 1) 253, 260–61; further Nic Shuibhne (n 1) 902–03.

[40] *cf* for an emphasis on a transition in the understanding of the key aim of the Directive from facilitating free movement to preventing burdens on the national welfare systems Kramer (n 37) 290; Nic Shuibhne (n 1) 903; Thym, 'The Elusive Limits of Solidarity' (n 25) 25; Thym, 'When Union Citizens Turn into Illegal Migrants' (n 1) 254–55.

[41] See also Nic Shuibhne (n 1) 916; Thym, 'When Union Citizens Turn into Illegal Migrants' (n 1) 252ff.

[42] *Alimanovic* (n 32) para 52.

The same must apply to other economically inactive persons with regard to Article 14(3) Directive 2004/38/EC.

This has been confirmed by the Court in the *García-Nieto* judgment handed down on 25 February 2016:

> In that context, it must also be stated that, although Directive 2004/38 requires the host Member State to take account of the individual situation of the person concerned before it adopts an expulsion measure or finds that the residence of that person is placing an unreasonable burden on its social assistance system [Brey], no such individual assessment is necessary in circumstances such as those at issue in the main proceedings.[43]

The circumstances of the *García-Nieto* case were characterised by the fact that a period of residence not exceeding three months was at stake for which Article 24(2) Directive 2004/38/EC explicitly (and in line with primary EU law) excludes an entitlement to social assistance.[44]

Hence, the proportionality test continues to apply for economically inactive Union citizens residing between three months and five years in the host Member State. Not only may *Dano*—in view of the Court's established case law from the pre-*Dano* era and its subsequent confirmation in *Alimanovic* and *García-Nieto*—be understood to the contrary;[45] such an understanding would also require an amendment of Articles 7(3)(b) and 14(3) of Directive 2004/38/EC.[46] It has to be added, though, that the scope of application of the proportionality test is rather limited in view of the specific provisions of the Directive regarding certain economically inactive persons, notably students (Article 24(2) Directive 2004/38/EC), first-time jobseekers (Article 24(2) Directive 2004/38/EC; *cf* III.E.i below) and former workers (Article 7(3) Directive 2004/38/EC; *cf* below III.E.ii); moreover, it has to be recalled that the threshold for being qualified as worker is relatively low,[47] so that, for instance, an employed person having to rely on in-work benefits supplementing her or his salary to the minimum level of subsistence would count as a worker, but not as an economically inactive person.[48]

[43] *García-Nieto* (n 31) para 46.

[44] See above (n 31).

[45] *cf* also Kramer (n 37) 294–95.

[46] *cf* also Verschueren (n 37) 379, 383ff, 388.

[47] See only ECJ, Case C-27/91 *URSSAF*, EU:C:1991:441, para 8; Case C-3/90 *Bernini*, EU:C:1992:89, paras 15f; Case C-213/05 *Geven*, EU:C:2007:438, para 7; Case C-53/81 *Levin*, EU:C:1982:105, paras 11ff; Case C-139/85 *Kempf*, EU:C:1986:223, paras 13ff; Case C-14/09 *Genc*, EU:C:2010:57, paras 19ff; for an overview, Wollenschläger, *Grundfreiheit ohne Markt* (n 7) 60ff. Despite the theoretically wide concept, O'Brien (n 1) 937ff, 953ff, identifies a tendency towards a restrictive understanding in the Member States' legislation and practice which is considered particularly problematic in view of changing patterns in the labour market and the proliferation of low-paid and insecure employment (like zero-hours contracts).

[48] See also Peers (n 37) 198.

C. Assessment of Proportionality

Undoubtedly, making the right of residence dependent on an assessment of proportionality in each individual case entails legal uncertainty. This problem is mitigated by the fact that the ECJ has refrained from questioning clear rules in the Directive[49] by requiring or applying a proportionality test, notably in the case of students,[50] economically inactive persons residing for less than three months[51] and former workers (seeking a job).[52,53] However, in cases in which the Directive contains ambiguous provisions—like in the case of the right to residence for economically inactive persons before having acquired a right to permanent residence with regard to expulsion not being the automatic consequence of a person having recourse to the social assistance system—the issue of legal uncertainty remains; it may only be mitigated by a gradual consolidation of the case law.[54] Against the background of this distinction between settled and open issues with regard to Directive 2004/38/EC, it seems wrong to parallelise *Dano* (regarding the latter) on the one hand and *Alimanovic* and *García-Nieto* (regarding the former).[55]

With regard to the proportionality test, one open issue is whether the claimant's becoming an unreasonable burden on the Member State's social assistance system has to be assessed with regard to the individual claimant or the impact on the social system as such.[56] The latter reading might be supported by the *Brey* judgment asking for an 'overall assessment of the specific burden which granting that benefit would place on the national social assistance system as a whole'.[57] However, such a test can hardly be met as the ECJ rightly stressed in *Alimanovic*:

> Moreover, as regards the individual assessment for the purposes of making an overall appraisal of the burden which the grant of a specific benefit would place on the national system of social assistance at issue in the main proceedings as a whole, it must be observed that the assistance awarded to a single applicant can scarcely be described as an 'unreasonable burden' for a Member State, within the meaning of Article 14(1) of Directive 2004/38. However, while an individual claim might not place the Member State concerned under an unreasonable burden, the accumulation of all the individual claims which would be submitted to it would be bound to do so.[58]

[49] See from a general perspective in terms of separation of powers Iliopoulou-Penot (n 1) 1030ff.
[50] *cf* ECJ, Case C-158/07 *Förster*, EU:C:2008:630—even before the Directive entered into force.
[51] *García-Nieto* (n 31).
[52] *Alimanovic* (n 32).
[53] See for a critical view in terms of the one-sided outcome Iliopoulou-Penot (n 1) 1023 ff. See also Kramer (n 37) 294f, 299.
[54] On the issue of legal certainty, Iliopoulou-Penot (n 1) 1025ff.
[55] See, eg, Farahat (n 1) 49ff; O'Brien (n 1) 948ff; Iliopoulou-Penot (n 1) 1015ff, 1028—relativised, however, at ibid, 1023ff.
[56] In more detail, Thym, 'The Elusive Limits of Solidarity' (n 25) 27ff.
[57] *Brey* (n 34) para 63.
[58] *Alimanovic* (n 32) para 62. *Cf* for a critical view Iliopoulou-Penot (n 1) 1027ff. *Cf* also *Dano* (n 32) para 74; *García-Nieto* (n 31) para 50.

Hence, it seems preferable to relate unreasonableness to the situation of the individual claimant.[59]

D. Relevance of the Fundamental Right to Social Assistance (Article 34 CFR)

Article 34 of the Charter of Fundamental Rights of the European Union contains a (social) right to social security and social assistance:

> (1) The Union recognises and respects the entitlement to social security benefits and social services providing protection in cases such as maternity, illness, industrial accidents, dependency or old age, and in the case of loss of employment, in accordance with the rules laid down by Union law and national laws and practices.
> (2) Everyone residing and moving legally within the European Union is entitled to social security benefits and social advantages in accordance with Union law and national laws and practices.
> (3) In order to combat social exclusion and poverty, the Union recognises and respects the right to social and housing assistance so as to ensure a decent existence for all those who lack sufficient resources, in accordance with the rules laid down by Union law and national laws and practices.

While it is true that deriving social entitlements directly from fundamental rights must be the exception, notably in view of the primacy of the democratically legitimised legislator, which is also reflected by the numerous references to EU and national law and practices in the aforementioned Charter provision,[60] and moreover the difficult question of how to distribute the social responsibility between the home and the host Member State has to be answered, the relevance of this Charter right in view of entitlement of economically inactive persons has to be nonetheless determined (this issue is discussed in more detail in the contribution of Niamh Nic Shuibhne in this volume).

In *Dano*, the Court avoided addressing this fundamental rights issue by a *limine* denying the applicability of the Charter. For, Member States would not be implementing EU law as required by Article 51(1) CFR which has to be interpreted strictly:

> In paragraph 41 of the judgment in Brey (EU:C:2013:565), the Court confirmed that Article 70 of Regulation No 883/2004, which defines the term 'special non-contributory cash benefits', is not intended to lay down the conditions creating the right to those benefits. It is thus for the legislature of each Member State to lay down those conditions.
>
> Accordingly, since those conditions result neither from Regulation No 883/2004 nor from Directive 2004/38 or other secondary EU legislation, and the Member States thus

[59] *cf* also—understanding 'the individual standard as a proxy for the systemic argument'—Thym, 'The Elusive Limits of Solidarity' (n 25) 30ff. See for a critical view O'Brien (n 1) 950.

[60] *cf* only F Wollenschläger, 'Grundrechtsschutz und Unionsbürgerschaft' in A Hatje and P-C Müller-Graff (eds), *Enzyklopädie Europarecht*, vol 2 (Baden-Baden, Nomos, 2014) § 8 para 48.

> have competence to determine the conditions for the grant of such benefits, they also have competence, as the Advocate General has observed in point 146 of his Opinion, to define the extent of the social cover provided by that type of benefit.
>
> Consequently, when the Member States lay down the conditions for the grant of special non-contributory cash benefits and the extent of such benefits, they are not implementing EU law.[61]

Denying an implementation of EU law within the meaning of Article 51(1) CFR despite extensive deliberations in the judgment on the interpretation of EU law regarding access of economically inactive persons to social assistance, may be considered surprising.[62] Moreover, this approach contrasts with the ECJ's *Kamberaj* judgment of 24 April 2012 in which the Court reverted to Article 34 CFR to interpret EU secondary law:

> Article 11(4) of Directive 2003/109 must be understood as allowing Member States to limit the equal treatment enjoyed by holders of the status conferred by Directive 2003/109, with the exception of social assistance or social protection benefits granted by the public authorities, at national, regional or local level, which enable individuals to meet their basic needs such as food, accommodation and health.
>
> In that regard, it should be recalled that, according to Article 34 of the Charter, the Union recognises and respects the right to social and housing assistance so as to ensure a decent existence for all those who lack sufficient resources. It follows that, in so far as the benefit in question in the main proceedings fulfils the purpose set out in that article of the Charter, it cannot be considered, under European Union law, as not being part of core benefits within the meaning of Article 11(4) of Directive 2003/109. It is for the referring court to reach the necessary findings, taking into consideration the objective of that benefit, its amount, the conditions subject to which it is awarded and the place of that benefit in the Italian system of social assistance.[63]

Moreover, the German Supreme Social Court (Bundessozialgericht) has advocated an even stricter reading of fundamental rights, inter alia, in its judgment in the *Alimanovic* case referred to the ECJ, by granting economically inactive Union citizens whose residence has become stable (which is usually assumed after a stay of six months) access to social assistance according to § 23(1) sentence 3 Social Code XII in view of the constitutional guarantee of a minimum subsistence level.[64]

[61] *Dano* (n 32) paras 89ff.

[62] See for a critical view Nic Shuibhne (n 1) 914–15; Thym, 'The Elusive Limits of Solidarity' (n 25) 48; Verschueren (n 37) 386–87; A Wallrabenstein, 'Wie Florin zwischen die Stühle rutschte—Die Unionsbürgerschaft und das menschenwürdige Existenzminimum' (2016) *JuristenZeitung* 109, 116–17; R Zahn, '"Common Sense" or a Threat to EU Integration? The Court, Economically Inactive EU Citizens and Social Benefits' (2015) 44 *Industrial Law Journal* 573, 583–84.

[63] ECJ, Case C-571/10 *Kamberaj*, ECLI:EU:C:2012:233, paras 91–92.

[64] German Supreme Social Court (Bundessozialgericht), Decision of 3 December 2015, B 4 AS 44/15 R, paras 36ff; *cf* also Decisions of 20 January 2016, B 14 AS 15/15 R and B 14 AS 35/15 R, Press Release no 1/16 of the German Supreme Social Court referring to social assistance for jobseekers.

This jurisprudence is controversially debated[65] and questioned by some lower social courts;[66] moreover, in a recent amendment to the Social Code II,[67] the legislator has explicitly rejected this jurisprudence—the compatibility of this legislation with (national) fundamental rights (and, by the way, also with EU law) remains to be seen, though.[68]

E. Situation of Jobseekers and Former Workers

i. First-Time Jobseekers

First-time jobseekers enjoy an unconditional right of residence in economic terms. Hence, there is no issue regarding fulfilment of economic criteria. The only limitation refers to the chances of finding a new job. They 'may not be expelled for as long as the Union citizens can provide evidence that they are continuing to seek employment and that they have a genuine chance of being engaged' (Article 14(4)(b) Directive 2004/38/EC). The downside of this privileged position in terms of economic residence criteria is, however, a complete exclusion from access to social assistance (Article 24(2) Directive 2004/38/EC)—a situation which corresponds to the pre-citizenship Acquis as confirmed in the *Lebon* ruling of 18 June 1987.[69]

Yet, the partial extension of the claim to social solidarity to economically inactive persons, as a consequence of the introduction of Union citizenship (see above, II), raised the question whether this development had to be transferred to the treatment of jobseekers, which seemed all the more justified since jobseekers, unlike other economically inactive persons, may be qualified as potential market actors

[65] I Kanalan, 'Das Menschenrecht auf das Existenzminimum ernst genommen—Sozialleistungsansprüche von Unionsbürger_innen' (*Verfassungsblog*, 1 March 2016): verfassungsblog.de/das-menschenrecht-auf-das-existenzminimum-ernst-genommen-sozialleistungsansprueche-von-unions-buerger_innen/; F Wilksch, 'Das BSG und die Existenzsicherung arbeitssuchender und wirtschaftlich inaktiver Unionsbürger*innen' (*Juwiss-Blog*, 15 December 2015 and 16 December 2015): www.juwiss.de/89-2015/ and: www.juwiss.de/90-2015/.

[66] Social Court of Second Instance Rheinland-Pfalz (Landessozialgericht Rheinland-Pfalz), Decision of 11 February 2016, L 3 AS 668/15 B ER, paras 22ff; Social Court of First Instance Dortmund (Sozialgericht Dortmund), Decision of 11 February 2016, S 35 AS 5396/15 ER, paras 23ff; Social Court of First Instance Berlin (Sozialgericht Berlin), Decision of 11 December 2015, S 149 AS 7191/13, paras 26ff; Social Court of Second Instance Niedersachsen-Bremen (Landessozialgericht Niedersachsen-Bremen), Decision of 17 March 2016, L 9 AS 1580/15 B ER.

[67] Gesetz zur Regelung von Ansprüchen ausländischer Personen in der Grundsicherung für Arbeitsuchende nach dem Zweiten Buch Sozialgesetzbuch und in der Sozialhilfe nach dem Zwölften Buch Sozialgesetzbuch vom 22. Dezember 2016, BGBl 2016 I, 3155 (Act regulating the access of foreigners to social assistance for jobseekers according to the Social Code II and on social benefits according to the Social Code XII, 22 December 2016).

[68] *cf* on the Dutch model of a 'sliding scale' Kramer (n 37) 283ff.

[69] ECJ, Case 316/85 *Lebon*, EU:C:1987:302, paras 25–26. For a critical view: M Dougan, 'Free Movement: The Workseeker as Citizen' (2001) 4 *Cambridge Yearbook of European Legal Studies* 93, 98–99.

and thus enjoy a janus-faced status.[70,71] The Court adopted this position and explicitly overruled *Lebon* in its *Collins* judgment handed down on 23 March 2004:

> In view of the establishment of citizenship of the Union and the interpretation in the case-law of the right to equal treatment enjoyed by citizens of the Union, it is no longer possible to exclude from the scope of [Art 45 para 2 TFEU]—which expresses the fundamental principle of equal treatment, guaranteed by [Art 18 TFEU]—a benefit of a financial nature intended to facilitate access to employment in the labour market of a Member State. The interpretation of the scope of the principle of equal treatment in relation to access to employment must reflect this development, as compared with the interpretation followed in Lebon.[72]

There were, however, limits to this claim to equal treatment as the Member States were allowed to introduce conditions for access to such benefits securing a 'connection between persons who claim entitlement to such an allowance and [the host Member State's] employment market'.[73]

The conflict of this jurisprudence with the explicit and complete exclusion of jobseekers from entitlement to social assistance in Article 24(2) Directive 2004/38/EC was evident.[74] In recent rulings, however, the Court—after having had confirmed and even widened the *Collins* jurisprudence[75]—has narrowed it down by findings not always in line with former judgments and notably by excluding social assistance within the meaning of Article 24(2) Directive 2004/38/EC from the scope of application of the *Collins* jurisprudence.[76] Thus, the only question which remains (open) is whether the complete exclusion of jobseekers from access to social assistance provided for by Article 24(2) Directive 2004/38/EC conflicts with the proportionality-based concept regarding economically inactive persons not seeking employment and is therefore in line with EU primary law.[77]

[70] *cf* also ECJ, Joined Cases C-22 and C-23/08 *Vatsouras and Koupatantze*, EU:C:2009:150, Opinion of AG Colomer, para 55: jobseekers 'are midway between being engaged in economic activity and not being so engaged'.

[71] See on this development F Wollenschläger, 'The Judiciary, the Legislature and the Evolution of Union Citizenship' in P Syrpis (ed), *The Judiciary, the Legislature and the EU Internal Market* (Cambridge, Cambridge University Press, 2012) 315ff.

[72] ECJ, Case C-138/02 *Collins*, EU:C:2004:172, paras 63–64.

[73] ibid paras 67–68.

[74] See only Wollenschläger, 'The Judiciary, the Legislature and the Evolution of Union Citizenship' (n 71) 324ff; further Iliopoulou-Penot (n 1) 1009ff.

[75] See ECJ, Case C-258/04 *Ioannidis*, EU:C:2005:559; Joined Cases C-22 and C-23/08 *Vatsouras and Koupatantze*, EU:C:2008:201; Case C-367/11 *Prete*, ECLI:EU:C:2012:668.

[76] *Alimanovic* (n 32) paras 40ff; further *García-Nieto* (n 31) para 37. See, however, *Vatsouras and Koupatantze* (n 76) paras 42ff. *Cf* for a critical view on *Alimanovic* in this respect O'Brien (n 1) 947–48; Iliopoulou-Penot (n 1) 1019–20; Wallrabenstein, 'Die Gleichheit der Freiheit' (n 1) 354.

[77] Disagreeing (proportionate): ECJ, Case C-67/14 *Alimanovic*, ECLI:EU:C:2015:210, Opinion of AG Wathelet, para 98, and *García-Nieto* (n 31) paras 73ff. *Cf* also *Alimanovic* (n 32) para 58: 'It follows from the express reference in Article 24(2) of Directive 2004/38 to Article 14(4)(b) thereof that the host Member State may refuse to grant any social assistance to a Union citizen whose right of residence is based solely on that latter provision.' See, however, O Golynker, 'Jobseekers' Rights in the European

ii. Former Workers (Unemployment)

Regarding former and now unemployed workers (whether looking for a new job or not), Article 7(3) Directive 2004/38/EC contains a distinction in terms of the retention of their status as worker (associated with an unconditional right of residence and access to social benefits), which is based on the duration of previous employment:

> For the purposes of paragraph 1(a), a Union citizen who is no longer a worker or self-employed person shall retain the status of worker or self-employed person in the following circumstances …
>
> (b) he/she is in duly recorded involuntary unemployment after having been employed for more than one year and has registered as a job-seeker with the relevant employment office;
>
> (c) he/she is in duly recorded involuntary unemployment after completing a fixed-term employment contract of less than a year or after having become involuntarily unemployed during the first twelve months and has registered as a job-seeker with the relevant employment office. In this case, the status of worker shall be retained for no less than six months.

In *Alimanovic*, the Court has confirmed this clear distinction as proportionate and not required a further individual assessment for persons having worked for less than one year (lit c):

> It must be stated in this connection that, although the Court has held that Directive 2004/38 requires a Member State to take account of the individual situation of the person concerned before it adopts an expulsion measure or finds that the residence of that person is placing an unreasonable burden on its social assistance system …, no such individual assessment is necessary in circumstances such as those at issue in the main proceedings.
>
> Directive 2004/38, establishing a gradual system as regards the retention of the status of 'worker' which seeks to safeguard the right of residence and access to social assistance, itself takes into consideration various factors characterising the individual situation of each applicant for social assistance and, in particular, the duration of the exercise of any economic activity.
>
> By enabling those concerned to know, without any ambiguity, what their rights and obligations are, the criterion referred to both in Paragraph 7(1) of Book II, read in conjunction with Paragraph 2(3) of the Law on freedom of movement, and in Article 7(3)(c) of Directive 2004/38, namely a period of six months after the cessation of employment during which the right to social assistance is retained, is consequently such as to guarantee a significant level of legal certainty and transparency in the context of the

Union' (2005) 30 *EL Rev* 111, 119; HM Heinig, 'Art 18 i.V.m. Art 12 EG als Schlüssel zur Teilhabe von arbeitsuchenden Unionsbürgern aus anderen Mitgliedstaaten an steuerfinanzierten Sozialleistungen in Deutschland' (2008) *Zeitschrift für europäisches Sozial- und Arbeitsrecht* 472, 473; further Wollenschläger, *Grundfreiheit ohne Markt* (n 7) 272ff.

award of social assistance by way of basic provision, while complying with the principle of proportionality.[78]

This interpretation is convincing. Not only does Article 7(3) Directive 2004/38/EC contain a clear rule. Moreover, with this distinction, the legislator has balanced the competing interests in a proportionate manner. Notwithstanding the rejection of a claim to social assistance in the case of Mrs Alimanovic in view of the one-year threshold, the rules of Directive 2004/38/EC for former workers may be considered rather generous; it grants an unemployed person having worked for more than one year and looking for a new job the same rights as a worker and thus full and unconditional entitlement to all forms of social assistance (and presumably for an unlimited period of time). This mitigates the criticism sparked off by the outcome of the *Alimanovic* judgment.[79]

IV. CONCLUSION: CONSOLIDATING THE ACQUIS

With the right to non-discrimination depending on enjoyment of a right to residence, the latter's criteria determine access of economically inactive persons to social assistance. While requiring self-sufficiency as a residence criterion would mean an exclusion of non-economic actors from equal access to social assistance, a more generous approach would broaden respective claims. Positioning the EU law framework in this context, the result is ambivalent. For, on the one hand, it demands sufficient resources but, on the other, not possessing them does not necessarily mean losing the right of residence; rather, a proportionality test is ultimately decisive. This tension brings legal uncertainty into the free movement regime—a situation for which not only the Court's jurisprudence on Union citizenship may be blamed, but also the Union legislator having transformed it into indeterminate provisions of secondary law. Notably recent judgments of the ECJ have in many respects done what could be done in court rulings to bring more clarity into the legal framework and thus consolidated it:[80] clear rules in the

[78] *Alimanovic* (n 32) paras 59ff. Disagreeing: *Alimanovic*, Opinion of AG Wathelet (n 77) paras 97ff.

[79] See for such a criticism, eg, Farahat (n 1) 50–51; Iliopoulou-Penot (n 1) 1015ff; further O'Brien (n 1) 959; T Kingreen, 'In Love with the Single Market? Die EuGH-Entscheidung Alimanovic zum Ausschluss von Unionsbürgern von sozialen Grundsicherungsleistungen' (2015) 21 *Neue Zeitschrift für Verwaltungsrecht* 1503, 1504–05. Moreover, in *Saint Prix*, the ECJ (Case C-507/12 ECLI:EU:C:2014:2007) has interpreted Art 7(3) Directive 2004/38/EC not as exhaustive in terms of grounds for retention of the worker status (*in casu*: extension to pregnancy)—*cf* on this judgment only S Currie, 'Pregnancy-related Employment Breaks, the Gender Dynamics of Free Movement Law and Curtailed Citizenship: *Jessy Saint Prix*' (2016) 53 *CML Rev* 543; this shows, by the way, that the Court is, as stated earlier (see Wollenschläger, 'The Judiciary, the Legislature and the Evolution of Union Citizenship' (n 71) 322), 'when secondary law is considered to leave room for manoeuvre, … still prepared to continue its integrationist jurisprudence and to find citizenship- and free movement-friendly solutions'.

[80] See for a distinction of three phases in the development of EU citizenship Wollenschläger, 'The Judiciary, the Legislature and the Evolution of Union Citizenship' (n 71) 305ff: (1) the Court's reassessment of the acquis in light of Union citizenship introduced in 1993; (2) the reception of the Court's

Directive have been confirmed as proportionate and thus have not been subjected to an individual assessment (*contra legem*) when applying them (access to social assistance for students, economically inactive persons residing for less than three months and former workers seeking a job); moreover, it has been stressed that self-sufficiency is the rule and deviating from this requirement the exception. The ECJ's recent jurisprudence, notably the *Dano* case, should, however, not be misunderstood as restoring the economic residence criteria as conditions *strictu sensu*. Rather, with regard to the right of residence of non-market actors for stays exceeding three months, they are still subject to a proportionality test; a contrary understanding would, as explained (above III.B.iii), not only contradict established case law, but also require an amendment of Articles 7(3)(b) and 14(3) of Directive 2004/38/EC. Considering this—and in addition, the generous treatment of former workers having become unemployed after a period of work of more than a year and the wide understanding of the concept of worker—economically inactive persons still enjoy an—albeit limited—claim to social solidarity in the host Member State. Against this background and in view of the fact that the aforementioned limitations on free movement rights of economically inactive persons contained in Directive 2004/38/EC, which have been explicitly confirmed by the Court so far, may hardly be considered disproportionate in view of the free movement guarantees enshrined in EU primary law, parts of the criticism the recent jurisprudence has drawn seem to go too far.[81] Rather, these limitations reflect the current state of integration in a politically sensitive area—a status quo which leaves room for and requires further consolidation.

jurisprudence in the new Citizenship Directive 2004/38/EC enacted in 2004; (3) the Directive's careful interpretation by the Court, however, not precluding citizenship- and free movement-friendly solutions beyond the scope of its application.

[81] See, eg, Nic Shuibhne (n 1) 908ff, quotation 909, further 926ff: 'That method turns the standard approach to conditions and limits on its constitutional head—the latter no longer *temper* equal treatment rights; they *constitute* the rights.'

10

Back to the Roots? No Access to Social Assistance for Union Citizens who are Economically Inactive

PAUL MINDERHOUD AND SANDRA MANTU

I. INTRODUCTION

ACCESS TO SOCIAL assistance benefits for economically inactive European Union (EU) citizens in other Member States has become an increasingly disputed issue in the EU. This issue is regulated by Directive 2004/38, which deals with the right of citizens of the Union and their family members to move and reside freely within the territory of the Member States. In the last three years, five important judgments of the Court of Justice of the EU (ECJ) have been delivered on this topic in the *Brey*, *Dano*, *Alimanovic*, *García-Nieto* and *Commission v UK* cases. This recent case law of the ECJ has drastically changed the landscape concerning access to social assistance benefits for inactive EU citizens.

Our contribution provides a legal analysis of these cases with the aim of charting the boundaries of social citizenship for mobile EU citizens. We argue that the Court's approach in the *Brey*, *Dano*, *Alimanovic*, *García-Nieto* and *Commission v UK* cases will have an impact upon how fundamental the status of EU citizenship is. An interpretation where economically inactive EU citizens must always have sufficient resources so that they do not need any social assistance benefit may effectively limit the number of inactive citizens exercising free movement rights since Member States may set a high threshold for having sufficient resources in their national legislation. Moreover, the Court's recent jurisprudence stresses that the objective of Directive 2004/38 is 'preventing Union citizens who are nationals of other Member States from becoming an unreasonable burden on the social assistance system' of their host State.[1] Yet, the Court has failed to engage in an analysis where it explains how this new found objective can be reconciled with

[1] Case C-333/13 *Dano*, EU:C:2014:2358, para 74; Case C-67/14 *Alimanovic*, EU:C:2015:597, para 50; Case C-299/14 *García-Nieto*, EU:C:2016:114, para 39.

the objective to facilitate and strengthen the right of free movement and residence of all Union citizens as emphasised in the *Metock* case based on the preamble of Directive 2004/38.[2] This chapter is organised as follows: section II discusses the link between economically inactive EU citizens' right to reside on the basis of Directive 2004/38 and the condition to have sufficient resources; section III examines the legal entitlement of mobile EU citizens to equal treatment based on Article 24 of Directive 2004/38; section IV provides a legal analysis of the *Brey*, *Dano*, *Alimanovic*, *García-Nieto* and *Commission v UK* cases with a focus on EU citizens' entitlement to social rights; finally, section V concludes this contribution with a discussion of the impact of the Court's shift in interpreting the social rights of mobile EU citizens on the notion of EU citizenship. Methodologically, this contribution offers a systematic review of recent ECJ decisions addressing the entitlement of economically inactive EU citizens to social rights in their host State with a view to assess the coherence, predictability and future implications of this case law for the mobility of EU citizens.

II. FREE MOVEMENT AND SOCIAL RIGHTS UNDER DIRECTIVE 2004/38

Directive 2004/38/EC makes a distinction between residence up to three months, residence from three months to five years, and residence for longer than five years. Different conditions for residence apply in each of these three categories. All EU citizens have the right to enter any EU Member State without any conditions or formalities, other than the requirement to hold a valid identity card or passport, for three months (Article 6). The treatment of economically inactive persons differs from the treatment of economically active persons. For residence longer than three months, economically inactive EU citizens must have sufficient resources in order not to become an unreasonable burden on the social assistance system of the host Member State during their period of residence and have a comprehensive medical insurance.

These conditions regarding sufficient resources and comprehensive sickness insurance do not apply to workers, self-employed persons, or persons who stopped being economically active but who retain worker or self-employed status pursuant to Article 7(3) Directive 2004/38.[3] Jobseekers who enter the territory of the host Member State in order to seek employment are another category of citizens for whom sufficient resources and sickness insurance are not relevant. Such persons may not be expelled for as long as they can provide evidence that they are continuing to seek employment and that they have a genuine chance of being engaged. Union citizens who have resided legally and for a continuous period of

[2] Case C-127/08 *Metock*, EU:C:2008:449, para 59.

[3] S Mantu, 'Protecting EU Workers in Case of Involuntary Unemployment: Retention of Worker Status' (2014) 7 *Online Journal on Free Movement of Workers within the European Union* 15.

five years in the host Member State have a right of permanent residence there. Union citizens (and their family members) enjoy this right without any further conditions, even if they no longer have sufficient resources or comprehensive sickness insurance cover.

It has never been entirely clear what the Directive means by 'sufficient resources', an issue that led to several debates during the negotiation of the Directive.[4] The most disputed aspects concerned the contradiction between prohibiting the use of a fixed amount of money to define sufficient resources and the use of the level of social assistance benefit as an indication of (a lack of) sufficient resources. This ambivalence is reflected in the practice of various Member States that relied on fixed amounts to set the threshold for sufficient resources.[5] However, *Commission v Netherlands* made clear that Member States could not require standard norms regarding sufficient resources.[6]

ECJ jurisprudence regarding the notion of sufficient resources further highlights two important issues: the level and the origin of the resources. Underpinning these issues is the relation between sufficient resources and reliance on the host State's social assistance system. At the moment, the Court's biggest challenge is to find a balance between the requirement to fulfil the condition of sufficient resources and the possibility to apply for social assistance, as shown by the *Brey* and *Dano* cases.[7] Regarding the origin of the resources, it is clear from the case law of the ECJ that to 'have' sufficient resources means that these resources are available to the Union citizen, regardless of their origin. While they can be derived from another person, including a third national family member (*Zhu and Chen*),[8] it is still disputed whether the prospect of future earnings is enough to fulfil the condition of sufficient resources (Opinion of AG Mengozzi in *Alopka*).[9] In July 2015, the Court reaffirmed its position in the *Zhu and Chen* judgment that the text of Article 7(1)(b) of Directive 2004/38 must be interpreted as meaning that a Union citizen has sufficient resources for himself and his family members not to become a burden on the social assistance system of the host Member State during his period of residence even where those resources derive in part from those of his spouse who is a third-country national.[10]

[4] P Minderhoud, 'Sufficient Resources and Residence Rights Under Directive 2004/38' in H Verschueren (ed), *Residence, Employment and Social Rights of Mobile Persons: On How EU Law Defines Where They Belong* (Cambridge, Intersentia, 2016).

[5] European Citizen Action Service, *Comparative study on the application of Directive 2004/38/EC of 29 April 2004 on the right of citizens of the union and their family members to move and reside freely within the territory of the member states*, European Parliament's Committee on Legal Affairs, PE 410.650 (Brussels, 2009) 165.

[6] Case C-398/06 *Commission v Netherlands*, EU:C:2008:214.

[7] Case C-140/12 *Brey*, EU:C:2013:565; *Dano* (n 1).

[8] Case C-200/02 *Zhu and Chen*, EU:C:2004:639.

[9] Case C-86/12 *Alopka*, EU:C:2013:645.

[10] Case C-218/14 *Kuldip Singh and Others*, EU:C:2015:476.

III. THE LIMITS OF EQUAL TREATMENT FOR EU CITIZENS

According to Article 24 of the Directive, Union citizens who reside on the basis of the Directive (ie, they fulfil the conditions attached to the type of residence rights as discussed above) enjoy equal treatment with nationals of the host Member State within the scope of the Treaty. However, a series of exceptions are envisaged: during the first three months of residence EU citizens are not entitled to any social assistance. EU citizens who move in search of employment can be excluded from social assistance for as long as they are looking for a job. Finally, a host Member State is not obliged to award maintenance aid for studies (student grants and student loans) to EU citizens who have not obtained a right to permanent residence in the host State. EU citizens who are EU workers, self-employed or retain these statuses in line with the provisions of the Directive and their family members are not covered by this exception from equal treatment in respect of maintenance aid.

The wording of the Directive in relation to the social rights of economically inactive mobile citizens has been criticised for lacking clarity.[11] On the one hand, the Directive only allows inactive persons to use their free movement rights if they have the necessary resources. On the other hand, it equally suggests that when inactive persons apply for a social assistance benefit, they should be able to get such a benefit without having to fear automatic expulsion due to a lack of sufficient resources. The Directive fails to offer a clear definition as to when an EU citizen becomes an 'unreasonable burden' on the social assistance system of his host State. Leeway is given to Member States to examine whether financial difficulties may be temporary, which some States duly used by developing their own definitions.[12] The categorisation of a benefit as social assistance is an equally contested issue. According to the ECJ in the *Vatsouras* case, a benefit of a financial nature intended to facilitate access to the labour market is not a social assistance benefit in the sense of Directive 2004/38.[13] This raised questions about the character of social assistance benefits in several countries (France, Germany, the UK and the Netherlands) which all have the intention of facilitating labour market access.[14] It was precisely some of these Member States that complained to the Commission about abuse of their welfare systems, although it is not clear whether the free movement rules encourage abuse or if the nature and rules of attribution of the benefits make it easier for economically inactive citizens to claim those benefits. Some of the cases analysed in this contribution offered the Court of

[11] K Hailbronner, 'Union Citizenship and Access to Social Benefits' (2005) 42 *CML Rev* 1245; P Minderhoud, 'Directive 2004/38 and Access to social Assistance' in E Guild, C Gortazar Rotaeche and D Kostakopoulou (eds), *The Reconceptualization of European Union Citizenship* (Leiden, Martinus Nijhoff, 2014); D Thym, 'The Elusive Limits of Solidarity: Residence Rights of and Social Benefits for Economically Inactive Union Citizens' (2015) 52 *CML Rev* 17.

[12] Minderhoud, 'Directive 2004/38 and Access to Social Assistance' (n 11).

[13] Case C-22/08 and C-23/08 *Vatsouras and Koupatantze*, EU:C:2009:344.

[14] H Verschueren, 'Do National Activation Measures Stand the Test of European Law on the Free Movement of Workers and Jobseekers?' (2010) 12 *European Journal of Migration and Law* 81.

Justice an opportunity to revisit its own jurisprudence on what constitutes a social assistance benefit. The Court chose to change the *Vatsouras* line of interpretation by enlarging the scope of the notion of 'social assistance' found in Article 24 of Directive 2004/38. A wider notion of 'social assistance' has implications for the range of benefits from which jobseekers are excluded on the basis of Article 24(2) of Directive 2004/38. It equally impacts the retention of a right to reside in the case of economically inactive EU citizens since if they claim such a benefit they may be seen as lacking sufficient resources.

In July 2009, the Commission published a Communication on guidance for better transposition and application of Directive 2004/38/EC on the right of citizens of the Union and their family members to move and reside freely within the territory of the Member States.[15] It repeated that, in assessing whether an individual whose resources can no longer be regarded as sufficient and who was granted the minimum subsistence benefit is or has become an unreasonable burden, the authorities of the Member States must carry out a proportionality test. To this end, Member States may develop a points-based scheme as an indicator. Recital 16 of Directive 2004/38 provides three sets of criteria for this purpose:

1. Duration: For how long is the benefit being granted? Is it likely that the EU citizen will get out of the safety net soon? How long has the residence lasted in the host Member State?
2. Personal situation: What is the level of connection of the EU citizen and his/her family members with the society of the host Member State? Are there any considerations pertaining to age, state of health, family and economic situation that need to be taken into account?
3. Amount: Total amount of aid granted. Does the EU citizen have a history of relying heavily on social assistance? Does the EU citizen have a history of contributing to the financing of social assistance in the host Member State?

The Communication emphasises that as long as the beneficiaries of the right of residence do not become an unreasonable burden on the social assistance system of the host Member States, they cannot be expelled for this reason, an interpretation reflecting Article 14(3) of the Directive. Concerning jobseekers, by way of exception from the general rule that EU citizens retain their right to reside for longer than three months if they meet the conditions of Article 7, Article 14(4) states that they 'may not be expelled for as long as the Union citizens can provide evidence that they are continuing to seek employment and that they have a genuine chance of being engaged'. Although this Guide and Communication were meant for clarification, Member States are given leeway to define the concept of unreasonable burden. Several questions remain relevant: when is it a case of temporary

[15] COM(2009)313/4 on guidance for better transposition and application of Directive 2004/38/EC on the right of citizens of the Union and their family members to move and reside freely within the territory of the Member States (Brussels).

difficulties, what is the required length of residence, which personal circumstances should be relevant, and how much granted aid is too much? After the introduction of Directive 2004/38, one can argue that an inactive EU citizen applying for a social assistance benefit because he lacked sufficient resources, kept a right of residence under Directive 2004/38 until the moment this right was withdrawn, on the ground that he was supposed to have become an unreasonable burden to the social assistance system. A combined reading of Articles 14, 24 and of paragraph 16 of the preamble of Directive 2004/38 suggests that access to social assistance is not out of the question as long as the citizen does not become an unreasonable burden on the social assistance system of the host Member State.

So far, based on the Court's jurisprudence it is not possible to argue that EU citizens enjoy unconditional access to social assistance benefits in their host State. First, applicants must show they reside legally in the host State. Second, in its jurisprudence the ECJ has formulated additional conditions to the extent that the applicant should 'have a genuine link with the employment market of the State concerned'[16] or 'need to demonstrate a certain degree of integration into the society of the host State'.[17] Likewise, the Court recognises the right of the host Member State to withdraw the right of residence of the person concerned, as long as this is not 'the automatic consequence of relying on the social assistance system'.[18]

IV. THE COURT'S VIEW ON ENTITLEMENT OF EU CITIZENS TO SOCIAL RIGHTS

In the last three years, five important judgments of the Court of Justice of the EU (ECJ) have been delivered on this topic in the *Brey*, *Dano*, *Alimanovic*, *García-Nieto* and *Commission v UK* cases. This recent case law of the ECJ has drastically changed the landscape concerning access to social assistance benefits for inactive EU citizens.

All cases deal with the entitlement of EU citizens to social benefits in their host State and explore the limits of social solidarity to which mobile EU citizens are entitled. In the *Brey* case the Court emphasised that Directive 2004/38 allows host Member States to impose legitimate restrictions in connection to social assistance benefits to Union citizens who are not workers so that those citizens do not become an unreasonable burden on the social assistance system of that Member State. The *Dano*, *Alimanovic* and *García-Nieto* cases all concern the same German provisions of the Social Code that restrict access to social allowances to EU citizens who move to Germany either to seek employment (the situation in *Alimanovic* and *García-Nieto*) or to seek social benefits (the situation in *Dano*). According to the Court,

[16] Case C-138/02 *Collins*, EU:C:2004:172, paras 67–69.

[17] Case C-209/03 *Bidar*, EU:C:2005:169, para 57.

[18] Case C-184/99 *Grzelczyk*, EU:C:2001:458, para 43; Case C-456/02 *Trojani*, EU:C:2004:488, para 36.

in these cases a Union citizen can claim equal treatment with nationals of the host State under Article 24(1) Directive 2004/38 *only* if his residence in the territory of the host Member State complies with the conditions of Directive 2004/38. In its decision in *Commission v UK*, the Court expands further the restrictive interpretation of equal treatment between EU citizens and its own citizens by allowing the Member States to make the access of economically inactive Union citizens to social *security* benefits[19] conditional on having a right to reside in their country.

A. The *Brey* Case

The *Brey* case of 19 September 2013 gives the first signals of an altering position in the ECJ regarding the tension between satisfying the condition as to sufficient resources and applying for a social assistance benefit.[20] This case concerned a German national, who was in receipt of a German invalidity pension of €1.087,74 and who had moved to Austria with his wife. He applied for an Austrian compensatory supplement which aimed at guaranteeing the person concerned a minimum subsistence income in Austria. The Austrian authorities refused to grant this benefit because, in their view, Mr Brey did not meet the conditions required to obtain the right to reside as he lacked sufficient resources. According to the Court, the fact that an economically inactive national from another Member State may be eligible, in the light of a low pension, to receive that compensatory supplement benefit, could be an indication that the national in question does not have sufficient resources to avoid becoming an unreasonable burden on the social assistance system of the host Member State for the purposes of obtaining or retaining the right to reside under Article 7(1)(b) of Directive 2004/38.

It is important to stress that we are only in the presence of an 'indication', not of an established fact. To this end, the Court recalls that the first sentence of Article 8(4) of Directive 2004/38 expressly states that Member States may not lay down a fixed amount which they will regard as 'sufficient resources', but must take into account the personal situation of the person concerned. Therefore, it follows that, although Member States may indicate a certain sum as a reference amount, they may not impose a minimum income level below which it will be presumed that the person concerned does not have sufficient resources, irrespective of a specific examination of the situation of each person concerned. National authorities must carry out an overall assessment of the specific burden which granting that benefit would place on the national social assistance system as a whole by reference to the personal circumstances characterising the individual situation of the person concerned. The ECJ stressed that any limitation upon the freedom of movement as a fundamental principle of EU law must be construed narrowly

[19] Emphasis added by authors.
[20] *Brey* (n 7).

and in compliance with the limits imposed by EU law and the principle of proportionality. The Member States' room for manoeuvre may not be used in such a manner as to compromise the attainment of the objective of Directive 2004/38, more specifically its objective to facilitate and strengthen the primary right to free movement. Relying on these elements, the Court confirms that EU law recognises a certain degree of solidarity between nationals of a host Member State and nationals of other Member States. The mere fact that a national of a Member State receives social assistance is not sufficient to demonstrate that he constitutes an unreasonable burden on the social assistance system of the host Member State. For that reason, the Austrian legislation, by virtue of which the mere fact that an economically inactive migrant EU citizen has applied for the 'compensatory supplement' is sufficient to preclude that citizen from receiving it, is not compatible with EU law. The Court stresses that the automatic character of the refusal prevents the national authorities from carrying out an overall assessment of the specific burden.

In his case note under the *Brey* judgment, Verschueren refers to the final judgment of the the Austrian Supreme Court after the ruling of the ECJ.[21] The Austrian Supreme Court recognised that the host Member State of a migrant economically inactive Union citizen may limit this person's right to reside on its territory when he becomes an unreasonable burden on its social assistance system.[22] In order to assess this unreasonableness, the national authorities must take into account the various elements to which the ECJ refers in *Brey*. A mechanism, as in place in the Austrian legislation, whereby nationals of other Member States who are economically inactive are automatically barred from receiving a particular social security benefit, does not enable the competent authorities of the host Member State to carry out such an assessment. The Austrian Supreme Court concluded that as long as Union citizens reside lawfully in Austria, they may rely on EU law, including as regards the principle of equal treatment, to receive social benefits, even if this could subsequently compromise their right of residence. In the case of Mr Brey, until the competent national authorities end his residence right by issuing a formal decision withdrawing his residence certificate in accordance with the provisions of Directive 2004/38, he continues to enjoy a right to equal treatment with Austrian nationals in relation to receiving a compensatory pension supplement.

B. The *Dano* Case

A year after *Brey*, the ECJ delivered its judgment in the *Dano* case where it took a different approach.[23] In *Dano*, two Romanian nationals, mother and son, living in

[21] H Verschueren, 'Free Movement or Benefit Tourism: The Unreasonable Burden of Brey' (2014) 16 *European Journal of Migration and Law* 147.

[22] OGH 17 December 2013, ECLI:AT:OGH0002:2013:010OBS00152.13W.1217.000: www.ris.bka.gv.at.

[23] *Dano* (n 1).

Germany were refused access to the SGB II benefit under the German basic provision rules. Ms Dano had not entered Germany to seek employment, and although she applied for a benefit reserved to jobseekers, the case file showed that she had not been looking for a job. She had no professional qualifications and had never exercised any profession in Germany or Romania. As regards access to social benefits, the Court held that nationals of other Member States are only entitled to be treated equally with nationals of the host Member State if their residence in the territory of the host Member State meets the requirements of Directive 2004/38. According to the Court, the Directive thus seeks to prevent Union citizens from using the host Member State's social assistance system to fund their means of subsistence. The fact that Union citizens who have used their freedom of movement and of residence are being treated differently from the host Member State's own nationals with regard to social benefits is described as an inevitable consequence of Directive 2004/38 (paragraphs 77 and 78). This potentially unequal treatment is in fact based on the link between sufficient resources being a residence requirement on the one hand and, on the other, the desire to prevent the burden on the social assistance system of the Member States, established by the Union legislature in Article 7 of that Directive. A Member State must therefore, in accordance with Article 7, have the possibility of refusing to grant social benefits to economically inactive Union citizens who exercise their right to free movement for the sole purpose of obtaining another Member State's social assistance, although they do not have sufficient resources in order to qualify for a right of residence. According to the Court, Ms Dano and her son lack sufficient resources and, pursuant to Directive 2004/38, are therefore not entitled to a right of residence in Germany, nor are they entitled to the SGB II benefit.

The *Dano* decision seems to imply that when economically inactive EU citizens (residing for less than five years in another Member State) apply for a social assistance benefit, it automatically means that they have no sufficient resources (any more), and consequently no residence right under Directive 2004/38.[24] Thus, if in *Brey* applying for a benefit was only an 'indication' of lack of sufficient resources, in *Dano* this has become 'certainty'. Where Mr Brey still had a right of residence under Article 7, Ms Dano is considered never to have had such a right. The reasoning in *Dano* leads to the paradoxical situation where a Union citizen would only be entitled to social assistance if he has sufficient resources and therefore is not in need of any social assistance.[25] We seem to be in the presence of a real Catch-22 situation. This position is also a long way from (pre-Directive 2004/38) cases such as *Martínez Sala*[26] and *Trojani*[27] where the Court ruled that an EU citizen, legally residing on the basis of national legislation in the territory of a host Member State, could rely on the equal treatment provision of (now) Article 18 of

[24] See, for a different analysis, see chapter 9 by F Wollenschläger in this volume.

[25] H Verschueren, 'Preventing "Benefit Tourism" in the EU: A Narrow or Broad Interpretation of the Possibilities offered by the ECJ in *Dano*?' (2015) 52 *CML Rev* 363, 381.

[26] Case C-85/96 *Martínez Sala*, EU:C:1998:217.

[27] *Trojani* (n 18).

the Treaty on the Functioning of the European Union in all situations which fall within the scope *ratione materiae* of EU law, including access to social assistance.[28] In this respect it is important to stress that Ms Dano had been granted a residence certificate of unlimited duration in Germany.[29] Based on this previous ECJ jurisprudence Ms Dano would in our view have been entitled to equal treatment.

C. The *Alimanovic* Case

Ms Alimanovic and her three children are all Swedish nationals.[30] The three children were born in Germany. After living abroad for 10 years, the family re-entered Germany in June 2010. Between then and May 2011, Ms Alimanovic and her eldest daughter worked for less than a year in short-term jobs or under employment-promotion measures in Germany. The two women have not worked since. From 1 December 2011 to 31 May 2012, they received subsistence allowances for beneficiaries fit for work ('SGB II benefit', the same benefit Ms Dano applied for), while the other children received social allowances for beneficiaries unfit for work. Subsequently, the competent German authority stopped paying those allowances, because according to the German legislation, non-nationals (and members of their family), whose right of residence arises solely out of the search for employment, may not claim such benefits.

First, the ECJ began by explicitly accepting the position of the referring court that the benefits in question are social assistance (and not social security) benefits. Overruling its 2009 finding in the *Vatsouras and Koupatantze*[31] case, the ECJ now found that the same German SGB II benefit, which is a 'special non-contributory cash benefit' within the meaning of Article 70(2) of Regulation 883/2004 is not primarily intended to facilitate access to the labour market. Social assistance benefits that facilitate access to the labour market do not fall under the equal treatment exception of Article 24(2) of Directive 2004/38, which excludes jobseekers from entitlement to social assistance benefits in general. The Court notes that the SGB II benefits at issue, even if they form part of a scheme that also provides for benefits to facilitate the search for employment, are intended to cover subsistence costs for persons who cannot cover those costs themselves and are not financed through contributions, but through tax revenue.

The ECJ reiterates that only EU nationals who have a right of residence under Article 7 of the Directive are entitled to equal treatment with nationals of the host Member State. Hence, the ECJ had to determine whether Ms Alimanovic was 'lawfully resident' in Germany under Article 7 Directive 2004/38. According to

[28] M Cousins, 'Social Assistance and the Right to Residence at the European Court of Justice—Dano v Jobcenter Leipzig' (2015) 22 *Journal of Social Security Law* 94.

[29] *Dano* (n 1) para 36.

[30] *Alimanovic* (n 1).

[31] *Vatsouras and Koupatantze* (n 13).

the Court, she was not because she and her daughter were no longer covered by the Directive as they were 'former workers'. On the basis of Article 7(3)(c) of the Directive, Union citizens who have worked in a host Member State for less than a year retain their right of residence for at least six months after becoming unemployed, after which the Member State (as Germany did) can terminate worker status. It is only for those six months that they are entitled to equal treatment with nationals of the host State. This does not mean, however, that Ms Alimanovic and her daughter can be expelled. As long as they are jobseekers and continue to have a genuine chance of being engaged in work, expulsion is not possible. But after six months of job-seeking, they no longer retain the status of worker and go back to being first-time jobseekers who are not entitled to social assistance.[32] Interestingly, according to the ECJ, in this situation Ms Alimanovic and her daughter can rely on a right of residence directly on the basis of Article 14(4)(b) Directive 2004/38.

The Court avoids any reflections on the importance of a possible demonstration of the existence of a 'genuine link' for the access to social benefits and ignores its previous case law in this respect completely.[33] Although Ms Alimanovic had a work history of 11 months, the Court treated her as a first-time jobseeker failing to attach any extra significance to her work history besides the rights she enjoyed based on Article 7(3)(c). This approach is understandable given the wording of Article 24(2) of Directive 2004/38 and the Court's emphasis on the need for a significant level of legal certainty and transparency.[34] But what is less comprehensible is why the Court does not stop here and adds an extra paragraph that states:

> Moreover, as regards the individual assessment for the purposes of making an overall appraisal of the burden which the grant of a specific benefit would place on the national system of social assistance at issue in the main proceedings as a whole, it must be observed that the assistance awarded to a single applicant can scarcely be described as an 'unreasonable burden' for a Member State, within the meaning of Article 14(1) of Directive 2004/38. However, while an individual claim might not place the Member State concerned under an unreasonable burden, the accumulation of all the individual claims which would be submitted to it would be bound to do so.[35]

Based on this paragraph, it appears that the Court holds the view that the mere fact that EU citizens could be an unreasonable burden on the social assistance system as a group is enough to regard the individual claimant as an unreasonable burden. This is in glaring contrast to the approach in the *Brey* case where the Court followed the suggestion of the Commission and decided that in order to ascertain more precisely the extent of the burden which the relevant grant in this case would place on the national social assistance system, it may be relevant to determine the proportion of beneficiaries of that benefit who are Union citizens

[32] *Alimanovic* (n 1) para 58.

[33] See *Collins* (n 16), paras 67–69; *Bidar* (n 17) para 57; *Grzelczyk* (n 18), para 43; *Trojani* (n 18) para 36.

[34] *Alimanovic* (n 1) para 61.

[35] *Alimanovic* (n 1) para 62.

in receipt of (in this case) a retirement pension in another Member State.[36] Minderhoud has suggested that one way of reconciling this issue is to consider that EU citizens in a host Member State should be seen as an unreasonable burden if they make in relative terms more use of social assistance benefits than native citizens of that host Member State. This is based on the assumption that most EU citizens contribute to taxes and premiums in the host Member State.[37] The approach chosen by the Court in *Alimanovic* fails to do justice to the fact that there is no empirical evidence showing that EU citizens make excessive use of the social assistance system of the host Member State and the fact that the whole discussion on 'welfare tourism' is built on quicksand.[38] The *Dano* and *Alimanovic* cases illustrate the fragmentation of EU citizenship status along economic lines. Job-seeking and economically inactive citizens are excluded from social assistance benefits but the act of asking for such benefits has different consequences for their right to reside. Even if job-seeking EU citizens enjoy a limited right to equal treatment,[39] they remain legally resident in their host State, whereas economically inactive ones risk being labelled as lacking resources and being an unreasonable burden on the host State.

D. The *García-Nieto* Case

This case[40] can be seen as the final piece of a triptych together with the *Dano* and *Alimanovic* cases, since all three cases deal with entitlement to the same benefit—the German SGB II benefit.[41] The *García-Nieto* case concerns a Spanish couple with two children. Ms García-Nieto and her daughter moved to Germany in April 2012 and shortly after the mother began working as a kitchen assistant. In June 2012, her unmarried and not registered partner, Mr Peña Cuevas, and

[36] *Brey* (n 7) para 78.

[37] P Minderhoud, 'Case Note under ECJ 19 September 2013, C-140/12, *(Brey)*' no 84, *Rechtspraak Vreemdelingenrecht* (Nijmegen, Ars Aequi, 2013) 511–13.

[38] For more details on this, see SA Mantu and PE Minderhoud, 'Solidarity (still) in the making or a bridge too far?' Nijmegen Migration Law Working Papers Series no 2015/01(2015): repository.ubn.ru.nl/handle/2066/143178.

[39] See for a critical view in this regard also A Iliopoulou-Penot, 'Deconstructing the Former Edifice of Union Citizenship? The Alimanovic Judgment' (2016) 53 *CML Rev*, 1007, 1015. Wollenschläger, chapter 9 in this volume is milder in his analysis.

[40] *García-Nieto* (n 1).

[41] Part of the problems dealt with in these cases is caused by the fact that the German social assistance system is complicated. It consists of two basic social benefits. The SGB II, which was the contested benefit in all three cases, provides a basic social benefit for jobseekers who have no rights to the usual unemployment benefit scheme (*Grundsicherung für Arbeitsuchende*). Additionally, the SGB XII (Social Code Book XII) provides a basic social benefit for jobless people who are not capable of work (*Sozialhilfe*). Section 21 of SGB XII however states that nobody should be entitled to this *Sozialhilfe* if they are in principle entitled to the *Grundsicherung für Arbeitsuchende*. Based on Articles 1 and 20 of the German Basic Law (*Grundgesetz*), there is however a right to a minimum level of dignified existence for everyone legally residing in Germany. See Bundesverfassungsgericht (Federal Constitutional Court) 18 July 2012, DE:BVerfG:2012:ls20120718.1bvl001010.

his son joined the other two in Germany. In July, the family applied for SGB II benefits, which were refused for Mr Peña Cuevas and his son, because at the time of the application Mr Peña Cuevas had resided in Germany for less than three months and did not have the status of worker or self-employed person. The Court upheld its *Dano* and *Alimanovic* decisions and restated that a Union citizen can claim equal treatment with nationals of the host Member State under Article 24(1) Directive 2004/38 only if his residence in the territory of the host Member State complies with the conditions of the Directive. The applicant could base his right of residence on Article 6(1) of the Directive, since this Article provides that Union citizens have the right of residence in the territory of another Member State for a period of up to three months without any conditions or any formalities other than the requirement to hold a valid identity card or passport. However, in such a case, the host Member State may rely on the derogation in Article 24(2) of Directive 2004/38 in order to refuse to grant that citizen the social assistance sought. Thus, *García-Nieto* appears as a confirmation of the Court's jurisprudence on this issue, while it also clarifies the derogation found in Article 24(2) in relation to residence for up to three months.

Even if the judgments in *Dano* and *Alimanovic* had not been given, it seems logical that EU citizens, who move to another Member State and have a right of residence based on Article 6 Directive 2004/38, cannot ask for social assistance during these first three months. Article 24(2) is clear on this. There are no conditions attached to their right of residence, but they do not derive any substantial rights from it as well. Even if we agree with this conclusion, the Court's reasoning in this case seems to miss a number of legal issues that are relevant for clarifying the legal framework applicable to mobile EU citizens asking for social benefits from their host State. In our view, it is unclear why Mr Peña Cuevas receives an SGB II benefit as from October 2012, after he has fulfilled his initial three-month residence period. In line with the Court's jurisprudence and the position of the German authorities in the previous cases discussed in this contribution,[42] he should be excluded from this benefit on the basis of point 2 of the second sentence of paragraph 7(1) of Book II of the Social Code. This provision excludes foreign nationals whose right of residence arises solely out of the search for employment, and their family members from receiving such benefits.[43]

[42] See the position of the national authorities in the *Alimanovic* case.

[43] Mr Peña Cuevas was excluded in the first three months of his residence on the basis of point 1 of the second sentence of Paragraph 7(1) of Book II of the Social Code. The relevant text read at that moment:

> Paragraph 7 of Book II of the Social Code, entitled 'Beneficiaries', provides as follows in subparagraph 1:
>
> 'Benefits under this Book shall be received by persons:
>
> 1. who have attained the age of 15 years and have not yet reached the age limit referred to in Paragraph 7a,
> 2. who are fit for work,

In other words: what is the basis of residence of Mr Peña Cuevas after three months? If he only has a residence right as a jobseeker, he should not have been given the SGB II benefit. If he is seen as a family member of Ms García-Nieto, although they are not married nor registered partners,[44] he could base his right of residence on Article 7(1)(d) Directive 2004/38 as the family member of an EU worker. And Ms García-Nieto is definitely a worker as she was compulsorily affiliated to German social security, and received a monthly net salary of €600.[45] In our view, if this is the correct basis for his right to reside Mr Peña Cuevas enjoyed a right to reside as a family member based on Article 7(1)(d) Directive 2004/38 from the moment Ms García-Nieto became a worker (1 July 2012) and should have been entitled to SGB II benefit from that moment as well. Thus, while the Court's clarification in relation to access to social assistance for EU citizens other than workers during the first three months of residence is welcomed, the judgment fails to give an answer based on the facts of the case.

E. The *Commission v UK* Case

The European Commission challenged the UK legislation regulating access to child benefit and child tax credit, which are both social security (not social assistance) benefits falling under Regulation 883/2004. The UK legislation made the grant of these benefits conditional upon having a right to reside in the UK, in addition to being habitually resident.[46] The case before the ECJ was confined to the question whether relevant authorities can verify the lawful residence of economically inactive Union citizens when they claim child benefit or child tax credit. The Commission contended that the UK had added a condition that does not appear in Regulation 883/2004, namely having a right to reside. Second, it argued that the right to reside test is a form of direct discrimination based on nationality

3. who are in need of assistance, and
4. whose ordinary place of residence is in the Federal Republic of Germany (beneficiaries fit for work).

The following are excluded:

1. foreign nationals who are not workers or self-employed persons in the Federal Republic of Germany and do not enjoy the right of freedom of movement under Paragraph 2(3) of the Law on freedom of movement of Union citizens [(Freizügigkeitsgesetz/EU, "the Law on freedom of movement")], and their family members, for the first three months of their residence,
2. foreign nationals whose right of residence arises solely out of the search for employment, and their family members (see Case C-299/1 *García-Nieto*, EU:C:2016:114, para 16 and 31)'.

[44] See Art 3(2) Directive 2004/38.

[45] See para 28.

[46] Case C-308/14 *Commission v United Kingdom*, EU:C:2016:436.

and as such in breach of Article 4 Regulation 883/2004 because UK nationals satisfy this condition automatically.

The Court dismissed the action of the Commission.[47] Regarding the first ground, the Court decided that Article 11(3)(e) Regulation 883/2004, which provides that a non-active person is subject to the legislation of the Member State of residence (which is defined in the Regulation as the place where a person habitually resides), is 'only' a conflict of law rule. It does not affect the power of Member States to determine their own conditions. This leads to the strange construction that the concept of residence first counts for determining the applicable legislation under Regulation 883/2004 (*in casu*, of the UK) and then is used to deny access to the benefits which fall under that same Regulation.

The Court agreed with the Commission that the condition requiring a right to reside in the UK gives rise to unequal treatment because UK nationals can satisfy it more easily than nationals of the other Member States. However, it considered the UK legislation as indirectly (not directly) discriminatory, thus opening up the possibility of justifying it.[48] The Court considers that this difference in treatment can be justified by a legitimate objective such as the need to protect the finances of the host Member State, provided that it does not go beyond what is necessary to attain that objective. In this regard, the Court finds that the UK authorities verify whether residence is lawful in accordance with the conditions laid down in the Directive on the free movement of citizens. This verification is not carried out systematically by the UK authorities for each claim, but only in the event of doubt. Therefore, it follows that the condition does not go beyond what is necessary to attain the legitimate objective pursued by the UK, namely the need to protect its finances 'as such grant could have consequences for the overall level of assistance which may be accorded by that State'.[49]

The *Commission v UK* case raises the question whether the line of the German cases (*Dano*, *Alimanovic* and *García-Nieto*) dealt with in this chapter, is now not only extended to Special Non-Contributory Benefits (SNCBs) under Regulation 883/2004, which are categorised as 'social assistance' within the meaning of Directive 2004/38, but also to certain social security benefits under Regulation 883.[50] This seems to be the intention of the Commission given its recent proposal to revise the coordination of social security systems.[51] Reflecting the rulings of the

[47] For a critical assessment of the case, see M Cousins, 'The Baseless Fabric of this Vision: EU Citizenship, the Right to Reside and EU Law'(2016) 23 *Journal of Social Security Law* 89; H Verschueren, 'Economische niet-actieve migrerende Unieburgers: enkel recht op sociale uitkeringen indien zij over verblijfsrecht beschikken' (2017) 65 *SEW* 36; C O'Brien, 'The ECJ Sacrifices EU Citizenship in Vain: *Commission v United Kingdom*' (2017) 54 *CML Rev* 209.

[48] *Commission v United Kingdom* (n 46) para 77.

[49] ibid para 80.

[50] See C O'Brien: eulawanalysis.blogspot.ie/2016/06/dont-think-of-children-cjeu-approves.html.

[51] COM(2016) 815 proposal for a Regulation of the European Parliament and the Council amending Regulation (EC) No. 883/2004 on the coordination of social security systems and regulation EC No 987/2009 laying down the procedure of implementing Regulation (EC) No 883/2004.

Court discussed in this chapter, the Commission wants to make possible the exclusion of economically inactive citizens from all social benefits, irrespective of their qualification as social assistance or social security. To achieve this, the Commission proposes to add a second paragraph to the equal treatment provision of Article 4 Regulation 883/2004 stating that:

> A Member State may require that the access of an economically inactive person residing in that Member State to its *social security* benefits be subject to the conditions of having a right to legal residence as set out in Directive 2004/38/EC.[52]

V. CONCLUSION

This contribution has analysed the case law concerned with the entitlement of economically inactive EU citizens to social rights in their host States and shown how it is undergoing some profound changes. The shift we note in the case law—from asking for social assistance being an 'indication' of lack of resources to becoming a 'certainty' that no longer requires an individualised examination of the case—raises some fundamental questions about the scope of EU citizenship and forms a breach with the Court's well-established way of interpreting EU citizenship rights and its usual emphasis on proportionality and the need for individual assessment. This legal shift in the interpretation of the Citizens Directive takes place in a context of rising political debates about free movement which are increasingly focusing on the mobility of poor or economically inactive EU citizens.

The Court's approach in the *Dano*, *Alimanovic* and *García-Nieto* judgments that a Union citizen can claim equal treatment with nationals of the host State under Article 24(1) *only* if his residence in the territory of the host Member State complies with the conditions of Directive 2004/38 will undoubtedly have an impact upon how fundamental the status of EU citizenship is. An interpretation where economically non-active EU citizens must always have resources sufficient not to qualify for any social assistance benefit may lead to an effective exclusion of most economically non-active EU citizens since in their national legislation Member States may set a high threshold regarding sufficient resources. Take for instance as example the Romanian pensioners who have an average old-age pension of around €175. Such pensioners would meet the requirement of sufficient resources only in eight of the 27 Member States (Bulgaria, Croatia, the Czech Republic, Estonia, Latvia, Lithuania, Poland and Slovakia). The area of free movement in which such Romanian pensioners may exercise their fundamental right to move and reside freely would shrink to less than one-third of the EU.[53]

This new case law also shows a change in the order of the assessment. Where in the cases of *Martínez Sala*, *Grzelczyk* and *Trojani* the Court first assessed whether

[52] Emphasis added by the authors.

[53] M Meduna et al, 'Institutional Report' in U Neergaard et al (eds), *Union Citizenship: Development, Impact and Challenges, The XXVI FIDE Congress in Copenhagen* (Copenhagen, DJØF Publishing, 2014).

the exclusion of the social benefit relevant in those cases was an act of discrimination and then looked at the possible consequences for the right of residence, in the new judgments the Court first assesses whether an EU citizen fulfils the conditions under which a right of residence arises, before it decides upon the question of a right to equal treatment.[54]

The emphasis of the Court that an objective of the Directive is 'preventing Union citizens who are nationals of other Member States from becoming an unreasonable burden on the social assistance system'[55] is disconcerting. This is difficult to reconcile with the objective of the Directive to facilitate and strengthen the right of free movement and residence of all Union citizens as was emphasised by the Court in the *Metock* case.[56]

The recent ECJ jurisprudence allowing the Member States to refuse social rights to mobile EU citizens in order to protect their national welfare systems rolls back decades of EU citizenship construction and harms its original meaning.[57] It devaluates the principle that there should be a certain degree of financial solidarity between nationals of a host Member State and nationals of other Member States resident there.[58] We agree with Neuvonen that the status of EU citizenship is now fundamentally defined by those substantive limitations and exceptions that are used to restrict the de facto enjoyment of EU citizenship rights in those cases that jurisdictionally fall into the scope of equal treatment under EU law.[59] In our view, a narrow type of solidarity is being promoted in the EU, since it is available only for those who do not need it and only when they do not need it. Moreover, if the political discussion is to continue along the line of problematising the working poor, while also bearing in mind the structural changes undergone by national labour markets that increasingly rely on part-time, poorly paid jobs to generate growth, some EU citizens will find it increasingly difficult to move freely within the EU.

[54] See also in this respect, F Pennings, 'EU-burgerschap en de vrees voor sociaal toerisme: de zaak Dano (2015) 21 *Nederlands Tijdschrift voor Europees recht* 39.

[55] *Dano* (n 1) para 74; *Alimanovic* (n 1) para 50; *García-Nieto* (n 1) para 39.

[56] *Metock* (n 2) para 59.

[57] Also N Nic Shuibhne, 'Limits Rising, Duties Ascending: The Changing Legal Shape of Union Citizenship' (2015) 52 *CML Rev* 889; C O'Brien, 'The Pillory, the Precipice and the Slippery Slope: The Profound Effects of the UK's Legal Reform Programme Targeting EU Migrants' (2015) 37 *Journal of Social Welfare and Family Law* 111; S Guibboni, 'Free Movement of Persons and European Solidarity: A Melancholic Eulogy' in H Verschueren (ed), *Residence, Employment and Social Rights of Mobile Persons. On How EU Law Defines Where They Belong* (Cambridge, Intersentia, 2016).

[58] *Grzelczyk* (n 18) para 44.

[59] PJ Neuvonen, *Equal Citizenship and its Limits in EU Law: We the Burden?* (Oxford, Hart Publishing, 2016) 2.

11

Integrating Union Citizenship and the Charter of Fundamental Rights

NIAMH NIC SHUIBHNE*

I. INTRODUCTION

FUNDAMENTAL RIGHTS AND Union citizenship are both, on their own terms, essential elements of the European Union's constitutional profile. In a legal sense, they also combine in three main ways. First, the opening words of Directive 2004/38/EC assert that '[c]itizenship of the Union confers on every citizen of the Union a primary and individual right to move and reside freely within the territory of the Member States'.[1] The fundamental nature of that right is underlined by its restatement in Article 45(1) of the Charter. Second, beyond the right *to* move and reside, wider fundamental rights questions can arise *when* a Union citizen moves and resides. For example, the right to respect for family life had shaped the outcome of citizenship case law even before the Charter acquired binding effect.[2] This second interaction accounts for the most typical assessment of fundamental rights in conjunction with citizenship rights, and sustains an enduring legacy for the vision outlined by Advocate General Jacobs in *Konstadinidis*.[3] Third, in exceptional circumstances, Union citizenship can also

* This work was partly funded by a Leverhulme Trust Major Research Fellowship. Sincere thanks to Daniel Thym for valued comments on an earlier draft.

[1] Directive 2004/38/EC on the right of citizens of the Union and their family members to move and reside freely within the territory of the Member States [2004] OJ L158/77, recital 1.

[2] eg Case C-127/08 *Metock*, EU:C:2008:449; building on Case C-60/00 *Carpenter* EU:C:2002:434 (freedom to provide services). Exploring these links soon after Maastricht, see S O'Leary, 'The Relationship between Community Citizenship and the Protection of Fundamental Rights in Community Law' (1995) 32 *CML Rev* 519.

[3] Writing before Maastricht, AG Jacobs proposed that 'a Community national who goes to another Member State as a worker or self-employed … is entitled not just to pursue his trade or profession and to enjoy the same living and working conditions as nationals of the host State; he is in addition entitled to assume that, wherever he goes to earn his living in the European Community, he will be treated in accordance with a common code of fundamental values, in particular those laid down in the European Convention on Human Rights. In other words, he is entitled to say "civis europeus sum" and to invoke that status in order to oppose any violation of his fundamental rights' (AG Jacobs in Case C-168/91, EU:C:1992:504, para 46 of the Opinion).

be engaged when there is no movement from the citizen's home State at all[4] and can therefore, in turn, engage Union standards on the protection of fundamental rights.[5]

But rights can be legitimately limited too. The general rule is that rights should be interpreted broadly and derogations from or exceptions to them construed narrowly.[6] The right to move and reside is qualified at a general level by the statement that it is conferred 'subject to the limitations and conditions laid down in the Treaty and to the measures adopted to give it effect' (Article 21(1) of the Treaty on the Functioning of the European Union (TFEU)).[7] Directive 2004/38 is the main 'measure' in that respect. For fundamental rights, Articles 50–54 of the Charter are the 'general provisions' that govern its 'interpretation and application'. Article 51(1) states that the Charter is 'addressed to the institutions, bodies, offices and agencies of the Union with due regard for the principle of subsidiarity and to the Member States *only when they are implementing Union law*'. Article 51(2) emphasises that the Charter 'does not extend the field of application of Union law beyond the powers of the Union or establish any new power or task for the Union, or modify powers and tasks as defined in the Treaties'. Article 52(1) outlines four basic criteria for establishing that limitations on Charter rights are legitimate.[8] And Article 52(2) provides that '[r]ights recognised by this Charter for which provision is made in the Treaties shall be exercised under the conditions and within the limits defined by those Treaties'.

Determining the scope of citizenship and fundamental rights therefore requires that both realising rights and recognising appropriate limitations must be carefully accommodated in accordance with the framework rules set down in the Treaty and in the Charter. Reflecting the significance of judicial interpretation for that task, this chapter investigates how the Court of Justice has undertaken it since the Charter became legally binding.[9] To frame the analysis of relevant case law, the chapter examines the interplay between rights and limits in two key ways: first, how the provisions that limit the scope of the Charter apply in citizenship law; and, second, how limits on citizenship rights are measured for compliance with

[4] eg Case C-135/08 *Rottmann*, EU:C:2010:104; Case C-34/09 *Ruiz Zambrano*, EU:C:2011:124.

[5] eg Joined Cases C-356/11 and C-357/11 *O and S*, EU:C:2012:776, paras 58–59.

[6] eg Joined Cases C-482 & 493/01 *Orfanopoulos and Oliveri*, EU:C:2004:262 paras 64–65.

[7] See similarly, Art 20(2) TFEU: 'Citizens of the Union shall enjoy the rights and be subject to the duties provided for in the Treaties ... These rights shall be exercised in accordance with the conditions and limits defined by the Treaties and by the measures adopted thereunder'.

[8] It provides: '[a]ny limitation on the exercise of the rights and freedoms recognised by this Charter must be provided for by law and respect the essence of those rights and freedoms. Subject to the principle of proportionality, limitations may be made only if they are necessary and genuinely meet objectives of general interest recognised by the Union or the need to protect the rights and freedoms of others'.

[9] Art 6(1) of the Treaty on European Union (TEU), as amended by the Lisbon Treaty, provides: '[t]he Union recognises the rights, freedoms and principles set out in the Charter of Fundamental Rights of the European Union of 7 December 2000, as adapted at Strasbourg, on 12 December 2007, which shall have the same legal value as the Treaties'.

Charter rights. The judgments presented are analysed with respect to both internal consistency—ie, assessing how case law on citizenship rights and Charter rights is developing in each respective sphere—and systemic consistency—ie, assessing whether case law on citizenship rights and Charter rights fit together

Following a brief overview of how Articles 51 and 52 of the Charter are interpreted in a general sense (section II), the chapter then traces how both provisions are applied in citizenship case law. Two main problems are identified. First, the determination that certain citizenship cases fall outside the scope of the Charter for the purposes of Article 51 is difficult to predict or rationalise and apparently out of sync with how the scope of the Charter is determined more generally (sections III.A and III.B respectively). Second, the relationship between primary law and secondary law, already complicated because of Article 21(1) TFEU, is even more difficult to systematise when we also consider Article 52 of the Charter (section IV).

At one level, both problems fit with the generally restrictive trends evident in recent citizenship case law, where we see stronger endorsement of Member State interests and concerns; adjustment of the threshold at which proportionality analysis becomes necessary, by accounting for the (potential) systemic implications of free movement over evaluation of individual case circumstances; and a sharpening of citizenship's access conditions, ie, the criteria connecting situations to the equal treatment promised by the Treaty.[10] However, counterintuitively against the developments just outlined, it will also be seen that fundamental rights clout is materialising in other parts of citizenship case law, where the right to move has either not been exercised at all or appraisal of the conditions under which it has been exercised is overlooked. The fragmented case law picture that results renews questions about what kind of affiliation this complicated and unpredictable status of Union citizenship is turning out to be.[11] Conversely, how fundamental rights are treated in citizenship cases also has implications for how the system of Charter law proceeds.

The chapter argues overall that Union citizenship and fundamental rights protection should be *integrated* more consistently and more effectively. This statement exhibits both a normative claim and a concrete objective, reflecting the centrality of both citizenship and fundamental rights protection to the Union's claims to constitutionalism—and indeed to constitutional credibility. The Charter is not a stand-alone instrument for all-inclusive fundamental rights protection. That is neither its purpose nor its goal. But the exercise of Union citizenship rights provides the necessary trigger for the required integrated approach. The conferring of legal effect on the Charter through the Lisbon Treaty was just one innovation among many in that reform process, in respect of which '[t]he main

[10] These issues are discussed comprehensively in several contributions to this volume; see esp chapter 5 by U Šadl and S Sankari; and chapter 9 by F Wollenschläger, in this volume.

[11] See, eg, recently, C O'Brien, 'Civis Capitalist Sum: Class as the New Guiding Principle of EU Free Movement Rights' (2016) 53 *CML Rev* 937.

intended beneficiaries … were neither the Member States nor the institutions, but individuals'.[12] In citizenship case law, fundamental rights are treated too erratically. It is not yet sufficiently clear either *when* the Charter will apply or *what* its guarantees might then mean in substance. Article 2 of the Treaty on European Union (TEU) tells us that the Union is 'founded' on respect for human rights. In particular, therefore, when it is decided that Union standards of fundamental rights protection do not apply, the criteria used to make that determination need to be explicit, objective and methodically applied. Both citizenship and fundamental rights protection ask at least this.

II. ARTICLES 51 AND 52 OF THE CHARTER: THE BASIC FRAMEWORK

In essence, Articles 51 and 52 govern, respectively, when Charter rights are relevant and when limits placed on them are legitimate. It is not surprising that the Court was asked questions about both provisions soon after they acquired binding legal effect.

A. Article 51 and the Reach of Charter Rights

A crucial aspect of Article 51 concerns when Member States are 'implementing' Union law since it is there made clear that the Charter is (only) then addressed to them. The Explanations relating to the Charter[13]—to which the Court is required by Article 6(1) TEU to have 'due regard'—assert that it 'follows unambiguously from the case-law of the Court of Justice that the requirement to respect fundamental rights defined in the context of the Union is only binding on the Member States when they act *in the scope of* Union law'.[14] In *Åkerberg Fransson*, the Court confirmed that position.[15] The idea of Member States acting 'in the scope' of Union law suggests a broad conception of Article 51.[16] Conversely, the limits of

[12] D Sarmiento and E Sharpston, 'European Citizenship and Its New Union: Time to Move On?' in D Kochenov (ed), *EU Citizenship and Federalism: The Role of Rights* (Cambridge, Cambridge University Press, 2017) 226–242.

[13] [2007] OJ C303/2.

[14] Emphasis added; citing Case 5/88 *Wachauf*, EU:C:1989:321; Case C-260/89 *ERT*, EU:C:1991:254; and Case C-309/96 *Annibaldi*, EU:C:1997:631, which evidences an aim to ensure continuity between the pre-Lisbon and post-Lisbon approach.

[15] Case C-617/10 *Åkerberg Fransson*, EU:C:2013:105, para 19: '[The Court] has no power to examine the compatibility with the Charter of national legislation lying outside the scope of European Union law. On the other hand, if such legislation falls within the scope of European Union law, the Court, when requested to give a preliminary ruling, must provide all the guidance as to interpretation needed in order for the national court to determine whether that legislation is compatible with the fundamental rights the observance of which the Court ensure'. In para 20, the Court refers to the Explanations on this point.

[16] For discussion, see E Hancox, 'The Meaning of "Implementing" EU Law under Article 51(1) of the Charter: *Åkerberg Fransson*' (2013) 50 *CML Rev* 1411.

the term are not self-evident.[17] For example: the Charter applies to 'all situations governed by European Union law'[18] and it does not apply when national legislation 'falls outside the framework of EU law'.[19] But how might these situations actually be distinguished?

In *Julian Hernández*, the Court elaborated:

> [T]he concept of 'implementing Union law'... presupposes *a degree of connection* between the measure of EU law and the national measure at issue which *goes beyond the matters covered being closely related* or one of those matters having an *indirect impact* on the other.[20]

Therefore, it is necessary to determine

> whether the national legislation *is intended to* implement a provision of EU law; the *nature* of the legislation at issue and *whether it pursues objectives other than those covered by EU law*, even if it is capable of indirectly affecting EU law; and also whether there are *specific rules of EU law* on the matter or rules which are *capable of affecting* it.[21]

Here, the criteria were expressed cumulatively but in *Siragusa*, the phrasing changed to '*some of the points to be determined are* whether that legislation is intended to implement a provision of EU law' etc.[22] In the next paragraph, the Court noted:

> *[i]n particular*, the Court has found that fundamental EU rights could not be applied in relation to national legislation because the provisions of EU law in the subject area concerned did not impose any obligation on Member States with regard to the situation at issue in the main proceedings.[23]

The Court therefore seeks more than 'an overlap or coincidence of subject matter'[24] to find that a Member State is implementing Union law. But pinning down the necessary 'degree of connection' remains, perhaps inevitably, open to interpretation.

B. Article 52 and the Nature of Limits

It was noted at the outset of this chapter that an EU citizen's right to move and reside freely is expressed in the Treaty (in Articles 20(2) and 21(1) TFEU) but

[17] For extensive analysis, see M Dougan, 'Judicial Review of Member State Action under the General Principles and the Charter: Defining the "Scope of Union Law"' (2015) 52 *CML Review* 1201.

[18] Case C-45/12 *Hadj Ahmed*, EU:C:2013:390, para 56.

[19] Case C-418/11 *Texdata Software*, EU:C:2013:588, para 72.

[20] Case C-198/13 *Julian Hernández*, EU:C:2014:2055, para 34 (emphasis added).

[21] ibid para 37 (emphasis added). The final criterion appears in slightly altered expression in, eg, Case C-265/13 *Torralbo Marcos*, EU:C:2014:187, para 32: 'European Union law does not contain any specific rules in that area or any which are *likely to affect* that national legislation' (emphasis added).

[22] Case C-206/13 *Siragusa*, EU:C:2014:126, para 25 (emphasis added).

[23] *Siragusa* (n 22) para 26 (emphasis added).

[24] Dougan (n 17) esp 1221–28.

also in Article 45(1) of the Charter. When assessing restrictions on the relevant Treaty rights, the Court has applied the justification framework developed for free movement law generally, ie, the restriction 'must be appropriate for securing the attainment of a legitimate objective and must not go beyond what is necessary to attain that objective'.[25] Article 52(1) of the Charter encompasses these criteria, but it adds that any limitation on Charter rights 'must be provided for by law and respect the essence of those rights and freedoms' and includes 'the need to protect the rights and freedoms of others' alongside its recognition of limitations that protect 'objectives of general interest recognised by the Union'. Consequently, in *ZZ*, the Court alluded to the added weight of scrutiny that Article 52(1) seems to require.[26]

However, Article 52(2) then provides that '[r]ights recognised by this Charter for which provision is made in the Treaties shall be exercised under the conditions and within the limits defined by those Treaties'—bringing us back for citizenship law to Article 21(1) TFEU and remembering, in particular, the instruction clearly spelled out there that the right to move and reside freely may be limited by secondary legislation as well as by provisions elsewhere in the Treaties. In *Pfleger*, concerning a restriction on the free provision of services and building on the approach summarised in section II.A above, the Court first confirmed a significant point of continuity with pre-Charter case law, ie, aiming to derogate from or restrict free movement rights constitutes 'implementing' Union law for the purposes of Article 51 of the Charter.[27] But it then suggested an absorptive effect for Article 52(2), concluding that 'an unjustified or disproportionate restriction of the freedom to provide services under Article 56 TFEU is also not permitted under Article 52(1) of the Charter in relation to Articles 15 to 17 of the Charter'.[28] In other words,

> *in the present case*, an examination of the restriction represented by the national legislation at issue in the main proceedings from the point of view of Article 56 TFEU *covers also* possible limitations of the exercise of the rights and freedoms provided for in Articles 15 to 17 of the Charter, so that a separate examination is not necessary.[29]

In one sense, the approach taken in *Pfleger* was uncontroversial because a restriction of rights was established under Article 56 TFEU. However, had the national measure been excused, would its examination under the additional criteria in Article 52(1) then be redundant? It would seem so. For example, in *ONEm*, the Court ruled that since the contested EU legislation 'complies with Article 45

[25] Case C-20/12 *Giersch*, EU:C:2013:411, para 46.
[26] Case C-300/11 *ZZ*, EU:C:2013:363, para 51.
[27] Case C-390/12 *Pfleger*, EU:C:2014:281, para 35.
[28] ibid para 59, referring to paras 63–70 of the Opinion of AG Sharpston (EU:C: 2013: 747).
[29] *Pfleger* (n 27) para 60 (emphasis added).

TFEU and Article 48 TFEU, *it also complies with* Article 15(2) of the Charter'.[30] In support, the Court cited its previous finding in *Gardella* that Article 52(2)

> provides that rights recognised by the Charter for which provision is made in the treaties are to be exercised under the conditions and within the limits defined therein. In that vein, Article 15(2) of the Charter reiterates inter alia the free movement of workers guaranteed by Article 45 TFEU, as confirmed by the explanations relating to that provision.[31]

Interestingly, the Explanations outline that Article 51(2)

> refers to rights which were already expressly guaranteed in the [EC Treaty] and have been recognised in the Charter, and which are now found in the Treaties (*notably the rights derived from Union citizenship*). It clarifies that such rights remain subject to the conditions and limits applicable to the Union law on which they are based, and for which provision is made in the Treaties. The Charter does not alter the system of rights conferred by the EC Treaty and taken over by the Treaties' (emphasis added).

This text indicates a protective purpose for Article 51(2). But if its application removes aspects of citizenship law from autonomous Charter review, then what seems initially like an absorptive effect might be more accurately described as an exclusionary one. But then, while Article 6(1) TEU sets the Treaties and the Charter at the same legal level, the particular construction of Articles 20 and 21 TFEU could signal a secondary law route out of both. That would in turn render the first statement confirmed in *Pfleger*—that derogating from or justifying restrictions on free movement rights does constitute implementing EU law—all the more important to ensure compliance with EU fundamental rights standards. After all, one function of fundamental rights is to construct boundaries around the choices of the legislator.

III. CITIZENSHIP AND ARTICLE 51: DELIMITING THE SCOPE OF THE CHARTER THROUGH THE CONDITION OF IMPLEMENTING UNION LAW

This section assesses the extent to which application of the Charter in citizenship case law aligns with the framework rules on Article 51 outlined in section II.A above, ie, the Charter should apply when there is a sufficient 'degree of connection' between EU law and national law that 'goes beyond the matters covered being closely related or one of those matters having an indirect impact on the other'. That threshold ought to be reached when Member State activity is connected to derogation from or justification of restrictions on free movement rights, as

[30] Case C-284/15 *ONEm*, EU:C:2016:220, para 34 (emphasis added).
[31] Case C-233/12 *Gardella*, EU:C:2013:449, para 39.

examined in section III.A. In section III.B, the discussion considers situations in which EU fundamental rights standards apply even though the right to move and reside has not been exercised.

A. To Move: Article 21 TFEU

Since the Lisbon Treaty came into force, national courts and tribunals habitually frame questions about the interpretation of EU citizenship rights by reference to Charter provisions.[32] These preliminary ruling requests raise interesting questions about what Charter rights mean in substance. For example, in *ZZ*, the Court provided detailed guidance on the right to effective judicial protection and the rights of the defence, triggered by a requested interpretation of Article 30 of Directive 2004/38. Similarly, as might be expected, cases about respect for private and family life (Article 7 of the Charter) continue to be referred.[33] Through this case law, the guarantees articulated in the Charter acquire meaning and substance. At one level, national disputes on the right to move and reside should be straightforward for the purposes of Article 51 of the Charter, since EU legislation—principally (but, as will be seen below, not exclusively) Directive 2004/38—is normally engaged. However, the imprint of the Charter on this line of case law is fainter than might be anticipated.

Three points of concern can be suggested: framing, silence and consistency.

First, how the Court of Justice frames the dispute before it can make a critical difference for the applicability of the Charter. For example, in *Iida*, the case concerned whether the applicant—the Japanese father of a German child, the latter now residing in Austria with her mother—could derive a right to (continue to) reside in Germany from his daughter's status as a Union citizen. In its judgment, the Court focused on any connection that might be established between the *applicant* and Union law, finding no such connection and therefore ruling that

> the German authorities' refusal to grant Mr Iida a 'residence card of a family member of a Union citizen' does not fall within the implementation of European Union law within the meaning of Article 51 of the Charter, so that its conformity with fundamental rights cannot be examined by reference to the rights established by the Charter.[34]

But concentrating the analysis on the third-country national family member in this way, as the bearer only of derived rights,[35] is unusual in free movement law.

[32] See, eg, the list of Charter-framed questions in para 32 of Case C-40/11 *Iida*, EU:C:2012:691; for a pending case, see eg, Case C-366/16 *H*.

[33] See, eg, Case C-145/09 *Tsakouridis*, EU:C:2010:708, para 52 (justification of national measures restricting free movement); Case C-208/09 *Sayn-Wittgenstein*, EU:C:2010:806, para 52 (names as a constituent element of identity and private life).

[34] *Iida* (n 32) para 81; see generally, paras 73ff.

[35] eg Case C-87/12 *Ymeraga and Others*, EU:C:2013:291, para 35: 'Any rights conferred on third-country nationals by the Treaty provisions on Union citizenship are not autonomous rights of those nationals but rights derived from the exercise of freedom of movement by a Union citizen'.

In contrast, Advocate General Trstenjak had followed the conventional approach, examining the question from the perspective of a potential restriction on the free movement rights of the Union citizen, ie, Mr Iida's daughter, and finding in consequence that an assessment of the national decision did have to be undertaken, as a potential restriction of those rights, to check for compliance with Article 7 of the Charter.[36]

Second, the circumstances of some cases seem inescapably connected to fundamental rights, yet there is an odd 'Charter silence' on this in the judgment of the Court. The decision in *Ruiz Zambrano* is a classic example and will be discussed in section III.B below. But we can find instances of the same silence in case law on the exercise of free movement rights. For example, in *Singh*, concerning the scope of rights retained by a third-country national in a host State following his divorce from a Union citizen who had left that State, the Court applied a (disputable) interpretation of Article 13(2) of Directive 2004/38 without any consideration of how the protection of fundamental rights might affect it.[37] Subsequently, in *NA*, where the Court was asked once again to interpret Article 13(2) of the Directive—and here in a case that involved domestic violence—there is again no reference to the Charter or to fundamental rights more generally. Adopting a 'literal, systematic and teleological interpretation' of Article 13(2), the Court concluded that

> when [Directive 2004/38] was adopted, the EU legislature declined to make provision, in the event of the departure from the host Member State of the Union citizen, for specific safeguards that would be available, on account of, inter alia, particularly difficult situations, to his family members who do not have the nationality of a Member State, that would be comparable to those provided for in Article 13(2)(c) of Directive 2004/3.[38]

Advocate General Wathelet applied the same interpretative method, ie, examining the context and objectives of Article 13(2), and the intention of the legislator through discussion of the measure's drafting history. But he reached the opposite conclusion.[39]

What the Court did not consider in *NA* is whether the EU legislature 'declining' to make such provision is itself Charter compliant.[40] Neither did the Court draw from previous case law in which the implications of legislation-compliant

[36] AG Trstenjak in *Iida* (EU:C:2012:296) esp paras 72–87 of the Opinion.

[37] Case C-218/14 *Singh*, EU:C:2015:476; for critique, see F Strumia, 'Divorce Immediately, or Leave. Rights of Third Country Nationals and Family Protection in the Context of EU Citizens' Free Movement: *Kuldip Singh and Others*' (2016) 53 *CML Review* 1373 esp 1387–88. Drawing softer and harder implications from the judgment, see respectively the Opinion of AG Wathelet (EU:C:2016:259) and judgment of the Court (EU:C:2016:487) in Case C-115/15 *NA*, discussed further below.

[38] *NA*, paras 49 and 44 respectively.

[39] AG Wathelet in *NA* (n 37) paras 60ff of the Opinion; explicitly addressing the context of domestic violence, he concluded that 'requiring a third country national to show that her ex-spouse was exercising Treaty rights in the host Member State at the time of the divorce in order to be able to retain a right of residence would therefore be manifestly contrary to the objective of legal protection pursued by that provision' (para 73 of the Opinion).

[40] It did, however, establish a derived right of residence for the applicant on the basis of what is now Art 10 of Regulation (EU) No 492/2011; see paras 53–67.

national decisions were nevertheless checked against the general principles of EU law.[41] Legislation being treated as the beginning and the end of the matter bridges then to the third point of concern: even where the Court does engage with the applicability of the Charter more overtly, case law indicates problematic inconsistency with both the *Åkerberg Fransson*/*Julian Hernández* framework outlined in section II.A and the premise established in section II.B that derogation/justification *itself* constitutes implementation of EU law and thus triggers consideration of the Charter.

The judgment in *Dano* exemplifies this point for rights exercised under Article 21 TFEU. In this case, there is undeniable cross-border movement—a Romanian national moved to and resided in Germany. The Court first recited its standard approach to cross-border situations, stating that

> [e]very Union citizen may … rely on the prohibition of discrimination on grounds of nationality laid down in Article 18 TFEU in all situations falling within the scope *ratione materiae* of EU law. These situations include those relating to the exercise of the right to move and reside within the territory of the Member States conferred by … Article 20(2) TFEU and Article 21 TFEU.[42]

However, as presented in more detail in other contributions to this volume, the Court then found that the applicant's eligibility for social assistance in the host State could not fall within the scope of Article 21(1) of Directive 2004/38—which it examined as a 'more specific expression' of the principle of non-discrimination—since she did not reside lawfully in Germany; moreover, the conditions for lawful residence were linked exclusively to Article 7(1) of the Directive in the circumstances of the case.[43] By dispensing with consideration of Ms Dano's Treaty rights through this method, the Court also dispensed with the need for classic public interest justification and proportionality analysis.

The referring court had also asked

> whether Articles 1 [human dignity], 20 [equality before the law] and 51 of the Charter [require] the Member States to grant Union citizens non-contributory cash benefits by way of basic provision such as to enable permanent residence or whether those States may limit their grant to the provision of funds necessary for return to the home State.[44]

This question connects to the fact that the benefits at issue fell within the scope of both Directive 2004/38 as social assistance and Article 70 of Regulation 883/2004 as non-contributory cash benefits.[45] On this question, the Court responded:

> [Regulation 883/2004] is not intended to lay down the conditions creating the right to those benefits. It is thus for the legislature of each Member State to lay down those conditions. Accordingly, since those conditions result neither from Regulation No 883/2004

[41] eg Case C-413/99 *Baumbast*, EU:C:2002:49.

[42] Case C-333/13 *Dano*, EU:C:2014:2358.

[43] ibid paras 68–76.

[44] ibid para 85.

[45] Regulation 883/2004 on the coordination of social security systems, 2004 OJ L166/1; see further, *Dano* (n 42) esp paras 46–55 and 63.

> nor from Directive 2004/38 or other secondary EU legislation, and the Member States thus have competence to determine the conditions for the grant of such benefits, they also have competence … to define the extent of the social cover provided by that type of benefit. Consequently, when the Member States lay down the conditions for the grant of special non-contributory cash benefits and the extent of such benefits, they are not implementing EU law.[46]

The Court further recalled that 'the Charter, pursuant to Article 51(2) thereof, does not extend the field of application of EU law beyond the powers of the European Union or establish any new power or task for [it] or modify powers and tasks as defined in the Treaties' and reiterated the limitation built into Article 51(1).[47]

It is difficult to conceive how national rules that determine the level of social assistance to which EU citizens are entitled falls outside the scope of EU law. Through its analysis, the Court closed down two different lines of case law that would result in the *Dano* circumstances establishing the necessary 'degree of connection' required by Article 51 for triggering the applicability of the Charter. First, on the nature of Regulation 883/2004, Dougan draws an analogy with the contrasting approach taken to age discrimination in *Kücükdeveci*,

> the logic of which should have led the Court to affirm the applicability of the Charter in *Dano*: regardless of whether or not the detailed conditions for and extent of special non-contributory cash benefits are defined by Union law, such benefits are nevertheless certainly defined and regulated by Regulation 883/2004.[48]

Similarly, the Directive at issue in *Åkerberg Fransson* empowered States to apply sanctions for VAT offences; but it did not itself lay down the penalties that must be applied in such situations.[49] As expressed in a general sense by Sarmiento, 'it is not the *intention* of the State, but the *function* of the State act regarding the implementation of EU law which matters'.[50]

Second, as already alluded to above, by pushing the dispute exclusively through secondary law premises, the Court sidesteps the need for analysis that probes restrictions on primary rights and corresponding arguments about justification on grounds of public interest, which is normally undertaken where Article 21 TFEU is engaged.[51] Here, a national of one Member State had moved to and

[46] *Dano* (n 42) paras 89–91.

[47] ibid paras 87–88. The Court's depiction of what the Regulation does *not* preclude vis-a-vis the Directive has implications beyond the applicability of the Charter: see Case C-308/14 *Commission v UK*, EU:C:2016:436; for discussion, see C O'Brien, 'The ECJ Sacrifices EU Citizenship in Vain: *Commission v UK*' (2017) 54 *CML Rev* 209.

[48] Dougan (n 17) 1225; Case C-555/07 *Kücükdeveci*, EU:C:2010:21.

[49] Council Directive 2006/112/EC on the common system of value added tax [2006] OJ L347/1.

[50] D Sarmiento, 'Who's Afraid of the Charter? The Court of Justice, National Courts and the New Framework of Fundamental Rights Protection in Europe' (2013) 50 *CML Review* 1267, 1279 (emphasis in original).

[51] *cf* eg Case C-503/09 *Stewart*, EU:C:2011:500, para 81: 'Situations falling within the material scope of EU law include those involving the exercise of the fundamental freedoms guaranteed by the Treaties, in particular those involving the freedom to move and reside … as conferred by Article 21 TFEU'.

resided in another Member State. That fact sparks an unambiguous cross-border connection. Examining the restriction placed on her free movement rights in light of fundamental rights committed to in the Charter could have applied, in the first instance, to the legislative choices expressed in Directive 2004/38 itself. In other words, what the Court does not address here is that the Directive implements Article 21 rights. Moreover, the national court's question was not framed around the Regulation—it was framed around the benefit. And the Court had itself insisted that the benefit in question fell within the scope of the Directive as well as of the Regulation.

Alternatively, the Court could have applied the Charter to an assessment of the contested national rules, especially since it provided an implicit indication of the relevant public interest underpinning those rules in the statement that the objective of Article 7 of the Directive is 'to prevent economically inactive Union citizens from using the host Member State's welfare system to fund their means of subsistence'.[52] On this point, there is also, once again, a missed linkage between the concern in *Dano* to equip the Member States to address possible abuse of free movement rights and the objective of 'preventing [VAT] evasion' applied in *Åkerberg Fransson*.[53] Additionally, Directive 2004/38 signals other objectives too: ensuring, for example, that the right to move and reside freely is 'to be exercised under objective conditions of freedom and dignity' (recital 5) and that the Directive in its entirety 'respects the fundamental rights and freedoms and observes the principles recognised in particular by the Charter of Fundamental Rights of the European Union' (recital 31).

In contrast, drawing from the terminology outlined in section II.A, the Court seems to be saying in *Dano* that where the conditions for lawful residence set down in the Directive are not met, there is never a *sufficient degree of connection* between national measures that exclude EU citizens from eligibility to social assistance and EU law; there are no *specific rules of EU law* on the matter or rules *capable of or likely to affect* it; the subject area concerned *does not impose any obligations* on the Member States. In *Commission v UK*, which builds on the reasoning applied in *Dano*, justification analysis of national measures that result in discrimination against EU citizens was restored.[54] The more recent judgment pierces even further into equal treatment rights through its finding that attaching a lawful residence condition to eligibility for non-contributory social benefits—ie, *not* social assistance—before EU citizens may claim them is justified by 'the need to protect the finances of the host Member State'.[55] And here, once again, there is no discussion of fundamental rights or the Charter at all.

How might the *outcome* in *Dano* have ended up differently? It is first important to acknowledge that application of the Charter might not have altered the

[52] *Dano* (n 42) para 76; confirmed in Case C-67/14 *Alimanovic*, EU:C:2015: 597, para 50.
[53] *Åkerberg Fransson* (n 15) para 25; *Dano* (n 42) paras 76–78.
[54] *Commission v UK* (n 47) paras 74–80.
[55] ibid para 80.

substantive outcome at all. However, consideration of the relevant provisions would have provided guidance for national courts faced with similar questions. Moreover, engagement with the Charter for legislation on the rights of third-country nationals demonstrates some potential for substantive implications even in the controversial area of social rights.[56] For example, national authorities are bound by the Charter 'when determining the social security, social assistance and social protection measures defined by their national law' in connection with Directive 2003/109.[57]

How might the *approach* taken in *Dano* have ended up differently? In striking contrast, to locate a citizenship dilemma squarely within the Charter in *Petruhhin*, what is left out of the discussion is the *Directive*—demonstrating the exasperating inconsistency that has come to define the evolution of EU citizenship law. The applicant in *Petruhhin* is an Estonian national who was arrested in Latvia in September 2014 and placed in provisional custody there in October. Later that month, the Latvian authorities received an extradition request from Russia, which was authorised by the Public Prosecutor in Latvia. Appealing against the decision to extradite him, the applicant raised equal treatment under Articles 18 and 21 TFEU, since Latvian nationals are protected from extradition in similar circumstances. In its judgment, the Court adopts the fact of movement approach absent from *Dano*;[58] and it cites a judgment delivered before the Directive took effect on that point.[59] Significantly for present purposes, the Court speaks only on Articles 18 and 21 TFEU, ie, it never questions whether the applicant meets the conditions for lawful residence under Directive 2004/38 so that he can, in turn, benefit from equal treatment with home State nationals under Article 24(1) of that measure. Instead, it states that the Latvian rules result in nationality discrimination that can only be justified 'where it is based on objective considerations and is proportionate to the legitimate objective of the national provisions'.[60] It then finds that

> the decision of a Member State to extradite a Union citizen, in a situation such as that of the main proceedings, comes within the scope of Article 18 TFEU and Article 21 TFEU and, therefore, of EU law for the purposes of Article 51(1) of the Charter.[61]

[56] See further chapter 13 in this volume by K de Vries.

[57] Case C-571/10 *Kamberaj*, EU:C:2012:233, paras 79–80, addressing Art 34(3) of the Charter in particular, ie, 'In order to combat social exclusion and poverty, the Union recognises and respects the right to social and housing assistance so as to ensure a decent existence for all those who lack sufficient resources, in accordance with the rules laid down by Union law and national laws and practices'. Directive 2003/109/EC on the status of third-country nationals who are long-term residents [2004] OJ L16/44.

[58] Case C-182/15 *Petruhhin*, EU:C:2016:630, para 30: 'in order to determine the scope of application of the Treaties within the meaning of Article 18 TFEU, that article must be read in conjunction with the provisions of the FEU Treaty on citizenship of the Union. The situations falling within their scope of application include, therefore, those involving the exercise of the freedom to move and reside within the territory of the Member States, as conferred by Article 21 TFEU'.

[59] Case C-209/03 *Bidar*, EU:C:2005:169, paras 31–33.

[60] *Petruhhin* (n 58) para 34.

[61] ibid para 52; citing *Åkerberg Fransson* (n 15). The Court goes on to provide guidance to the national court in connection with Arts 1, 4 and 19 of the Charter. It is also interesting to note that the

A fact of movement approach also comes through in the Opinion of Advocate General Wathelet. He observed that

> the Member States have reiterated … the classic position in this type of situation, namely that in order for the FEU Treaty rules on citizenship of the Union to be applicable the facts of the main proceedings must relate to a matter governed by EU law and that it is not sufficient that the citizen of the Union concerned has exercised his freedom of movement.[62]

But he continued:

> [I]t is settled case-law that the situations falling within the scope of EU law *include those involving the exercise of the fundamental f*reedoms guaranteed by the FEU Treaty, in particular those involving the freedom to move and reside within the territory of the Member States, as conferred by Article 21 TFEU … Thus, in matters falling within the competence of the Member States, a relevant link with EU law may consist in the exercise by a national of one Member State of his right to move and reside on the territory of another Member State.[63]

He then stated that 'Mr Petruhhin, who was arrested in Latvia, made use of his freedom to move and reside in another Member State, guaranteed by Article 21(1) TFEU'.[64] Interestingly, he also observed that 'in the absence of rules of EU law on the extradition of nationals of the Member States to Russia, the Member States retain the power to adopt such rules and to conclude agreements on such extradition with the Russian Federation'.[65] An analogy can surely be seen here with the reasoning of the Court in *Dano* as regards the powers that Member States retain notwithstanding Regulation 883/2004. However, in *Petruhhin*, AG Wathelet recalled instead the standard case law principle that

> the Member States are required *to exercise that power in a manner consistent with EU law*, and in particular with the provisions of the FEU Treaty on freedom to move and reside on the territory of the Member States, as conferred by Article 21(1) TFEU on every citizen of the Union.[66]

Court stayed outside citizenship rights altogether to develop the substance of the right to vote; see Case C-650/13 *Delvigne*, EU:ECLI:2015:648; here, Art 14(3) TEU provides the trigger for consideration of Arts 39(2) and 49(1) of the Charter.

[62] AG Wathelet in *Petruhhin* (EU:C:2016:330), para 38 of the Opinion.

[63] ibid para 39 (emphasis added).

[64] ibid para 40.

[65] ibid para 41.

[66] ibid para 42. In footnote 15, the Advocate General cited extensive supporting case law, reproduced here in full to underline its widespread influence in citizenship law: 'See, in particular, concerning national provisions on compensation for victims of assaults carried out on national territory … *Cowan* (186/87, EU:C:1989:47, paragraph 19); regarding national rules on criminal matters and criminal procedure … *Bickel and Franz* (C-274/96, EU:C:1998:563, para 17); on national rules governing a person's surname … *Garcia Avello* (C-148/02, EU:C:2003:539, para 25), and … *Runevič-Vardyn and Wardyn* (C-391/09, EU:C:2011:291, para 63 and the case-law cited); regarding an enforcement procedure for the recovery of debts … *Pusa* (C-224/02, EU:C:2004:273, point 22); as regards national rules on direct taxation … *Schempp* (C-403/03, EU:C:2005:446, para 19); concerning national rules defining

In its judgment, the Court made a similar point, framed around the duty of sincere cooperation.[67] On the question of Charter scope, how then can *Petruhhin* be reconciled with *Dano*?

Commenting on *Åkerberg Fransson*,[68] Sarmiento observes that the Court

> rejects the possibility that Member States might act within the scope of application of EU law but with no duty to respect the Charter. A strict interpretation of Article 51(1) would have confirmed the existence of areas in which EU law would be applicable, but not the Charter.[69]

In parts of citizenship case law, precisely this disjointed result has materialised. In *Dano*, not even the possibly softer *Melloni* prescription, ie,

> where a court of a Member State is called upon to review whether fundamental rights are complied with by a national provision or measure which, in a situation *where action of the Member States is not entirely determined by European Union law*, implements the latter for the purposes of Article 51(1) of the Charter, national authorities and courts remain free to apply national standards of protection of fundamental rights, *provided that* the level of protection provided for by the Charter, as interpreted by the Court, and the primacy, unity and effectiveness of European Union law are not thereby compromised[70]

was considered as a possible reflection of Regulation 883/2004's paradigm of coordination. Neither does the judgment in *Dano* explain how precluding recourse to equal treatment in a host State unless the conditions of Directive 2004/38 are met[71] fits with the commitment in Article 52(1) of the Charter that restrictions must 'respect the essence of those rights and freedoms'. Limits may not, in other words, go so far as to negate the existence of the right in the first place.

There is also a problematic distinction as regards citizens who reside in a host State on another legal basis—for example, the children of migrant workers who reside on the basis of the right to complete their education under Regulation 492/2011.[72] These citizens may remain outside certain rights conferred by

the persons entitled to vote and stand as a candidate in elections to the European Parliament … *Spain* v *United Kingdom* (C-145/04, EU:C:2006:543, para 78); regarding the definition of the conditions for the acquisition and loss of nationality … *Rottmann* (C-135/08, EU:C:2010:104, paras 39 and 41); as regards the Member States' power to organise their social security schemes … *Reichel-Albert* (C-522/10, EU:C:2012:475, para 38 and the case-law cited), and … *Commission* v *Austria* (C-75/11, EU:C:2012:605, para 47 and the case-law cited); and, as regards the content of teaching and the organisation of the education systems of the Member States … *Martens* (C-359/13, EU:C:2015:118, para 23 and the case-law cited)'.

[67] *Petruhhin* (n 58) para 47.

[68] And, in particular, on the statement in para 21 that 'the applicability of European Union law entails applicability of the fundamental rights guaranteed by the Charter'.

[69] Sarmiento (n 50) 1278.

[70] *Åkerberg Fransson* (n 15) para 29, citing Case C-399/11 *Melloni*, EU:C:2013:107, para 60 (emphasis added) and Art 53 of the Charter.

[71] On this point, see D Thym, 'When Union Citizens Turn into Illegal Migrants: The Dano Case' (2015) 40 *EL Rev* 249, 257–58.

[72] See, eg, Case C-480/08 *Teixeira*, EU:C:2010:83.

the Directive, such as the possibility to achieve permanent residence rights if they or their family members do not meet the Directive's monetary criteria for lawful residence.[73] However, since rights based on Regulation 492/2011 stem from Article 45 TFEU, they would still fall within the scope of the Charter. So here, for example, does exclusion of a parent from qualification for permanent residence in a host State, even though he or she was residing lawfully there with Union citizen child(ren) under non-Directive premises of EU law, align with the requirement in Article 24(2) of the Charter that the child's best interests must be a primary consideration in decisions taken by public authorities? Asking the question in this way would require consideration of what public interest is served by the exclusion and whether it is achieved proportionately. In *Ruiz Zambrano,* AG Sharpston remarked that

> [i]t would be paradoxical (to say the least) if a citizen of the Union could rely on fundamental rights under EU law when exercising an economic right to free movement as a worker, or when national law comes within the scope of the Treaty (for example, the provisions on equal pay) or when invoking EU secondary legislation (such as the services directive), but could not do so when merely 'residing' in that Member State'.[74]

But that paradoxical place is precisely where we seem to have ended up in EU citizenship law.

In *Dano,* Advocate General Wathelet had offered another argument to remove the case from the reach of the Charter. Looking to Article 52(2)—which was described above as generating at least an absorptive and possibly also an exclusionary effect on the evaluation of limits placed on Charter rights—there was, in his view, no need for the Court to deal with equal treatment under Article 20 of the Charter.[75] In one sense, that reasoning confirms the approach of the Court in *Pfleger* and *ONEm,* outlined in section II.B above. What becomes clearer by reflecting on it in the light of *Dano* is that Article 52(2) of the Charter would then deprive equal treatment (protected by Article 20 of the Charter) of *any* possible effect in cases connected to Article 21 TFEU. In other words, by folding not just the Charter's promise of a right to move and reside freely (in Article 45(1)) back into Articles 20 and 21 TFEU, but also the right to equal treatment in Article 20 of the Charter back into the same Treaty provisions,[76] parallel expressions of the right to move and reside become conflated with what we normally think of as ancillary rights, ie, the rights that represent the *conditions* under which the right to move and reside is exercised. Is it not supposed to be precisely the other way around, ie, that the Charter sets parameters for the interpretation of legislation; not that legislation can bypass the requirements of the Charter?

[73] Case C-592/11 *Alarape and Tijani,* EU:C:2013:290, paras 36–47.

[74] AG Sharpston in *Ruiz Zambrano* (EU:C:2010:560) para 84 of the Opinion.

[75] AG Wathelet in *Dano* (EU:C:2014:341), paras 149–51 of the Opinion.

[76] At para 149 of the Opinion, AG Wathelet stated: 'the principle of equal treatment referred to in Article 20 of the Charter is also laid down in Articles 20 TFEU and 21 TFEU'.

This question is picked up again in section IV below, but it is worth underlining as a preliminary point that even something falling within the scope of Union law per Article 51 will not necessarily engage Charter applicability where Article 52(2) needs to be considered too. For now, we do not know whether the Charter's commitments to human dignity or the combating of social exclusion and poverty have concrete implications for a State's decision, based on a framework set by the EU legislature, not to extend social assistance to Union citizens in certain circumstances. But

> [c]itizens deserve to know if the Court is willing to uphold a strong Charter of rights or, on the contrary, whether the Charter is merely destined to enunciate generic and low-level standards for a wide community of twenty-eight Member States. The Member States also deserve to know what threshold of rights protection the Court is willing to attribute to the Charter.[77]

If the Court wishes to avoid accusations of selective, issue-based or policy-driven application of the Charter—or indeed, recalling *Petruhhin*, of the Directive—a more systematic framework for determining the Charter's applicability should be drawn. In particular, the determinations made in citizenship case law need to align more coherently with case law that develops the framework of Article 51 at a more general level. Application of fundamental rights can make a powerful difference in some cases, but in a system founded on 'the values of respect for human dignity, freedom, democracy, equality, the rule of law and respect for human rights' (Article 2 TEU), that power is not of itself a good reason to avoid applying them. It is vital to remember once again that engaging the Charter does not necessarily mean that the outcome of a case will be different. As we saw in section II, Charter rights are not absolute and may legitimately be limited, both by the Union institutions and by the Member States when their authorities act in the scope of EU law. But Article 2 TEU does I think require that how the outcome of a case fits with Union thresholds for and understandings of fundamental rights protection should be clearly articulated, carefully explained and consistently applied. It requires that the fundamental rights question is addressed, at least. We cannot claim that case law on Article 21 TFEU meets these benchmarks yet. In section III.B, it will be shown that we cannot claim it for case law on Article 20 TFEU either; but it will be seen that the trajectory here is more promising.

B. To Stay: Article 20 TFEU

When Union citizens remain in their State of nationality but nevertheless trigger Union citizenship rights under Article 20 TFEU—a line of case law built on *Rottmann*—when does the Charter apply? There is a critical difference between

[77] Sarmiento and Sharpston (n 12).

disingenuous appeals to citizenship to attract EU fundamental rights protection in what are, in reality, situations purely internal to one Member State that are not otherwise connected to Union law; and attributing appropriate substance to fundamental rights when EU citizenship is legitimately engaged. In *Ruiz Zambrano*, the Court's silence on the Charter could perhaps be explained by uncertainty about that very dilemma.[78] It ruled that third-country national family members may derive a residence right from static Union citizens in the latter's home State when not granting that derived right would 'have the effect of depriving citizens of the Union of the genuine enjoyment of the substance of the rights conferred by virtue of their status as citizens of the Union'.[79] The fact of dependency between minor Union citizens and their parents suggested to the Court that 'such a refusal would lead to a situation where those children, citizens of the Union, would have to leave the territory of the Union in order to accompany their parents'.[80] The Court rationalised the granting of a work permit on the same basis. Otherwise, the children's father, in this case,

> would risk not having sufficient resources to provide for himself and his family, which would also result in the children, citizens of the Union, having to leave the territory of the Union. In those circumstances, those citizens of the Union would, in fact, be unable to exercise the substance of the rights conferred on them by virtue of their status as citizens of the Union.[81]

In *Iida*, the 'intrinsic connection with the freedom of movement of a Union citizen' informing the Court's reasoning and the exceptional nature of the 'very specific situations' to which it applies were underlined.[82]

The referring court in *Ruiz Zambrano* connected its citizenship questions to Articles 21, 24 and 34 of the Charter,[83] but the Court stayed clear of explaining how or to what extent the circumstances of the case constituted the 'implementation' of Union law. Soon afterwards, it addressed the question in *Dereci*. First,

[78] Other considerations have been suggested to explain this 'Charter silence'—see, eg, S Iglesias Sánchez, 'The Court and the Charter: The Impact of the Entry into Force of the Lisbon Treaty on the ECJ's Approach to Fundamental Rights' (2012) 49 *CML Rev* 1565, 1577 (observing that 'the controversial or adventurous solutions arrived at by the Court could somehow have a negative impact in the attitude of national authorities or private actors towards the Charter').

[79] *Ruiz Zambrano* (n 4) para 42; capturing the resulting 'crossroads' moment for potential further development of both citizenship and fundamental rights law, see S Iglesias Sánchez, 'Fundamental Rights and Citizenship of the Union at a Crossroads: A Promising Alliance or a Dangerous Liaison? (2014) 20 *European Law Journal* 464; and MJ van den Brink, 'EU Citizenship and EU Fundamental Rights: Taking EU Citizenship Rights Seriously?' (2012) 39 *Legal Issues of Economic Integration* 273.

[80] *Ruiz Zambrano* (n 4) para 44.

[81] ibid.

[82] *Iida* (n 32) paras 72 and 71 respectively; for analysis, see S Reynolds, 'Exploring the "Intrinsic Connection" between Free Movement and the Genuine Enjoyment Test: Reflections on EU Citizenship after *Iida*' (2013) 38 *EL Rev* 376.

[83] *Ruiz Zambrano* (n 4) para 35, raising the non-discrimination, rights of the child, and social security and social assistance provisions of the Charter respectively.

considering further when a Union citizen might be forced to leave the Union territory, the Court ruled that

> the mere fact that it might appear desirable to a national of a Member State, for economic reasons *or in order to keep his family together in the territory of the Union*, for the members of his family who do not have the nationality of a Member State to be able to reside with him in the territory of the Union, *is not sufficient in itself* to support the view that the Union citizen will be forced to leave Union territory if such a right is not granted.[84]

But, second, the Court suggested that this was 'without prejudice to the question whether, on the basis of other criteria, inter alia, by virtue of the right to the protection of family life, a right of residence cannot be refused'.[85]

Considering the rights protected under Article 7 of the Charter to be 'the same' in meaning and scope as the rights protected under Article 8 ECHR,[86] but also recalling Article 51(1) of the Charter, the Court advised that

> if the referring court considers … that the situation of the applicants in the main proceedings is covered by European Union law, it must examine whether the refusal of their right of residence undermines the right to respect for private and family life provided for in Article 7 of the Charter. On the other hand, if it takes the view that that situation is not covered by European Union law, it must undertake that examination in the light of Article 8(1) of the ECHR.[87]

What that circular statement does not address is the stage at which, in the determination of a *Ruiz Zambrano* residence right, EU standards of fundamental rights become relevant for national authorities. Moreover, in *Ruiz Zambrano*, both parents were third-country nationals, but from *Dereci* onwards we see the variation that dependent Union citizens were connected to at least one carer himself or herself possessing Union citizenship: could such situations ever reach the threshold of forced departure from the Union territory? And how might that be determined in connection with the protections provided by the Charter, Article 24(2) of which provides that '[i]n all actions relating to children, whether taken by public authorities or private institutions, the child's best interests must be a primary consideration'? Additionally, Article 24(3) establishes that '[e]very child shall have the right to maintain on a regular basis a personal relationship and direct contact with both his or her parents, unless that is contrary to his or her interests'.

Citizenship case law has started to answer some of these critical questions. In *CS*, the Court ruled that the Charter is relevant when a Member State seeks to deport a

[84] Case C-256/11 *Dereci*, EU:C:2011:734, para 68 (emphasis added); for analysis, see S Adam and P Van Elsuwege, 'Citizenship Rights and the Federal Balance between the European Union and its Member States: Comment on *Dereci*' (2012) 37 *EL Review* 176.

[85] *Dereci* (n 84) para 69.

[86] ibid para 70.

[87] ibid para 72.

third-country national family member who resides there with a dependent Union citizen on the basis of *Ruiz Zambrano* but has been convicted of a criminal offence,

> since [the applicant's] situation falls within the scope of EU law, assessment of her situation must take account of the right to respect for private and family life, as laid down in Article 7 of the Charter of Fundamental Rights … an article which must be read in conjunction with the obligation to take into consideration the child's best interests, recognised in Article 24(2) of the Charter.[88]

In this case, it was found that the contested legislation 'seems to establish a systematic and automatic link between the criminal conviction of the person concerned and the expulsion measure applicable to him or, in any event, there is a presumption that the person concerned must be expelled'.[89] In such circumstances, the child's rights under Article 7 of the Charter are part of the 'balancing exercise required' of national courts, against the Member State's public policy or public security interest in seeking deportation of the family member.[90] To assess proportionality, and referring to case law of the European Court of Human Rights (ECtHR), the Court directed that '[p]articular attention must be paid to [the child's] age, his situation in the Member State concerned and *the extent to which* he is dependent on the parent'.[91]

What is far less clear is the role that fundamental rights should play in determining the existence of *Ruiz Zambrano* residence rights in the first place. In *Dereci*, Advocate General Mengozzi indicated that the substance of EU citizenship rights criterion articulated in *Ruiz Zambrano* does not per se 'include the right to respect for family life'.[92] Moreover, under the case law of the Strasbourg Court,

> Article 8 of the ECHR does not guarantee foreign nationals 'a right to choose the most suitable place to develop family life' and does not impose on a State 'a general obligation to respect immigrants' choice of the country of their matrimonial residence and to authorise family reunion in its territory'.[93]

In *Iida*, however, Advocate General Trstenjak argued that

> if it were to transpire in a particular case that denying a right of residence would rule out the possibility of maintaining regular personal relations, this could constitute interference with a fundamental right, the justification for which would have to been assessed from the standpoint of proportionality.[94]

[88] Case C-304/14 *CS*, EU:C:2016:674, para 36. At para 31, the Court had explained that 'CS's child has the right, as a Union citizen, to move and reside freely within the territory of the European Union, and any limitation of that right falls within the scope of EU law'.

[89] ibid para 44.

[90] ibid para 48 (and see also, paras 46–47).

[91] ibid para 49 (emphasis added), citing *Jeunesse v The Netherlands* (App no 12738/10) judgment of 3 October 2014, para 118.

[92] AG Mengozzi in *Dereci* (EU:C:2011:626), para 37 of the View.

[93] AG Bot in Case C-83/11 *Rahman*, EU:C:2012:174, para 72 of the Opinion, citing *Ahmut v The Netherlands* (1996) 24 EHRR 62, paras 71 and 67 and *Gül v Switzerland* (1996) 22 EHRR 93, para 38.

[94] AG Trstenjak in *Iida* (n 36) para 85 of the Opinion, which continued: 'it would be necessary to consider, among other things, whether the child's father who is a third-country national also actually exercises his right of custody and endeavours to fulfil his parental duties'.

The minor Union citizen in *Iida* had exercised cross-border movement; should the same line of reasoning apply when determining whether a dependent Union citizen is being forced to leave the Union territory where one parent (or other carer)[95] is denied a residence permit in the citizen's home State?

In *O and S*, the Court repeated *Dereci* language about 'the mere fact that it might appear desirable to a national of a Member State to keep his family together in the territory of the Union', but it also seemed to soften that approach by construing dependency as potentially meaning 'legally, financially or emotionally dependent'.[96] In the context of EU legislation on family reunification for third-country nationals, the Court also confirmed that Article 7 of the Charter

> must also be read in conjunction with the obligation to have regard to the child's best interests, recognised in Article 24(2) of the Charter, and with account being taken of the need, expressed in Article 24(3), for a child to maintain on a regular basis a personal relationship with both parents.[97]

However, in *Ymeraga*—a judgment delivered without an Advocate General's opinion—the harder position re-emerged, in the finding that

> the refusal to confer a right of residence on [the applicant's] family members *does not have the effect of* denying him the genuine enjoyment of the substance of the rights conferred by virtue of his status as citizen of the Union. *In those circumstances*, the Luxembourg authorities' refusal to grant [his] family members a right of residence as family members of a Union citizen *is not a situation involving the implementation of European Union law within the meaning of Article 51* of the Charter, so that its conformity with fundamental rights cannot be examined in the light of the rights established by the Charter.[98]

In other words: the determination of dependency is made first; and only if dependency is established does the situation fall within the scope of EU law. But how can it be logical or proper to separate determinations of dependency from consideration of family life, and all the more from Article 24 of the Charter when children are involved? As argued by Advocate General Wathelet in *NA*,

> [i]f a Treaty provision does not preclude a Member State from refusing a right of residence subject to compliance with certain conditions, it follows by definition that the situation in question falls within the scope of that provision. If that were not the case, the Court would have to decline jurisdiction to answer the question referred.[99]

Advocate General Sharpston has agreed that

> it is necessary to look at a legal situation through the prism of the Charter if, but only if, a provision of EU law imposes a positive or negative obligation on the Member State (whether that obligation arises through the Treaties or EU secondary legislation).[100]

[95] *O and S* (n 5) para 55.
[96] ibid para 56.
[97] ibid para 76; addressing Directive 2003/86/EC on the right to family reunification [2003] OJ L251/12.
[98] *Ymeraga* (n 35) paras 42–43.
[99] AG Wathelet in *NA* (n 37) para 122 of the Opinion.
[100] AG Sharpston in Case C-456/12 *O* (EU:C:2013:837) and Case C-457/12 *S* (EU:C:2013:842) para 61 of the Opinion.

How is the requirement to make an assessment of whether or not a *Ruiz Zambrano* residence right might exist, a requirement based on Article 20 TFEU, *not* an obligation imposed by EU law on national authorities? In the same Opinion, she continued:

> [A] provision such as Article 20 or 21 TFEU is not simply a basis for residence status separate from Article 7 of the Charter. Rather, considerations regarding the exercise of the right to a family life permeate the substance of EU citizenship rights. Citizenship rights under Article 20 or 21 TFEU must thus be interpreted in a way that ensures that their substantive content is 'Charter-compliant'. That process is separate from the question of whether a justification advanced for a restriction of EU citizenship rights … is consistent with the Charter. Such an approach does not 'extend' the scope of EU law and thus violate the separation of competences between the Union and its constituent Member States. It merely respects the overarching principle that, in a Union founded on the rule of law, all the relevant law (including, naturally, relevant primary law in the shape of the Charter) is taken into account when interpreting a provision of that legal order. When viewed in that light, taking due account of the Charter is no more 'intrusive', or 'disrespectful of Member State competence', than interpreting free movement of goods correctly.[101]

In *NA*, Advocate General Wathelet expressly endorsed her argument, adding that

> the inclusion of Article 7 of the Charter in the national court's reflection on the application of Article 20 TFEU is not such as to have the effect of extending the scope of EU law in a manner that would be contrary to Article 51(2) of the Charter. After all, it is European citizenship as provided for in Article 20 TFEU that triggers the protection afforded by the fundamental rights … not the other way round.[102]

That analysis then leads to another crucial question: 'must the obligation to leave the territory of the European Union be measured from a legal perspective or *in concreto*, in relation to the facts?'[103] In Advocate General Wathelet's view, a theoretical ('legal') possibility of having to leave the territory of the Union has to be distinguished from the factual circumstances of an individual case.[104] For example, in the *NA* case,

> although, 'as German nationals', NA's daughters 'enjoy an unconditional right of residence in Germany, it is also common ground that neither they nor [their] mother can reasonably be expected to live there, and, on this basis, the domestic courts have held that they could not be removed [from the United Kingdom to Germany] without violating the ECHR'. [I]f that information were to be confirmed by the referring court, it would fall to that court to recognise MA and IA as having a right of residence in the United Kingdom on the basis of Article 20 TFEU, with NA herself, by extension, obtaining a derived right of residence.[105]

[101] AG Sharpston in *O* and *S*, paras 62–63 of the Opinion.
[102] AG Wathelet in *NA* (n 37) para 125 of the Opinion.
[103] ibid para 98.
[104] ibid esp paras 105–09.
[105] ibid paras 116–17 of the Opinion.

The Court's implicit guidance in *Dereci* and explicit ruling in *Ymeraga* had contrasted vividly with the *integrated* approach later promoted by Advocates General Sharpston and Wathelet. Their logic is compelling. Article 20 TFEU requires national authorities to consider a derived residence right in a Union citizen's home State where the denial of that right might deprive the Union citizen of the genuine enjoyment of the substance of their citizenship rights. That requirement in turn imposes an obligation on national authorities, which accords with the *Åkerberg Fransson* et al understanding of implementing Union law per Article 51(1) of the Charter. The instinct to limit the reach of EU law in situations that are factually confined to one Member State is understandable. But, as already argued in section III.A for situations involving the exercise of free movement rights, developing a fragmented approach to what does or does not fall within the scope of Union law does not provide a defensible solution to a more general scope of Union law problem. Where the Article 20 TFEU door is opened—and the Court itself opened it—the Charter applies in consequence.

As seen, the Court tends to encourage national courts to reflect on the lawfulness of deprivation of residence rights for family members under Article 8 ECHR where it rules out the application of the Charter.[106] The paradoxical position that national judges may then find themselves in is that a situation acknowledged to breach Article 8 ECHR is removed from the ambit of Article 7 of the Charter even though the national judge is partly ascertaining the existence of rights under Article 20 TFEU—a reflection itself required by the *Ruiz Zambrano* case law. A brief look at national case law helps to demonstrate the logic of a more integrated framework. For example, consider the reasoning in a Court of Appeal judgment (England and Wales), interpreting national rules implementing *Ruiz Zambrano*:

> [T]he welfare of the child cannot be the paramount consideration because that would be flatly inconsistent with the statutory test which is whether the child would be unable to reside in the UK if the mother left. It will, in normal circumstances, be contrary to the interests of a child for one of its parent carers, whether the primary carer or not, to be taken away from him or her. *It would certainly be contrary to article 24(3) of the Charter* … The only basis upon which the reviewer was considering the adequacy of the father's ability to care for [the child] was because *it was obvious that it would be a bad thing for him to have to leave his mother*, and the reviewer needed to establish whether the effect would be so bad that Brandon would be unable to remain in the UK. At one end of the spectrum, there would be a situation in which the father would refuse or be unable to care for Brandon at all—in that case he would obviously be compelled to leave to follow his mother. At the other end of the spectrum, the father would offer a very satisfactory home for Brandon which would not seriously impair his quality or standard of life, in which case he would be well able to stay in the UK. [It] was not surprising that the reviewer did not spend much time explaining how bad it would be for a 4-year old child to be separated from his mother. That was a given.[107]

[106] eg *Dereci* (n 84) paras 72–73.

[107] Vos LJ in *Hines v Lambeth LBC*, Court of Appeal (Civil Division) [2014] EWCA Civ 660, paras 22 and 27 (emphasis added).

And citing *Dereci,* it was starkly observed that 'only a limited importance is given to the right to respect for family life'.[108] Similarly, in *Harrison*, the national judge concluded that

> the right to reside in the territory of the Union is not a right to any particular quality or life or to any particular standard of living. Accordingly, there is no impediment to exercising the right to reside if residence remains possible as a matter of substance, albeit that the quality of life is diminished.[109]

Reflecting on the *Dereci* exclusion of 'economic reasons or in order to keep his family together in the territory of the Union', the *Harrison* judgment then presents the resulting dilemma:

> In practice these are the most likely reasons why the right of residence would be rendered less beneficial or enjoyable. If these considerations do not engage this wider principle, it seems to me extremely difficult to identify precisely what will. What level of interference with the right would fall short of de facto compulsion and yet would constitute a form of interference which was more than simply the breakdown of family life or the fact that the EU citizens are financially disadvantaged by the removal of the non EU national family member?[110]

It is difficult to recognise how we normally conceive the fundamentals of the EU legal order in these statements. Yet they are apparently consistent with the guidance issued to national courts by the Court of Justice.[111]

Disconnecting the determination of dependency from fundamental rights analysis might also lead to outcomes inconsistent with the European Convention on Human Rights. For example, in *Jeunesse v The Netherlands*, the ECtHR reflected on a family situation involving a Surinamese mother and Dutch father as follows:

> Noting that the applicant takes care of the children on a daily basis, it is obvious that their interests are best served by not disrupting their present circumstances by a forced relocation of their mother from the Netherlands to Suriname or by a rupturing of their relationship with her as a result of future separation. In this connection, the Court observes that the applicant's husband provides for the family by working full-time in a job that includes shift work. He is, consequently, absent from the home on some evenings. The applicant—being the mother and homemaker—is the primary and constant carer of the children who are deeply rooted in the Netherlands of which country—like their father—they are nationals. The materials in the case file do not disclose a direct link between the applicant's children and Suriname, a country where they have never been.[112]

[108] ibid para 22.

[109] Elias LJ in *Harrison v Secretary of State for the Home Department*, Court of Appeal (Civil Division) [2012] EWCA Civ 1736, para 67.

[110] ibid para 68.

[111] See further, eg, the report on the Netherlands (prepared by J Langer and A Schrauwen) for the XXVI FIDE Congress (Copenhagen, 2014) in U Neergaard, C Jacqueson and N Holst-Christensen (eds), *Union Citizenship: Development, Impact and Challenges*: fide2014.eu/pdf/FINAL-Topic-2-on-Union-Citizenship.pdf, 695 at 705–08.

[112] *Jeunesse v The Netherlands* (n 91) para 119. Interestingly, in *NA*, the Secretary of State did not appeal a finding at first instance that refusing a right to reside to the applicant would, since it would compel the children to leave the *United Kingdom*, breach the children's ECHR rights. AG Wathelet

But following *Dereci*, and thus without applying the Charter, it would be difficult to demonstrate forced departure from the Union noting the father's Dutch nationality.

It is therefore both significant and welcome to discern glimmers of the integrated approach in the Court of Justice's recent judgment in *Rendón Marín*. The applicant is a Colombian national and the sole carer of two children. His son is a Spanish national and his daughter is a Polish national, but both children have always lived in Spain. The children's mother is a Polish national but it was not known where she resided at the time of the case. The applicant has a criminal record in Spain, which resulted in his 2010 application for a temporary residence permit being rejected.[113] The Court assessed the applicant's claim to derived residence rights under two different strands of EU law. It was first considered whether he had a right to reside in Spain on the basis of Directive 2004/38, as the father of a Polish daughter. On this question, the Court applied standard free movement analysis: the Union citizen's residence rights must first be established on the basis of the conditions set down in Article 7(1)(b) of the Directive; if those conditions are met, the situation falls within the scope of Union law; consequently, when determining

> the possible expulsion of Mr Rendón Marín [in accordance with Article 27 of the Directive], it is necessary, first, to take account of the fundamental rights whose observance the Court ensures, in particular the right to respect for private and family life, as laid down in Article 7 of the Charter of Fundamental Rights of the European Union.[114]

Should the conditions of Article 7(1)(b) not be met, the Court also considered whether a residence right might be derived from Mr Rendón Marín's Spanish son under Article 20 TFEU and *Ruiz Zambrano*. Here, we are reminded of Advocate General Wathelet's distinction between a possibility to reside in another State in law and that possibility in reality. Cases such as *Dereci* and *Ymeraga*, and also *Alokpa and Moudoulou*,[115] suggested that possibility in law was enough to defeat a *Ruiz Zambrano* claim. However, in *Rendón Marín*, the Court is strikingly more nuanced:

> Several Member States which have submitted observations have contended that Mr Rendón Marín and his children could move to Poland, the Member State of which his

indicated in his Opinion that a right to reside under EU law should still be considered, since 'it is not inconceivable that the Court's answers to the various questions put to it will determine whether NA is eligible for certain social security benefits and special non-contributory benefits which she is currently denied because of the restriction of the rights conferred by a right of residence based on Article 8 ECHR' (para 30 of the Opinion).

[113] Case C-165/14 *Rendón Marín*, EU:C:2016:675, para 16. In the same paragraph, it was also observed that '[o]n the date of the order for reference … he was awaiting a decision on an application for mention of his criminal record to be removed from the register'.

[114] ibid para 66.

[115] Case C-86/12 *Alokpa and Moudoulou*, EU:C:2013:645; here, the fact of the French nationality of a Togolese national's children was deemed to preclude a *Ruiz Zambrano*-based right to reside in Luxembourg, notwithstanding the applicant's submission that 'she was unable to settle with her

> daughter is a national. Mr Rendón Marín, for his part, stated at the hearing that he maintains no ties with the family of his daughter's mother, who, according to him, does not reside in Poland, and that neither he nor his children know the Polish language. In this regard, it is for the referring court to check whether, in the light of all the circumstances of the main proceedings, Mr Rendón Marín, as the parent who is the sole carer of his children, may in fact enjoy the derived right to go with them to Poland and reside with them there, so that a refusal of the Spanish authorities to grant him a right of residence would not result in his children being obliged to leave the territory of the European Union as a whole.[116]

Without prejudice to the final say being left to the national court, the Court continued,

> it seems to be clear from the information before the Court that the situation at issue in the main proceedings is capable of resulting, for Mr Rendón Marin's children, in their being deprived of the genuine enjoyment of the substance of the rights which the status of Union citizen confers upon them, and that it therefore falls within the scope of EU law.[117]

The Court was then free to follow the logic of its judgment in *CS*, delivered on the same day:

> Article 20 TFEU does not affect the possibility of Member States relying on an exception linked, in particular, to upholding the requirements of public policy and safeguarding public security. However, in so far as Mr Rendón Marin's situation falls within the scope of EU law, assessment of his situation must take account of the right to respect for private and family life, as laid down in Article 7 of the Charter, an article which … must be read in conjunction with the obligation to take into consideration the child's best interests, recognised in Article 24(2) of the Charter.[118]

If the approach tested in this judgment continues to take root, displacing *Dereci* and *Ymeraga* in future *Ruiz Zambrano* situations, it would show that appropriate integration of citizenship rights and fundamental rights *is* feasible.[119]

children in France, or reside with their father on the ground that she had no relations with the latter and that those children required follow-up medical treatment in Luxembourg as a result of their premature birth' (para 15).

[116] *Rendón Marín* (n 113) para 78. For similar tendencies in UK case law see, eg, *R (on the application of Zewdu) v Secretary of State for the Home Department* [2015] EWHC 2148 (Admin) para 27 ('as to the suggestion that there might be some other carer in the [UK] who could take charge of the boy, this is mere speculation'); *Secretary of State for the Home Department v AQ (Nigeria)* [2015] EWCA Civ 250, para 77 ('I cannot accept the Secretary of State's position that the tribunal was only required to consider the ability of others to care for the child in the UK and was bound to ignore questions such as whether a family member would be willing to provide care or was under any familial or other responsibility to do so … In the present case … it seems that none of the witnesses were asked whether she would care for AQ's son if the only alternative was that he would be required to leave the UK with his mother').

[117] *Rendón Marín*, n 113 para 80.

[118] ibid, para 81.

[119] Note, eg, the Opinion of AG Szpunar (EU:C:2016:659) in Case C-133/15 *Chavez-Vilchez and Others* (EU:C:2017:354).

IV. CITIZENSHIP AND ARTICLE 52: RECONCILING THE CHARTER AND THE TREATY

We saw in section II.B that derogating from free movement rights constitutes implementing Union law for the purposes of Article 51 of the Charter and that Article 52(1) establishes how Charter rights may be limited. Additionally, Article 52(3) requires that where Charter rights correspond to ECHR rights, 'the meaning and scope of those rights shall be the same as those laid down by the said Convention'. The fact that recent citizenship case law has retracted the parameters within which an assessment of the *impact* of limitations in individual cases must be undertaken is considered in several contributions to this volume.[120] Previously, however, Advocate General Geelhoed had linked that obligation to the Charter:

> [I]t should also be possible to apply [national criteria and conditions] with sufficient flexibility to take account of the particular individual circumstances of applicants, where refusal of [social] assistance is likely to affect what is known in German constitutional law as the 'Kernbereich' or the substantive core of a fundamental right granted by the Treaty, such as the rights contained in Article [21(1) TFEU] ... [T]his principle has been laid down in Article [52(1)] of the Charter of Fundamental Rights of the Union ... This provides that any limitation on the exercise of the rights and freedoms recognised by the Charter must respect the essence of these rights and freedoms. Article [45(1)] of the Charter guarantees the freedom of EU citizens to move and reside within the territory of the Member States in terms which are essentially identical to Article [21(1) TFEU].[121]

However, as also seen in section II, Article 52(2) provides that '[r]ights recognised by this Charter for which provision is made in the Treaties shall be exercised under the conditions and within the limits defined by those Treaties'—drawing a line back to Articles 20(2) and 21(1) TFEU, which explicitly authorise the limitation of rights by legislation. But how do all these instructions relate to each other?

Before the Charter had binding legal effect, the language of fundamental rights already characterised how limits on free movement should be evaluated. For example, in *Trojani*, Advocate General Geelhoed was clear that 'the right of residence is a fundamental right of every European citizen, and it should be possible actually to exercise this fundamental right' while acknowledging that '[a]t the same time, the right of residence may be limited or subjected to conditions only on the grounds of compelling national interest'.[122] In *Baumbast*, the Court emphasised that 'the application of the limitations and conditions acknowledged in Article [21(1) TFEU] in respect of the exercise of that right of residence is subject to judicial review'.[123] The implications of citizenship as a status bearing rights

[120] See esp the contributions in this volume, chapter 9 by F Wollenschläger; and chapter 10 by P Minderhoud and S Mantu.

[121] AG Geelhoed in Case C-209/03 *Bidar* (EU:C:2004:715) para 32 of the Opinion. Describing the 'primary and individual right to move and reside freely' as being 'reaffirmed' by Art 45 of the Charter, see, eg, Case C-162/09 *Lassal*, EU:C:2010:592, para 29.

[122] AG Geelhoed in Case C-456/02 *Trojani* (EU:C:2004:112) paras 12–13 of the Opinion.

[123] *Baumbast* (n 41) para 86.

were also recognised through the idea that 'a particularly restrictive interpretation of the derogations from [freedom of movement] is required by virtue of a person's status as a citizen of the Union'.[124]

As flagged in section III.A, the strained translation of that logic to the binding Charter environment, coinciding with diminished appetite for progressing citizenship rights, is well illustrated by Advocate General Wathelet's reasoning in *Dano*. He first referred to 'the principle of equal treatment ... in Article 20 of the Charter [as] also laid down in Articles 20 TFEU and 21 TFEU' and acknowledged that 'Regulation No 883/2004 and Directive 2004/38 flesh out the meaning and scope of the principle of equality established by those provisions'.[125] Then he continued:

> Under Article 52(2) of the Charter, rights recognised by the Charter for which provision is made in the Treaties are to be exercised under the conditions and within the limits defined by those Treaties. As the [relevant questions referred] concern provisions of secondary law defining the conditions and limits of the rights protected by Articles 20 TFEU and 21 TFEU, it seems to me to be sufficient to examine those questions for the purpose of providing the referring court with a useful answer.[126]

We have also seen legislative limits applied 'by analogy' even when the case falls outside the scope of the Directive but within the scope of primary Treaty rights.[127]

The newer approach depletes the practice of testing the provisions of secondary legislation for compliance with fundamental rights. The case law has moved towards a starting point that the provisions of secondary legislation are legitimate on the basis that Articles 20 and 21 TFEU infer that they must be. The reach of judicial review is then significantly reduced. In *Alokpa*, Advocate General Mengozzi considered

> the possibility that the provisions of the Charter ... might result in [the] conditions [in Article 7(1)(b) of Directive 2004/38 being relaxed or even disregarded, in particular with a view to ensuring that account is taken of the child's best interests (Article 24 of the Charter) and respect for family life (Articles 7 and 33 of the Charter).[128]

Even the language here—'relaxed or even disregarded'—is interesting. It already conveys that something would be awry with such an investigation. But surely being 'subject to judicial review' is just a more neutral expression of the same enquiry? It is not, in other words, a question of the requirement to have sufficient resources being 'relaxed' by consideration of Charter rights; such conditions are just being examined for compliance with Charter, ie, primary law rights.

[124] eg *Orfanopoulos and Oliveri* (n 6) para 65.

[125] AG Wathelet in *Dano* (n 75) para 149 of the Opinion.

[126] ibid paras 150–51.

[127] eg Case C-456/12 *O*, EU:C:2014:135, para 50; criticising this approach, see AG Szpunar in Case C-202/13 *McCarthy* (EU:C:2014:345) para 82 of the Opinion.

[128] AG Mengozzi in *Alokpa* (EU:C:2013:197) para 34 of the Opinion.

Advocate General Mengozzi concluded in *Alokpa* that

> it appears difficult to envisage such a possibility, since this would mean disregarding the limits laid down by Article 21 TFEU on the right of citizens of the Union to move and reside freely ... and would therefore ... result in the modification of the powers and tasks defined in the Treaties, in breach of Article 51(2) of the Charter.[129]

Even though Article 6(1) TEU confers equal status on the Treaties and the Charter, the Charter's final provisions seem to create an exception: for rights conferred on EU citizens, the Treaties have a superior status; which means, in actual fact, that legislation has a superior status.[130] It is not self-evident, though, why merely *enabling* restriction of rights by legislation, as Articles 20 and 21 TFEU do, should also provide enhanced shelter from judicial review for the legislative choices made. Nevertheless, the capacity of legislation to set limits on citizenship rights but also on fundamental rights was well demonstrated in the February 2016 Decision negotiated in the context of the UK's referendum on withdrawal from the European Union. A Declaration attached to the Decision on 'issues related to the abuse of the right of free movement of persons' outlined various questions that the Commission intended to re-examine. In particular,

> [t]he Commission intends to adopt a proposal to complement Directive 2004/38 ... in order to exclude, from the scope of free movement rights, third country nationals who had no prior lawful residence in a Member State before marrying a Union citizen or who marry a Union citizen only after the Union citizen has established residence in the host Member State. Accordingly, in such cases, the host Member State's immigration law will apply to the third country national.[131]

That proposal was interesting because, if adopted, it would reverse the Court's decision in *Metock*. In that judgment, two levels of analysis can be identified. First, the Court reasoned that since the EU legislator did not include a condition on prior lawful residence for such family members in Directive 2004/38, no such requirement could then be read into the measure. On that basis, it is plainly conceivable

[129] ibid para 35; for the avoidance of doubt, he also pointed out: '[b]y way of a reminder ... Article 21(1) TFEU provides that that right exists "subject to the limitations and conditions laid down in the Treaties and by the measures adopted to give them effect" and, therefore, to those laid down in Directive 2004/38' (footnote 15 of the Opinion).

[130] This position can be contrasted further with arguments about an even 'higher rank' for the Charter vis-a-vis the Treaties notwithstanding the wording of Art 6(1) TEU; on this point, see J Kokott and C Sobotta, 'The Charter of Fundamental Rights of the European Union after Lisbon' EUI Working Papers, AEL 2010/6: cadmus.eui.eu/bitstream/handle/1814/15208/AEL_WP_2010_06.pdf?sequence=3, 6. Adding a caution around extending autonomous status to Art 18 TFEU for the purposes of Charter trigger, see D Thym, 'Separation Versus Fusion—or: How to Accommodate National Autonomy and the Charter? Diverging Visions of the German Constitutional Court and the European Court of Justice' (2013) 9 *European Constitutional Law Review* 391, 414–18.

[131] Annex VII to the Decision of the Heads of State or Government, meeting within the European Council, concerning a new settlement for the United Kingdom within the European Union, 18–19 February 2016.

that an amendment of the Directive is all that would be needed to change things. But second, the right to respect for family life infuses the judgment throughout.[132] What recent case law seems to suggest is that this wider environmental dimension can be legislated away too, suggesting once again that the binding effect of the Charter can make it easier in some respects, and even if counterintuitively, to accomplish reduced protection of rights. That is not, for the integrity of either citizenship rights or fundamental rights, a constitutionally safe place to be.

V. CONCLUSION

This chapter examined how the Charter of Fundamental Rights has been applied in citizenship case law since the Lisbon Treaty acquired binding legal effect. Three main conclusions can be summarised. First, the relationship between free movement rights and fundamental rights has become more complicated. Citizenship law is already complex on its own terms. Similarly, how the provisions of the Charter fit together internally, never mind with the provisions of the Treaties, has become less and not more clear. Second, it is difficult to assess how Charter rights might affect free movement rights in substance, since Article 51 of the Charter has been applied with notable strictness in citizenship case law—at odds with how it is construed in case law more generally. In fact, citizenship cases that most transmit what we might describe as Charter ethos tend not to mention the instrument at all. Third, the largely unchecked force of legislation arguably exceeds what Articles 20 and 21 TFEU, read in conjunction with Article 52 of the Charter, would compel. In this respect, there is more reluctance to undertake substantive judicial review when limitations on free movement rights are challenged; conversely, the baseline (Directive) conditions of free movement might be glossed over when a Charter solution is preferred.

Three discussion points can be highlighted in consequence. First, the analysis presented here confirms a theme evident in several contributions to this volume: that citizenship law seems now to be more about the State than the citizen.

Second, the chapter advocates an integrated understanding of citizenship rights and fundamental rights—pursued initially by Advocates General trying to inject Charter considerations into the *Ruiz Zambrano* case law, but seen recently to have had some influence on the reasoning of the Court too. Ironically, though, the

[132] See *Metock* (n 2) para 56 ('Even before the adoption of Directive 2004/38, the Community legislature recognised the importance of ensuring the protection of the family life of nationals of the Member States in order to eliminate obstacles to the exercise of the fundamental freedoms'); para 62 ('if Union citizens were not allowed to lead a normal family life in the host Member State, the exercise of the freedoms they are guaranteed by the Treaty would be seriously obstructed'); and para 89 ('Where a Union citizen founds a family after becoming established in the host Member State, the refusal of that Member State to authorise his family members who are nationals of non-member countries to join him there would be such as to discourage him from continuing to reside there and encourage him to leave in order to be able to lead a family life in another Member State or in a non-member country').

Charter seems less visible in more conventional, ie, free movement-based citizenship case law. It was emphasised that the Charter is not a stand-alone fundamental rights instrument and that its application might not change certain substantive case outcomes at all. But engaging with its guarantees more consistently is as much about 'elevat[ing] the constitutional tone of the reasoning'.[133] Furthermore, it is simply a fact that national judges and national authorities are asking Charter questions; and they need guidance to manage their decision-making effectively and appropriately. We tend to pitch EU and national fundamental rights standards against each other. But we can also conceive 'a variety of autonomous legal orders coexisting in a common space and with *common* objectives'.[134] In that light, if national courts are more frequently locating citizenship questions within the system of the Charter, they may need clearer answers not because national or indeed ECHR law does not provide any protection; but just to check whether the Charter might provide *different* protection.

Third, questions about how to balance judicial and legislative contributions to the realisation of citizenship rights have inevitably intensified through consideration of the Charter. This is another long-standing story in citizenship law. But it has broader implications for the Union's system of judicial review and for what it means to 'found' that system on respect for fundamental rights and on the rule of law. Neither the initial phase of citizenship-charged case law nor the more recent phase of State-charged case law pleases everyone. However, the incline of the corrective balance, in either direction, as well as the methods developed to realise it offer useful standards for the assessment of constitutional quality that could be shared more widely. In that light, what we may take for granted as foundational premises of the EU legal order could be more vulnerable than we might realise. A key strand of understanding the relationship between the Union and the role of law in its shaping was articulated as the idea of integration through law. We should be careful not to bring about the disintegration *of* that law. Neither Treaty nor Charter guarantees should be evaded on account of the sheer power that their integration might produce. If primary law is part of that problem,[135] then primary law is what needs to be changed.

[133] Iglesias Sánchez, 'The Court and the Charter' (n 78) 1579.

[134] Sarmiento (n 50) 1302 (emphasis added).

[135] See, eg, J Snell, 'Fundamental Rights Review of National Measures: Nothing New under the Charter?' (2015) 21 *European Public Law* 285, 308 ('if the Masters of the Treaties do wish to alter the law, they need to do so in the clearest of terms, which was not the case for Article 51(1)').

Part III

The Citizenship–Immigration Nexus

12

The Constitutional Status of Foreigners and European Union Citizens: Loopholes and Interactions in the Scope of Application of Fundamental Rights

SARA IGLESIAS SÁNCHEZ[1]

I. INTRODUCTION

WHEN IT COMES to discussing what the 'fundamental status' of European Union (EU) citizenship should consist of, academic debate focuses much on the equal treatment of nationals and citizens of other Member States and on what differences may or may not still be admitted. Fundamental limits to the content of the common citizenship are widely discussed, ie, the boundaries of solidarity or the lack of absolute security of residence. With a citizenship still 'in the making', and in a situation where the nationality divide is far from having been superseded by equality, the status of those who do not enjoy EU citizenship might be considered a somewhat secondary issue. Yet, paradoxically, the status of third-country nationals has come to play a central role in EU citizenship studies, particularly when those third-country nationals are family members of Union citizens.

In recent times, however, the status of third-country nationals in EU law has become a genuine topic of interest in its own right, from the point of view of its overreaching repercussions on the status of EU citizenship.[2] Indeed, the basic status granted by EU law to those who are not citizens of the Union necessarily

[1] The opinions in this chapter are purely personal to the author.

[2] See, eg D Thym, 'Citizens and Foreigners in EU Law: Migration Law and its Cosmopolitan Outlook' (2016) 22 *ELJ* 296; F Strumia 'European Citizenship and EU Immigration: A Demoi-cratic Bridge between the Third Country Nationals' Right to Belong and the Member States' Power to Exclude' (2016) 22 *European Law Journal (ELJ)* 417; S Iglesias Sánchez, 'Fundamental Rights Protection for Third Country Nationals and Citizens of the Union: Principles for Enhancing Coherence' (2013) 15 *European Journal of Migration and Law* 137.

reflects on the construction and proper understanding of the status of EU citizenship itself. This exercise of broader reflection has only been made possible since a solid body of EU legislation on the status of third-country nationals has been set up, pre-defining a generally applicable burgeoning status of 'EU foreigner', international agreements and family related rights notwithstanding.

Twenty years after the communitarisation of asylum and migration policies through the Treaty of Amsterdam, there is still much uncertainty about the impact of EU law on the legal status of different persons, depending on their nationality and whether or not they have crossed an internal or external border. This question requires a broad study of secondary law and EU international agreements, which goes beyond the possibilities of this chapter. It does not engage with either the normative or philosophical underpinnings of the constitutional articulation of the status of citizens and foreigners in EU law. The present analysis has a more modest objective: it focuses on the systematisation of the most basic layer underlying the interaction of the status of third-country nationals and EU citizens: the scope of application of EU fundamental rights with regard to EU citizens and third-country nationals. It looks at the dissection of the complex scenario of EU fundamental rights through the lens of the citizen/foreigner divide.

After a brief account of the structure of the provisions of the Charter of Fundamental Rights of the EU (the Charter) and the role of nationality in the determination of entitlement to fundamental rights (II), the question of the impact of the different competences of the Union with regard to EU citizens and EU foreigners will be explored (III). This third section deals, first, with the areas of competence where in principle no distinction on the basis of nationality exists in the application of EU secondary law (A). Subsequently two main areas where such nationality-based differentiation exists will be considered: free movement law and EU migration law (B). The final section of this chapter (IV) is devoted to exploring how the different structure and reach of EU competences and their development by secondary law in the above-mentioned fields projects onto the scope of EU fundamental rights. It will be posited that the specificity of the structure of EU fundamental rights protection, combined with the scope of competences of EU law in citizenship and migration issues—and the different development of those areas through secondary law—leads to a particular constitutional scenario, where the scope of fundamental rights protection does not correspond to preconceived expectations based on national conceptions of the status of citizens and foreigners.

II. NATIONALITY AND THE CHARTER

From the point of view of EU law, the scope of EU fundamental rights is governed by the horizontal provisions of the Charter, in particular, by its Article 51(1). That provision makes an emphasis on *who is obliged* to comply with the provisions of the Charter. It does not however explicitly indicate *who the beneficiaries* of those rights are. It is therefore necessary to refer to the wording of each Article of the Charter.

This exercise of determination of the beneficiaries of Charter rights shows, with some punctual exceptions, that the great majority of EU fundamental rights are proclaimed with regard to 'everybody'.[3] Far from being the result of an attempt to leave open the issue of entitlement to fundamental rights, the wording of the Charter demonstrates a deliberate choice for comprehensive inclusion of all individuals whose situation falls within the scope of EU law, notwithstanding nationality. This is attested by the fact that, when the drafters of the Charter wanted to establish a differentiation on the basis of nationality, they clearly did so in the wording of specific provisions. Indeed, several provisions in the Charter contemplate differentiations on the basis of nationality. Some of the rights contained in the Charter are proclaimed only with regard to EU citizens. Those are mostly provisions enunciating rights connected with the 'basic core' rights of European citizenship: free movement and political rights. However, when it comes to determine differences of entitlement to fundamental rights for citizens and foreigners, nationality is not the only relevant criterion. The Charter relies on further differentiating elements, such as residence and legal status.

Finally, besides the narrow issue of entitlement, the actual impact of Charter rights on citizens and foreigners may be affected by considerations which appertain to the material content of some fundamental rights, where nationality plays a role (eg, with regard to the admitted grounds for deprivation of liberty, the non-discrimination principle or the rights connected to asylum or non-refoulement). Additionally, there are some fundamental rights that become particularly relevant in migration/asylum-related contexts. Some of them refer to the protection against dangers where third-country nationals seem to be particularly affected, or that evoke particular problems connected to migration and asylum. The following lines explore the references of the Charter to nationality, residence and status, as well as the content-wise specificities of fundamental rights which are relevant for the citizen/foreigner divide.

A. Nationality-Based Entitlements

Article 45(1) of the Charter recognises the right to move and reside freely within the territory of the Member States only to EU citizens. Through that provision, free movement rights have been confirmed as fundamental rights. However, the Explanation on Article 45 of the Charter reminds us that, in accordance with Article 52(2) of the Charter, free movement rights have to be applied under the

[3] See, generally, S Peers, 'Immigration, Asylum and the European Union Charter of Fundamental Rights' (2001) 3 *European Journal of Migration and Law* 141, 146.

conditions and within the limits of the Treaties.[4] Therefore, through the connection to Article 20(2)(a) of the Treaty on the Functioning of the European Union (TFEU), the fundamental right of EU free movement seems to add very little to the traditional EU free movement rights.[5] As a consequence, EU free movement rights remain linked to the beneficiaries determined by EU law and secondary legislation who, according to established case law, are the nationals of the Member States.[6]

However, it has to be noted that the wording of Article 45 of the Charter is unclear as to whether it covers the fundamental right to free movement *within* a State. Advocate General Cruz Villalón expressed the view, in a case related to the limitations imposed on the freedom to choose a residence within a Member State to beneficiaries of subsidiary protection, that the right to free movement within a State could be considered 'in accordance with Article 6(3) TEU, a general principle of EU law resulting both from the constitutional traditions of the Member States and from Article 2 of Protocol No 4 to the ECHR'.[7] Determining the beneficiaries of that right could then arguably follow criteria different from those of Article 45 of the Charter, in light of the prohibition of discrimination.[8]

In the same vein, Article 15(2) of the Charter contains the freedom to seek employment, to work, to provide services and to exercise the right of establishment in any Member State. Only EU citizens benefit from these rights according to the wording of that provision, which is conceived as a reinstatement of EU free movement rights.[9]

With regard to political rights, there are different mentions of nationality in the Charter. Article 12(2) of the Charter, mirroring Article 10(4) TFEU, provides that 'political parties at Union level contribute to expressing the political will of the citizens of the Union'. Articles 39 and 40 of the Charter enunciate, respectively, the right to vote and stand as a candidate at election to the European Parliament and at the municipal elections of the Member State of residence only with regard to EU citizens. The right to the diplomatic and consular protection of Article 46 is also exclusively proclaimed with regard to citizens of the Union.

[4] See, eg, Case C-162/09 *Lassal*, EU:C:2010:592, para 29; Case C-434/09 *McCarthy*, EU:C:2011:277, para 27; Case C-543/12 *Zeman*, EU:C:2014:2143, para 39.

[5] See, for further discussion, chapter 11 by N Nic Shuibhne in this volume.

[6] Case 238/83 *Meade*, EU:C:1984:250, para 7; Case C-230/97 *Awoyemi* EU:C:1998:521, para 29; Case C-147/91 *Ferrer Laderer*, EU:C:1992:278, para 9. For the early debate see I Lirola Delgado, *El ámbito de aplicación subjetivo del principio de libre circulación de personas en el proceso de integración europea* (Santiago de Compostela, Universidad de Santiago de Compostela, 1992).

[7] Opinion of Advocate General Cruz Villalón in Joined Cases C-443/14 and C-444/14 *Kreis Warendorf and Osso* EU:C:2015:665, para 46. The Court has referred to Art 2 of Protocol 4 of the European Convention on Human Rights (ECHR) in its judgment in Case 36/75 *Rutili*, EU:C:1975:137, para 49, declaring that 'in the case of partial prohibitions on residence, limited to certain areas of the territory, persons covered by Community law must, under Article 7 of the Treaty and within the field of application of that provision, be treated on a footing of equality with the nationals of the Member State concerned'. See also Case C-100/01 *Oteiza Olazabal*, EU:C:2002:712.

[8] Advocate General Cruz Villalón in *Kreis Warendorf and Osso* (n 7) para 71ff.

[9] See, eg, Case C-284/15 *ONEm and M*, EU:C:2016:220, para 54; and Case C-233/12 *Gardella*, EU:C:2013:449, para 39.

However, even if the Charter relies on nationality in the framework of citizenship rights, it also decouples the rights of citizenship from the citizenship of the Union (understood as intrinsically dependent upon Member States' nationality). Indeed, the majority of the rights brought together under the heading of 'citizenship rights' of the Charter do not establish any distinction regarding their beneficiaries with regard to nationality, as some of them rely on residence. Third-country nationals see themselves recognised, to a limited extent, a certain role as 'citizens' of the supranational polis.

Moreover, the non-exclusionary character of Charter rights is shown by the fact that the rights that are restricted to EU citizens can be 'extended' to third country nationals.[10] Article 45(2) of the Charter provides that free movement may be granted to legally residing third-country nationals. This reflects the existing EU competence contained in Article 79(2)(c) TFEU, to define 'the rights of third-country nationals residing legally in a Member State, including the conditions governing freedom of movement and of residence in other Member States'.[11] Similarly, the Treaty provisions on freedom to provide services also foresee the possibility to extend that freedom to nationals of third countries established in the Union.[12] This therefore portrays free movement rights as fundamental rights whose personal scope of application depends on legislative choice,[13] which is somehow at odds with its nature as a fundamental right.

Additionally, in the field of political rights, the non-exclusionary character of EU fundamental citizenship rights has also been shown by case law. The Court of Justice has ruled that Member States may extend to third-country nationals the right to vote and stand as a candidate in European Parliament elections (as of course, they can do with regard to municipal elections):

> [W]hile citizenship of the Union is destined to be the fundamental status of nationals of the Member States, enabling those who find themselves in the same situation to receive the same treatment in law irrespective of their nationality, subject to such exceptions as are expressly provided for ... that statement does not necessarily mean that the rights recognised by the Treaty are limited to citizens of the Union.[14]

[10] Iglesias Sánchez, 'Fundamental Rights Protection for Third Country Nationals and Citizens of the Union' (n 2) 140.

[11] It shall however not be forgotten that some key rights linked to free movement had already been extended to third-country nationals that are family members of EU citizens. The validity of the inclusion of stateless persons or refugees residing in the territory of the Member States in the scope of Council Regulation (EEC) No 1408/71 of 14 June 1971 on the application of social security schemes to employed persons, to self-employed persons and to members of their families moving within the Community, as amended and updated by Council Regulation (EEC) No 2001/83 of 2 June 1983 [1983] OJ L230/6, was confirmed by the Court. See Case C-95/99 to C-98/99 and C-180/99 *Khalil and others*, EU:C:2001:532.

[12] Art 56 TFEU.

[13] The Explanation on this Article states that 'Paragraph 2 refers to the power granted to the Union by Articles 77, 78 and 79 of the Treaty on the Functioning of the European Union'. Consequently, the granting of this right depends on the institutions exercising that power.

[14] Case C-145/04 *Spain/United Kingdom*, EU:C:2006:543. On the extension of EU political rights to third-country nationals, A Schrauwen, 'Granting the Right to Vote for the European Parliament to Resident Third-Country Nationals: Civic Citizenship Revisited' (2013) 19 *ELJ* 201.

B. Residence-Based Entitlements

Some of the rights enumerated under the heading of 'citizens' rights' define their beneficiaries with regard to residence and not nationality. This is the case of the right of access to documents (Article 42); the right to refer to the European Ombudsman (Article 43); and the right to petition the European Parliament (Article 44), which are recognised for EU citizens and to natural or legal persons residing or having their registered office in a Member State. The precise understanding of 'residence' for the purposes of those rights has, however, still not been clarified by case law. Whether residence relates to a broader notion of stay/physical presence (including, therefore, irregularly staying third-country nationals, temporary visitors on short-term visas or asylum seekers) or whether it is linked with a specific status of legal residence remains uncertain, even though, lacking any other indications, a broad scope should arguably be presumed. Institutional practice by the European Parliament and by the European Ombudsman has extended in certain cases the right to petition and the right to refer to non-citizens and non-residents.[15]

C. Status-Based Entitlements

Besides nationality and residence as criteria for differentiation, other elements may play a role in modulating or limiting entitlement to EU fundamental rights protection, such as legal status or authorisation to work. Article 34(2) of the Charter restricts entitlement to social security benefits and social advantages to 'everyone residing and moving legally within the European Union'. This theoretically excludes not only irregular third-country nationals, but potentially EU citizens who do not reside or move 'legally'. However, having in mind the content and nature of residence rights for citizens and foreigners, the limitation is liable to have a considerably greater impact on third-country nationals. An entitlement defined on the basis of authorisation to work is to be found in Article 15(3) of the Charter, according to which only 'nationals of third countries who are authorised to work' are entitled to working conditions equivalent to those of EU citizens. Be that as it may, both limitations rely on concepts whose material content is far from being unequivocal—'legal residence' and 'authorisation to work'. It remains unclear whether those concepts are to be interpreted by reference to secondary law or whether implementing national acts may further the content of those restrictions.

[15] See below section IV.A and n 66.

D. Nationality and the Material Content of Fundamental Rights

Even if no differentiation regarding nationality or status is made in certain rights, nationality may still play a role in determining their material content. First, nationality has a specific treatment as a suspect ground for the fundamental right to non-discrimination. Second, there are some fundamental rights that relate to migration/asylum-related contexts, where nationality plays an important part.

Of particular relevance are the principle of equality and the prohibition of discrimination. Discrimination on the basis of nationality receives specific treatment in Article 21(2) of the Charter. The Explanations of this provision state that this right corresponds with the prohibition of discrimination on grounds of nationality in Article 18 of the TFEU. According to settled case law, the prohibition of discrimination on grounds of nationality, as enunciated by that provision, is restricted to nationals of the Member States.[16] The inclusion of a common migration and asylum policy has led to a doctrinal debate on the need to extend the scope of the prohibition of discrimination on grounds of nationality. Some authors now propose that this prohibition should be extended to third-country nationals covered by EU rules, since they are now 'within the scope of the Treaties'.[17] The scope of the equality principle of Article 20 and of the general non-discrimination prohibition of Article 21 of the Charter, with regard to the consideration of nationality as a suspect ground, remains unclear.[18] The Court has resorted, without mention of the Charter, to enunciating a general principle of equal treatment in a case concerning the differentiation of treatment between third-country nationals who are long-term residents and EU citizens.[19] Beyond this debate, some of the prohibited grounds of discrimination explicitly enumerated in Article 21(1) of the Charter may prove relevant for asylum and migration cases: race, colour, ethnic origin,

[16] See Cases C-22/08 and C-23/08 *Vatsouras and Koupatantze*, EU:C:2009:344, para 52. See also, Case C-45/93 *Commission/Spain*, EU:C:1994:101, para 10; *Khalil and others* (n 11) para 40; and Case C-45/12 *Hadj Ahmed*, EU:C:2013:390, paras 39–41. With regard to companies, see Case C-291/09 *Francesco Guarnieri & Cie* EU:C:2011:217, para 20.

[17] On this debate, C Hublet, 'The Scope of Article 12 of the Treaty of the European Communities vis-à-vis Third-Country Nationals: Evolution at last' (2009) 12 *ELJ* 575. See, more recently, E Brouwer and K de Vries, 'Third-Country Nationals and Discrimination on the Ground of Nationality: Article 18 TFEU in the Context of Article 15 ECHR and EU Migration Law: Time for a New Approach' in M van den Brink, S Burri and J Goldschmidt (eds), *Equality and Human Rights: Nothing but Trouble? Liber amicorum Titia Loenen* (Utrecht, SIM, 2015).

[18] See, in particular, Opinion of AG Bot in Case C-311/13 *Tümer*, EU:C:2014:2337, point 70ff where he considered that 'making the right to the guaranteed settlement of pay claims conditional, in the case of an employee who is a third-country national, upon legal residence is not, to my way of thinking, consistent with the principle of equal treatment and non-discrimination' of Articles 21 and 20 of the Charter. The judgment of the Court in that case did not rule on the issue of non-discrimination. For this debate see, more recently, Brouwer and de Vries (n 17).

[19] Case C-579/13 *P and S*, EU:C:2015:369. See, in this connection, chapter 13 by K de Vries in this volume.

language, religion or belief, membership of a national minority or birth.[20] The practical relevance of this provision is reinforced by the fact that secondary law developing the principle of non-discrimination exists.[21]

Furthermore, some Charter provisions evoke situations or realities particularly linked to migration and asylum contexts. Even if not specifically addressed to third-country nationals, Article 5(3) of the Charter, which prohibits trafficking in human beings, covers cases of trafficking through illegal migration networks.[22] Article 19 of the Charter prohibits collective expulsions and codifies the non-refoulement principle. Those rights inevitably have a greater impact in asylum/migration-related contexts, although it has been made clear that non-refoulement also plays an important role with regard to EU citizens, ie, in extradition-related situations.[23] In the same vein, Article 18 of the Charter establishes that the right to asylum shall be guaranteed with due respect for the Geneva Convention. That right does not contain any distinction on the basis of nationality, albeit that this issue constitutes a crucial element in the debate concerning the application of the safe country rule,[24] applied with particular rigour with regard to EU citizens.[25]

Other important consequences attached to migration-related contexts are to be found within the permitted grounds for deprivation of liberty. Even if Article 6 of the Charter has a very brief wording (everyone has the right to liberty and security of person), the Explanations to the Charter 'import' the content of Article 5 ECHR. Article 5(1)(f) ECHR allows deprivation of liberty in accordance with a procedure prescribed by law for 'the lawful arrest or detention of a person to prevent his effecting an unauthorized entry into the country or of a person against whom action is being taken with a view to deportation or extradition'.

[20] The Court has recently declared that a criterion of differentiation (used by a credit institution, requiring persons applying for a loan to provide additional proof of identity in the form of a copy of a passport or residence permit) based on the person's country of birth, is not generally more likely to affect persons of a 'given ethnicity' than 'other persons', so it does not give rise to indirect discrimination based on ethnic origin. Case C-668/15 *Jyske Finans*, EU:C:2017:278, paras 33–35.

[21] Council Directive 2000/43/EC of 29 June 2000 implementing the principle of equal treatment between persons irrespective of racial or ethnic origin [2000] OJ L180/22. Council Directive 2000/78/EC of 27 November 2000 establishing a general framework for equal treatment in employment and occupation [2000] OJ L303/16.

[22] According to the Explanations to the Charter, 'Paragraph 3 stems directly from human dignity and takes account of recent developments in organised crime, such as the organisation of lucrative illegal immigration or sexual exploitation networks'. They also refer to Art 27(1) of the Convention implementing the Schengen Agreement, which refers to illegal immigration networks: 'The Contracting Parties undertake to impose appropriate penalties on any person who, for financial gain, assists or tries to assist an alien to enter or reside within the territory of one of the Contracting Parties in breach of that Contracting Party's laws on the entry and residence of aliens'.

[23] See Case C-182/15 *Petruhhin*, EU:C:2016:630.

[24] With regard to nationality distinctions on the basis of the safe third-country principle, see Case C-175/11 *D and A*, EU:C:2013:45, paras 71ff.

[25] It ought to be noted that Protocol (No 24) on asylum for nationals of Member States of the European Union restricts the possibility for nationals of the Member States to very specific circumstances on the basis that Member States shall be regarded as constituting safe countries of origin in respect of each other.

That provision has proven to be a central element in the interpretation of migration and asylum legislation, which contain detention-related stipulations.[26]

Finally, purely in terms of 'impact', it shall be added that other provisions of the Charter have a potential to be of particular importance for non-nationals, as they are liable to open avenues for migration and residence rights.[27]

III. THE SCOPE OF EU LAW AND THE NATIONALITY DIVIDE

The previous account of entitlement to fundamental rights on the basis of nationality, residence or status is, however, a misleading indicator of the potential impact of EU fundamental rights on the legal situation of third-country nationals and EU citizens. The scope of application of EU fundamental rights is defined, primarily, on the basis of a *connection* with EU law. The determination of what that connection should be is one of the most challenging exercises in the interpretation of EU law. The complexity of the EU system of allocation of competences and the close intertwinement of EU law and national law defies any doctrinal attempt at systematising the scope of EU fundamental rights in a definitive matter.[28] What is clear, in any case, is that being a national of a Member State is not enough to trigger that connection. Nationality, however, does play an important part as it may define not only the scope of the fundamental right at issue, but also the scope of the rule of EU law triggering the applicability of EU fundamental rights.

According to Article 51(1) of the Charter, its provisions are, first, addressed 'to the institutions, bodies, offices and agencies of the Union with due regard for the principle of subsidiarity' and, second, 'to the Member States only when they are

[26] In particular, point (e) of the first subparagraph of Art 8(3) of Directive 2013/33/EU of the European Parliament and of the Council of 26 June 2013 laying down standards for the reception of applicants for international protection [2013] OJ L180/96. See, as to the validity of this provision, Case C-601/15 PPU *N*, EU:C:2016:84. With regard to Art 28 of Regulation (EU) No 604/2013 of the European Parliament and of the Council of 26 June 2013 establishing the criteria and mechanisms for determining the Member State responsible for examining an application for international protection lodged in one of the Member States by a third-country national or a stateless person [2013] OJ L180/31, see Case C-528/15 *Al Chodor* EU:C:2017:213. See also Directive 2008/115/EC of the European Parliament and of the Council of 16 December 2008 on common standards and procedures in Member States for returning illegally staying third-country nationals [2008] OJ L348/98.

[27] Such as Art 7, on the right to family life, see K Hailbronner and D Thym 'Constitutional Framework and Principles for Interpretation' in K Hailbronner and D Thym (eds), *EU Immigration and Asylum Law, A Commentary*, 2nd edn (Munich/Oxford/Baden-Baden, CH Beck/Hart/Nomos, 2016) 25.

[28] Just to name a few studies, see: X Groussot, L Pech and GT Petursson, 'The Scope of Application of EU Fundamental Rights on Member States' Action: In Search of Certainty in EU Adjudication' 1/2011 *Eric Stein Working Paper*; M Safjan, 'Areas of Application of the Charter of Fundamental Rights of the European Union: Fields of Conflict?' 2012/22 *EUI WP Law*; D Sarmiento, 'Who's Afraid of the Charter? The Court of Justice, National Courts and the New Framework of Fundamental Rights Protection in Europe' (2013) 50 *CML Rev* 1267; A Ward, 'Article 51—Field of Application' in S Peers, T Hervey, J Kenner and A Ward (eds), *The EU Charter of Fundamental Rights: A Commentary* (Oxford, Hart Publishing, 2014) 1456.

implementing Union law'. The case law of the Court of Justice of the European Union (CJEU) has interpreted the meaning of this provision when applied to both the institutions and to the Member States. With regard to the institutions, the Court has recently declared that the Charter 'is addressed to the EU institutions, including … when they act outside the EU legal framework'.[29] With regard to the applicability of the Charter to the Member States, the landmark judgment is *Åkerberg Fransson*.[30] The Court confirmed its previous case law, declaring that EU fundamental rights 'are applicable in all situations governed by European Union law'. Since the Charter must be complied with 'where national legislation falls within the scope of European Union law, situations cannot exist which are covered in that way by European Union law without those fundamental rights being applicable'. As a consequence, 'the applicability of European Union law entails applicability of the fundamental rights guaranteed by the Charter'.[31]

Having in mind this system of determination of the scope of application of the Charter, its practical effects on a given case will depend on whether there is an EU rule relevant to the situation at hand. Therefore, even if the scope of EU fundamental rights cannot be equated to the scope of EU competences,[32] the existing Treaty competences and their development through secondary legislation applicable in a given case entail a higher likelihood of applicability of EU fundamental rights.

In this connection, the different Treaty layout of EU competences on EU citizens and third-country nationals becomes relevant. EU citizenship law and EU immigration and asylum law follow different rationales. The development of those EU competences entails the progressive determination of the scope of EU law. As a consequence, the way in which those competences are developed through secondary law makes apparent the divide through the different legal mechanisms and dynamics, which projects, in turn, on the scope of application of EU fundamental rights. A first task is, therefore, analysing the scope of the competences of the Union, and how broadly they have been exercised with regard to these groups of subjects. An examination from this point of view indicates that two fields of differentiation can be identified: those areas of EU action where no difference is made between EU citizens and third-country nationals; and those which establish that differentiation. EU law related to the status of EU citizenship and EU immigration and asylum law are good examples of this latter category.

[29] Cases C-8/15 P to C-10/15 P *Ledra Advertising/Commission and ECB*, EU:C:2016:701, para 67.

[30] Case C-617/10 *Åkerberg Fransson*, EU:C:2013:105.

[31] ibid paras 19 and 21. See also, Case C-206/13 *Siragusa*, EU:C:2014:126; Case C-265/13 *Torralbo Marcos*, EU:C:2014:187; Case C-198/13 *Julian Hernández and others*, EU:C:2014:2055; or Case C-40/11 *Iida*, EU:C:2012:691.

[32] The case law shows this difficulty, see eg, Case C-23/12 *Zakaria*, EU:C:2013:24; or Case C-638/16 PPU *X and X*, EU:C:2017:173.

A. EU Law Applied Regardless of Nationality

EU law applies, to a great extent, regardless of nationality. The first studies on the status of third-country nationals under EU law brought to the fore the inclusive character of EU law, indicating that, outside the specific realm of free movement of persons, third-country nationals could generally avail themselves of EU law.[33] That is particularly the case, as those authors put forward, of consumer law, workers' protection-related measures, as well as data protection rules or environmental law.[34] That is also the case, for example, of transport policy. The Court declared in *Awoyemi*,[35] that the Driving Licences Directive[36] applied not only to nationals of the Member States 'but also to holders of a driving licence issued by a Member State, irrespective of nationality'. In the same vein, EU law applies, in principle, regardless of nationality, in the field of judicial cooperation in civil[37] and criminal matters,[38] which are particularly relevant in terms of their potential impact on fundamental rights. Even though free movement of persons is tied to nationality, the other fundamental freedoms—goods and capital—remain inclusive.[39]

[33] See, particularly, K Groenendijk, E Guild and R Barzilay, *Legal Status of Third Country Nationals who are Long-Term Residents in a Member State of the European Union* (Nijmegen, European Community, 2000). See also E Guild and S Peers, 'Out of the Ghetto? The Personal Scope of EU Law' in S Peers and N Rogers (eds), *EU Immigration and Asylum Law: Text and Commentary*, 1st edn (Leiden, Martinus Nijhoff, 2006) 95.

[34] With regard to Directive 95/46/EC of the European Parliament and of the Council of 24 October 1995 on the protection of individuals with regard to the processing of personal data and on the free movement of such data [1995] OJ L281/31 see Cases C-141/12 and C-372/12 *YS and others*, EU:C:2014:2081.

[35] *Awoyemi* (n 6), paras 20ff.

[36] Council Regulation (EEC) No 2913/92 of 12 October 1992 establishing the Community Customs Code [1992] OJ L302/1, thereafter replaced by Regulation (EC) No 450/2008 of the European Parliament and of the Council of 23 April 2008 laying down the Community Customs Code [2008] OJ L145/1.

[37] See however, Council Directive 2002/8/EC of 27 January 2003 to improve access to justice in cross-border disputes by establishing minimum common rules relating to legal aid for such disputes [2003] OJ L26/41. Its Art 4, entitled 'Non-discrimination', provides that 'Member States shall grant legal aid without discrimination to Union citizens and third-country nationals *residing lawfully* in a Member State' (emphasis added).

[38] eg the European arrest warrant is applied to third-country nationals, even though not so many cases so far have arrived at the CJEU. (See, eg, Case C-453/16 PPU *Özçelik*, EU:C:2016:860.)

[39] See, eg, with regard to free movement of capital, Art 63(1) gives effect to the liberalisation of capital between the Member States and between Member and non-Member States, see: C-163/94, C-165/94 and C-250/9 *Sanz de Lera and Others*, EU:C:1995:451; and C-101/05 *A*, EU:C:2007:804. See also C-484/93 *Svensson and Gustavsson*, EU:C:1995:379. Interestingly, in this last case, Advocate General Elmer (EU:C:1995:140) examined the issue from the perspective of free movement of services and the rights of recipients of services, concluding that those rights could not be claimed by third-country nationals. Art 56 TFEU provides that the provisions on free movement of services may be extended to third-country nationals who are established within the Union. Directive 2006/123/EC of the European Parliament and of the Council of 12 December 2006 on services in the internal market [2006] OJ L376/36 provides in its 36 recital with regard to the concept of 'service recipient' that it 'should also cover third country nationals who already benefit from rights conferred upon them by Community acts such as Regulation (EEC) No 1408/71, Council Directive 2003/109/EC of

To cite just one relevant example in the field of consumer protection, the *Aziz* case is noteworthy. This case was about the interpretation of the powers of national judges in the realm of the Directive on unfair terms in consumer contracts,[40] a domain in which the relevance of fundamental rights has been made even more apparent in recent case law.[41] The *Aziz* case, which concerned the inclusion of unfair terms in a mortgage contract concluded by a Moroccan national who had been working in Spain, has given rise to a subsequent stream of case law leading to very significant legislative modifications in the law governing the enforcement of mortgage proceedings (with the subsequent eviction) in the Member State affected.[42]

Protection of workers' rights is another field in which the inclusive nature of EU law is of particular relevance in terms of individual rights. The entitlement of third-country nationals to the protection of the Directive on insolvency of the employer[43] was explicitly addressed in the *Tümer* case.[44] The significance of this case is even greater because it concerned a third-country national who was unlawfully residing in a Member State. The Court of Justice first confirmed the broad scope of the Treaty competence to adopt minimum requirements to improve living and working conditions as including third-country nationals.[45] It further declared, after noting that illegal third-country nationals were not excluded from the scope of the Directive, that Member States were not entirely free to define the concept of 'employee' for the purposes of the Directive, and that they could not disregard its social objectives.[46]

B. Where Nationality Matters

The nationality divide occupies centre stage in the field of EU Law concerning free movement of persons, borders, migration and asylum. Despite an ever-growing

25 November 2003 concerning the status of third-country nationals who are long-term residents, Council Regulation (EC) No 859/2003 of 14 May 2003 extending the provisions of Regulation (EEC) No 1408/71 and Regulation (EEC) No 574/72 to nationals of third countries who are not already covered by those provisions solely on the ground of their nationality and Directive 2004/38/EC of the European Parliament and of the Council of 29 April 2004 on the right of citizens of the Union and their family members to move and reside freely within the territory of the Member States. Furthermore, Member States may extend the concept of recipient to other third country nationals that are present within their territory'.

[40] Council Directive 93/13/EEC of 5 April 1993 on unfair terms in consumer contracts [1993] OJ L95/29.

[41] See, eg, Case C-34/13 *Kušionová*, EU:C:2014:2189; and Case C-169/14 *Sánchez Morcillo and Abril García*, EU:C:2014:2099.

[42] Case C-415/11 *Aziz*, EU:C:2013:164.

[43] Council Directive 80/987/EEC of 20 October 1980 relating to the protection of employees in the event of the insolvency of their employer [1980] OJ L283/ 23, as amended by Directive 2002/74/EC of the European Parliament and of the Council of 23 September 2002 [2002] OJ L270/10.

[44] *Tümer* (n 18).

[45] ibid para 32.

[46] ibid paras 42ff.

impact of derivative rights, mostly for third-country nationals who are family members of Union citizens,[47] the rights concerning free movement of persons—both as economic and citizenship rights—are based on the nationality of a Member State.[48] As indicated above, the prohibition in the Treaty of discrimination on grounds of nationality has been interpreted so far as only applying to those having the nationality of a Member State.

The role of free movement and citizenship as a trigger for the protection of EU fundamental rights is difficult to delimit. This issue is examined in more depth by the contribution of Niamh Nic Shuibnhe (chapter eleven in this volume). Here it suffices to say that the exercise of free movement rights does not invariably trigger EU fundamental rights protection. Notwithstanding other potential connections to EU law there needs to be an obstacle or limitation to the exercise of Treaty rights in order to trigger the protection of EU fundamental rights on the basis of free movement. Mere speculation on the potential impact of a measure or situation on free movement do not suffice. For example, the allegation that the execution of a penalty of imprisonment would be a restriction of EU free movement rights was readily rejected by the Court as a sufficient connection with EU law to trigger the protection of EU fundamental rights.[49] Internal controls on citizens which are not connected with border controls or where the person did not show an intention to cross the internal border are not within the scope of the Charter.[50] What is more, not every national rule affecting access to benefits of EU citizens residing in another Member State fall within the scope of EU fundamental rights.[51]

The effective protection of EU citizenship rights has given rise to an innovative line of case law on the basis of Article 20 TFEU, which in very exceptional situations triggers the protection of that provision—and consequently, of EU

[47] 'Derivative rights' also include the rights derived from the provision of services of companies employing workers who are third-country nationals. (See, eg, C-113/89 *Rush Portuguesa*, EU:C:1990:142 and Case C-43/93 *Vander Elst* EU:C:1994:310), including third-country nationals who act as intermediaries in the provision of services of companies established in a Member States. (See Case C-336/14 *Ince*, EU:C:2016:72, paras 41–44.)

[48] See, on the initial debate on the personal scope of free movement of persons: T Hartley, 'The International Scope of the Community Provisions Concerning the Free Movement of Workers' in FG Jacobs (ed), *European Law and the Individual* (Amsterdam, North-Holland Publishing, 1976) 24; R Plender, 'Competence, European Community Law and Nationals of Non-Member States' (1990) 39 *ICLQ* 599, 605; M-P Lanfranchi, *Droit communautaire et Travailleurs migrants des Etats tiers: Entrée et Circulation dans la Communauté Européenne* (Paris, Economica, 1994); A Evans, 'Third Country Nationals and the Treaty on European Union' (1994) 5 *European Journal of International Law* 199, 207; C Tomuschat, 'The Legal Status of Non-Citizens of the EU: General Introduction' (1995) *European Review of Public Law* 544, 549.

[49] See Case C-299/95 *Kremzov*, EU:C:1997:254, where the Court declared, citing Case 180/83 *Moser*, EU:C:1984:233, para 18, that 'Whilst any deprivation of liberty may impede the person concerned from exercising his right to free movement, the Court has held that a purely hypothetical prospect of exercising that right does not establish a sufficient connection with Community law to justify the application of Community provisions' (see in particular to this effect, para 16).

[50] Order in Case C-14/13 *Cholakova*, EU:C:2013:374.

[51] See Case C-333/13 *Dano*, EU:C:2014:2358, para 87ff, concerning the application of the equal treatment principle with regard to economically inactive citizens and their access to special non-contributory cash benefits. See on that case, D Thym, 'When Union Citizens Turn into Illegal Migrants: The *Dano* Case' (2015) 40 *EL Rev* 249, 259–60.

fundamental rights.[52] The debate on the role of EU fundamental rights as a potential component of the substance of EU citizenship rights has been very broad in the literature.[53] However, the Court has confirmed that Article 20-based protection is only triggered in situations of 'deprivation' of the genuine enjoyment of the substance of the rights conferred by virtue of their status as Union citizens. The bar is higher, since, to date, 'mere affection'—not merely limitations or obstacles—is considered sufficient.[54]

With regard to EU law on migration and asylum, its scope of application is linked with the notion of 'third-country nationals', ie, absence of EU citizenship. The connection with EU law is ascertained in this field not on the basis of intra-EU free movement, but on the fact of falling within the scope of the pertinent instrument of EU secondary law. This usually will happen through the status of the third-country national as either an 'applicant' or a 'holder'. Regarding the former category, being an applicant for a visa or permit is a sufficient connection, allowing the applicability of procedures governed by EU law—which bring with them important procedural rights.[55] With regard to the latter category, third-country nationals who are holders of residence rights guaranteed through EU migration law harmonised rules are entitled to a specific status, generally based on a limited equal treatment clause.[56] Contrary to free movement and EU citizenship-based rights, however, permits it would seem hold a 'constitutive' nature, notwithstanding fulfilment of the material conditions of a given status.[57]

The strict dividing line between EU citizenship and EU migration law is shown by the fact that some of secondary law instruments of the common EU migration policy even exclude from their scope of application third-country nationals who are family members of Union citizens,[58] or family members of Union

[52] See, eg, Case C-34/09 *Ruiz Zambrano*, EU:C:2011:124; Case C-165/14 *Rendón Marín*, EU:C:2016:675; and Case C-304/14 *CS*, EU:C:2016:674.

[53] See, eg, A von Bogdandy et al, 'Reverse *Solange*—Protecting the Essence of Fundamental Rights Against EU Member States' (2012) 49 *CML Rev* 489; D Kochenov, 'The Right to Have What Rights? EU Citizenship in Need of Clarification' (2013) 19 *ELJ* 502; S Iglesias Sánchez, 'Fundamental Rights and Citizenship of the Union at a Crossroads: A Promising Alliance or a Dangerous Liaison?' (2014) 20 *ELJ* 464; D Düsterhaus, 'EU Citizenship and Fundamental Rights: Contradictory, Converging or Complementary?' in D Kochenov (ed), *EU Citizenship and Federalism: The Role of Rights* (Cambridge, Cambridge University Press, 2017); MJ van den Brink, 'EU Citizenship and EU Fundamental Rights: Taking EU Citizenship Rights Seriously?' (2012) 39 *Legal Issues of Economic Integration* 273.

[54] K Lenaerts and JA Gutiérrez Fons, 'Ruiz-Zambrano (C-34/09) o de la emancipación de la Ciudadanía de la Unión de los límites inherentes a la libre circulación' (2011) 40 *Revista española de derecho europeo* 493.

[55] See, for a general overview, F Ippolito, 'Migration and Asylum Cases before the Court of Justice of the European Union: Putting the EU Charter of Fundamental Rights to Test?' (2015) 1 *European Journal of Migration and Law* 1.

[56] See S Morano-Foadi and K de Vries, 'The Equality Clauses in the EU Directives on Non-discrimination and Migration/Asylum' in S Morano-Foadi and M Malena (eds), *Integration for Third Country Nationals: The Equality Challenge* (Cheltenham, Edward Elgar Publishing, 2012).

[57] See *Iida* (n 31) paras 45–48.

[58] Council Directive 2003/86/EC of 22 September 2003 on the right to family reunification [2003] OJ L251/12.

citizens who have exercised their free movement rights.[59] This is the case for the Family Reunification Directive. This exclusion relies on the fact that the status of family members is covered by Directive 2004/38. The fact that EU migration law may cover, in some cases, family members of EU citizens has proven to be highly relevant. Indeed, in cases where the situation was not found to be covered by free movement rights enshrined in the Treaty or in the Citizenship Directive, the fact that the Long-term Residents Directive does not exclude family members of EU citizens was hinted at by the Court as a possible legal solution for Mr Iida.[60]

IV. THE SCOPE OF EU FUNDAMENTAL RIGHTS FOR CITIZENS AND FOREIGNERS

The scope of application of the Charter regarding the protection of fundamental rights of EU citizens and foreigners is a function of the two previously discussed issues: the entitlement to fundamental rights as determined by the specific Articles of the Charter; and the extent to which a specific situation falls within the scope of EU law in the sense of its Article 51(1). This section is not aimed at providing a general analysis of the immensely rich and vast constellation of fundamental rights implications for citizens and foreigners. Rather, it aims at offering the results of an exercise of joint consideration of the two aspects discussed in the two sections above. The ensuing analysis offers the overall structural picture of the impact of EU Charter rights with regard to both EU citizens and foreigners. As a result, the scenario of applicability of EU fundamental rights is fraught with peculiarities, which show the unique way in which EU law is redefining the common understanding of the status of individuals who fall, under certain circumstances, within its scope. The following lines aim just at uncovering some of these particularities, which lead to uncertainty and interpretative challenges inasmuch as they challenge preconceived ideas of the correlation between the status of citizens and aliens when taking state citizenship and the state-construed status of foreigners as a point of reference.

[59] That is the case in Council Directive 2009/50/EC of 25 May 2009 on the conditions of entry and residence of third-country nationals for the purposes of highly qualified employment [2009] OJ L155/17; of Directive 2011/98/EU of the European Parliament and of the Council of 13 December 2011 on a single application procedure for a single permit for third-country nationals to reside and work in the territory of a Member State and on a common set of rights for third-country workers legally residing in a Member State [2011] OJ L343/1; of Directive 2014/36/EU of the European Parliament and of the Council of 26 February 2014 on the conditions of entry and stay of third-country nationals for the purpose of employment as seasonal workers [2014] OJ L94/375); and of Directive 2016/801 of the European Parliament and of the Council of 11 May 2016 on the conditions of entry and residence of third-country nationals for the purposes of research, studies, training, voluntary service, pupil exchange schemes or educational projects and au pairing [2016] OJ L132/21.

[60] See *Iida* (n 31).

A. EU Fundamental Citizenship Rights Entitlements Based on Nationality, Residence or Status

One would expect that where EU fundamental rights entitlements are determined by reference to citizenship/nationality to the exclusion of third-country nationals, the protection of the latter rights would fall outside the scope of EU law. This assumption is somewhat buttressed by the fact that 'exclusive-citizenship' rights of the Charter correspond with secondary law and Treaty provisions in which the exclusion of third-country nationals is already entrenched. Where potential extensions of 'exclusive-citizenship' rights are contemplated by primary law—both the Treaty and the Charter, as is the case with free movement of persons—the actual enactment of secondary law developing these possibilities would constitute the necessary avenue to bring the situation of third-country nationals within the scope of EU law. There are, however, some situations where the equation of entitlement of a right and the scope of EU law still present some uncertainties.

First, in the event that Member States unilaterally proceed to extend EU fundamental rights beyond the 'entitlements' predetermined by the Charter, are they acting outside the scope of EU law? This question is indeed not as theoretical as it might appear. What if a Member State proceeds to extend voting rights to the European Parliament to third-country nationals? Would the basic safeguards of the Charter then apply (eg, imagine a Member State extending that right to third-country nationals, but then limiting it on the basis of sex, sexual orientation or ethnicity)?[61]

Second, the limitations of the scope of Charter rights based on status—legal residence or authorisation to work—may give rise to interpretative difficulties. Primarily these are difficulties regarding the interaction of those rights with other provisions of the Charter, interpreted in accordance with the corresponding rights of the European Convention on Human Rights (ECHR or the Convention). It could be argued that Articles 34(2) and 15(2) of the Charter do not correspond with rights of the ECHR, hence there is no link with the Convention in terms of interpretative coherence, in the sense of Article 52(3) of the Charter.[62] However, social security/assistance benefits as well as certain working conditions such as wages or pension rights could well be understood as covered under the right to property declared in Article 1 of the First Protocol to the ECHR, which corresponds to Article 17 of the Charter.[63] The prohibition of discrimination of

[61] In Case C-650/13 *Delvigne*, EU:C:2015:648, paras 25–33, the Court declared that the determination of the beneficiaries of the right to vote falls within the competence of each Member State in 'compliance with EU law'. Member States, when organising the elections to the European Parliament, in implementing its obligation under Art 14(3) TEU and Art 1(3) of the 1976 Act, are implementing EU law within the meaning of Art 51(1) of the Charter.

[62] The ECHR is neither mentioned in the Explanations to these rights, nor in the Explanation to Art 52 of the Charter.

[63] The ECtHR has also declared some work-related rights comprised within the right to private life under Art 8 ECHR. For an account of that case law, see Factsheet elaborated by the Press Unit of the ECtHR on Work-related rights: www.echr.coe.int/Documents/FS_Work_ENG.pdf (February 2017).

Article 14 ECHR—which corresponds, partially, to Article 21 of the Charter[64]—could then arguably be triggered. In this regard, the European Court of Human Rights (ECtHR) has not only considered nationality as one of the categories under which discrimination is prohibited,[65] but also migration status—even if in a much more nuanced way.[66]

Third, it ought to be noted that, by establishing nationality/residence-based entitlements for specific fundamental rights, the Charter has introduced an additional element to the general rule of applicability of Article 51(1) of the Charter. The question arises as to whether there may be situations in which EU law is applicable or is being implemented, but that are left outside the scope of a given fundamental right because of a restriction based on status or residence. Particularly relevant are the residence-based entitlements concerning the right to petition the European Parliament or reference to the European Ombudsman. This mismatch between entitlement and applicability of EU law has led both the European Parliament and the European Ombudsman to come up with strategies aimed at broadening the practical exercise of those EU fundamental rights.[67]

Moreover, where secondary EU law applies to citizens and foreigners regardless of nationality or status, the limitation of entitlements of Charter rights on the basis of nationality leads to fragmentation in the interpretation of EU secondary law. The exclusion of third-country nationals from free movement rights and from the principle of non-discrimination on the basis of nationality also has an important impact on the spheres where EU law is applicable irrespective of nationality. Indeed, even where EU law expands to third-country nationals, the legal effects of free movement related considerations or those connected with Article 18 TFEU do not expand to them.[68]

[64] The Explanations to the Charter only mention Art 14 ECHR with regard to Art 21.

[65] See, eg, *Gaygusuz v Austria* ECHR Reports of Judgments and Decisions 1996–IV; *Koua Poirrez v France* App no 40892/98 (ECHR, 30 September 2003); *Luczak v Poland* App no 77782/01 (ECHR, 27 November 2007); *Andrejeva v Latvia* App no 55707/00 (ECHR, 18 February 2009); or *Dhabhi v Italy* App no 17120/09 (ECHR, 8 April 2014).

[66] See, in particular, *Ponomaryovi v Bulgaria* App no 5335/05 (ECHR, 21 June 2011); and *Bah v United Kingdom* App no 56328/07 (ECHR, 27 September 2011).

[67] Rule 215(15) of the Rules of Procedure of the European Parliament (January 2017, provisional edition) provides: 'Petitions addressed to Parliament by natural or legal persons who are neither citizens of the European Union nor reside in a Member State nor have their registered office in a Member State shall be registered and filed separately. The President shall send a monthly record of such petitions received during the previous month, indicating their subject-matter, to the committee responsible for petitions, which may ask to see those which it wishes to consider.' This rule was already introduced in 1993, see E Marias, 'The Right to Petition the European Parliament after Maastricht' (1994) 19 *EL Rev* 175. The European Ombudsman uses its own-initiative power to investigate maladministration cases brought by non-citizens or non-residents. See *Annual Report of the European Ombudsman* (2009) 24. This practice has explicitly been the object of the Memorandum of Understanding between the European Ombudsman and the European Investment Bank concerning information on the Bank's policies, standards and procedures and the handling of complaints, including complaints from non-citizens and non-residents of the European Union [2008] OJ C244/1.

[68] eg in *Francesco Guarnieri & Cie* (n 16), a case concerning a Monégasque company, the Court had declared that, as the result of the assimilation operated by Council Regulation (EEC) No 2913/92 of 12 October 1992 establishing the Community Customs Code [1992] OJ L302/1, thereafter replaced by

Probably, the most well-known and commented case in this regard is *Awoyemi*.[69] In that case, even if, as commented above, Mr Awoyemi could rely on the Driving Licences Directive,[70] he could not rely on the principle of proportionality with regard to the sanction imposed on him. The reason for that was that the application of the principle of proportionality of sanctions, in the *Skanavi* case,[71] was linked to free movement: even though the Directive did not regulate sanctions and that aspect was therefore a national competence, Member States had to act in such a way as not to impinge upon free movement and therefore had to apply the principle of proportionality when imposing sanctions. This principled statement could not, however, be applicable in the case of Mr Awoyemi, a third-country national, who could not rely on free movement.

Having in mind the relevant legal effects of the principle of non-discrimination on grounds of nationality and of the prohibition of obstacles to free movement in connection with other material rules in EU law, the exclusion of third-country nationals from these two fundamental rights reintroduces an important difference in the operation of the rules of EU law which are applicable regardless of nationality, described in the previous subsection.

B. Fundamental Rights Applicable Regardless of Nationality

Where the Charter of fundamental rights enunciates a right regardless of nationality/residence or status, can secondary law or implementing national law introduce differentiations based on those criteria? This is an important question, which has so far not received a full and definitive answer, and which is closely interlinked with the challenges regarding the uncertain consideration of nationality or status as prohibited grounds for discrimination under the Charter.

Far from being a purely theoretical hypothesis, status-based distinctions have materialised in several secondary law instruments in areas where EU law traditionally applied regardless of nationality or status. Some examples are the limitations on the application of non-discrimination rights to 'legally resident' consumers,[72]

Regulation (EC) No 450/2008 of the European Parliament and of the Council of 23 April 2008 laying down the Community Customs Code [2008] OJ L145/1, goods originating in Monaco were covered by free movement of goods. However, the Monégasque company could not usefully rely on Art 18 TFEU for the purposes of claiming equal treatment with nationals of a Member State with regard to the provision of security pending judgment.

[69] *Awoyemi* (n 6) para 20f.

[70] First Council Directive 80/1263/EEC of 4 December 1980 on the introduction of a Community driving licence [1980] OJ L375/1 and of Arts 1(2) and 8(1) of Council Directive 91/439/EEC of 29 July 1991 on driving licences [1991] OJ L237/1.

[71] Case C-193/94 *Skanavi and Chryssanthakopoulos*, EU:C:1996:70.

[72] Directive 2014/92/EU of the European Parliament and of the Council of 23 July 2014 on the comparability of fees related to payment accounts, payment account switching and access to payment accounts with basic features [2014] OJ L257/214, introduces some relevant limitations—in its recitals.

or the limitations of the application of the principle of non-discrimination with regard to legal aid to 'lawful residents'.[73] The interesting point, for the purposes of this discussion, is whether those limitations may suffice to place a situation outside the scope of the instrument at issue, and therefore outside the scope of EU law. In this connection, it ought to be recalled that, in the framework of interpretation of secondary law and the limitations imposed by it on particular enactments of the equal treatment principle, the effects of the Charter are not only deployed after a connection with EU law has been triggered. The Charter is an element of interpretation of the scope of EU law acts per se, and as such, it operates also as an element liable to influence the construction of the scope of EU law as determined by secondary law. The paradigmatic example of this is the case of *Kamberaj*,[74] where the Court had recourse to the Charter in order to determine the material scope of the equal treatment principle enshrined in the Long-term Residents Directive.[75] If mere reference to the Charter does not suffice to establish a sufficient connection with EU law, the Charter itself decisively influences how that scope is to be determined through the interpretation of EU acts of secondary law.

Equally challenging may be the consideration of national provisions implementing EU law in the event that they introduce distinctions based on nationality or status. Where those distinctions are not provided for in the EU act itself, a first way to look at this would arguably be to examine whether that limitation is compatible with the instrument of secondary law at issue.[76] The issue of compatibility of such limitations with primary law could give rise to different interpretative options, having in mind that there are several Articles of the Charter which enunciate rights with regard to the conditions set up in EU law and in national laws and practices. The doctrine has identified the potentiality of this reference

According to recital 35: 'Consumers who are legally resident in the Union should not be discriminated against by reason of their nationality or place of residence, or on any other ground referred to in Article 21 of the Charter of Fundamental Rights of the European Union (the "Charter") when applying for, or accessing, a payment account within the Union. Furthermore, access to payment accounts with basic features should be ensured by Member States irrespective of the consumers' financial circumstances, such as their employment status, level of income, credit history or personal bankruptcy.' Interestingly, recital 36 defines 'legally resident in the Union' as both Union citizens and third-country nationals who already benefit from rights conferred upon them by Union acts. It also contemplates that Member States should be able to extend the concept of 'legally resident in the Union' to other third-country nationals that are present on their territory.

[73] Council Directive 2002/8/EC of 27 January 2003 to improve access to justice in cross-border disputes by establishing minimum common rules relating to legal aid for such disputes [2003] OJ L26/41. According to its Art 4, entitled 'Non-discrimination', 'Member States shall grant legal aid without discrimination to Union citizens and third-country nationals residing lawfully in a Member State'.

[74] Case C-571/10 *Kamberaj*, EU:C:2012:233.

[75] ibid, para 92, where the Court declared that 'according to Article 34 of the Charter, the Union recognises and respects the right to social and housing assistance so as to ensure a decent existence for all those who lack sufficient resources. It follows that, in so far as the benefit in question in the main proceedings fulfils the purpose set out in that article of the Charter, it cannot be considered, under European Union law, as not being part of core benefits within the meaning of Article 11(4) of Directive 2003/109'.

[76] See, in particular, *Tümer* (n 18).

to serve as a way of introducing further differences in treatment regarding fundamental rights on the basis of nationality or status.[77] With the general application of the equal treatment principle with regard to distinctions made on the basis of (third-country) nationality and migration status being far from clear, there is still uncertainty as to how to tackle differentiations based on those grounds if established through secondary law and national implementing acts. It could be argued that this question does not seem to be relevant for the purposes of determining the scope of application of EU fundamental rights; rather it could be regarded as an issue connected with the permissible limitations under the criteria of Article 52(1) of the Charter.[78]

C. Generally Applicable EU Fundamental Rights and EU Law Distinguishing on the Basis of Nationality

A third set of issues arise when considering the scope of EU fundamental rights from the perspective of specific nationality divides reflected in Treaty and secondary law on EU citizenship and migration law. The different legal bases and their development through secondary law with regard to EU citizens' rights—mostly, those based on free movement—and those of third-country nationals—under the common migration policy—give rise to a different range of situations in which EU fundamental rights are applicable. The different 'origins' of these two fields of EU law in primary law are relevant here. The provisions concerning the status of the citizenship of the Union, the fundamental freedoms and the common migration and asylum policy are placed in different parts of the Treaty. The legal bases concerning migration and asylum law do not connect with the provisions on free movement as an extension of that regime to third-country nationals, but are placed under a different Title, that of the Area of Freedom, Security and Justice. According to their genealogy, their raison d'être corresponds more to the need to adopt compensatory measures in order to secure the good functioning of the fundamental freedoms than to the idea of extending the scope of those freedoms.

However, and in a rather paradoxical fashion, the progressive development of EU law has led to a situation in which EU law on free movement of persons is still reminiscent of an internationalist approach, whereas the EU migration policy seems to have adopted a constitutional approach. As a result of the structure of primary law the status of EU citizens is mostly based on equal treatment and free movement between States. Free movement rights rest on the nationality divide—they liberalise movement between the nationals of contracting parties, and they grant national treatment. For third-country nationals, the logic of EU law competences is different. The Union engages with the determination of minimum

[77] See, in this regard, Peers (n 3) 146.
[78] ibid.

fundamental status of foreigners in the host Member State not as a matter of free movement (there is no intra-EU free movement for-third country nationals),[79] but as a material competence. This competence includes not only the power to regulate conditions of entry and residence,[80] but generally, 'the definition of the rights of third-country nationals residing legally in a Member State',[81] regardless of what their nationality is and what the relationships between the Union and the State of origin are.[82] As a result, the extension of the equal treatment principle does not depend on a previous liberalisation of movement rights. EU migration policy, after the subsequent reforms culminating in the Lisbon Treaty fulfils, rather, a constitutional mandate to give 'fair treatment' to third-country nationals.[83]

This structure necessarily projects in the way EU competences have been developed. Whereas the core instrument on free movement of EU citizens, Directive 2004/38 constitutes the cornerstone of a regime of free movement across the Member States, the legal migration Directives are centred on governing first entry and second minimum content of status. EU legal migration instruments cover therefore a different ground from EU free movement law. As a result, and despite the clear conceptual parallelism between EU free movement law and EU migration law, the development of the latter is inspired by different objectives. As a consequence, there is no fluidity in status—both areas of law evolve without a clear organic connection. Even though there are some instances of analogical interpretation,[84] there is not a clear distinguishable rationale based on considerations of equal treatment or 'preferential' treatment of citizens of the Union.[85]

[79] See S Iglesias Sánchez, La Libre Circulación de los Extranjeros en la Unión Europea: el régimen de movilidad en las directivas europeas en materia de inmigración (Madrid, Reus, 2010); S Iglesias Sánchez 'Free Movement of Third Country Nationals in the European Union? Main Features, Deficiencies and Challenges of the New Mobility Rights in the Area of Freedom, Security and Justice' (2009) 15 ELJ 791; A Kocharov, 'What Intra-community Mobility for Third-country Workers?' (2008) 33 ELJ 913; A Wiesbrock, 'Free Movement of Third-country Nationals in the European Union: The Illusion of Inclusion' (2010) 35 EL Rev 455. See also, Intra-EU Mobility of third-country nationals (European Migration Network Study, 2013).

[80] Art 79(2)(a) TFEU.

[81] Art 79(2)(b) TFEU.

[82] Of course, we are not considering the specific international law-rooted specific rights awarded by the different agreements of the Union with third states. For an account of that and their interaction with the common migration policy, see P García Andrade, 'Privileged Third-country Nationals and their Right to Free Movement and Residence to and in the European Union: Questions of Status and Competence' in E Guild, C Gortázar Rotaeche and D Kostakopoulou (eds), *The Reconceptualization of European Union Citizenship* (Leiden, Brill/Nijhoff, 2014); S Iglesias Sánchez, 'Migration Agreements between the European Union and Third States' in GS Goodwin-Gill and P Weckel (eds), *Migration and Refugee Protection in the 21st Century International Legal Aspects* (Leiden, Martinus Nijhoff, 2015) 167.

[83] See Arts 67(2) and 79(1) TFEU.

[84] See, eg, Case C-578/08 *Chakroun*, EU:C:2010:117, paras 46 and 64.

[85] The paradigmatic case is *Vatsouras and Koupatantze* (n 16), where the Court found, that since Art 18 TFEU (ex- Article 12 TCE) is only applicable to cases concerning differences in treatment between nationals of the Member States, national rules excluding EU citizens from benefits granted to third-country nationals were not precluded. However, some elements of 'preferential' treatment might be hinted at in some judgments. In Case C-127/98 *Metock and others*, EU:C:2008:449, para 69, the Court found 'paradoxical' an interpretation leading to the outcome that a Member State would be

Against this background, it is not surprising that the contents of EU free movement law and the EU law instruments regarding legal migration do not overlap. Those different legal and theoretical backgrounds entail that the citizen–foreigner cleavage in the Union does not follow the logics found on nation-states.[86] This makes it possible that, in certain respects, the common migration policy goes further than EU free movement law. The paradigmatic case is the EU regulation of family reunification where, for third-country nationals, there is a general instrument, whereas for Union citizens that right is still dependent on free movement. The radical clear-cut separation between EU citizenship and EU migration law has been made even more apparent by the fact that family members of EU citizens have been excluded from the scope of application of the family reunification Directive.[87] This obviously projects on the scope of application of the fundamental right to family life of the Charter.

V. CONCLUDING REMARKS

This chapter has attempted to provide an overview of the scope of EU fundamental rights regarding EU citizens and third-country nationals. Approaching the scope of EU fundamental rights from this point of view may seem not systematically appropriate, since the determination of the scope of application of Charter rights, as defined by its Article 51(1), does not rely on nationality. However, looking at how the provisions of the Charter—and the particular entitlements based on citizenship, residence and status—interact with the scope of EU law is a useful exercise for the purposes of advancing the ongoing discussion of the relationship between EU citizenship and the EU status of third-country nationals.

The current scenario ensues from two separate structural peculiarities of EU law. First, the way in which the protection of EU fundamental rights is triggered. Second, the different structures and developments of EU citizenship law and EU migration law. More precisely, the outcome of the analysis undertaken in this chapter is the function of two sub-elements of the above-mentioned structural

obliged, under the family reunification Directive 'to authorise the entry and residence of the spouse of a national of a non-member country lawfully resident in its territory where the spouse is not already lawfully resident in another Member State, but would be free to refuse the entry and residence of the spouse of a Union citizen in the same circumstances'. With regard to transitional periods imposed on workers of new Member States and the principle of 'community preference' with regard to instruments of the common migration policy, see C-15/11 *Sommer*, EU:C:2012:371.

[86] On this debate, D Thym, 'Ambiguities of Personhood, Citizenship, Migration and Fundamental Rights in EU Law' in L Azoulai, S Barbou des Places and E Pataut (eds), *Constructing the Person: Rights, Roles, Identities in EU Law* (Oxford, Hart Publishing, 2016) 111.

[87] See, in particular, Case C-256/11 *Dereci and Others*, EU:C:2011:734, paras 47–49, explaining that 'although the proposal for a Council Directive on the right to family reunification … included within its scope Union citizens who have not exercised their right to free movement, that inclusion was deleted in the course of the legislative process leading to Directive 2003/86'.

peculiarities: the fundamental rights entitlements of the Charter—some of which establish differentiations on the basis of nationality, status or residence—and the scope of the different instruments/EU law policies—some of which also strongly rely on the nationality divide, such as EU free movement, citizenship and migration law. The combination of those elements leads to a complex and discontinuous coverage map of EU fundamental rights for citizens and third-country nationals.

The consequences of this unique structure explain the peculiarities in the correlation of the status between the positions that an individual may hold with regard to the Union. In a given case, the results of this operation may appear surprising or counterintuitive. Consideration of parallel factual situations of third-country nationals and EU citizens may lead to very different results, and the ensuing differences do not evoke a traditional construction based on the progressiveness of status. Some of the uncertainties and interpretative challenges emanating from the structure described above have been outlined on the last section of this chapter.

First, the establishment of differentiations based on nationality, residence or status through the specific entitlements in particular provisions of the Charter presents normative tensions. The rights proclaimed as exclusively 'citizen' rights—free movement or political rights—are far from having an 'exclusive' nature. Charter rights establishing limitations on the basis of status present challenges in their joint interpretation with other Charter provisions which in turn have to be interpreted in line with Convention rights. The provisions of the Charter which rely on residence as a criterion for fundamental rights entitlement have led to institutional initiatives to overcome those limitations.

Second, the exclusion of third-country nationals from free movement rights and from the principle of non-discrimination on the basis of nationality—which compose the pillars of the development of EU law in terms of individual rights—leads to fragmentation in the interpretation of EU secondary law even in situations where secondary EU law applies to citizens and foreigners regardless of nationality or status.

Third, the uncertain constitutional status of the non-discrimination principle with regard to third-country nationals, and of (third-country) nationality and status as a prohibited ground of discrimination under the Charter and EU general principles still does not offer a solid framework for addressing those situations where differences in treatment are introduced by secondary law or implementing national law.

Fourth, the projection of the system of EU competences in the fields of free movement and migration law and, more precisely, their different development through secondary law in a disconnected fashion, prevents the possibility of establishing any logical correlation between the regulation of the status of citizens and third-country nationals, as the well-known example of family reunification rights demonstrates.

Those problematic lines modulate the perception of EU citizenship and migration law, challenging common wisdom about the way in which a political entity engages with the fundamental rights of citizens and foreigners. Indeed, doctrinal debate on the correlation between EU citizen status and the emerging status of 'EU foreigners' has necessarily as a point of reference preconceptions based on the interaction of the status of citizens and foreigners in States, be that to identify similarities or to justify the differences with the peculiar regime of citizenship and migration in the Union. The analysis of the scope of application of EU fundamental rights from this vantage point offers an account of the impact of EU law on the most fundamental layer of the status of individuals. It makes it possible to identify the difficulties, uncertainties and counterintuitive results ensuing from the projection of the different competences of the Union with regard to different groups of individuals. It unveils the specificity of the reconstruction of the concepts of citizens and migrants in the European Union as two parallel but disconnected statuses, where any attempt at reintroducing conceptual dynamics inherited from the State encounters rigid structural limitations in the current primary law design.

13

The Integration Exception: A New Limit to Social Rights of Third-Country Nationals in European Union Law?

KM (KARIN) DE VRIES

I. INTRODUCTION

SINCE THE TREATY of Amsterdam, the European Union (EU) has been working towards the realisation of a common policy on immigration and asylum. For almost 20 years the EU institutions, together with the Member States, have been debating the conditions governing the entry and residence of third-country nationals (TCNs) and the rights to be accorded to them. The body of EU migration law today comprises a substantial number of legislative instruments setting common standards in most areas of immigration law, including asylum, family reunification, labour migration and long-term residence. Yet the field of EU immigration and asylum policy is still under construction. Besides new legislative initiatives, the EU Court of Justice (CJEU) is called upon to provide guidance on the interpretation of existing directives and to provide answers to questions left undetermined by the EU legislator.

One of these questions concerns the relationship between Member States' integration policies and TCNs' access to social rights, as determined by the EU migration directives. This question came to the fore in two recent judgments of the CJEU: *P & S*, concerning Dutch integration measures for long-term resident TCNs, and *Alo & Osso*, on equal access to social assistance for persons benefiting from international protection. In both cases the CJEU postulated an 'integration exception', accepting that the guarantees of equal treatment, provided in the EU migration directives, do not preclude differences in treatment in national legislation where the aim of such measures is to promote integration. These judgments suggest that the need for integrated and socially cohesive societies is gaining force as an argument to limit solidarity with TCNs residing in the Member States. In considering this development, the present chapter complements the analysis earlier in this volume of the limitations to free movement and social rights of EU citizens. It shows that concerns over integration and social cohesion play a role in EU migration law as well as in EU citizenship law; developments in both fields are likely to influence each other and cannot therefore be considered in isolation.

This contribution both signals the Court's introduction of the 'integration exception' and provides a legal and conceptual analysis of its potential consequences for the protection of TCNs' social rights in EU migration law. It combines a doctrinal analysis of EU migration law, including recent case law, with a theoretical exploration, examining the consequences of legal developments for the conceptualisation of integration and solidarity with TCNs at the EU level. Section II lays the theoretical groundwork, providing a brief consideration of the origins of welfare state citizenship and its development in relation to international migration. It is then shown how integration is emerging as a potential new limitation to equal social rights for TCNs under EU law. Section III outlines the principal standards set by EU immigration and asylum law as regards TCNs' access to social rights and measures in the field of integration, followed in section IV by a detailed examination of the *P & S* and *Alo & Osso* judgments to determine the scope and nature of the integration exception as constructed in the case law. Section V sets out some doctrinal objections to the exception and reflects on its implications for solidarity with TCNs in the field of EU immigration law.

II. INTEGRATION, SOLIDARITY AND CITIZENSHIP

In modern welfare states, the notion of citizenship crucially includes protection against poverty and access to social rights. TH Marshall famously argued that social rights were extended to all members of the national community as the final step in the process of the creation of national citizenship.[1] On this view, the provision of welfare by the state is considered the basis for the participation and allegiance of those citizens who did not already have a stake in the national order as property holders. Conversely, the extension of rights to all citizens also reflects a growing underlying sense of national identity and belonging.[2] Citizenship in welfare states thus entails a relationship of solidarity in which access to social rights and a commitment to the national community constitute mutually reinforcing elements. This implies, however, that the boundaries of the national community also form the boundaries of the welfare state. The link between community and solidarity has been explained as being twofold: besides a sense of allegiance that can exist only within a discernable community and that morally justifies the redistribution of resources, the boundaries of the welfare state also serve to maintain

[1] TH Marshall, 'Citizenship and Social Class' in TH Marshall and T Bottomore (eds), *Citizenship and Social Class* (London, Pluto Press, 1992).

[2] N Mussche, 'Social Citizenship *vs* the Territoriality Principle: Lessons for Flanders' Solidarity Circle' in B Cantillon, P Popelier and N Mussche (eds), *Social Federalism: The Creation of a Layered Welfare State. The Belgian Case* (Cambridge, Intersentia, 2011) 174–75, with references to further literature.

its financial viability, as collective resources are only distributed to those belonging to the community.[3]

If welfare state citizenship has developed in close relation to national communities (as opposed to local or supranational communities), this explains why it is challenged by international migration.[4] Conceptually, welfare state citizenship presupposes a closed community of individuals whose allegiance may be aligned to their share in the redistribution of resources but who are not bound by loyalties to other national groups. Put differently: welfare state citizenship sought to overcome the divisions of class, not nationality. Meanwhile, the reciprocal relationship between welfare provision and commitment to the national community that characterises welfare state citizenship also indicates that there are two ways in which the challenge of international migration can be met. If the influx of non-nationals upsets the balance between redistribution and commitment, this can be resolved either by excluding international migrants from welfare schemes or by accepting that nationality is not the sole determinator of allegiance.[5]

In practice, inclusion has been the solution for at least some categories of migrants. While the idea of welfare state citizenship may have developed in a national setting, in many welfare states eligibility for social rights has not been strictly tied to nationality.[6] Contributory benefit schemes, including old-age pensions and unemployment and disability benefits, have generally been available to all contributing participants and have thus been tied to employment relationships rather than nationality. Eligibility for non-contributory benefits, including social assistance and family benefits, is typically granted to immigrants who have acquired a right of permanent residence.[7] Finally, in the EU context the introduction of EU citizenship has greatly facilitated access to social rights for EU citizens moving to other Member States as well as their family members. In reality,

[3] M Dougan and E Spaventa, 'Wish You Weren't Here … New Models of Social Solidarity in the European Union' in E Spaventa and M Dougan (eds), *Social Welfare and EU Law* (Oxford, Hart Publishing, 2005) 184–85.

[4] M Bommes and A Geddes, 'Introduction: Immigration and the Welfare State' in M Bommes and A Geddes (eds), *Immigration and Welfare: Challenging the Borders of the Welfare State* (London, Routledge, 2000) 1–2.

[5] ibid 2.

[6] WR Brubaker, 'Membership Without Citizenship: The Economic and Social Rights of Noncitizens' in WR Brubaker (ed), *Immigration and the Politics of Citizenship in Europe and North America* (Lanham, MD, University Press of America, 1989) 155–56. The overall trend towards the diminished relevance of nationality for the attainment of rights is highlighted in chapter 3, Dimitry Kochenov's contribution to this volume. While Kochenov rightly documents a shift towards 'personhood' as the foundation for rights entitlements, it is important to keep in mind that, also in the case of social rights, this rarely concerns personhood as such but rather situated personhood, taking the form of (long-term, lawful) residence and/or a participation in the society of the host state. For an illustrative example see L Slingenberg, *The Reception of Asylum Seekers under International Law* (Oxford, Hart Publishing 2014).

[7] Slingenberg (n 6) 156. See also G Vonk and S van Walsum, 'Access Denied. Towards a New Approach to Social Protection for Formally Excluded Migrants' in G Vonk (ed), *Cross-Border Welfare State: Immigration, Social Security and Integration* (Antwerp, Intersentia, 2012) 11–18.

therefore, welfare state citizenship is not strictly limited to those who possess the nationality of the welfare state. To the extent that loyalty to the national community has been considered a condition for access to social rights, in particular non-contributory benefits, this has been implicit in the requirements for permanent residence status, notably the requirement of long-term lawful residence.[8]

In recent years, however, the 'loyalty' side of the coin has received more explicit attention as concerns about immigrant integration and perceived cultural incompatibilities between immigrant minorities and majority populations in the host states have come up high on the political agendas of many EU Member States. Integration policies based on multiculturalism and recognition of cultural and religious diversity have been discarded in the face of a new ideological consensus emphasising cultural uniformity and national identity.[9] One result of this ideological shift has been the introduction of integration requirements and tests in the immigration and naturalisation laws of various Member States. Immigrants are confronted with such conditions when they apply for admission, especially in the field of family reunification, for a secure residence status and/or when they apply for naturalisation.[10]

In some cases, moreover, we now see integration requirements being inserted directly into the domain of social rights. Under the Flemish integration policy, non-compliance with mandatory integration programmes can be sanctioned by temporary cuts of welfare benefits and a refusal of access to social housing.[11] In Germany, besides the rules that were disputed in the *Alo & Osso* judgment (see section IV below), Article 44(2) of the Residence Act (*AufenthaltsGesetz*) provides that certain categories of foreigners can be compelled to attend an integration course if they are recipients of jobseekers' allowances and the attendance of a course is foreseen in an integration agreement. And as of 2016 recipients of social assistance in the Netherlands who cannot demonstrate a sufficient command of the Dutch language must participate in a language course, failing which social assistance benefits are reduced and ultimately stopped.[12] Other examples may be available. The point is, however, that integration conditions are emerging as a new means of demarcating, directly or indirectly, immigrants' eligibility for social rights and hence of defining the boundaries of the welfare state in a context where the presumption of a closed national community has been defied by the reality of international migration and loyalty to the nation is no longer taken for granted.

[8] WR Brubaker (ed), *Immigration and the Politics of Citizenship in Europe and North America* (Lanham, MD, University Press of America, 1989) 149–52.

[9] D Kostakopoulou, 'Introduction' in R van Oers, E Ersbøll and D Kostakopoulou (eds), *A Re-definition of Belonging? Language and Integration Tests in Europe* (Leiden, Martinus Nijhoff, 2010) 1–3. See also R Rubio-Marín, 'Integration in Immigrant Europe: Human Rights at a Crossroads' in R Rubio-Marín (ed), *Human Rights and Immigration* (Oxford, Oxford University Press, 2014) 73–74.

[10] For a broad overview of practices in different Member States, see R van Oers, E Ersbøll and D Kostakopoulou (eds), *A Re-definition of Belonging?* (Leiden, Martinus Nijhoff, 2010).

[11] S Ganty and P Delgrange, 'Heurs et malheurs des parcours d'accueil et d'intégration des étrangers en Belgique' (2015) *Revue du droit des étrangers* 511, 514–15.

[12] See Art 18b of the Dutch Participation Act (*Participatiewet*).

III. INTEGRATION AND SOLIDARITY IN EU IMMIGRATION AND ASYLUM LAW

A. The Treaty Framework

Following this conceptual analysis, I will now turn to the legal framework of EU immigration and asylum law to examine TCNs' access to social rights and the role of (national) integration measures. The legal basis for EU action in the field of immigration and asylum is found in Articles 77–80 of the Treaty on the Functioning of the European Union (TFEU), in Title V on the 'Area of Freedom, Security and Justice'. Article 78 TFEU provides the competence for the elaboration of a common policy on asylum, in accordance with the 1951 Refugee Convention. Article 79 mandates the development of a common immigration policy aimed at, inter alia, efficient management of migration flows and fair treatment of TCNs residing legally in the Member States. The common immigration and asylum policy is to include secondary legislation establishing a uniform status of asylum and of subsidiary protection as well as legislative measures to define the rights of legally resident TCNs.[13] Article 79(4) creates a basis for EU legislation to support the actions of the Member States aimed at promoting the integration of TCNs but excludes harmonisation of Member States' laws and regulations in this field.

The constitutional direction of EU immigration and asylum law has been convincingly qualified as 'cosmopolitan'.[14] This qualification points towards two important principles emerging from the Treaty provisions. First, EU immigration and asylum law aims to harmonise the immigration laws and policies of the Member States without pushing for open borders or full equal treatment of TCNs and Member State nationals. Unlike the rules on free movement of EU citizens, the Treaty provisions on EU immigration and asylum do not grant TCNs a fundamental right to enter and reside in the Member States.[15] They call instead for the joint regulation of the conditions under which TCNs have access to the Member States, taking into account the public interests of those Member States and the EU as a whole. Also, the applicability of Article 18 TFEU, prohibiting discrimination on the grounds of nationality, has thus far been limited to EU citizens to the exclusion of TCNs.[16] As a second principle, however, EU immigration and asylum law does reflect a commitment towards the protection of TCNs' fundamental rights. Measures on immigration and the legal status of TCNs must be in conformity with the rights set out in the Charter of Fundamental Rights and the European Convention on Human Rights (ECHR),

[13] Arts 78 (2)(a) and (b) and 79 (2)(b) TFEU [2016] OJ C202.

[14] D Thym, 'EU Migration Policy and its Constitutional Rationale: A Cosmopolitan Outlook' (2013) 50 *CML Rev* 709.

[15] ibid 718–19. See also L Azoulai and K de Vries, 'Introduction' in L Azoulai and K de Vries (eds), *EU Migration Law: Legal Complexities and Political Rationales* (Oxford, Oxford University Press, 2014) 3–4.

[16] ECJ, C-22/08 and C-23/08 *Vatsouras & Koupatantze*, ECLI:EU:C:2009:344, para 52.

including the prohibition of inhuman treatment, the right to family life and the prohibition of discrimination. Still, to the extent that fundamental rights norms leave a margin of appreciation, the exact level of protection to be accorded to TCNs is not determined in the Treaty provisions; this is left to the discretion of the EU legislator.[17]

B. Access to Social Rights

Turning now to the question of TCNs' access to social rights, it appears that many of the directives adopted pursuant to Articles 78 and 79 TFEU, determining the residence statuses of different categories of TCNs, contain some provisions according equal treatment in the field of social rights. The term 'social rights' is used broadly here, including not only social security and social assistance but also access to other state-supported facilities such as education and vocational training, healthcare and housing. Where equal treatment is granted in the directives, this is most often equal treatment with nationals of the Member States and in some cases with other categories of TCNs.

The number of EU migration directives calling into existence residence statuses for different categories of TCNs has increased steadily since the adoption of the Family Reunification Directive in 2003.[18] Other directives according some form of social protection to TCNs are the Long-term Residents Directive (establishing a permanent residence status for TCNs after five years of lawful residence in a Member State),[19] the Human Trafficking Directive,[20] the recast Qualification Directive (concerning international protection)[21] and several directives in the field of labour migration.[22] The Single Permit Directive, adopted in 2011, sets out a

[17] Thym, 'EU Migration Policy and its Constitutional Rationale' (n 14) 721.

[18] Directive 2003/86/EC on the right to family reunification [2003] OJ L 251/12 (Family Reunification Directive).

[19] Directive 2003/109/EC concerning the status of third-country nationals who are long-term residents [2004] OJ L16/44 (Long-term Residents Directive) as amended by Directive 2011/51/EU to extend its scope to beneficiaries of international protection [2011] OJ L132/1.

[20] Directive 2004/81/EC on the residence permit issued to third-country nationals who are victims of trafficking in human beings or who have been subject of an action to facilitate illegal immigration, who cooperate with the competent authorities [2004] OJ L261/19.

[21] Directive 2011/95/EU on standards for the qualification of third-country nationals or stateless persons as beneficiaries of international protection, for a uniform status for refugees or for persons eligible for subsidiary protection, and for the content of the protection granted [2011] OJ L337/9 (Qualification Directive).

[22] Directive 2005/71/EC on a specific procedure for admitting third-country nationals for the purposes of scientific research [2005] OJ L289/15 (Researchers Directive); Directive 2009/50/EC on the conditions of entry and residence of third-country nationals for the purposes of highly qualified employment [2009] OJ L155/17 (Blue Card Directive); Directive 2014/36/EU on the conditions of entry and stay of third-country nationals for the purpose of employment as seasonal workers [2014] OJ L94/375 (Seasonal Workers Directive); and Directive 2014/66/EU on the conditions of entry and residence of third-country nationals in the framework of an intra-corporate transfer [2014] OJ L157/1 (Directive on Intra-Corporate Transferees).

procedure for the issue of a single permit allowing the holder to reside and work in a Member State as well as a common set of rights.[23] These rights are available to third-country workers irrespective of the purposes for which they were admitted (this may include, for example, family members admitted under the Family Reunification Directive), provided that they are allowed to take up employment in the host Member State.[24]

It is impossible, within the scope of this contribution, to discuss each of the above-mentioned directives in detail.[25] A global assessment shows that there exists a good deal of variation between the different statuses, both in terms of the conditions for admission and termination of residence and of rights provided. To a certain extent the specificities of a particular residence status dictate the need for certain rights or benefits. Thus, the Seasonal Workers Directive, instead of conferring equal treatment in the field of housing, has a separate provision on accommodation adapted to the distinctive housing needs of TCNs who come to work on a seasonal basis.[26] Apart from such arrangements, however, the body of legislation on social rights for TCNs reveals that the challenge to national welfare systems is addressed in two main ways.

First, the conditions under which a right of residence is granted (and may be withdrawn) often already contain conditions aimed at excluding applicants who are likely to become welfare state dependents. Under the various directives that have been adopted in the field of labour migration, admission is conditional upon employment in a Member State.[27] TCNs admitted under these directives are thus, in principle, secured of an income which precludes them from having to rely on income-replacing welfare provisions. This approach to income requirements resembles the approach taken by the CJEU towards the conditions of residence for economically inactive EU citizens in recent cases such as *Dano* and *Alimanovic*, discussed elsewhere in this volume.[28] Other residence requirements in the labour

[23] Directive 2011/98/EU on a single application procedure for a single permit for third-country nationals to reside and work in the territory of a Member State and on a common set of rights for third-country workers legally residing in a Member State [2011] OJ L343/1.

[24] Art 2(b) Single Permit Directive [2011] OJ L343/1. The overview just presented does not include the recast Receptions Conditions Directive (2013/33/EC), as it concerns asylum seekers whose right to residence has not yet been determined. Also left out are the Temporary Protection Directive (2001/55/EC), which can be applied in situations of mass influx but has been left unused during the Syrian refugee crisis, and the Students Directive which does not contain any social rights other than limited labour market access.

[25] For discussions of individual directives see, amongst others, L Halleskov, 'The Long-term Residents Directive: A Fulfilment of the Tampere Objective of Near-Equality?' (2005) 7 *European Journal of Migration and Law* 181; A Beduschi, 'An Empty Shell? The Protection of Social Rights of Third-Country Workers in the EU after the Single Permit Directive' (2015) 17 *European Journal of Migration and Law* 210; B Fridriksdóttir, 'What Happened to Equality? The Construction of the Right to Equal Treatment of Third-Country Nationals in European Union Law on Labour Migration' (dissertation defended at the Radboud Universiteit Nijmegen, 21 November 2016).

[26] Art 20 Seasonal Workers Directive (n 22).

[27] This applies to the Researchers Directive, Blue Card Directive, Seasonal Workers Directive, and Intra-Corporate Transferees Directive.

[28] See notably chapter 9 by Ferdinand Wollenschläger in this volume.

migration directives include sufficient healthcare insurance and/or the requirement that the person concerned must have sufficient resources to maintain himself or herself without recourse to the social assistance system.[29] The availability of healthcare insurance and sufficient resources is also a condition for admission under the Family Reunification Directive and for the acquisition of the status of long-term resident.[30] The only statuses that are granted regardless of economic considerations are international protection under the Qualification Directive and protection for victims of human trafficking.

Second, the level of social rights granted to TCNs under the various directives falls well short of that available to Member State nationals. The lowest level of guarantees is found in the Directive on victims of human trafficking, which requires only that Member States provide a minimum level of subsistence and necessary medical care and adopt measures on access to the labour market, vocational training and education, without stipulating equal treatment. The Family Reunification Directive orders equal treatment, but only with the sponsor (not Member State nationals) and in a limited number of fields (education, employment and vocational training). Other directives prescribe equal treatment with Member State nationals in a broader field of rights, including access to social security, social assistance and/or social protection. The most far-reaching provisions are laid down in the Long-term Residents Directive and the recast Qualification Directive, both of which include a right to equal treatment in respect of social assistance. More modest equal treatment provisions are included in the labour migration directives and the Single Permit Directive. Still, the equal treatment provisions in each of these directives allow for important derogations which again detract from equal treatment with Member State nationals. To give but two examples: Article 12(2)(a) Single Permit Directive allows the Member States to restrict equal access to education and vocational training for students and unemployed persons and to maintain differences in treatment regarding grants and loans, including for the purposes of study and maintenance. Article 11(4) Long-term Residents Directive permits the limitation of equal treatment in the fields of social assistance and social protection to core benefits.

As mentioned above, the EU migration directives, as well as acts of the Member States implementing them, must comply with the fundamental rights norms of the Charter, the ECHR and the general principles of EU law (section III.A. above). A potential challenge to existing standards may be based on the right to equal treatment, including on the grounds of nationality, as laid down in Article 21(2) of the Charter of Fundamental Rights. However in the case of *Kamberaj*, concerning equal access to housing benefits for a long-term resident TCN, the CJEU did

[29] eg Art 5(e) Blue Card Directive (n 22); and Art 6(3) Seasonal Workers Directive (n 22).

[30] Art 7(1)(c) Family Reunification Directive (n 18); and Art 5(1) Long-term Residents Directive (n 19).

not apply the Charter provisions on non-discrimination.[31] The European Court of Human Rights has repeatedly held that non-nationals who were long-term lawful residents of the host state were entitled to equal social rights compared to nationals.[32] On the other hand, it acknowledged that access to 'resource-hungry public benefits', such as healthcare and social assistance, may be restricted for temporary immigrants and those without legal residence.[33] The specific question of whether non-nationals' eligibility for social rights may be conditioned upon integration criteria has not come before the Strasbourg Court.

C. Integration Measures

i. The Division of Competences between the EU and the Member States

Having assessed the standards set at EU level on TCNs' access to social rights, this subsection examines the room for integration measures especially in relation to such rights. I first address the division of competences between the EU and the Member States in the field of integration, before turning to the role that integration measures have played thus far in EU immigration law.

As mentioned above, Article 79(4) TFEU delineates the EU's competence in the field of integration. This provision states that the EU legislator may 'establish measures to provide incentives and support for the action of Member States a view to promoting the integration of third-country nationals residing legally in their territories, excluding any harmonisation of the laws and regulations of the Member States'. Article 79 (4) TFEU was introduced in the Lisbon Treaty and provides a legal basis for measures such as the European Asylum, Migration and Integration Fund.[34] It also makes clear that integration is primarily a competence of the Member States. The EU's competence in this field is only supportive, confirmed by Article 5(2) TFEU, and may not be directed towards harmonisation of Member States' legislation.

While the legal distribution of competences may thus be clear, policies on immigrant integration are in practice closely tied up with other policy areas. The process of immigrant integration in any Member State will be affected by measures in the fields of employment, welfare policy and non-discrimination, to name but a

[31] ECJ (GC), Case C-571/10 *Kamberaj*, ECLI:EU:C:2012:233. In the same judgment, the Court did rely on Art 34 of the Charter (on the right to social security and social assistance) to determine that housing assistance is a 'core benefit', in respect of which equal treatment is required, where it serves to ensure a decent existence for persons lacking sufficient resources (para 92).

[32] eg *Gaygusuz v Austria* App no 17371/90 (ECHR, 16 September 1996); *Dhahbi v Italy* App no 17120/09 (ECHR, 8 April 2014).

[33] eg *Ponomaryovi v Bulgaria* App no 5335/05 (ECHR 21 June 2011) para 54.

[34] Regulation 516/2014 establishing the Asylum, Migration and Integration Fund [2014] OJ L150/168.

few, to the extent that these measures influence the position of immigrants in the host society and its institutions. A strong connection also exists between integration and immigration policies, especially with regard to immigrants who stay for a longer period of time. This is clearly visible at the EU level: legislative measures adopted by the EU in the field of immigration have had the express aim, amongst others, to support the integration of TCNs in the societies of the Member States.[35]

While Article 79(4) TFEU precludes harmonisation of national integration laws, it does not affect the validity of EU legislative measures that are taken on the basis of other legal competences, such as the competence to establish a common policy on asylum and immigration. In acting upon its immigration competence, the EU legislator may be guided by objectives regarding immigrant integration provided that the use of another legal basis does not circumvent the express exclusion of harmonisation in Article 79(4).[36] It follows that integration tests or other integration criteria can be imposed on TCNs in the EU migration directives as conditions for the acquisition of a residence permit and/or any other rights pertaining to their immigration status. At the same time, the discretion of the Member States to adopt such integration conditions is circumscribed by EU immigration law. While the Member States may, in principle, require that TCNs pass integration tests or comply with other integration measures, such obligations may not detract from the rights granted to TCNs under EU legislation. Furthermore, integration requirements that do not affect TCNs' enjoyment of any specific rights laid down in the directives must still be applied in such a manner as not to jeopardise the directives' objectives and so to deprive them of their effectiveness.[37]

ii. Integration and Access to Rights

Having established the limits of the EU's competence in the field of integration, it can now be asked how considerations of integration policy have guided the development of EU immigration law. Conceptually, the relationship between integration and TCNs' access to residence and equal rights can be imagined in two opposite ways.[38] The 'inclusive' approach sees a secure residence status and equal treatment as coming before integration. On this view, integration is perceived primarily in terms of access to rights while additionally such access may be seen as

[35] See, notably, recitals (3), (4) and (15) of the preamble, Family Reunification Directive (n 18); and recitals (4) and (15), preamble, Long-term Residents Directive (n 19).

[36] ECJ, Case C-376/98 *Germany v Council & Parliament*, ECLI:EU:C:2000:544, para 79; see also the discussion in D Thym, 'Legal Framework for EU Immigration Policy' in K Hailbronner and D Thym (eds) *EU Immigration and Asylum Law, A Commentary*, 2nd edn (Munich/Oxford/Baden-Baden, CH Beck/Hart/Nomos, 2016); Treaty Guidance under Article 79 TFEU [2016] OJ C202, MN 25.

[37] ECJ, Case C-579/13 *P & S*, ECLI:EU:C:2015:369, para 45.

[38] These concepts are broadly similar to those identified by Groenendijk; see K Groenendijk, 'Legal Concepts of Integration in EU Migration Law' (2004) 6 *European Journal of Migration and Law* 111. A third concept proposed by Groenendijk, integration as a condition for naturalisation, is less relevant for the purpose of this contribution. *cf* also the distinction between a 'residence' and an 'integration model' in Daniel Thym's chapter 6 on the evolution of EU citizenship rights earlier in this volume.

instrumental to the formation of social ties and a sense of belonging in the host society. By contrast, the 'exclusive' approach to integration considers that a certain degree of integration or integration capacity is a condition that must be fulfilled before access to rights is granted. In this approach 'integration' or 'integration capacity' is generally defined in terms of social and/or cultural affiliation to the host State, to be established through integration tests or criteria such as duration of residence, employment or language proficiency.

The Treaty provisions establishing the EU's competence on immigration do not point in the direction of one or other approach to integration, nor has an unequivocal choice been made by the EU legislator in this regard.[39] Instead several of the migration directives clearly reflect elements of both an inclusive and an exclusive approach to integration, reflecting the political compromises fettered between the Member States in the course of the legislative process. This is especially visible in the Family Reunification and Long-term Residents Directives.[40] The preambles of both directives express that the right to family reunification and the possibility of a permanent residence status, including the right to equal treatment in a number of fields, are intended to support the integration of TCNs in the host Member States.[41] This integration objective has been confirmed by the CJEU and guided its interpretation of the directives.[42] This notwithstanding, both directives also contain derogatory clauses allowing the Member States to make the entry of family members, and the acquisition of long-term residence status, conditional upon the fulfilment of integration criteria.[43] The CJEU, in the case of *K & A*, confirmed that Article 7(2) Family Reunification Directive allows for integration tests, subject to the principle of proportionality.[44]

It follows that EU immigration law, while not prescribing an exclusive approach to integration, allows Member States to take such an approach in relation to the admission of family members and the granting of long-term residence status. Indirectly, therefore, integration can be one of the conditions that TCNs must meet in order to gain access to equal treatment and social rights in the Member States.[45] On the other hand, once a (long-term) residence permit has been granted, it would seem that eligibility for equal treatment no longer depends on the fulfilment of integration requirements.

[39] D Thym, 'Legal Framework for EU Immigration Policy' in K Hailbronner and D Thym (eds), *EU Immigration and Asylum Law, A* Commentary, 2nd edn (Munich/Oxford/Baden-Baden, CH Beck/Hart/Nomos, 2016) MN 44.

[40] See further K de Vries, 'Integration Requirements in EU Migration Law' EUI Working Paper MWP 2012/20 (San Domenico di Fiesole, European University Institute, 2012).

[41] See above (n 35).

[42] eg *Kamberaj* (n 31) para 86.

[43] See Art 7(2) Family Reunification Directive (n 18); and Art 5(2) Long-term Residents Directive (n 19). Art 15(3) of the Long-term Residents Directive moreover allows for integration conditions for long-term residents moving to a second Member State.

[44] ECJ, Case C-153/14 *K & A*, ECLI:EU:C:2015:453.

[45] As described in section III.B, the Family Reunification Directive (n 18) contains very few equal treatment provisions. TCNs admitted under this Directive are, however, entitled to the equal treatment rights set out in the Single Permit Directive if they are allowed to work.

IV. THE 'INTEGRATION EXCEPTION'

Recently, however, the CJEU has introduced an exception in its case law with the potential of greatly increasing the room for Member States to set integration requirements as conditions for equal treatment, and so to adopt an exclusive approach to integration also in relation to social rights. The exception first appeared in the case of *P & S* in and again in *Alo & Osso*. This section introduces both cases, followed by an assessment of the scope of the integration exception and its applicability to different categories of TCNs.

A. Introducing the Exception: *P & S* and *Alo & Osso*

The *P & S* case originated in proceedings started by two TCNs, *P* and *S*, who had obtained the status of long-term residents in the Netherlands.[46] While P and S did not have to fulfil integration conditions to get a long-term residence permit, they were nevertheless obliged under Dutch law to pass an integration exam within a legally determined period.[47] This obligation applies, in principle, to all TCNs with permanent residence status in the Netherlands who have not already passed the integration exam or are able to show equivalent diplomas.[48] Non-compliance does not result in a loss of permanent residence status, but is sanctioned by a fine of up to €1250 that is repeated every two years until the exam has been successfully taken.[49]

Preliminary questions were asked by the Dutch court to find out whether the obligation imposed on P and S was compatible with their status under the Long-term Residents Directive. One of the questions concerned compatibility with Article 11(1)(a) and (b) of the Directive, on the right to equal treatment with Member State nationals in the fields of employment and education and vocational training. It is observed that the impact of the integration obligation on the field of employment in particular was not strongly argued by the referring court.[50] This point was not, however, addressed by the CJEU. Instead the Court raised the issue

[46] *P & S* (n 37).

[47] Since 1 January 2010 the integration exam is one of the conditions for the acquisition of long-term resident status in the Netherlands. This is laid down in Art 45b(2)(g) of the Dutch Aliens Act (*Vreemdelingenwet* 2000). *P & S* obtained long-term resident status in 2008 and 2007 respectively, hence before the integration requirement was introduced.

[48] See Art 3(1) of the Dutch Integration Act (*Wet Inburgering*). Art 5 of the Act states some exceptions, including for TCNs who are under 18 or of pensionable age and those for whom the obligation to integrate would contravene international agreements.

[49] Arts 31–34 Dutch Integration Act.

[50] The referring court stated that TCNs would need to invest time and money to prepare for the exam, which could temporarily influence their availability in the labour market. It acknowledged, however, that this impact would be minimal and comparable to that experienced by other employees seeing to improve their labour market position through education. See Central Appeals Tribunal (*Centrale Raad van Beroep*) 13 November 2013, ECLI:NL:CRVB:2013:2269, para 7.4.

of comparability, stating that equal treatment is only warranted in comparable situations.[51] It then continued to say that

> the integration measures at issue consist, in essence, in the obligation to acquire and/ or demonstrate oral and written proficiency in the Dutch language and knowledge of Netherlands society. Whereas it may be presumed that nationals have such proficiency and knowledge, that is not the case as regards third-country nationals.
>
> Therefore, since those situations are not comparable, the fact that the civic integration obligation at issue in the main proceedings is not imposed on nationals does not infringe the right of third-country nationals who are long-term residents to equal treatment.[52]

The Court thus held that, in as far as language proficiency and host country knowledge are concerned, TCNs and Member State nationals are not in a comparable situation. While this may not seem a particularly far-fetched conclusion, it shows that the right to equal treatment in the Long-term Residents Directive is subject to a comparability test, which is not necessarily met in the case of integration measures. This was confirmed, in rather bolder terms, in the *Alo & Osso* judgment some nine months later.

The case of *Alo & Osso*, decided by the CJEU in the aftermath of the Syrian refugee crisis, concerned two Syrian nationals who had been granted subsidiary protection in Germany.[53] The conditions attached to their residence permits specified that Alo had to reside in the city of Ahlen, whereas Osso was required to live in the region of Hannover with the exception of Hannover city. Under the applicable German legislation, such geographic restrictions could be imposed on holders of temporary residence permits or settlement permits who received jobseeker allowances, social assistance or asylum seeker benefits.[54] Before the court, Alo and Osso claimed that the geographic restrictions imposed on them violated Articles 29(1) and 33 of the Qualification Directive. Under these provisions, beneficiaries of international protection are entitled to social assistance as provided to the nationals of the Member State and to freedom of movement, within the Member State that granted the protection, under the same conditions and restrictions as those provided for other legally resident TCNs.

The CJEU confirmed that the German rules created a difference in treatment between beneficiaries of subsidiary protection, on the one hand, and refugees and German citizens who could obtain social assistance without any geographic restrictions being imposed.[55] However, it added that equal treatment is not called

[51] *P & S* (n 37) para 41.

[52] ibid paras 42–43.

[53] CJEU (GC), Joined Cases C-443/14 and C-444/14 *Alo & Osso*, ECLI:EU:C:2016:127.

[54] § 12(2) German Residence Act (*AufenthaltsGesetz*).

[55] *Alo & Osso* (n 53) paras 52–53. According to the Advocate General there was no evidence that the geographic restrictions imposed by Germany had the actual effect of limiting access to social assistance (Opinion of the Advocate General, para 66). For the Court, however, the possibility of geographic restrictions being imposed sufficed to conclude that there had been a difference in treatment.

for in case the groups concerned are not in an objectively comparable situation as regards the objectives pursued by the measures at stake.[56] Applying this exception to the case at hand, the Court observed that the stated aim of the restrictions imposed on Alo and Osso was to prevent a concentration in certain areas of welfare-dependent foreign nationals, so as to avoid social tensions that would negatively affect their integration. Also, the restrictions could be applied to tie foreign nationals with specific integration needs to places where those needs could be met.[57] This led the CJEU to conclude that: 'Article 29 of [the Qualification Directive] is not relevant … since beneficiaries of subsidiary protection and German nationals are not in a comparable situation so far as the objective of facilitating the integration of third-country nationals is concerned'.[58] Hence, the Court confirmed that the right of TCNs to equal treatment with Member State nationals is subject to an integration exception: where the purpose of a difference in treatment is to facilitate integration, there are no comparable situations and so no claims to equal treatment can be made. Because the comparability test is linked directly to the principle of equal treatment, the same reasoning can be applied to other equal treatment provisions in the various migration directives. The integration exception therefore has the potential of substantially weakening the level of equal treatment and social rights accorded to TCNs by the EU legislator.

B. Limits to the Integration Exception?

The scope of the integration exception, and therefore the impact it may have on TCNs' access to social rights, is partly determined by the type of measures or conditions that qualify as integration measures. In *P & S*, the CJEU took care to explain that knowledge of the host country and its language could '[encourage] interaction and the development of social relations' between TCNs and Member State nationals, besides making it easier for TCNs to access the labour market and vocational training.[59] It thus argued that the Dutch integration exam could have a positive effect on the integration of TCNs. This stance was later repeated in the case of *K & A*, concerning pre-entry integration exams.[60] Moreover, the Court's finding in *P & S* that TCNs and Member State nationals were not in comparable situations specifically concerned their language proficiency and host country knowledge, leaving open the possibility of comparability in other areas (eg, job skills or levels of education). Finally, it was decided in *P & S* that integration

[56] *Alo & Osso* (n 53) para 54.

[57] ibid para 58. These aims are expressed in paras 12.2.5.2.1 and 12.2.5.2.2 of the Administrative Instruction (*Allgemeine Verwaltungsvorschrift*) implementing the Residence Act.

[58] *Alo & Osso* (n 53) para 59.

[59] *P & S* (n 37) para 47.

[60] *K & A* (n 44) para 53.

conditions imposed on long-term residents must respect the principle of non-discrimination and must not undermine the effectiveness of the Long-term Residents Directive by imposing too heavy a burden on long-term resident TCNs.[61]

Looking at the *P & S* case in isolation, the scope of the integration exception appears limited. The judgment can be understood as allowing restrictions to equal treatment only in the form of integration conditions aimed at addressing a lack of language proficiency and not imposing an unreasonable burden on TCNs. In *Alo & Osso*, however, the exception is considerably widened. The geographic restrictions faced by the applicants in this case were not meant to address their language skills or knowledge of German society; instead they were based on rather speculative notions concerning social tensions that would erupt if beneficiaries of international protection were granted a free choice of residence. Yet the CJEU, contrary to its approach in *P & S*, simply accepted that the restrictions served to promote the integration of TCNs. It also failed to explain why the free choice of residence by TCNs would increase the chance of social tensions whereas this is not the case for nationals of the host Member State who were also recipients of welfare benefits. Lastly, the Court did not assess whether the 'matching' of TCNs to integration facilities could not have been achieved by offering those facilities in places with large concentrations of TCNs. In all, the Court's reticent approach in *Alo & Osso* indicates that the Member States have substantial room to formulate integration measures without running into the equal treatment guarantees of the migration directives.[62] Finally, there is no mention in the *Alo & Osso* judgment of the proviso previously formulated in *P & S*—that integration measures may not be implemented in such a way as to deprive the applicable directive of its effectiveness.

C. Residence as Integration?

Also relevant for determining the scope of the integration exception is its applicability to different categories of TCNs. Underlying the exception is the assumption that TCNs are not already integrated in the host Member State and therefore not comparable to nationals. Nevertheless, it follows from the *Alo & Osso* judgment that this assessment of comparability is influenced by the duration of residence in the host Member State.

It is recalled that Alo and Osso relied on Article 33 Qualification Directive, which guarantees to beneficiaries of international protection freedom of movement 'under the same conditions and restrictions as those provided for other legally

[61] *P & S* (n 37) paras 44–45 and 54.

[62] Compare, to contrast, the Opinion of AG Cruz Villalón. Applying a fundamental rights analysis with a strict proportionality test, the AG found that any difference in treatment in respect of the right to free movement would only be justified by considerations of immigration or integration policy that are 'sufficiently serious and linked to concrete situations' (Opinion of the AG in *Alo & Osso*, para 105).

resident TCNs'.[63] Having already determined that the application of this provision requires a comparability test, the CJEU had to decide whether the applicants, as beneficiaries of subsidiary protection, were in an objectively comparable situation to other legally resident TCNs receiving social assistance, or whether they faced greater difficulties relating to their integration. While leaving this question to be answered by the referring court, the CJEU observed that other TCNs generally become eligible for social assistance only after having fulfilled 'a certain period of continuous legal residence in the host Member State' and that it may be assumed from such a period of residence that they are sufficiently integrated in the host State.[64]

It follows that 'a certain period of continuous legal residence' is relevant to the assumption of (non-)integration and therefore to the applicability of the integration exception. This connection between residence and integration also appears elsewhere in the case law. In *Tahir*, the CJEU stated concerning EU long-term resident status that: 'it is the five-year duration of the legal and continuous residence that shows that the person concerned has put down roots in the country and therefore that that person is a long-term resident'.[65] Nevertheless, it cannot be concluded that after five years of legal residence the integration exception no longer applies. After all, the applicants in *P & S* were both long-term residents who had, moreover, legally resided in the Netherlands for over 10 years. Still, the CJEU considered their situation 'not comparable' to that of Dutch nationals because they lacked the necessary language skills. It must the case that, while duration of residence may be a relevant to determining the level of integration between different categories of TCNs, it does not as such suffice to give TCNs equal access to social rights as compared to nationals of the Member States.

V. INTEGRATION AS A NEW LIMIT TO TCNS' SOCIAL RIGHTS

A. Doctrinal Objections

After the analysis conducted in the foregoing sections, it is now time to take stock of the legal and conceptual implications of the integration exception. From a doctrinal perspective, the Court's introduction of the exception is not particularly convincing. As explained earlier, the exception is based on the assumption of incomparability of TCNs and Member State nationals in respect of their integration. The use of the comparability test reflects one of the basic tenets of the legal principle of equality, namely that equal treatment is required only in equal cases.[66]

[63] Other provisions of the Qualification Directive (n 21) also require equal treatment with legally residing TCNs instead of host State nationals. See Art 27(2) on access to adult education and Art 32(1) on access to accommodation. See also Art 14(1) of the Family Reunification Directive (n 18) which guarantees to incoming family members equal treatment with the *sponsor*.

[64] *Alo & Osso* (n 53) para 63.

[65] ECJ, Case C-469/13 *Tahir*, ECLI:EU:C:2014:2094, para 33.

[66] eg AF Bayefsky, 'The Principle of Equality or Non-Discrimination in International Law' (1990) 11 *Human Rights Law Journal* 1, 11.

However, it does not follow from this premise that comparability must always be assessed by the Court. Regarding the equality principle as a general principle of EU law, the CJEU has consistently held that: 'the principle of equal treatment requires that comparable situations must not be treated differently and that different situations must not be treated in the same way unless such treatment is objectively justified'.[67] Clearly, this very open formulation of the equality principle cannot be applied by the Court without any subsequent determination of what constitutes 'comparable situations'. In the cases of *P & S* and *Alo & Osso*, however, the CJEU was not called upon to apply the principle of equal treatment as a general principle of EU law. Both cases concerned, instead, specific provisions on equal treatment laid down in the Long-term Residents and Qualification Directives. Expressed in each of these provisions is a precisely circumscribed right to equal treatment, for a particular category of TCNs, in one or more specified fields and, in some cases, subject to specific derogations.

Where equal treatment rights are clearly confined, as in the migration directives, to specific groups and/or situations, it must be understood that the issue of comparability has already been decided by the EU legislator. To take the example of Article 29(1) Qualification Directive: the meaning of this provision is precisely to determine that, for the purpose of granting social assistance, TCNs who are beneficiaries of international protection are comparable to nationals of the Member States. Equal treatment is thus required, except where the derogation of Article 29(2) applies.[68] Given the availability of a specific norm in secondary legislation, it is both unnecessary and undesirable for the CJEU to introduce a further comparability test. The creation of this judicial exception is moreover surprising in light of the Treaty objective of achieving a common policy on immigration and asylum. Instead of enhancing the level of harmonisation already achieved at the legislative level, the integration exception creates additional room for the Member States to adopt national measures derogating from the common standard.

This critique of the integration exception is not to say that the Member States can no longer introduce mandatory integration measures. In the *P & S* case, for example, the CJEU could have resolved the issue by pointing out that the obligation to pass the integration exam did not affect the applicants' equal access to employment or education. Integration measures, including integration tests, can therefore still be imposed as long as they do not detract from the social rights granted to TCNs under the various migration directives.

B. Conceptual Implications: Integration and Solidarity

The introduction of the integration exception shows that, also in the field of EU immigration law, questions about the boundaries of solidarity are intertwined with

[67] eg ECJ, Case C-210/03 *Swedish Match*, ECLI:EU:C:2004:802, para 70.

[68] Under Art 29(2) of the Qualification Directive (n 21) the Member States may limit social assistance for beneficiaries of subsidiary protection to core benefits.

questions about integration, participation and national identity. This relationship is not new: it was shown above that the idea of welfare state citizenship rests upon a connection between redistribution and social rights on the one hand, and loyalty and commitment to the national community on the other. What is noteworthy about the integration exception, however, is that the direction of this relationship is being reversed. Whereas in traditional welfare state theory the extension of social rights to all citizens is instrumental to furthering a sense of community, the integration exception instead allows the Member States to withdraw social rights from TCNs who do not comply with normative prescriptions adopted for the purpose of creating an integrated society. This reflects the exclusive approach to integration identified above in section III.C.ii, and also its expansion beyond the fields of family reunification and long-term residence, into the domain of social rights.

Meanwhile, the integration exception does not direct the Member States towards any substantive understanding of integration. This is exemplified by the different integration measures at stake in the cases of *P & S* and *Alo & Osso*. In *P & S* the applicants had to pass a language and country knowledge test which, the Court stressed, would support their ability to participate in the labour market and education as well as interaction with the majority population. By contrast, the applicants in *Alo & Osso* were compelled to live in a particular region. While this may have enabled them to access integration facilities, the primary reason for these geographic restrictions appears to have been the prevention of social tensions. For this reason, the *Alo & Osso* case can more easily be seen as one where the applicants' access to social rights was traded off against a general integration interest instead of being instrumentalised to further their individual participation capacity. This notwithstanding, it remains the case that in *P & S* as well as *Alo & Osso* the applicants faced exclusion from equal access to social rights for reasons of integration.

C. Repercussions Beyond the Common Immigration Policy?

As a final remark, it is observed that the introduction of the integration exception for TCNs may, at least theoretically, have repercussions beyond the area of the common immigration policy in the field of free movement law. The right to free movement for EU citizens is based on the fundamental freedom to move between the Member States and the constitutional principles underpinning free movement law are therefore different from those supporting the common policy on immigration and asylum.[69] Nevertheless, as a matter of legal interpretation the question of comparability in terms of integration can also be raised in relation to equal treatment rights of EU citizens as laid down in the Residence Directive[70] or in

[69] Thym, 'EU Migration Policy and its Constitutional Rationale' (n 14). See also section III.A.

[70] Directive 2004/38 on the right of citizens of the Union and their family members to move and reside freely within the territory of the Member States [2004] OJ L158/77.

Article 18 TFEU. Indeed, existing CJEU case law already shows some indications that the level of integration in the host Member State is relevant to determining EU citizens' equal access to social rights.[71] A follow-up question might be whether, in the context of free movement, the criterion of integration can also refer to language proficiency. This question is pushed to the fore by the Court's statements in *P & S*, to the effect that TCNs and Member State nationals are in relevantly different situations because the latter are assumed to have a command of the host State's official language. While in abstract terms the possession of EU citizenship may be relied upon to support a presumption of comparability as to integration, it is clear that in terms of language proficiency EU citizens from other Member States and TCNs are equally different. It follows that the *P & S* judgment has, perhaps unwittingly, raised questions about the level of solidarity to be extended to EU citizens as well as to long-term residents TCNs.

VI. CONCLUDING REMARKS

This contribution signalled the introduction of the integration exception in two recent cases decided by the CJEU and assessed the legal and conceptual implications of this development. The combination of a legal and theoretical approach allowed both to evaluate the doctrinal quality of the cases discussed and to envision their influence on the direction of EU law as it proceeds to determine TCNs' access to social rights and, hence, their claims to solidarity and welfare state citizenship.

On the doctrinal level, it was argued that the Court's introduction of the integration exception is not convincing. Looking beyond doctrinal considerations, however, the integration exception does provide an instrument for the Court to cope with increasingly restrictive attitudes in the Member States towards immigrants and immigrant integration. Some of the migration directives, in particular the Long-term Residents Directive, were adopted in the early phase of the EU's common immigration policy which was characterised by a greater emphasis on inclusiveness and rights than would probably be supported today. Nevertheless, following the *P & S* and *Alo & Osso* judgments the Member States can rely on the integration exception to introduce measures which tie eligibility for social rights to conditions in the field of integration. Consequently, the exclusive approach to integration that was already visible with regard to residence rights of family migrants and long-term residents is now also present in the domain of social rights. It remains to be seen whether this development will be continued in future case law. However, it is clear that the introduction of the integration exception signals a new limit to TCNs' access to social rights as determined by EU immigration law with potentially far-reaching impact.

[71] D Thym, 'The Elusive Limits of Solidarity: Residence Rights of and Social Benefits for Economically Inactive Union Citizens' (2015) 52 *CML Rev* 17, 34–39. The point made here is most clearly illustrated by the *Förster* case, Case C-158/07, ECLI:EU:C:2008:630.

14

Membership without Naturalisation? The Limits of European Court of Human Rights Case Law on Residence Security and Equal Treatment

CLÍODHNA MURPHY

CARENS ARGUES THAT once an individual has been settled in a state for a reasonable period of time, they are morally entitled to all of the rights that citizens enjoy, 'except for perhaps the right to vote, the right to hold high public office, and the right to hold high policymaking positions'.[1] For Carens, this means that it is more appropriate, in a democratic state, to speak of 'rights of membership' rather than 'rights of citizenship'.[2] He reaches this conclusion even within the constraints of the conventional closed-borders view that states are entitled to regulate immigration. The text of the European Convention on Human Rights (ECHR) would appear to support Carens' vision of membership without naturalisation, with Article 1 extending the rights contained in the ECHR to 'everyone' within the jurisdiction of the Contracting State.[3] Moreover, the bases of Carens' theory are closely aligned with the universalist foundations of

[1] JH Carens, 'An Overview of the Ethics of Immigration' (2014) 17 *Critical Review of International Social and Political Philosophy* 538, 546. See also JH Carens, *The Ethics of Immigration* (Oxford, Oxford University Press, 2013); and scholarly responses and discussion, including those contained in A Abizadeh, D Miller, R Bauböck and J Carens, 'Review Symposium: The Ethics of Immigration by Joseph Carens' (2015) 43 *Political Theory* 380; and contributions to symposium (2016) 33 *Journal of Applied Philosophy*. See also I Honohan, 'Reconsidering the Claim to Family Reunification in Migration' (2009) 57 *Political Studies*; M Blake, 'Immigration' in Frey and Wellman (eds), *A Companion to Applied Ethics* (Oxford, Blackwell, 2003) 228.

[2] Carens, 'An Overview of the Ethics of Immigration' (n 1) 547. See also the quite similar concept of 'civic citizenship' or 'denizenship', as discussed (for example) by M Jesse, *The Civic Citizens of Europe: The Legal Potential for Immigrant Integration in the EU, Belgium, Germany and the United Kingdom* (Leiden, Brill, 2017) 33f.

[3] Art 16 ECHR creates a very limited exception to this general rule to allow for restrictions on the political activity of aliens.

international human rights law.[4] Nonetheless, in the ECHR context, the continued importance of formal citizenship is clearly illustrated in two areas: the Article 8 case law of the European Court of Human Rights (ECtHR) on residence security and expulsion; and the interpretation of the Article 14 ECHR non-discrimination clause in cases taken by migrants.

This chapter considers whether, and to what extent, the ECtHR jurisprudence on residence security and equal treatment enshrines a 'membership without naturalisation' paradigm. It will use the work of Joseph Carens and the outputs of the UN human rights treaty bodies, respectively, as the theoretical and legal touchstones for the analysis. The primary focus is an examination of the jurisprudence of the ECtHR on the limits imposed by Article 8 ECHR on state powers of expulsion of non-citizens, concentrating on the impact on residence security of integration in the host State. As Thym has observed, the limits imposed by Article 8 on contracting states' powers of deportation constitute a remarkable restriction of state sovereignty through human rights law.[5] In perhaps the most groundbreaking strand of this case law, the Court has recognised that integration or social ties to the 'host State' will lead to an enhanced protection against expulsion under Article 8. In stating that expulsion severs ties to the community and potentially violates an individual's private life, the ECtHR has provided a legal recognition of membership which does not require naturalisation. However, scholars including Dembour[6] and Steinorth[7] have pointed out that the Court's jurisprudence in this area is flawed; it has been criticised as arbitrary and unpredictable.[8] Article 8 cases (and particularly those based largely on private life claims) rarely succeed and the Court has at times seemed overly cautious in respecting states' margin of appreciation in this sensitive policy area.[9]

[4] On the relationship between universal human rights norms, immigration and integration, see eg, A Xanthaki, 'Multiculturalism and International Law: Discussing Universal Standards' (2010) 32 *Human Rights Quarterly* 21; M Kjaerum, 'Human Rights for Immigrants and Immigrants for Human Rights' in E Guild and J van Selm (eds), *International Migration and Security: Opportunities and Challenges* (London, Routledge, 2005); E Guild, 'Cultural and Social Identity: Immigrants and the Legal Expression of National Identity' in E Guild and J van Selm (eds), *International Migration and Security: Opportunities and Challenges* (London, Routledge, 2005).

[5] D Thym, 'Residence as *de facto* Citizenship? Protection of Long-term Residence under Article 8 ECHR' in R Rubio-Marin (ed), *Human Rights and Immigration* (Oxford, Oxford University Press, 2014).

[6] M-B Dembour, 'Human Rights Law and National Sovereignty in Collusion: The Plight of Quasi-Nationals at Strasbourg' (2003) 21 *Netherlands Quarterly of Human Rights* 63; M-B Dembour, *When Humans Become Migrants: Study of the European Court of Human Rights with an Inter-American Counterpoint* (Oxford, Oxford University Press, 2015) including at ch 6.

[7] C Steinorth, '*Üner v the Netherlands*: Expulsion of Long-term Immigrants and the Right to Respect for Private and Family Life' (2008) 8 *Human Rights Law Review* 185.

[8] See the references above (n 6); and Thym, 'Residence as *de facto* Citizenship?' (n 5) 129.

[9] For a strong critique of the Court's approach in what she calls the 'Strasbourg reversal', see Dembour, *When Humans Become Migrants* (n 6) ch 4. See also A Farahat, 'The Exclusiveness of Inclusion: On the Boundaries of Human Rights in Protecting Transnational and Second Generation Migrants' (2009) 11 *European Journal of Migration and Law* 253.

This chapter identifies two key limitations of the ECtHR case law on residence security based on private life. These limitations, it is argued, deprive the case law of much of its cosmopolitan promise.[10] First, the conception of membership employed by the ECtHR is problematic, with one of the central focuses of the Court an examination of whether the individual has cut all ties to the country of nationality. Second, the doctrinal uncertainty within the case law, as identified by Dembour, Steinorth, Thym and others, poses significant problems for national decision-makers and courts trying to establish the scope of national obligations under the ECHR. It will be argued, using Ireland as a case study, that the vagueness and lack of clarity in the Court's approach leaves room for highly restrictive and statist approaches at the national level.

The chapter finishes by briefly considering the impact and potential of the non-discrimination clause contained in Article 14 ECHR in the context of challenging immigration rules under Article 8. It concludes that, despite the recent encouraging judgment of the Grand Chamber in *Biao v Denmark*, Article 14 arguments remain of limited utility. The approach of the Court in *Biao v Denmark* bolsters this chapter's overall argument that the ECtHR case law does not dislodge the reality that naturalisation remains the key to full security of legal status and residence in modern states.[11]

I. RESISTING EXPULSION ON THE GROUNDS OF ARTICLE 8 AND PRIVATE LIFE

Before turning to the limitations of the case law, it is useful to provide a summary of the basic legal principles in this area. It is well established that a decision to expel a non-citizen from a Contracting State may raise an issue under Article 8 ECHR if it would disrupt family or private life in that State. Many of the cases which have come before the Court have concerned 'integrated' or second-generation immigrants who have lived for long periods of time in the host State. The Strasbourg Court has placed a strong emphasis on integration, and in particular on the social aspects of integration, in deciding whether the expulsion fails to respect the individual's private and family life. The Court's jurisprudence has gradually evolved to the point of assessing complex questions of the applicant's social and cultural ties and economic links to the Contracting State, in addition to the more straightforward issue of family ties.

The Court assesses these applications on a case-by-case basis rather than treating long-term residents as a special category whose expulsion would require exceptional circumstances. In the early cases, there were strong dissenting voices within the Court itself which suggested either that long-term residents should be

[10] For some similar arguments, see Thym, 'Residence as *de facto* Citizenship?' (n 5).

[11] D Kostakopoulou, 'Why Naturalisation?' (2003) 4 *Perspectives on European Politics and Society* 85.

no more expelled than nationals;[12] or that expulsion of an integrated alien as a rule should only exceptionally be justified where the alien is convicted of very serious crimes (eg, such as serious crimes against the state, political or religious terrorism or holding a leading position in a drug trafficking organisation).[13]

This case-by-case approach led to particularly haphazard results in the early cases, which was described by Judge Martens in *Boughanemi v France*[14] as 'a source of embarrassment for the Court' and a 'lottery'.[15] No clear thread of logic underlining the importance of the seriousness of the offence or the applicant's degree of integration or the looseness of the family ties is apparent in these cases, with the Court emphasising different factors in each case.[16] Since the 2001 judgment in *Boultif v Switzerland*,[17] however, the Court has followed a more structured approach, applying a defined set of criteria to each case. At least three of these criteria are indirectly linked to the degree of integration of the individual and their family in the host State: the duration of the individual's stay; his or her family situation; and difficulties that would be faced by the spouse in settling in the country of origin. Regarding the duration of stay criterion, the Grand Chamber in *Üner v The Netherlands*[18] explained its rationale as based on the assumption that the longer the individual stays, the closer the ties between the individual and the host State must be. In addition, the Grand Chamber in *Üner v The Netherlands* added two further criteria to the list of matters to be considered in these cases:

1. The best interests and wellbeing of the children, in particular the seriousness of the difficulties which any children of the applicant are likely to encounter in the country to which the applicant is likely to be expelled.
2. The solidity of social, cultural and family ties with the host country and the country of destination.

Üner and subsequent case law have demonstrated that where a person has lived in the host State almost all their life, the integration factor will weigh heavily in the balancing exercise.[19] The basic implications of integration in terms of the ECHR are clear and far-reaching: integration has the potential to positively impact on the legal security of residence of certain immigrants in certain circumstances. This is particularly welcome in light of the trend among European states to

[12] See, eg, dissenting opinions in *Baghli v France* (2001) 33 EHRR 32; *Boughanemi v France* (1996) 22 EHRR 228; *Nasri v France* (1996) 21 EHRR 458.

[13] Dissenting Opinion of Judge Martens in *Boughanemi v France* (n 12) para 9.

[14] *Boughanemi v France* (1996) 22 EHRR 228.

[15] Para 4 of the Dissenting Opinion.

[16] See R Cholewinski, 'Strasbourg's "Hidden Agenda"? The Protection of Second Generation Migrants from Expulsion under Article 8 of the European Convention on Human Right' (1994) 12 *Netherlands Quarterly of Human Rights* 287.

[17] *Boultif v Switzerland* (2001) 33 EHRR 50.

[18] *Üner v The Netherlands* (2007) 45 EHRR 14.

[19] Post-*Üner*, see *Maslov v Austria* [2008] ECHR 546; *Emre v Switzerland (No 2)* App no 5056/10 (ECHR, 11 October 2011).

introduce integration requirements as a threshold for the entry and legal residence of non-EU nationals.[20] However, the next section will show that despite its positive aspects, the case law in this area is replete with theoretical, doctrinal and practical problems.

II. A PROBLEMATIC CONCEPTION OF MEMBERSHIP

In *Üner*, the ECtHR built on its existing jurisprudence to place increased emphasis on the fact of integration by including it as one of the express criteria to be applied in assessing a person's Article 8 claim. In expressly acknowledging that the Court can become involved in assessing the extent of a person's social and cultural ties, the case law enters the complex and contested arena of issues relating to attachment and belonging. The question of what it means to be 'integrated'—and the legal consequences that should flow for individuals from successfully integrating, or not—is among the most hotly debated issues in modern European societies. So how has the Court approached this part of the balancing test?[21]

A. Proving Membership: Putting the Onus on the Individual

The Strasbourg Court, in assessing social and cultural ties, looks at more than mere residence in the host State.[22] This means that in order to gain security of residence under Article 8 ECHR, even long-term legal residents must prove their active membership and engagement with society in the host country in a way in which citizens cannot be required to do. As Kochenov notes in chapter three in this volume, this assessment of membership is altogether more nuanced and meaningful than integration 'tests' as part of citizenship law. He states that: 'Under this logic a place in the nation is not 'deserved' by passing humiliating tests of

[20] For criticism of this trend, see, eg, M Jesse, 'The Unlawfulness of Existing Pre-departure Integration Conditions Applied in Family Reunification Scenarios—Urgent Need to Change National Laws in the European Union' (2017) 2 *International Journal of Migration and Border Studies* 1; A, 'Against Integration, for Human Rights' (2016) 20 *International Journal of Human Rights* 815; R van Oers, E Ersbøll and D Kostakopoulou, 'Mapping the Redefinition of Belonging in Europe' in R van Oers, E Ersbøll and D Kostakopoulou (eds), *A Re-definition of Belonging? Language and Integration Tests in Europe* (Leiden, Martinus Nijhoff, 2010) 318; E Guild, K Groenendijk and S Carrera, 'Understanding the Contest of Community: Illiberal Practices in the EU?' in E Guild, S Carrera and K Groenendijk (eds), *Illiberal Liberal States: Immigration, Citizenship and Integration in the EU* (Farnham, Ashgate, 2009) 3; S Carrera, *In Search of the Perfect Citizen? The Intersection between Integration, Immigration and Nationality in the EU* (Leiden, Martinus Nijhoff, 2009).

[21] The ideas in this section build upon my earlier article: C Murphy, 'The Concept of Integration in the Jurisprudence of the European Court of Human Rights' (2010) *European Journal of Migration and Law* 23.

[22] This approach is reinforced by the existence of a separate criterion in the balancing test specifically addressing 'the length of the applicant's stay in the country from which he or she is to be expelled'.

the knowledge of the non-existent cultural uniqueness or a random act of birth in particular circumstances, but by *being part of a society*'.[23] However, an individualistic requirement for active membership sits uneasily with equality-based conceptions of integration, which conceive of integration as a long-term gradual process of equalisation with existing members of society. Equality-based integration paradigms have been adopted as the basis for the best practice integration model at the Office of the UN High Commissioner for Refugees,[24] as well as the UN Human Rights Committees in their work.[25] The partly qualitative approach to membership taken by the ECtHR, which considers the quality of integration as well as mere presence in the state, also marks a point of departure from the Carens model, which requires simple residence to demonstrate membership in a particular society. As Carens notes, 'Living there gives them interests that visitors do not have, interests that deserve legal recognition. Living there makes them members of civil society'.[26] While idealised models of citizenship emphasise the importance of political participation and active membership of society, those born with citizenship are not required to demonstrate their active citizenship to achieve residence security, in contrast to long-term residents in the ECHR vision.

In its assessment of the solidity of social and cultural ties to the host State, the Court looks at a range of factors which vary from case to case, including the education and employment history of the person within the host State;[27] criminal record and seriousness of previous offences;[28] speaking the language;[29] and attempts to acquire nationality.[30] This provides a flexible method of approaching the question of integration, and also allows for a margin of appreciation for national authorities. However, the criteria used are lacking in objective justification and clarity. From a theoretical perspective, the key difficulty is that the Court is engaged in assessing a complex social phenomenon by way of a sole focus on the individual concerned, without considering structural factors within the host society; systemic discrimination against migrants or particular ethnic or social

[23] D Kochenov, 'The Citizenship of Personal Circumstances in Europe' University European Institute Working Paper 2017/7.

[24] R DaCosta, *Rights of Refugees in the Context of Integration: Legal Standards and Recommendations, UNHCR Legal and Protection Policy Research Series* (UNHCR, June 2006).

[25] See generally, C Murphy, *Immigration, Integration and the Law: The Intersection of International, EU and Domestic Regimes* (Farnham, Ashgate, 2013) 212–50.

[26] Carens, 'An Overview of the Ethics of Immigration' (n 1) 546. He acknowledges that during the early stages of settlement, it is permissible to limit rights to redistributive benefits and protection against deportation, but finds that the longer people stay in a society, the stronger their moral claims become to be treated like citizens in these respects.

[27] See, eg, *Salem v Denmark* App no 77036/11 (1 December 2016—referral to GC rejected 24 April 2017).

[28] See, eg, *Amrollahi v Denmark* App no 56811/00 (ECHR, 11 July 2002); *Dalia v France* (2001) 33 EHRR 26; *AA v The United Kingdom* App no 8000/08 (ECHR, 20 September 2011).

[29] See, eg, App no 38030/12 (23 April 2015). (Struck out by the Grand Chamber on 21 September 2016 upon the giving of assurances by Germany that they would not in fact expel the applicant under this deportation order.)

[30] See, eg, *Kaya v Germany* (1998) 28 EHRR 1.

groups; or the wider socio-economic context within which the integration process has taken place.[31] These difficulties were also highlighted from within the Court in the early case law. In *Nasri*, for example, Judge Morenilla argued that states which accept immigrant workers should become responsible for the education and social integration of such immigrants as it is for the children of its citizens.[32] Indeed, it is difficult to see how courts can ever appropriately assess a person's integration into society, given the limitations of the adversarial setting and the individualised nature of the evidence presented.

A further side effect of the Court's approach of focusing on individual efforts to integrate is that it lends legitimacy to the current trend for integration policy at the national level to shift the primary responsibility for integration from the State to migrant communities, including by way of integration testing. This tendency has been criticised by the UN Committee on the Elimination of All Forms of Racial Discrimination (CERD Committee) in respect of numerous European countries.[33] Most recently, in its concluding observations on the Netherlands in 2015, the CERD Committee expressed concern that shifting the primary onus of integration from the State to migrants in this way 'puts migrants in particularly vulnerable situations at risk of receiving insufficient attention and support, leaves them vulnerable to social exclusion, and hampers their integration and the full enjoyment of rights.' The Court of Justice (ECJ), in contrast, has expressly approved the use in principle of civic integration tests as a means of facilitating integration,[34] without discussing human rights.[35]

All of this means that the Court's approach aligns more closely with a 'liberal nationalism'[36]-type model as theorised by Miller,[37] for example, than the universalistic Carens or human rights-based models. Miller's core values of 'weak cosmopolitanism', national self-determination, fairness in distribution and social cohesion justify and prioritise the right of states to deal with immigrants according to community goals and preferences. Such preferences, according to Miller, would legitimately include the cost of integrating immigrants with different

[31] These are all factors which are identified by the UN treaty bodies as having an impact on integration.

[32] Para 3 of his partly Dissenting Opinion.

[33] See generally, C Murphy, 'Towards a Human Rights-Based Paradigm of Integration? The Contribution of International Law' (2013) *European Human Rights Law Review* 166.

[34] ECJ, Case C-57913 *P&S*, EU:C:2015:369, para 49; ECJ, Case C-153/14, EU:C:2015:453, paras 53 and 57.

[35] For commentary, see D Thym, 'Towards a Contextual Conception of Social Integration in EU Immigration Law: Comments on *P&S* and *K&A*' (2016) 18 *European Journal of Migration and Law* 89, 100–01.

[36] For an excellent overview, see P Kelly, 'Liberalism and Nationalism' in S Wall (ed), *The Cambridge Companion to Liberalism* (Cambridge, Cambridge University Press, 2015).

[37] See, in particular, D Miller, *Strangers in Our Midst: The Political Philosophy of Immigration* (Cambridge, MA, Harvard University Press, 2016). Reviewed by, among others, L Bosniak, 'Strangers in Our Midst: The Political Philosophy of Immigration: Immigration Ethics and the Context of Justice' (2017) 31 *Ethics & International Affairs* 93.

languages, religions or lifestyles;[38] as well as the desire to protect national cultures.[39] The structural dimensions of integration, and the duty of the State to facilitate integration, are given little weight under this analysis, which would allow for civic integration to be promoted through education and mandatory citizenship tests, for example. It is arguable that Miller's contextual approach, which would allow for the political dimensions of practical ethics to be taken into account, is an appropriate model for a supranational court bound by the principle of subsidiarity. Indeed, it should be acknowledged that the ECJ has recently adopted quite a similar 'contextual' approach in the context of EU migration law.[40] However, quite outside methodological difficulties with Miller's application of a contextual approach to the question of immigration,[41] this author believes that this argument is outweighed in the case of the ECtHR by the inherent moral and ethical dimensions of the task being performed by the Court (that of adjudicating individual human rights claims); as well as the universal application of the Convention as stated in Article 1.

B. Rejection of Social and Cultural Ties in the Country of Origin as a Prerequisite to Residence Security?

A second problematic feature of the Court's conception of membership stems from the second limb of the integration criterion set out in *Üner*: the assessment of 'social and cultural ties in the country of destination'.[42] *Maslov v Austria*[43] was a rare case in which the Court accepted that the applicant's principal social, cultural and family ties were within Austria, but also placed much emphasis on the fact that he had 'convincingly explained' that he could not speak Bulgarian or read and write in the Cyrillic alphabet.[44] This factor seemed to weigh significantly in the Court's overall decision that the exclusion of this young man (a minor) for 10 years to Bulgaria after a series of offences, including aggravated burglary, violated Article 8. Conversely, in many cases (a number of which are discussed here) the courts have found that tenuous links between the applicant and/or family members to the country of origin mean that integration in that society would not be 'impossible'.

The general hardening of the ECtHR's approach observable in recent Article 8 cases has coincided with ever more 'contrived'[45] assertions that it would

[38] Miller (n 37) 107.
[39] ibid 108.
[40] Thym, 'Towards a Contextual Conception of Social Integration' (n 35).
[41] Bosniak (n 37).
[42] For a discussion of similar issues, see Farahat (n 9).
[43] *Maslov v Austria* [2008] ECHR 546.
[44] Paras 96 and 97.
[45] *Balogun v The United Kingdom* [2012] ECHR 614, Dissenting Opinion of dissenting Judges Garlicki and Bjorgvinsson, para 6.

be possible for the person to resume a private life in the country of origin. In *Balogun v The United Kingdom*,[46] the applicant had been in the UK since the age of three, and was a settled migrant whose expulsion required compelling justification. However, in finding that the interference with private life here was proportionate, in addition to considering the seriousness of the offence the Court pointed out that his mother resided in Nigeria. Even though the applicant had asserted that he did not know where she was, this was seen as a relationship and link that 'could be pursued and strengthened by the applicant if he chose'. This was strongly criticised as 'highly speculative and artificial' by the dissenting Judge Garlicki and Judge David Thor Bjorgvinsson.[47] Similarly, in *Khan v Germany*,[48] the Court found that a woman suffering from a severe psychiatric illness could possibly reintegrate into Pakistani society, despite the fact that she had no social network there. Although the family had stated that they would not take her in or visit her in hospital, the Court was of the view that 'it does not appear impossible that contacts with the family in Pakistan could be pursued and ultimately strengthened'.[49] In *Sarkozi and Mahran v Austria*, the Court decided that a Slovakian national who had spent the formative years of her childhood in Austria retained 'at least cultural ties'[50] to Slovakia, in the absence of any concrete ties.[51] Overall, these cases show that it will be almost impossible for an applicant to show that the lack of ties to their country of origin constitutes an overwhelming obstacle to reintegration there.[52]

In order for this criterion to have any discernible impact on the overall balancing process, it seems that applicants are required to convince the Court that they have completely severed, or lost, all social and/or cultural ties with the country of origin. This method of analysis makes sense, to a certain point, in the context of the exercise in which the Court is engaged: assessing whether deportation to the country of origin would be a disproportionate interference with private life. It is at odds, however, with broader human rights norms which emphasise that each person has a human right to maintain their language and cultural identity without penalty. Article 27 of the International Covenant for Civil and Political Rights (ICCPR); Article 15 of the International Covenant for Social, Cultural and

[46] ibid.

[47] ibid.

[48] *Khan v Germany* App no 38030/12 (ECHR, 23 April 2015). Struck out by the Grand Chamber on 21 September 2016 upon the giving of assurances by Germany that they would not in fact expel the applicant under this deportation order.

[49] Para 52. See also *Savasci v Germany* App no 45971/08 (ECHR, 19 March 2013) para 29; *Trabelsi v Germany* App n. 41548/06 (ECHR, 13 October 2011) para 63.

[50] *Sarkozi and Mahran v Austria* App no 27945/10 (ECHR, 2 April 2015).

[51] Para 74.

[52] Although see, eg, *AW Khan v The United Kingdom* App no 47486/06 (ECHR, 12 January 2010); *Mehemi v France* App no 25017/94 (ECHR, 26 September 1997); *Beldjoudi v France* App no 12083/86 (ECHR, 26 March 1992).

Economic Rights (ICSCER);[53] and Article 27(1) of the Universal Declaration of Human Rights (UDHR) protect the rights of minorities (and others) to maintain their cultural identity, including to use their own language and to take part in cultural life.[54] Article 27 of the ICCPR, in particular, implies a positive obligation to enable minorities to both participate in the host society and also retain their own distinctive identity.[55] Even the EU's common basic principles for integration, which are often criticised as vague and depoliticised,[56] require the safeguarding of diverse cultural practices and religion.[57] When scrutinised alongside these international and EU instruments, the Court's approach to membership in the form of social and cultural ties appears closer to outdated ideas of assimilation, and ignores the value to human dignity of maintaining cultural and linguistic heritage, let alone family and social links.

A pragmatic reading of the cases suggests that these consequences are probably unintended: the artificiality of the Court's reasoning on this point has more to do with the doctrinal uncertainty caused by the flexible case-by-case approach than it does with a preference for a cultural assimilation model of integration. Overall, it seems that the criterion simply has comparatively little weight in the overall balancing exercise: the ECtHR will not allow an absence of real links to the home country to become a barrier to deportation where this seems proportionate on a consideration of all the other relevant factors. However, the Court is forced to fit this reality within its consistent mantra that the consideration of ties to the country of origin is one of a number of important factors in a holistic assessment of all the relevant circumstances of the case. Overall, while the reasoning of the Court in respect of 'social and cultural ties to the country of origin' may be of limited practical legal weight and value, it is still revealing of its understanding of membership. This conception of membership, constructed in the awkward attempt to reconcile state and individual interests in the sphere of deportation, unthinkingly legitimises exclusionary national narratives of integration which emphasise cultural and values integration.[58]

[53] See also CESCR General Comment No 21, 'The Right of Everyone to Take Part in Cultural Life' (UN Doc E/C.12/GC/21, 21 December 2009) para 34. See R O'Keeffe, 'The Right to Take Part in Cultural Life under Article 15 of the ICESCR' (1998) 47 *ICLQ* 904.

[54] P Thornberry, *International Law and the Rights of Minorities* (Oxford, Oxford University Press, 1991) 142; 187. S Poulter, 'The Rights of Ethnic, Linguistic and Cultural Minorities' (1997) 3 *European Human Rights Law Review* 254.

[55] See CCPR General Comment No 23, 'The rights of minorities (Art 27)' (8 April 1994).

[56] P Mac Einri, 'Integration Models and Choices' in B Fanning (ed), *Immigration and Social Change in the Republic of Ireland* (Manchester, Manchester University Press, 2007) 231.

[57] Common Basic Principle 8, Justice and Home Affairs Council Conclusions, *Common Basic Principles on Immigrant Integration*, Council Document 14615/04 (Brussels, 19 November 2004).

[58] For academic commentary see, eg, D Kostakopoulou, 'An Anatomy of Civic Integration' (2010) 73 *MLR* 933; S Mullally, 'Retreat from Multiculturalism: Community Cohesion, Civic Integration and the Disciplinary Politics of Gender' (2013) 9 *International Journal of Law in Context* 911; A Kundnani, 'The Death of Multiculturalism' (2002) 43 *Race & Class* 67.

III. DOCTRINAL UNCERTAINTY AND UNPREDICTABILITY OF OUTCOMES

A. The Balancing Test: In-Built Arbitrariness?

The Court follows a consistent formula in its Article 8 expulsion case law. It assesses whether the deportation would interfere with the applicant's private and/or family life; whether the measure is in accordance with law and pursues a legitimate aim; and then moves quickly to consider the proportionality of the removal under Article 8(2) by using the criteria expressly set down in *Boultif* and *Üner*. In spite of the seeming simplicity of this approach, as mentioned already, the application of the balancing test based on the *Boultif* criteria is notoriously vague and uncertain, particularly as regards the question of the relative weight of the various factors. As highlighted by Lady Justice Arden of the UK Court of Appeal in her extrajudicial writing, the primary duty of supranational European courts seeking to maintain respect and promote effectiveness in the domestic sphere is to provide a legitimate body of law for national authorities to apply. This implies creating a principled body of law within their jurisdiction, as well as quality of reasoning and ability to communicate clearly with their constituents.[59] The Article 8 private life case law arguably fails to achieve this threshold of legitimacy, as will be explained below in the Irish context.

As already mentioned, this aspect of the case law has been continually criticised by academic commentators.[60] It is worth nonetheless highlighting again here, briefly. The decisions of the Court in respect of two brothers (separately) claiming violations of Article 8 in respect of their deportations from the United Kingdom (for different offences) provides a striking illustration of some of the problems in the case law. The Khan brothers were Pakistani nationals and had lived in the UK for nearly 30 years, since childhood. In *AH Khan v the United Kingdom*,[61] it was decided that the applicant had not achieved 'a significant level of integration into British society', due to his limited family life with his six children, his long criminal record, his lack of a lengthy or consistent employment history, and his marriage in and travel to Pakistan on one other occasion.[62] His removal following a conviction for robbery was found to be permissible under Article 8. In contrast, in *AW Khan v The United Kingdom*,[63] the Court concluded that the deportation of the applicant on foot of a conviction for importation of heroin would violate Article 8, having particular regard to

> the length of time that the applicant has been in the United Kingdom and his very young age at the time of his entry, the lack of any continuing ties to Pakistan, the strength of his

[59] M Arden, 'Peaceful or Problematic? The Relationship between National Supreme Courts and Supranational Courts in Europe' (2010) 29 *Yearbook of European Law* 3.

[60] See nn 5, 6, 7 and 8.

[61] *AH Khan v the United Kingdom* App no 6222/10 (ECHR, 20 December 2011).

[62] Para 41.

[63] *AW Khan v The United Kingdom* App no 47486/06 (ECHR, 12 January 2010).

> ties with the United Kingdom, and the fact that the applicant has not reoffended following his release from prison in 2006.[64]

The key distinctions between the cases were that the older brother had visited Pakistan twice and had married there (although he claimed that he had lost contact with his wife); that he had offended over a long period of time; and that he maintained less contact with his extended family and his children in the UK. The distinctions based on the relative quality of social and cultural ties of the two brothers in the UK and in Pakistan are unconvincing: reading between the lines, the Court seemed to share the opinion of the UK Government that the older brother was a 'n'eer do well' who would resist reform and keep reoffending. It appears then to engage in a form of backward reasoning whereby the analysis of the criteria is made to fit what seems to be the correct decision. This is highly problematic from the perspective of legal principle. Even if it is felt that this critique goes too far, it is difficult to deny that national authorities would derive limited assistance from these two cases in understanding what the Court requires in an individual case.

B. Limiting the Impact of Residence: Precarious Legal Status

Aside from the problems caused in its application of the balancing test in individual cases, the ECtHR has employed a number of conceptual devices, such as the 'settled migrant' and 'precarious' legal status, in such a way as to potentially limit the impact of residence and leave a wide margin of appreciation for states in the area of expulsion of non-citizens, particularly those with an irregular status.[65] In cases including *ZH v Switzerland*,[66] *Jeunesse v Switzerland*[67] *and AS v* Switzerland,[68] the Court has clarified that the Court's Article 8 case law on settled migrants who have already been formally granted a right of residence in the host country cannot automatically be transposed to those who have not been granted a right of residence (eg, asylum seekers or irregular migrants). However, a violation of Article 8 is theoretically possible even in the case of a person with no formal legal status, as shown in the judgments in *Slivenko v Latvia*,[69] *Sisojeva v Latvia*[70] and *Jeunesse v The Netherlands*.[71] In adopting this stance, the Court is attempting to allow for distinctions between migrants in different legal and factual circumstances without

[64] Para 50.
[65] *Nnyanzi v The United Kingdom* App no 21878/06 (ECHR, 8 April 2008) para 76.
[66] *ZH v Switzerland* App no 60119/12 (ECHR, 8 December 2015) para 40.
[67] *Jeunesse v Switzerland* App no 12738/10 (ECHR, 3 October 2014).
[68] *AS v Switzerland* App no 39350/13 (ECHR, 30 June 2015) para 46.
[69] *Slivenko v Latvia* App no 48321/99 (9 October 2003 (GC)).
[70] *Sisojeva v Latvia* App no 60654/00 (15 January 2007 (GC)).
[71] These cases, and the issues raised, are thoroughly considered in D Thym, 'Respect for Private and Family Life under Article 8 ECHR in Immigration Cases: A Human Right to Regularize Illegal Stay?' (2008) 57 *ICLQ* 87.

creating strict categorical divisions between long-term legal residents and irregular migrants, for example. This fluid approach could fit with Carens' perspective on irregular migrants, which emphasises the moral importance of the length of stay, even if unauthorised. He states: 'When people settle in a country, they form connections and attachments that generate strong moral claims over time. After a while, the conditions of admission become irrelevant'.[72] However, theoretical justifications aside, just as in the case of the application of the *Boultif* criteria, above, these concepts introduce uncertainty and complexity into the Court's jurisprudence. The paragraphs below examine how the uncertainty as to the impact of irregular or 'precarious' immigration status affects the national level and can lead to very restrictive approaches which could impair the very essence of the right to a private life. Ireland is used as a as a case study.

C. Confusion at the National Level: Recent Developments in Ireland

The European Convention on Human Rights is indirectly incorporated into Irish law, at a sub-constitutional level, by the European Convention on Human Rights Act 2003. The Act places an obligation on administrative decision-makers to carry out their functions in compliance with the ECHR.[73] This means that Convention rights must be considered by the Minister for Justice in deciding whether to deport an individual, or to renew their permission to remain in the State. Such decisions of the minister can be challenged by way of judicial review and frequently end up in the courts.[74] The Supreme Court and the Court of Appeal have recently followed a restrictive approach when the applicant's private life in the State was developed in circumstances where their legal status was 'precarious'. In such cases, it seems that it will be very difficult for applicants to show that Article 8 is engaged at all, in such a way as to require justification and a proportionality analysis under Article 8(2). Even where Article 8 is found to be potentially engaged, it will require wholly exceptional circumstances to dislodge the presumption in favour of the State's entitlement to control immigration such that expulsion would be disproportionate and unlawful.

In *PO v Minister for Justice and Equality*,[75] the Supreme Court refused to restrain the deportation to Nigeria of a woman and her nine-year-old son, who was born, raised and educated in the State (although was not an Irish citizen). The Court considered Article 8 ECHR issues, among other issues raised by the applicants, who had unsuccessfully applied for asylum in Ireland. The majority judgments

[72] Carens, 'An Overview of the Ethics of Immigration' (n 1) 551.
[73] s 3, European Convention on Human Rights Act 2003.
[74] See generally, C Murphy, 'A Matter of Humanity? Emerging Principles Relating to Deportation and Human Rights' (2016) 39 *Dublin University Law Journal* 259. Some of the arguments in this section build on those made in that article.
[75] *PO v Minister for Justice and Equality* [2015] IESC 64.

focused on the entitlement of the State to control immigration, the precarious legal status of the applicants, their extensive ties to Nigeria, the absence of any family life issues, and the wide margin of appreciation of decision-making in all the circumstances.[76] It was suggested that the extent of the ties to Ireland would need to be 'overwhelming' to outweigh the entitlement of the State to control entry into its territory, in the circumstances where the applicants had had no right to be in the State since 2010. Charleton J discerned a number of legal principles from the ECHR case law, including that 'those who create uncertainty as to their status within the country to which they migrate, by claiming asylum rights that are unfounded, cannot rely on mere presence to invoke Article 8 rights'.[77] He could not find any evidence that the minister's findings were adverse to any of these principles.

The Court of Appeal followed a similar rationale—if a somewhat different line of reasoning—in *CI v Minister for Justice and Equality*[78] and *Dos Santos v Minister for Justice and Equality*,[79] both cases in which the elements of private life had been created during a period of 'precarious' residence in the State (the applicants in *CI* were unsuccessful Nigerian asylum applicants; and those in *Dos Santos* were a Brazilian man with an expired work permit and his wife and five children). On the Convention arguments made by the applicants in both cases, Finlay Geoghegan J drew a distinction between the nature of the consideration of the private life rights of settled migrants and those in the State unlawfully, focusing on the nature of the private life rights protected by Article 8 in each case. She noted that there was no ECtHR decision directly on the question of whether asylum seekers or irregular migrants can enjoy the type of private life experienced by settled migrants, in terms of integration into the State and specific social ties formed. Drawing on *Nnaynzi v UK*,[80] *Bensaid v UK*[81] and *Balogun v UK*,[82] as well as applying the five-step test laid down in the House of Lords decision in *R (Razgar) v Home Secretary*,[83] she found that in the case of residents without a legal right to reside, while the Court could take into account private life in the sense of ties established within the State, this would carry little weight in the overall balancing exercise. The most important question was whether the applicants' broader private life right to physical and moral integrity, and ability to form relationships, would be disproportionately interfered with by the deportation, such as to engage the operation of Article 8. In this case, a proportionality analysis was not required as the Court of

[76] Judgments of MacMenamin J and Charleton J (with whom Laffoy J concurred on the substantive issues).
[77] Para 35.
[78] *CI v Minister for Justice and Equality* [2015] IECA 192.
[79] *Dos Santos v Minister for Justice and Equality* [2015] IECA 210.
[80] *Nnaynzi v UK* (2008) 47 EHRR 18.
[81] *Bensaid v UK* (2001) 33 EHRR 10.
[82] *Balogun v UK* App no 60286/09 (ECHR, 10 April 2012).
[83] *R (Razgar) v Home Secretary* [2004] 2 AC 368.

Appeal found that the decision of the minister that the consequences of deportation were not of sufficient gravity to potentially engage Article 8 was fair.

It will be almost impossible for Article 8 private life claims to reach the high threshold set out in these cases. Following *Dos Santos* and *CI*, applicants without a legal permission to remain appear to face two obstacles. First, they must show that deportation will have consequences of sufficient gravity to potentially engage Article 8. Invoking *Bensaid* and *Nnyanzi*, the Court of Appeal found that this would require 'wholly exceptional circumstances' in the case of persons who were never lawfully allowed to reside in the State except for the purposes of pursuing an asylum claim. Thus, the Court seemed to find that while settled migrants can argue that their private life within the State is ruptured by the expulsion, more short-term migrants on specific-purpose visas, asylum seekers, or those who are undocumented are essentially confined to claims based on how their broad right to private life in the country of expulsion will be affected. This idea seems to be unrelated to ECHR case law and is an 'innovation' of the Irish Court of Appeal here. In subsequent cases involving the Article 8 private and family rights of international students to remain in Ireland, conflicting judgments were delivered by the High Court,[84] illustrating the continuing uncertainty around the issue of the 'engagement' of Article 8 and the threshold question of whether these rights apply in the case of those with precarious residence status. The Court of Appeal was again called upon to determine the matter,[85] and it clarified (among other things):

1. The situation of those with a subsisting permission to remain was different from that of irregular migrants, asylum seekers or failed asylum seekers such as the applicants in *PO*, *CI* and *Dos Santos*.
2. A decision not to renew a permission of a person who had been in the State lawfully for several years is *capable* of engaging Article 8 of ECHR. The question as to whether, on the particular facts of the application, a decision not to renew the permission would have consequences of such gravity for the person concerned, such that Article 8 is engaged in the sense that term is used in the *Razgar*, *CI* and *Dos Santos* judgments is a matter for determination by the minister subject only to judicial review by the courts.

In these circumstances, the Court of Appeal found, Article 8 rights to private and family life should have been considered by the minister in deciding upon an application for extension of permission to remain made by those who are, or have been, lawfully residing in the State under a student visa.

The Irish case law is difficult to follow, and one suspects that these precedents will continue to cause problems of interpretation and application. The question

[84] *Balchand & Ors v Minister for Justice and Equality* [2016] IEHC 132, para 21; *Luximon v Minister for Justice* [2015] IEHC 227.

[85] *Balchand & Ors v Minister for Justice and Equality* [2016] IECA 382; *Luximon v Minister for Justice* [2016] IECA 522. These cases are under appeal to the Supreme Court.

here is not so much the outcomes-based question of 'would the ECtHR have decided differently?'[86] For the purposes of the present discussion, two points are of note. First, the Supreme Court and Court of Appeal have drawn extensively on the jurisprudence of the ECtHR to justify a restrictive approach to the membership claims of families who have been in the State for considerable periods of time, and which in the *PO* case, included children born and educated in the State. Second, the lack of clarity in the Irish courts' approach reflects deep problems in the ECtHR's jurisprudential approach and reasoning, and the consequential impact on the precedential value of its case law for national authorities applying ECHR obligations. This in turn allows national authorities, in Ireland in this case study, the room to dilute the impact in practice of the Court's overall pioneering attitude to residence security based on private life membership claims.

IV. NATURALISATION WITHOUT MEMBERSHIP? *BIAO V DENMARK* AND THE LIMITED UTILITY OF ARTICLE 14-BASED ARGUMENTS

Having identified some of the limitations of the ECHR case law on residence security decided under Article 8, I will now turn to the question of equal treatment. The applicability and role of anti-discrimination provisions in the context of immigration measures is long debated, with the scope of the principle of non-discrimination on the grounds of race and nationality among the central questions.[87] A classic example of the limitations of the principle of equal treatment in the field of immigration is found in the EU Race Equality Directive, which,

> does not cover difference of treatment based on nationality and is without prejudice to provisions and conditions relating to the entry into and residence of third-country nationals and stateless persons on the territory of Member States, and to any treatment which arises from the legal status of the third-country nationals and stateless persons concerned.[88]

For its part, the record of the ECtHR in upholding the principle of equal treatment for migrants, particularly in the area of immigration law, has been mixed.

[86] The Court of Appeal in *CI and Dos Santos* certainly did not consider cases which might have been more favourable to those in the country illegally—*Slivenko and Sisojeva* (nn 69, 70), for example. It also did not consider that in *Balogun* (n 45), the Court effectively overlooked defects in the applicant's immigration status. See the detailed examination of these doctrinal questions in A McMahon, 'The Right to Respect for Private Life under Article 8 ECHR—the Irish cases of Dos Santos and CI' (*European Database of Asylum Law Blog*, 18 March 2016): www.asylumlawdatabase.eu/en/journal/right-respect-private-life-under-article-8-echr-%E2%80%93-irish-cases-dos-santos-and-ci.

[87] See, eg, M-B Dembour, 'Still Silencing the Racism Suffered by Migrants—The Limits of Current Developments under Article 14 ECHR' (2009) 11 *European Journal of Migration and Law* 221; M-B Dembour, '*Gaygusuz* Revisited: The Limits of the European Court of Human Rights' Equality Agenda' (2012) 12 *Human Rights Law Review* 689.

[88] Council Directive 2000/43/EC of 29 June 2000 implementing the principle of equal treatment between persons irrespective of racial or ethnic origin, Art 3(2).

In the field of social protection, the ECtHR has confirmed that 'very weighty reasons would have to be put forward ... before the Court could regard a difference of treatment based exclusively on the ground of nationality as compatible with the Convention'.[89] In *Gaygusuz v Austria*[90] and subsequent cases,[91] the Court confirmed the applicability of Article 14 ECHR, which provides for non-discrimination (in respect of the rights set out in the Convention) 'on any ground such as sex, race, colour, language, religion, political or other opinion, national or social origin, association with a national minority, property, birth or other status'. In the education segregation cases involving Roma children, the Court has emphasised that 'no difference in treatment based exclusively or to a decisive extent on a person's ethnic origin is capable of being justified in a contemporary democratic society'.[92]

By contrast, a restrictive approach has been taken to Article 14 discrimination in cases involving immigration rules: an approach which can be traced to the foundational principle of the Court's immigration jurisprudence that 'a State has the right to control the entry of non-nationals into its territory'. In the seminal case of *Abdulaziz, Balkandali and Cabales v The United Kingdom* (ABC),[93] the applicants' claim that the UK's immigration rules were discriminatory on the grounds of sex because they introduced stricter conditions for husbands to join their wives than vice versa was upheld by the Court. However, the claim that the rules constituted discrimination on the grounds of race and/or ethnicity because they disproportionately applied to immigrants from the New Commonwealth and Pakistan (in spite of being neutrally formulated) was rejected. One of the applicants was a UK citizen and she also argued that she had been discriminated against on the grounds of birth. This claim was rejected by the Court, which stated that '(t)here are general persuasive social reasons for giving special treatment to those whose links with a country stem from birth within it'.[94]

Against this background, the case of *Biao v Denmark* raised some stark questions on the limits of Article 14 in the immigration context. At issue here were Danish rules which provided that spousal family reunion could be granted only if both spouses were over 24 years of age and their aggregate ties to Denmark were stronger than the spouses' attachment to any other country (the 'attachment requirement'). The rules provided an exemption for persons who had held Danish

[89] *Gaygusuz v Austria* App no 17371/90 (ECHR, 16 Sept 1996) para 42.

[90] ibid.

[91] Including *Koua Poirrez v France*, App no 40892/98, § 46, ECHR 2003-X; *Andrejeva v Latvia* [GC], App no 55707/00, § 87, ECHR 2009; and *Ponomaryovi v Bulgaria*, App no 5335/05, § 52, ECHR 2011.

[92] *DH and Others v the Czech Republic* [GC] App no 57325/00, ECHR 2007-IV; *Sampanis and Others v Greece* App no 32526/05 (ECHR, 5 June 2008); *Oršuš and Others v Croatia* [GC] App no 15766/03, ECHR 2010- II; *Sampani and Others v Greece* App no 59608/09 (ECHR, 11 December 2012); *Horvath and Kiss v Hungary* App no 11146/11 (ECHR, 29 January 2013; and *Lavida and Others v Greece* App no 7973/10, (ECHR, 30 May 2013).

[93] *Abdulaziz, Balkandali and Cabales v The United Kingdom (ABC)* (1985) EHRR 471.

[94] Para 88.

citizenship for at least 28 years (the '28-year rule'). The applicants in this case were a Ghana-born, naturalised Danish citizen and his Ghanaian wife, who had been refused reunification. They argued that the 28-year rule indirectly discriminated against naturalised citizens on the basis of ethnicity, as they would have to wait a much longer period of time than citizens by birth until they could satisfy the 28-year requirement. The Chamber found no violation of either Article 8 alone or Article 14 in conjunction with Article 8, drawing extensively on the previous approach of the Court in *ABC*. The Grand Chamber overturned this finding to hold that Article 14 in conjunction with Article 8 was violated. It found that the 28-year rule constituted indirect discrimination, which the government had failed to justify by reference to compelling or very weighty reasons, unrelated to ethnic origin. The case is of interest from a number of perspectives, including the general principle of non-discrimination between citizens;[95] its clarification of some notions in the ECtHR's case law involving the distinction between direct and indirect discrimination;[96] and the application of indirect race discrimination outside the education segregation domain; and its apparent turn away from the *ABC* approach to discrimination between citizens on the basis of birth.[97] Here, I am interested in exploring what the *Biao* judgment tells us about the limits of the ECtHR's Article 14 jurisprudence in immigration cases, as well the Court's approach to the issues surrounding 'attachment' and membership thrown up by the facts.

The significance of the *Biao* judgment should not be underestimated, and the reasoning of the Court includes many positive elements. Its overall impact is strengthened by the fact that the majority does not get bogged down in the question of whether the 28-year rule pursued a legitimate aim, but rather re-emphasises that the key question for the Court is whether there are compelling and weighty reasons for the differential treatment in question.[98] It is also clear that stereotypes, such as those based on the integration potential of certain groups and marriage patterns of migrants, cannot constitute a compelling or weighty reason that would justify discrimination, including on the basis of ethnic origin.[99] Here, the 'general biased assumptions'[100] on which the preparatory work for the legislation were based included the following statement:

> With resident aliens and Danish nationals of foreign extraction it is a widespread marriage pattern to marry a person from their country of origin, among other reasons

[95] E Ersbøll, '*Biao v Denmark*; Discrimination among Nationals': eudo-citizenship.eu/commentaries/citizenship-blog/1646-biao-v-denmark-discrimination-among-nationals.

[96] M Moschel, 'The Strasbourg Court and Indirect Race Discrimination: Going Beyond the Education Domain' (2017) 80 *MLR* 121.

[97] KM de Vries, 'Rewriting *Abdulaziz*: The ECtHR Grand Chamber's Ruling in Biao v Denmark' (2016) 18 *European Journal of Migration and Law* 467.

[98] Para 121.

[99] Para 126.

[100] ibid.

> owing to parental pressure. This pattern contributes to the retention of these persons in a situation where they, more than others, experience problems of isolation and maladjustment in relation to Danish society.[101]

In addition to refusing to focus on the question of a legitimate aim, the Court does not require that discriminatory intent be proven in a case involving indirectly discriminatory rules. As Moschel notes, the Court seems more willing than in previous case law to look behind apparently neutral measures to consider whether is racial discrimination at play.[102] This could lead to a (welcome) comprehensive discrimination analysis of other apparently neutral civic integration and family reunification measures in the future.

Nonetheless, the judgment of the majority of the Grand Chamber in *Biao* could sow the seeds of future difficulties for migrants attempting to rely on Article 14 to challenge discriminatory immigration rules. First, the spectre of doctrinal uncertainty once again haunts the case law. The Grand Chamber sidestepped the finding in *ABC* that 'there are general persuasive reasons for giving special treatment to those whose links with a country stem from birth within it'. While it did not apply this principle in *Biao*, it did not overrule the *ABC* approach either, preferring to focus on its central message that distinctions in treatment between citizens must have compelling and weighty justification. While generalised stereotypes of migrants or particular ethnic groups are clearly not accepted by the Court, it remains an open question as to what could constitute a sufficiently compelling reason. All this leaves room for uncertain, or even restrictive, interpretations of the judgment.

Finally, the Court does not assess the legality of the attachment requirement itself, focusing rather on the 28-year rule exemption. Indeed, Article 8 would perhaps be the more appropriate doctrinal yardstick against which to assess the attachment requirement. However, it is notable that the Court does not reveal any discomfort with the basic principle of having an attachment requirement as part of the test for family reunification. In fact, if one refers back to the discussion of the Court's case law above, the idea of an assessment of ties to both countries is consistent with the Court's own theoretical approach. Also in line with its own previous pronouncements, the Court notes that integration or attachment is not measured by simple time of residence or nationality alone: it has a qualitative dimension.[103] It criticises the 'speculative arguments'[104] as to the time when the Danish national has created such strong ties with Denmark that reunification with a foreign spouse has a prospect of being successful from an integration perspective. In the view of the Grand Chamber, 'the answer to this question

[101] Reproduced at para 106 of the judgment.
[102] Moschel (n 96) 131.
[103] Para 125.
[104] ibid.

cannot … depend solely on the length of nationality'.[105] In this case, this approach benefitted Mr Biao: he had already proven knowledge of the Danish language and society in his application for naturalisation, as well as self-sufficiency. However, as mentioned above, these types of assessments of integration in the judicial context inherently place the focus on the individual, making it hard to measure the impact of the wider policy framework, and the political and socio-economic climate on individual integration. In this way, as argued above in the Article 8 expulsion context, the Court's position could be viewed as part of the broader legal and theoretical framework of civic integration, with its stigmatising effects for migrant groups.

V. CONCLUSION

This chapter has tried to look beyond the straightforward legal doctrinal implications of the ECtHR's case law on residence security and equal treatment, to examine the underlying conception of membership employed by the Strasbourg Court. This is not an easy task. It has argued that despite the avant-garde nature of the Court's decisions in the sphere of Article 8 and private life, the case law has been far from transformative, particularly when viewed in the light of the residence-as-membership model advocated by Carens. Doctrinal uncertainty and a problematic assessment of integration prevail—even in the most up-to-date, and broadly welcomed, anti-discrimination judgment of the Grand Chamber in *Biao v Denmark*. In addition, the ECtHR's approach is defective because it fails to acknowledge that 'the receiving society is the stronger partner in integration processes'[106] and that it is the receiving society which dictates the terms and conditions that will determine how immigrants can live in that society.[107]

The challenges for courts involved in assessing integration, and in developing a coherent approach to the requirements of societal membership, are not unique to the ECtHR. EU law seems to encompass multiple visions of integration depending on the context and the group of mobile persons in question.[108] In chapter 13, de Vries discusses in detail the 'integration exception' introduced by the ECJ, whereby Member States are given considerable latitude to set integration requirements as conditions for equal treatment of third-country nationals.[109] As mentioned above, the ECJ seems to have embraced a contextual approach to migrant integration, in contrast to the equality-based paradigm adopted to the question of Union citizens.[110]

[105] ibid.

[106] Jesse, *The Civic Citizens of Europe* (n 2) 361.

[107] ibid.

[108] Murphy, *Immigration, Integration and the Law* (n 25) ch 4.

[109] KM de Vries 'The Integration Exception: A New Limit to Social Rights of Third-Country Nationals in EU Law?', chapter 14, this volume.

[110] K Groenendijk, 'Legal Concepts of Integration in EU Migration Law' (2004) 6 *European Journal of Migration and Law* 111; Thym, 'Towards a Contextual Conception of Social Integration' (n 35); Murphy, *Immigration, Integration and the Law* (n 25) ch 4.

Of course, courts are not necessarily concerned with the theoretical bases of their decisions, rather with resolving a specific legal issue or achieving justice in a particular case. Nonetheless, given that language and civic integration requirements constitute an increasingly important part of migration law, courts at both the domestic and supranational levels will continue to be required to explore these complex social questions. For the ECtHR, the Article 8 balancing test appears to be here to stay. In the view of this author, in developing a legal approach to the open-ended and contested concept of 'integration', the Strasbourg Court ought to have more regard for the universalist foundations of the ECHR, and be mindful of the potentially stigmatising messages which its case law sends.

15

Conclusion: The Non-Simultaneous Evolution of Citizens' Rights

DORA KOSTAKOPOULOU AND DANIEL THYM

I. THE NON-SIMULTANEITY OF THE SIMULTANEOUS

UNION CITIZENSHIP is a pivotal component of the European Union's constitutional heritage and, yet, the chapters in this volume expose that its legal, political and social contours remain surprisingly fragile. Nothing has been inevitable in the evolution of supranational citizens' rights. In this conclusion, we want to demonstrate, on the basis of the arguments put forward by the contributors to this project, that the inherent instability can be rationalised as an expression of non-simultaneity. In doing so, we shall employ the concept of non-simultaneity in a threefold manner: as a heuristic device to describe the interaction between judicial interpretation and wider political or social processes (below II); as a diagnostic tool to illuminate the position of the Court of Justice (ECJ) on social benefits (III); and as a projective instrument to show how 'alternate takes' may direct the future evolution of supranational citizenship beyond the free movement paradigm (IV).

The concept of non-simultaneity, often used in the rhetorical phrase 'the simultaneity of the of the non-simultaneous' (German: 'Ungleichzeitigkeit des Gleichzeitigen'), is more than a play on words. It gained popularity through its use by philosopher Ernst Bloch, who coined it as a catchword in his cultural theory rejecting the rational impulse of historical teleology.[1] Bloch emphasised the coexistence of heterogeneous stages of social and economic tensions that may result in non-synchronous contradictions propelling the evolution of a given society in diverse directions.[2] In that respect, the concept of non-simultaneity reflects the

[1] See E Bloch, *Tübinger Einleitung in die Philosophie* (Frankfurt am Main, Suhrkamp, 1964) building on the terminology of the cultural historian W Pinder, *Das Problem der Generationen in der Kunstgeschichte Europa* (Frankfurt, Frankfurter Verlagsanstalt, 1926).

[2] E Bloch, *Erbschaft dieser Zeit* (Frankfurt am Main, Suhrkamp, 1962), which was published first in 1935, applied the concept initially to rationalise the collapse of Germany's Weimar Republic into Nazi Dictatorship.

basic message of postmodern deconstruction theory—highlighted in the introduction to this book—that values and concepts exhibit a synthesised character[3] and that institutions and practices influence their evolution.[4] This book about 'Questioning EU Citizenship' set out to describe and explain these processes.

This approach can be particularly meaningful in understanding the evolution of Union citizenship, whose two components—the supranational legal order and the citizenship idea—exhibit an in-built conceptual open-endedness. The chapters in this volume show that, notwithstanding the modernist vision of a quasi-linear move towards an 'ever closer union'[5] in the self-description of the European project, the legal foundations of Union citizenship provide a perfect backdrop against which to deconstruct the non-simultaneous forces behind the evolution of the European project. The Brexit referendum and ongoing public debates about migration highlight tangible expressions of a fundamental uncertainty at the heart of supranational citizenship, which replaces the modernist assumption of lineal progress by a 'multiversum'[6] of non-simultaneity. The initial designation of European Union (EU) citizenship as destined to become a 'fundamental status' (as the ECJ famously did in the early years of its groundbreaking citizenship judgments)[7] cannot prevent countervailing forces from complicating the realisation of this promise at a later stage.

The non-simultaneous evolution of supranational citizens' rights is defined, amongst other factors, by a twofold uncertainty of the relative weight of (con) federal elements in the construction of Europe and the conceptual openness of the citizenship ideal. These two uncertainties define the enquiry undertaken throughout the chapters in this book. The outcome of the Brexit referendum presents itself as a radical expression of a centripetal force which has always existed, favouring a confederal structure and accepting that the primary allegiance of citizens lies with solidary communities at national level.[8] This 'camp' has recently gathered momentum, as debates about lessons to be drawn from the euro crisis and—in the domain of EU citizenship—disputes about transnational access to social benefits, demonstrate. Chapters in this book chronicle this trend from different angles, but they do not limit themselves to passively observing this change of direction. Rather, they chart underlying reasons, which will be brought together below.

[3] See the Introduction by D Thym, section II.

[4] See D Kostakopoulou, 'Ideas, Norms and European Citizenship' (2005) 68 *MLR* 233; and D Kostakopoulou, 'Co-Creating European Union Citizenship' (2012/13) 15 *Cambridge Yearbook of European Legal Studies* 255, 259–66.

[5] Recital 1 of the preamble of the original EEC Treaty of 1957, the present Treaty on the Functioning of the European Union, and the Charter of Fundamental Rights.

[6] Bloch, Tübinger Einleitung in die Philosophie (n 1).

[7] ECJ, C-184/99 *Grzelczyk*, EU:C:2001:458, para 31.

[8] *cf* U Haltern, 'On Finality' in A von Bogdandy and J Bast (eds), *Principles of European Constitutional Law*, 2nd edn (Oxford, Hart Publishing, 2009); and, in the context of Union citizenship, R Bellamy, 'Evaluating Union Citizenship: Belonging, Rights and Participation within the EU' (2008) 12 *Citizenship Studies* 597.

For the purposes of this book, the conceptual uncertainty stretches further than the amorphous (con)federal structure of the EU. As mentioned in the introduction, the citizenship concept is defined by an in-built ambiguity: citizens' rights can serve, like human rights norms, as channels to substantiate legal debates with normative arguments.[9] The normative visibility of the citizenship ideal explains why its meaning is bound to be contested. In particular, one crucial element of Union citizenship is a subject of modern controversy, namely transnational mobility across borders (and, again, public discourse prior to the Brexit referendum provided an extreme expression of a general trend).[10] This is why several chapters in this volume take up broader debates about transnational mobility of third-country nationals in the EU and demonstrate, in doing so, striking conceptual and legal similarities with discussions about core features of Union citizenship.

II. HOW TO EXPLAIN THE CHANGE IN THE CASE LAW

In chapter two, Susanne Schmidt presents empirical data showing that publications written by legal academics on Union citizenship coincide with the number of corresponding court judgments. This is beneficial as an expression of academic division of labour, but can be problematic if the legal analysis of citizens' rights becomes self-referential. A holistic approach requires a broader outlook on how to study constitutional concepts such as Union citizenship and their judicial interpretation.[11] This is why the chapters in this volume have applied mixed methods to highlight factors which may explain the change in the ECJ's citizenship case law. Arguments put forward throughout the book reaffirm general hypotheses about the role of courts in democratic constitutional systems, while further revealing a number of specificities regarding Union citizenship. This section brings together the arguments on how to explain the change in the case law at a medium level of abstraction. The next section will focus on social benefits.

An examination of relations with political institutions is crucial for any analysis of constitutional courts, which can, like the ECJ, review the legality of legislative choices.[12] It is well established that judges in Luxembourg benefit from a privileged institutional position, since they are well protected against direct attempts at reversing the impact of specific rulings and against curbing their role

[9] See the introduction, this volume, section II; and D Kostakopoulou, *The Future Governance of Citizenship* (Cambridge, Cambridge University Press, 2008).

[10] While debates about immigration often serve as a projection sphere for wider unease concerning the effects of globalisation and are regrettably employed by populist parties with xenophobic intentions, they are also concerned with what people perceive, rightly or wrongly, as the effects of immigration for social cohesion, the labour market or public services; see S Castles et al, *The Age of Migration*, 5th edn (Basingstoke, Palgrave Macmillan, 2013) 307–12.

[11] See, again, the introduction to this volume, section IV.

[12] By way of example, see A Stone Sweet, 'The European Court of Justice' in P Craig and G de Búrca (eds), *The Evolution of EU Law*, 2nd edn (Oxford, Oxford University Press, 2011).

more generally.[13] That is not to say, however, that judges regularly ignore the position of the legislature or the preferences of political actors, including the Member States; empirical surveys show that this is not generally the case.[14] Against this background, the more restrictive recent twist of the case law on Union citizenship may be perceived as a pronounced form of judicial deference to the criticism of several powerful Member States, including the British Government. Various contributors to this volume have unearthed corresponding evidence which confirms this and will be taken up in more detail in the following section on social benefits. It might be too simple, however, to present the change in the case law as a response solely to political pressure. There are other factors at play.

Academics whose background is not in law and who analyse the position of judges often perceive the law as a dependent variable, the interpretation of which is influenced by extralegal factors. While we acknowledge the inherent open-endedness of constitutional reasoning, it should be noted, nonetheless, that the ECJ strives for an internal coherence of its case law. It does so by means of justifying the outcome with recourse to traditional styles of argumentation, mirroring the tradition of continental civil law jurisdictions.[15] If this is correct, the in-built ambiguity of legal rules on Union citizenship is an important factor that has contributed to the restrictive approach on the part of judges in Luxembourg.[16] Remember that Article 21 of the Treaty on the Functioning of the European Union (TFEU) concerning the freedom of movement of those who do not work has been phrased as 'subject to … limitations and conditions' ever since its introduction and that the EU legislature refrained from granting unambiguous equal treatment regarding access to social benefits when adopting Directive 2004/38/EC (see chapter nine by Ferdinand Wollenschläger, as well chapter ten by Paul Minderhoud and Sandra Mantu). The ECJ may have previously exploited this in-built ambiguity to enhance citizens' rights; however more recently it has moved in the opposite direction. In a telling expression of judicial deference to a supposedly clear will of the legislature, Advocate General Wathelet justified his Opinion in

[13] See D Kelemen, 'The Political Foundations of Judicial Independence in the European Union' (2012) 19 *Journal of European Public Policy* 43; and M Dawson, 'The Political Face of Judicial Activism' in M Dawson et al (eds), *Judicial Activism at the European Court of Justice: Causes, Responses and Solutions* (Cheltenham, Edward Elgar, 2013) 13–24.

[14] For relations with the EU legislature, see D Martinsen, *An Ever More Powerful Court? The Political Constraints of Legal Integration in the European Union* (Oxford, Oxford University Press, 2016); and for the interaction with the Member States, see C Carrubba and G Matthew, *International Courts and the Performance of International Agreements: A General Theory with Evidence from the European Union* (Cambridge, Cambridge University Press, 2014); in addition to the quantitative surveys, see the qualitative analysis by V Hatzopoulos, 'Actively Talking to Each Other: The Court and the Political Institutions' in M Dawson et al (eds), *Judicial Activism at the European Court of Justice* (Cheltenham, Edward Elgar, 2013) 112 et seq.

[15] See G Beck, *The Legal Reasoning of the Court of Justice of the EU* (Oxford, Hart Publishing, 2012); and J Bomhoff, 'Perfectionism in EU Law' (2014) 12 *Cambridge Yearbook of European Legal Studies* 75.

[16] See also T Horsley, 'Reflections on the Role of the Court of Justice as the "Motor" of European Integration' (2013) 50 *CML Rev* 931, 941–63.

Dano as an 'inevitable consequence of Directive 2004/38'.[17] This may be no coincidence given his service as Minister of Justice for Belgium—he is merely one of several reporting judges and Advocates General in recent judgments with a background in politics (see chapter five by Urška Šadl and Suvi Sankari).

A common thread running through many chapters in this volume is the path dependency of the case law, which builds on earlier judgments and takes them further in light of new developments.[18] While Susanne Schmidt highlights the constitutional implications of this, others concentrate on the internal consistency of judicial argument (see the chapter four by Stephanie Reynolds; chapter ten by Paul Minderhoud and Sandra Mantu; chapter eleven by Niamh Nic Shuibhne; and chapter twelve by Sara Iglesias Sánchez). In this context, Urška Šadl and Suvi Sankari demonstrate how the current, more restrictive outcome is based on an argumentative move from techniques focusing on the telos (purpose) and constitutional principles (human rights, significance of free movement) to those paying closer attention to the wording, general scheme and drafting history. The latter argumentative techniques traditionally signal greater deference to the legislature.[19] Such shift in the style of argumentation tends not to come out of the blue; strong incentives are required to overcome the path dependency of judicial argument.[20] Arguably, there were such incentives for the ECJ.

A first set of incentives relates to debates prior to the Brexit referendum and transnational access to social benefits, as discussed below. While many academic debates on Union citizenship revolve around free movement, this volume encourages a broader outlook, considering the position of third-country nationals under EU law.[21] The overlap relates to public debates and the dissemination of legal concepts. First, the general public will not always distinguish between Union citizens and other foreigners—an overlap the British Government willingly exploited when branding Union citizens as 'migrants' and warning against instances of 'benefits tourism', thereby directing public unease with immigration more generally against the European Union.[22] In this respect, a critical stance on Union citizenship may be a side-effect of the salience of immigration-related topics in public

[17] AG Wathelet, *Dano* C-333/13, EU:C:2014:384, paras 93 and 103 et seq; similarly ECJ, *Dano* C-333/13, EU:C:2014:2358, para 77.

[18] See, generally, M Jacob, Precedents and Case-Based Reasoning in the European Court of Justice: Unfinished Business (Cambridge, Cambridge University Press, 2014).

[19] See also D Thym, 'The Elusive Limits of Solidarity: Residence Rights of and Social Benefits for Economically Inactive Union Citizens' (2015) 52 *CML Rev* 17, 22–25; and N Nic Shuibhne, 'Limits Rising, Duties Ascending: The Changing Legal Shape of Union Citizenship' (2015) 52 *CML Rev* 889.

[20] See A Stone Sweet, 'Path Dependence, Precedent, and Judicial Power' in M Shapiro and A Stone Sweet (eds), *On Law, Politics, and Judicialization* (Oxford, Oxford University Press, 2002); and, in the context of EU citizenship, S Schmidt, 'Who Cares About Nationality? The Path-Dependent Case Law of the ECJ from Goods to Citizens' (2012) 19 *Journal of European Public Policy* 8.

[21] Generally on the interaction of both sets of rules D Thym, 'EU Migration Policy and its Constitutional Rationale: A Cosmopolitan Outlook' (2013) 50 *CML Rev* 709.

[22] J Shaw and N Miller, 'When Legal Worlds Cllide: An Exploration of What Happens when EU Free Movement Law meets UK Immigration Law' (2013) 38 *EL Rev* 137.

debates (see chapter eight by Francesca Strumia). Second, there is a conceptual overlap in the definition of membership rights, which fluctuates between equality-based reasoning and reasoning grounded on affiliation (see chapter fourteen by Clíodhna Murphy; and chapter six by Daniel Thym). This connection is tangible when considering the 'integration' yardstick, which takes centre stage in legal rules and corresponding case law on Union citizens and third-country nationals (see chapter thirteen by Karin De Vries).

Other contextual factors which might have motivated the Court include the implications of the euro crisis and the corresponding unease about the future direction of the European project at a time of resurging national self-confidence (see chapter eight by Francesca Strumia and chapter six by Daniel Thym). It is unsurprising that citizens' rights are affected by wider unease at the European project. As mentioned in the introduction, Union citizenship was always an integral part of attempts to forge some sort of federal union. Michael Dougan showed this impetus may explain the noteworthy parallelism between, on the one hand, the rise and fall of the Constitutional Treaty and, on the other, the switch from ambitious citizenship rulings to a cautious approach.[23] Flatly denying equal treatment to jobseekers and those without a right to reside in *Alimanovic* and *Dano* has brought that development full circle. This can be rationalised, as Strumia and Thym argue in their chapters, as an expression of the ECJ's loss of confidence in the potential of integration through law.

This decline of legally driven modification of social and economic realities suits the concept of non-simultaneity, which rejects the modernist vision of gradual progress towards a pre-defined better future. Critical voices, which have always been present, can now gain the upper hand and direct the interpretation of the law in a different direction. That is not to say that legal interpretation reflects only broader debates, as the reverse effect can also occur. Legal rules, court judgments and academic treatises may partake in the constant reconstruction of individual and collective identities, but they must be embedded into social structures and political life to influence patterns of identification[24]—something the free movement provisions have achieved only to a limited extent (see chapter seven by Ettore Recchi). Moreover, Recchi asserts the identificatory nexus between mobility and the EU may result in a backlash when the immobile (who also tend to be less economically well-off) associate mobility with the transnational elite and direct their opposition, as a result, at the European project.[25] This hypothesis is of intuitive plausibility in light of the Brexit referendum and attacks against the EU by populist parties across Europe.

[23] See M Dougan, 'The Bubble that Burst' in M Adams et al (eds), *Judging Europe's Judges: The Legitimacy of the Case Law of the European Court of Justice* (Oxford, Hart Publishing, 2013).

[24] See S Benhabib *The Rights of Others: Aliens, Residents, and Citizens* (Cambridge, Cambridge University Press, 2004) ch 5; and F Michelman, 'Law's Republic' (1988) 97 *Yale Law Journal* 1493.

[25] See also M Everson, 'A Citizenship in Movement' (2014) 15 *German Law Journal* 965.

While such criticism may define the delicate state of Union citizenship at this juncture, the status quo need not persist indefinitely. Alternative takes are possible, as considered in the final section. In any case, the contributions to this volume are a powerful reminder that legal academics should be careful not to overestimate the impact of legal rules and corresponding court judgments. If this is correct, legal academics must pursue a contextual analysis, and may adopt—as with many chapters in this volume—a critical stance exploring the normative achievements *and* deficits of Union law.[26] The evolution of citizens' rights will not be a linear process which will make the world a better place. Alternate takes, including retrogression and stalemates, coexist simultaneously.

III. SOCIAL BENEFITS AND THE EMERGENCE OF UNEQUAL CITIZENSHIP

The foregoing discussion demonstrated that 'generative moments', during which new legal templates or norms are developed, are followed by periods in which consolidation and crystallisation of legal developments takes place, as well as by periods in which backsliding occurs. The economic crisis in Europe, coupled with the rise in Euroscepticism and populism in several Member States (epitomised by the Brexit referendum), have had an impact on one area specifically, which is addressed by a number of this volume's contributors: access to social benefits. The ECJ recognised Member States as actors wielding significant influence in the regulation of the grant of social assistance. Their interests, be they real or discursive, in reducing migration and settlement of non-economically active EU citizens and jobseekers who might have to rely on short-term public assistance to resume full economic activity, have recently been accorded priority over the need to give EU citizenship a more universal and inclusive scope. This has been a tactical choice and a response to challenging extrinsic factors, including the pressure exerted by the UK Government in the pre-Brexit landscape (see chapter four by Stephanie Reynolds); however it also reflects the broader developments discussed above. This section will focus on factors which influenced the change of direction in the case law on access to social benefits.

First, it is noteworthy that the Court was careful not to appear like a political actor when it drew on Article 24(2) of Directive 2004/38 in order to provide reasons justifying the exclusion of economically inactive EU citizens who do not have a right of residence under the Directive, as well as jobseekers, from entitlement to certain special non-contributory cash benefits, so as to avoid becoming a burden on the host State's welfare system (see chapter ten by Paul Minderhoud and Sandra Mantu; and chapter nine by Ferdinand Wollenschläger). These judgments, which are a regression from the Court's case law decided before the entry into

[26] See Editorial Comments, 'The Critical Turn in EU Legal Studies' (2015) 52 *CML Rev* 881; and L Azoulai, 'Solitude, désoeuvrement et conscience critique' (2015) *Politiques européennes* 82, 82–86.

force of Directive 2004/38/EC,[27] ignore constitutional arguments judges might have used to correct the legislature,[28] such as an interpretation of the Directive in light of primary law including the Charter of Fundamental Rights (see chapter eleven by Niamh Nic Shuibhne). Judgments like *Dano* and *Alimanovic* present a marked shift towards doctrinal conservatism. The Court has abandoned earlier attempts to read political visions of a good life and just society into the Treaty notion of Union citizenship.

Concerning access to social benefits, the Court is no longer willing to function as an agent of systemic transformation. This is a manifestation of reflexivity.[29] Interaction of internal and external environments leads to the incorporation of new demands, suggestions and viewpoints— the Court brakes by means of the path dependency described above. The rulings in *García-Nieto*[30] and *Commission v UK*,[31] which were delivered a few weeks before the Brexit referendum on 25 February 2016 and 14 June 2016 respectively, legitimated the closure of national welfare systems against the demands of vulnerable non-national EU citizens and the emergence of lawful residence as an ordering principle of social closure. The 'interest of the states' emerged as a weighty principle out of the interplay between judicial decision-making and economic and socio-political phenomena in certain spatial and temporal contexts. The vulnerability of the ordinary individuals *qua* EU citizens is less important than the demands of national executives who are legitimately concerned about the future of their welfare systems in an age of economic austerity, notwithstanding the absence of tangible evidence supporting any claim of the significant impact of the grant of social benefits to EU citizens on national welfare budgets.[32]

Second, several chapters in this volume identify a difficulty at the heart of the court judgments on free movement and equal treatment: the prevalence of personal circumstances. Their significance is, however, not limited to the ECJ. Rather, it follows the distinction in the EU Treaties between resident statuses demarcating

[27] *cf*, inter alia, ECJ, C-85/96 *Martínez Sala*, EU:C:1998:217; ECJ, C-456/02 *Trojani*, EU:C:2004:488; and ECJ, C-138/02 *Collins*, EU:C:2004:172.

[28] See M Dougan, 'The Constitutional Dimension to the Case Law on Union Citizenship' (2006) 31 *EL Rev* 613.

[29] In 1990 Giddens referred to 'institutional reflexivity', that is, an outcome which is the result of a reflection on the dynamics surrounding an institution and its environment; see also D Kostakopoulou, 'Nested "Old" and "New" Citizenships in the EU: Bringing Forth the Complexity' (1999) 5 *Columbia Journal of European Law* 389; and D Kostakopoulou, *Citizenship, Identity and Immigration in the European Union: Between Past and Future* (Manchester, Manchester University Press, 2001).

[30] ECJ, C-299/14 *García-Nieto et al*, EU:C:2016:114.

[31] ECJ, C-308/14 Commission v United Kingdom, EU:C:2016:436.

[32] C Giulietti et al have shown that the link between social benefits and migration in the EU is not well established; *cf* C Giulietti et al 'Unemployment Benefits and Immigration. Evidence from the EU' (2010) *IZA Discussion Paper* no 6075; in the UK, the Government estimated that only 1% of EU citizens who were jobseekers were claiming Housing Benefit; *cf* ibid, 'The Removal of Housing Benefit from EEA Jobseekers. Impact Assessment' (27 February 2014).

an uneven distribution of rights and opportunities—a distinction Kochenov aptly describes as a 'medieval' citizenship of personal circumstance. As Verschueren has noted, 'EU citizenship is not for the poor'.[33] Human vulnerability and the needs of EU citizens to 'lead a life in keeping with human dignity'[34] are now viewed as less important than the Member States' reasoning. The poor are not permitted full institutional participation; their free movement options are restricted and their settlement in other Member States is discouraged.[35] This result stands in a striking contrast to the protective stance of the early internal market case law, which interpreted the free movement of workers in an inclusive manner so as to enhance the social protection of those engaged in marginal economic activities.[36] In chapter four, Stephanie Reynolds shows that we can even observe feedback loops between the more recent citizenship rulings and the internal market case law whereby the principled stance in favour of equal treatment of workers is undermined by a novel focus on personal circumstances.

Bringing together the arguments made by various authors, it can be argued that the emphasis placed on personal circumstances in both the legal rules and the ECJ case law has led to a breaking point preventing Union citizenship from achieving broader constitutional potential in the field of social benefits. There are several difficulties which stem from the salience of personal circumstances. At the macro level, the detailed prescription in earlier citizenship case law can result in an 'over-constitutionalisation', leaving little room for political contest and choice, and thereby destabilising the legitimacy structure of the European project (see chapter two by Susanne Schmidt).

Third, the ECJ's focus on personal circumstances when deciding individual cases can result in practical difficulties if domestic authorities struggle to apply the ECJ's parameters. This is complicated by the fact that the ECJ is not consistent when deciding which factors are to be decisive.[37] Practical complications were one element that motivated the ECJ to pursue a strict line in *Alimanovic* when it justified the restrictive outcome without the need for an individualised assessment as providing 'a significant level of legal certainty and transparency'.[38] This was in contrast to the widespread confusion among domestic authorities and courts about the practical implications of earlier rulings (see chapter ten by Paul Minderhoud and Sandra Mantu). Observers should be careful not to overestimate the power of

[33] H Verschueren, 'Free Movement of EU Citizens: Also for the Poor' (21st International Conference of Europeanists, Washington DC, 14–16 March 2014).

[34] ECJ, C-67/14 *Alimanovic*, EU:C:2015:597, para 45.

[35] See C O'Brien, 'Civis Capitalist Sum. Class as the New Guiding Principle of EU Free Movement Rights', (2016) 53 *CML Rev* 937.

[36] On cases such as *Levin*, *Kempf* and *Raulin*, see S Kadelbach, 'Union Citizenship' in A von Bogdandy and J Bast (eds), *Principles of European Constitutional Law*, 2nd edn (Oxford, Hart Publishing, 2009) 443–77, 449–52.

[37] See Thym, 'The Elusive Limits of Solidarity' (n 19) 45–47.

[38] *Alimanovic* (n 34) para 61.

the ECJ, whose success has always depended on the willingness of domestic actors to follow Luxembourg's guidance.[39]

Most importantly, fourth, the focus on personal circumstances (both in the case law and the EU Treaties) has normative implications, given it contradicts the quality-based foundations of prominent citizenship theories. Union citizenship may be available to all nationals of the Member States as a status de jure, but the legal implications are decidedly differentiated when it comes to free movement and equal treatment (see chapter three by Dimitry Kochenov). There is a fascinating parallel between the situation of Union citizens and third-country nationals, in relation to which the EU legislature and the ECJ have activated an 'integration exception' to justify the (un)equal treatment of third-country nationals in the application of recent immigration directives (see chapter thirteen by Karin de Vries). These legal developments turn the original vocation of equal citizenship as an instrument to overcome disparities on its head when factual differences vindicate the denial of equal treatment rights, thus exacerbating existing disparities. In contemporary EU law, membership rights are not grounded on equality-based reasoning, but on social affiliation (see chapter fourteen by Clíodhna Murphy; and chapter six by Daniel Thym).

The practical and conceptual significance of personal circumstances suggests a more general difficulty. The application of the citizenship concept has always been problematic in the EU, given the concept was developed in the context of the closed nation-state.[40] It was no foregone conclusion that the equality-based reasoning of the national welfare state would be resurrected indiscriminately at supranational level.[41] There were and are different takes at play, particularly considering social citizenship is simultaneously undergoing a profound reconceptualisation at national level.[42] Hybrid statuses are gaining ground (see chapter eight by Francesca Strumia). For several years, the Court of Justice employed citizens' rights as an instrument to counter this trend, but recently it has taken a different path—at least insofar as transnational access to social benefits is concerned.

[39] See G Davies, 'Activism Relocated. The Self-Restraint of the European Court of Justice in its National Context' (2012) 19 *Journal of European Public Policy* 76; and K Alter, 'The European Court's Political Power (1996)' in K Alter (ed), *The European Court's Political Power: Selected Essays* (Oxford, Oxford University Press, 1996) 99–105.

[40] See N Walker, 'The Idea of Constitutional Pluralism' (2002) 65 *MLR* 317, 328–31; and N Walker, 'Postnational Constitutionalism and the Problem of Translation' in JHH Weiler and M Wind (eds), *European Constitutionalism Beyond the State* (Cambridge, Cambridge University Press, 2003).

[41] On different options, see D Kostakopoulou, 'European Union Citizenship: Writing the Future' (2007) 13 *ELJ* 623; and D Kochenov, 'The Essence of EU Citizenship Emerging from the Last Ten Years of Academic Debate' (2013) 62 *ICLQ* 97.

[42] See Z Bauman, 'Freedom from, in and Through the State: TH Marshall's Trinity of Rights Revisited' (2005) 44 *Theoria: A Journal of Social and Political Theory* 13.

IV. 'ALTERNATE TAKES'[43]

It is in the nature of the concept of non-simultaneity described at the outset that there are always non-synchronous contradictions propelling the evolution of a given society in diverse directions. If this is correct, alternative outcomes remain possible. While it will be difficult for the Court to overrule its principled statements on social benefits, other fora might guide Union citizenship in the future—in the same way as popular anxiety concerning the European project accompanies the 'pulse of Europe' movement. The synthesised character of the citizenship concept may drive alternate takes to the fore. Indeed, the 'deconstruction' of Union citizenship in the field of social assistance was accompanied by its 'reconstruction' in other fields, such as political citizenship and the links between citizenship and fundamental rights.[44] In these policy areas, the Court has looked forward to the future and reimagined Union citizenship. In so doing, it has signalled that EU citizenship remains at the heart of the European project.

In five cases, two of which were adjudicated before the British referendum on 23 June 2016, the Court attributed more intelligibility and practical meaning to EU citizenship, confirming that institutional change is a fluctuating, selective and multi-threaded process. These cases show, by way of example, that deconstruction and reconstruction are inseparable processes: modifications and improvisations accompany both (almost) linear repetitions and regressions. These dimensions must coexist. Adjudication in the field of Union citizenship is both deconstructive and reconstructive—ie, it is in some respects continuous and in other respects discontinuous. In the latter case, judicial decision-making could lead to either transformative results (a *metabasis*) or to a backsliding (a *metaboli*).

A transformative result in the political dimension was achieved in the *Delvigne* case.[45] Delvigne, a French national convicted of murder and sentenced to 12 years' imprisonment, challenged his exclusion from the electoral roll with recourse to the Charter of Fundamental Rights.[46] Rejecting the Opinion of Advocate General Cruz Villalón, the Grand Chamber agreed on the applicability of the Charter, relying on the requirement of 'universal and direct' elections to the European Parliament contained in Article 14(3) TEU and the 1976 Act on the elections to the European Parliament in conjunction with Article 39 of the Charter. These provisions endow EU citizens with a specific right to vote in European Parliament elections—a right that may even be extended to third-country nationals in domestic law (see chapter twelve by Sara Iglesias Sánchez). There is no need

[43] This phrase is borrowed from John Coltrane's album released in 1975 on Atlantic Records.

[44] For a similar view, see D Sarmiento and E Sharpston, 'European Citizenship and Its New Union: Time to Move On?' in D Kochenov (ed), *EU Citizenship and Federalism: The Role of Rights* (Cambridge University Press, 2017).

[45] ECJ, C-650/13 *Delvigne*, EU:C:2015:648.

[46] Namely, Art 39(2) and Art 49(1).

for a cross-border element for the activation of this right, which can be exercised in the country in which one is a national. The Court here evidently attempted a *metabasis* on *Delvigne*.[47] It stepped in to guarantee the political rights of Union citizens in their home States by establishing its jurisdiction to review national restrictive measures and by affirming the importance of a proportionality test. The European *homo politicus* has thus been clearly established.[48]

A second case adjudicated in the pre-Brexit referendum period was *Bogendorff von Wolffersdorff*.[49] The Court ruled that the refusal of the German authorities to recognise the change of forenames and surname of a German national, which contained tokens of nobility, as obtained under the legislation of another Member State of which that national also held his nationality, restricted his right to move and reside freely within the territory of the Member States. Given that a person's name is, in line with established case law, a constitutive element of his or her identity and private life (as protected by Article 7 of the Charter of Fundamental Rights and Article 8 European Convention on Human Rights) and given there is 'serious inconvenience at administrative, professional and private levels'[50] caused by the refusal to recognise his surname and forenames, the national court must be convinced there exists a sound justification for any restriction imposed on public policy grounds and the test of proportionality is complied with. The judgment demonstrates the continued significance of free movement in areas other than access to social benefits. Here, the Court is more generous in assuming EU law and the Charter apply (see chapter eleven by Niamh Nic Shuibhne). Free movement thrives in the slipstream of human rights.

Following the Brexit outcome, the Court did not abandon its agenda of reconstruction. It continued to build the institutional stature of Union citizenship sequentially with normative integrity and compositional logic. It expanded the range of rights enjoyed by EU citizens and reinforced the layers of protection afforded by the Member States. In *Aleksei Petruhhin*,[51] the Grand Chamber enhanced the protection offered to EU citizens preventing their extradition to a third state and affirmed the centrality of the procedural safeguards of Article 19 of the Charter of Fundamental Rights (see chapter eleven by Niamh Nic Shuibhne). The Court's ruling in *Petruhhin* constituted a clear supranational innovation and demonstrates that the protection of individual citizens remains at the centre of the European integration project, despite the UK's rejection of it. It also shows that, notwithstanding the challenging political and economic environment in

[47] See K Lenaerts and JA Gutiérrez-Fons, 'Epilogue on EU Citizenship: Hopes and Fears' in D Kochenov (ed), *EU Citizenship and Federalism: The Role of Rights* (Cambridge University Press, 2017) 753–57, 775–79.

[48] See also J Shaw, 'Citizenship: Contrasting Dynamics at the Interface of Integration and Constitutionalism' in P Craig and G de Búrca (eds), *The Evolution of EU Law*, 2nd edn (Oxford, Oxford University Press, 2011) 597–608.

[49] ECJ, C-438/14 *Bogendorff von Wolffersdorff*, EU:C:2016:401.

[50] ibid para 38; building upon EuGH, C-208/09 *Sayn-Wittgenstein*, EU:C:2010:806, paras 52–71.

[51] ECJ, C-182/15 *Petruhhin*, EU:C:2016:630.

Europe, the Court continues to make principled innovations, and acts as an agent of institutional change in the field of individual rights—both for Union citizens and third-country nationals (see chapter twelve by Sara Iglesias Sánchez).

This combination of deconstructive and reconstructive logic in the case law on EU citizenship was confirmed in the *CS*[52] and *Rendón Marín*[53] cases, where the Court reiterated the significance of EU citizenship by anchoring its judgments in the *Ruiz Zambrano* ruling. In these cases, the Court prevented the expulsion of third-country national parents of EU citizens who are minors on the basis that this would deprive the young Europeans of the genuine enjoyment of the substance of their rights as Union citizens, which had been presumed largely irrelevant by many observers.[54] Things turned out differently. In an alternate take, the judgments highlight EU citizenship as a 'fundamental status'[55] in the post-Brexit landscape and serve to connect normative goals with the provision of concrete protection to, for instance, third-country national parents who have been convicted of a criminal offence (see, again, chapter eleven by Niamh Nic Shuibhne). As far as the process of institutional change is concerned and despite the pre-Brexit rulings on social assistance for needy EU citizens, it is now clear that EU citizenship remains ever evolving.

A common thread running through the aforementioned cases is that they move beyond the transnational, ie, they do not only concern citizens living in another Member State. This may be an important indication of where the 'new' citizenship concept might be heading—towards encompassing all citizens, not merely those on the move. This could be an indirect response to Ettore Recchi's observation that it was dangerous to associate the European project solely with transnational mobility. Rather, it must reach out to every citizen, including those who are immobile. While the debate about immobile Union citizens has traditionally be framed in terms of the (in)adequacy of the purely internal rule among legal academics,[56] the recent cases above show an alternative route is available. By this alternative route, one can activate the democratic potential of Union citizenship as a basis for political participation and the human rights in the Charter, which often apply without a cross-border element, thereby putting flesh on the bones of Union citizenship, which has always been constituted by 'the rights and … duties provided for *in the Treaties*'.[57] These rights and duties, by virtue of Article 6 of the Treaty on

[52] ECJ, C-304/14 *CS*, EU:C:2016:674.

[53] ECJ, C-165/14 *Rendón Marín*, EU:C:2016:675.

[54] See, by way of example, D Thym, 'Family as Link. Explaining the Judicial Change of Direction on Residence Rights of Family Members from Third States' in H Verschueren (ed), *Residence, Employment and Social Rights of Mobile Persons. On How EU Law Defines Where They Belong* (Antwerp, Intersentia, 2016).

[55] See *CS* (n 52) para 24; and *Rendón Marín* (n 53) para 69.

[56] For a rich discussion, see S Iglesias Sánchez, 'A Citizenship Right to Stay? The Right Not to Move in a Union Based on Free Movement' in D Kochenov (ed), *EU Citizenship and Federalism: The Role of Rights* (Cambridge, Cambridge University Press, 2017).

[57] First sentence of Art 20(2) TFEU (emphasis added).

European Union, now include the Charter of Fundamental Rights. Here, we are witnessing a remarkable meeting of two components of the supranational legal order that lie at the heart of the EU's constitutional self-image.

In light of what has been said, it is evident that Union citizenship continues to be multifaceted. These diverse facets are the natural consequence of various normative templates, the reconstruction of the past, different facts and demands and different surrounding conditions. Judicial incrementalism is both evolutionary and uneven. Whereas the pre-Brexit rulings in *Dano, Alimanovic, García-Nieto* and *Commission v the United Kingdom* signalled the deconstruction of EU citizenship, the unfolding EU citizenship story is a much more complex enterprise. A reconstruction is now emerging in policy fields other than the provision of social assistance. The non-simultaneity of the evolution of the EU citizenship case law is far from surprising. After all, flat processes and case law progressing in an orderly and linear fashion are species of fiction. Adjudication relies both on coherence and 'alternate takes'. Like jazz, judicial decision-making utilises both existing chords and outside notes. Contradictory strands often coexist and run parallel to one another. This is the non-simultaneity in the simultaneousness of the evolution of Union citizenship.

Index

www.ingramcontent.com/pod-product-compliance
Ingram Content Group UK Ltd.
Pitfield, Milton Keynes, MK11 3LW, UK
UKHW020238290926
15470UKWH00002B/600

9 781509 914685